BEST!
LETTERS FROM ASIAN AMERICANS
IN THE ARTS

Best! Letters from Asian Americans in the arts

EDITED BY CHRISTOPHER K. HO
AND DAISY NAM
WITH PAPER MONUMENT

EDITORS' LETTER

January 18, 2021

Dear Reader,

The anthology you hold suggested itself to us on a chilly afternoon in early 2020. As we sipped coffee on the Bowery, under the warm glow of globe lamps and surrounded by lunchtime chatter, we discussed parallel projects: Daisy was planning a live reading of letters of redress, motivated by her experiences of workplace gaslighting; Chris was drafting a letter of apology to his Asian-identifying former students, to whom he felt he had been an inadequate role model. Coincidentally or not, letters and racialized identity had intertwined for both of us, catalyzed by feelings of suspicion and guilt. Where did these "minor feelings" (to borrow a phrase from contributor Cathy Park Hong) come from? They intimated racial tensions just beneath the surface of our professional and artistic lives.

We wondered: *Was it just us?* Might other cultural workers want to process their experiences and exorcise their emotions, and could letter writing be a way to do this? We thought it could be. We reached out to artists, curators, educators, art historians, editors, writers, and designers in our communities and asked: Care to write a letter?

In letters, we can be vulnerable, provocative, and mundane. They carry the sound of the writer's voice. They can counter the bombastic self-presentation endemic to social media, and to the Internet's various echo chambers and funhouse mirrors. Sitting down to write a letter, with an addressee and signatory, is an intimate experience. And in the gap between writing and receiving, there's space for dreaming—and for change.

A letter can attempt to set the record straight. The art collective Godzilla's missive to the director of the Whitney Museum of American Art for its underrepresentation of Asian American artists remains as relevant today as when it was written in 1991. So too does Bill Clinton's 1992 redress letter to Japanese American survivors of US internment camps. He writes (vaguely), "[We] understand that the nation's actions were rooted deeply in racial prejudice, wartime hysteria, and a lack of political leadership." The dream of recognition and reparation remains unfinished.

We had several revelations while editing this anthology. First, in brainstorming potential contributors, we were astonished to see how *long* the list became. Asian Americans are active and thriving in every aspect of contemporary art; how had they remained invisible, even to us? And what does it mean to be seen by others, and to see each other in the art world?

Several contributors also expressed gratitude for being given, for the first time, a forum to explore their Asian American identity in relationship to their practice, their upbringing, their place in the world, and their aspirations for the future. Having known many of these contributors professionally for years, it dismayed us that one could work for decades in cultural fields and never be asked about one's culture on one's own terms.

This book is by no means comprehensive. We sought out contributors with strong ties to North America, and more or less followed the US Census's current definition of "Asian American," which includes people who trace their origins to East, Southeast, and South Asia and the Pacific Islands. We bent the rules for the occasional Asian Canadian, or Asian residents who spent significant time in the United States. We hope that the modest visibility afforded here sparks more correspondences to come, and that it foreshadows further conversations and communities.

Within months of embarking on this project, COVID-19 shattered our social systems and ruptured any remaining sense of national cohesion. Stoked by President Trump's rhetoric (he quickly labeled the coronavirus the "China virus"), xenophobia and racism against Asians and Asian Americans steadily escalated. By summertime, political unrest and mass protests against the ongoing murders of Black and Brown people by the police forced us to reevaluate what it means to be Asian American—a term influenced by the Black Power movement of the late 1960s, with a political agenda of equality, anti-racism, and anti-colonialism. How could we help dismantle the model minority myth? Are we complicit with White supremacy? With whom do our alliances lie? How can we thrive in our own unique ways and make way for others to do the same? Unfolding events brought urgency to these questions.

Our initial question—*Was it just us?*—was answered with a resounding no. We heard echoes of our own experiences in each letter. The individual narratives and viewpoints recounted here are diverse, reflecting the varied cultures, contested histories, vast geographies, and linguistic divisions that clumsily aggregate into the term "Asian American." What consistently struck us were the letters' emotional depth and range, and the authors' fearlessness. The letters are visceral, and their words will linger. We ached; we raged; we commiserated; we laughed out loud—sometimes within the space of a single letter.

Thank you for reading *Best! Letters from Asian Americans in the arts.* You play an important role. And should you be inspired to write a letter of your own, here is an excerpt of our prompt to contributors:

1. Write a letter to anybody, somebody, or something.

2. Respond directly, indirectly, tangentially, tacitly, and/or tactically, to any, all, or none of the following:

    - Who do you want to speak to most? Do you have their address?
    - When have you used your voice loudly or softly?
    - What does it mean to be Asian in the art world?
    - Tell us a secret.
    - Fill in the blanks: When I think about my race, ethnicity, class, and/or sexuality, I ____. This happens _ times a day.
    - How does it feel to be in your body?
    - Which do you prefer, Almond Roca or Ferrero Rocher?

3. Email or mail us your letter.

Best!
Christopher K. Ho and Daisy Nam

P.S. Letters to the editors are welcome.

BYRON KIM

3103 A Evening Way
La Jolla, CA 92037
July 1, 2020

July 1, 1984

Byron Kim
2615 C Magnolia St.
Oakland, CA 94607

Dear Byron,

Today, I'm making a landscape painting of the clear blue sky. The sky is still blue in 2020. Though it is square and depicts only the sky, I call it a landscape, because the brushstrokes are horizontal. In La Jolla, where we were born, I always have to add a little gray when I paint the sky. Other than that, we never saw La Jolla as gray.

In high school, a friend took you to the moon. You ran south in the dark along Windansea Beach until we got to where the moon's yellow light, itself a reflection of starlight, mixed with the blue algal chemistry, which we catalyzed with our bodies. The light mixed in the tidepool, which was like a crater, but did not make green.

You're going to China soon! I've been many times. Hong Kong first, always just passing through, or to meet a friend, or to make a friend. Hong Kong is a time portal centered on Kowloon, maybe Chungking Mansions, but that's an early 90s sentiment. In 1997, exactly between your time and mine, the lease runs out. The Hong Kong crucible continues to burn.

Worrying gets you nowhere. Yes, I know, that makes you worry. Twice, lots of people nearby are going to get sick. The first time is now. Reagan's lack of compassion will kill lots more people with AIDS. And the next time is now. There is always the problem of a we and a them. In the bigger picture we are making The Earth sick, but, really, we make ourselves sick. The Earth will be perfect even when the Sun burns out.

Advice never works, so I'm trying to stick to the facts. You are sitting in an empty room worrying about how useless it is to be an artist. Yet without art, we have to admit, life would hardly be worth living. Being able to bring new experiences, no matter how small, is a luxury worth pursuing. This kind of freedom is paramount. Of course, wherever freedom is concerned, there is always the problem of a we and a them. But it doesn't really need to be that way. I have only these few words, so this last claim will sound like advice, because it is. In the end you have only yourself, but it can be wonderful to ask for help.

Love, Byron

3103A Evening Way
La Jolla, CA 92037

July 1, 2020

July 1, 1984

Byron Kim
2615C Magnolia Street
Oakland, CA 94607

Dear Byron,

Today, I'm making a landscape painting of the clear, blue sky. The sky is still blue in 2020. Though it is square and depicts only the sky, I call it a landscape because the brushstrokes are horizontal. In La Jolla, where we were born, I always have to add a little gray when I paint the sky. Other than that, we never saw La Jolla as gray.

In high school, a friend took you to the moon. You ran south in the dark along Windansea Beach until we got to where the moon's yellow light, itself a reflection of starlight, mixed with the blue algal chemistry, which we catalyzed with our bodies. The lights mixed in the tide pool, which was like a crater, but did not make green.

You're going to China soon! I've been many times. Hong Kong first—always just passing through, or to meet a friend, or to make a friend. Hong Kong is a time portal centered on Kowloon, maybe Chungking Mansions, but that's an early 90s sentiment. In 1997, exactly between your time and mine, the lease runs out. The Hong Kong crucible continues to burn.

Worrying gets you nowhere. Yes, I know, that makes you worry. Twice, lots of people nearby are going to get sick. The first time is now. Reagan's lack of compassion will kill lots more people with AIDS. And the next time is now. There is always the problem of a we and a them. In the bigger picture, we are making the Earth sick, but really, we make ourselves sick. The Earth will be perfect, even when the Sun burns out.

Advice never works, so I'm trying to stick to the facts. You are sitting in an empty room worrying about how useless it is to be an artist. Yet without art, we have to admit, life would hardly be worth living. Being able to bring new experiences, no matter how small, is a luxury worth pursuing. This kind of freedom is paramount. Of course, wherever freedom is concerned, there is always the problem of a we and a them. But it doesn't really need to be that way. I have only these few words, so this last claim will sound like advice—because it is. In the end, you have only yourself, but it can be wonderful to ask for help.

Love,
Byron

DAWN CHAN
ADDRESSING PEOPLE OF PURPLE-HUED SKIN

You know when it comes to racism, people say: "I don't care if they're black, white, purple, or green." Uh, hold on now: purple or green?! You gotta draw the line somewhere! To hell with purple people! Unless they're suffocating, then help 'em.
—Mitch Hedberg

Wherever there are groups of strangers on social media arguing about race, disaster ensues. Often that disaster takes the form of somebody invoking a list of improbably-colored people. Blue people. Green people. Purple people.

For those of us molded by the blithe social norms of the 80s, the word *diversity* brings to mind a Benetton ad, or a chorus singing "We Are the World." How uncomplicated things were then. By contrast, when it comes to skin tones, we live now in an expanded field.

You, the people with purple-hued skin, may not know any of this. You seem to keep your own social media presence to a minimum.

Social media deters me too. But in the hopes of becoming better acquainted with you, I went where you are most often discussed by others: in the feeds of Twitter users making dubious claims about race and racism.

Reading the tweets of strangers shouting each other down is something few will find fun. To be fully honest, my research lasted about three minutes before exhaustion set in. But one fact did become clear: whenever someone rattles off a list of strangely colored people, there's about an 80 percent chance that Purple people can be found somewhere around the rear.

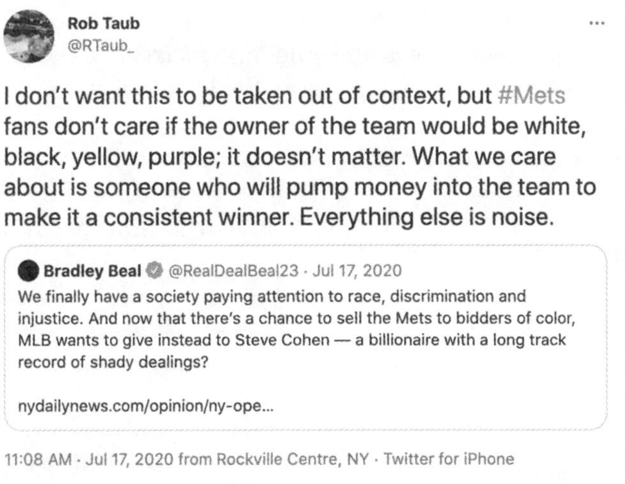

Rob Taub
@RTaub_

I don't want this to be taken out of context, but #Mets fans don't care if the owner of the team would be white, black, yellow, purple; it doesn't matter. What we care about is someone who will pump money into the team to make it a consistent winner. Everything else is noise.

Bradley Beal @RealDealBeal23 · Jul 17, 2020
We finally have a society paying attention to race, discrimination and injustice. And now that there's a chance to sell the Mets to bidders of color, MLB wants to give instead to Steve Cohen — a billionaire with a long track record of shady dealings?

nydailynews.com/opinion/ny-ope...

11:08 AM · Jul 17, 2020 from Rockville Centre, NY · Twitter for iPhone

Fig. 1: White, Black, Yellow, Purple

It is not always the case that Purple people appear last.

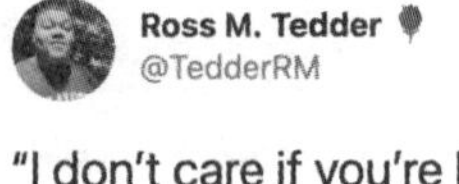

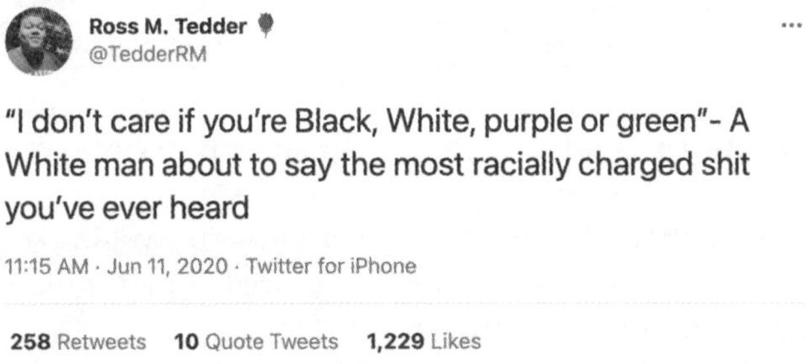

Ross M. Tedder
@TedderRM

"I don't care if you're Black, White, purple or green"- A White man about to say the most racially charged shit you've ever heard

11:15 AM · Jun 11, 2020 · Twitter for iPhone

258 Retweets **10** Quote Tweets **1,229** Likes

Fig. 2: Black, White, Purple, Green

But very often, it is a Purple person who is deployed as the rhetorical clincher.

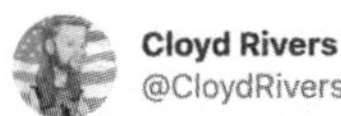

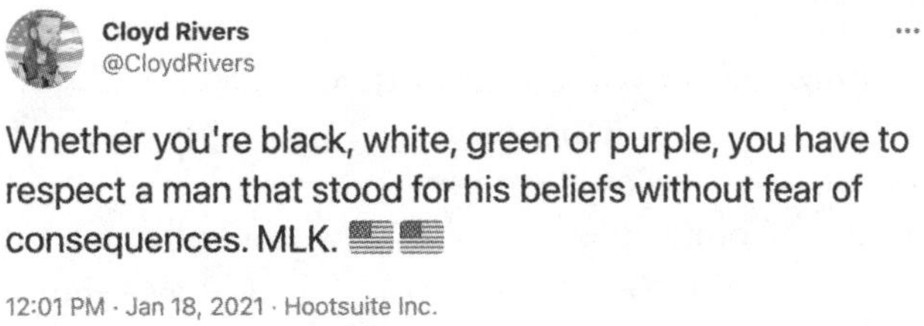

Cloyd Rivers
@CloydRivers

Whether you're black, white, green or purple, you have to respect a man that stood for his beliefs without fear of consequences. MLK. 🇺🇸🇺🇸

12:01 PM · Jan 18, 2021 · Hootsuite Inc.

Fig. 3:Back, White, Green, Purple

In fact, Purple people function almost as plot twists in these tweets. Because, indeed, a story is being told: a narrative with twists and turns galore. Let us look a little closer at that story—a story which emerges from a Twitter debate between two people whom, for argument's sake, we will call Alice and Bob.

At the outset, Bob typically establishes an ideological position. Alice proceeds to declare it (or him—or both it and him) racist.

Bob then responds with a defense, which begins: "I don't care if you're black or white."

Bob's words—which, as you'll note, paraphrase the refrain of Michael Jackson's 1991 hit song—express a desire to transcend the fraught binary through which most of America's ongoing structural racism is construed and propagated.

As we know, that binary is established via a recognizable cast of characters: Black people and White people.

But soon, more characters begin to enter Bob's story. Brown people. Red people.

Chaos unfolds:

Yellow people.

Yellow people! Has anyone else sounded this far-fetched before now? Yet Bob's tale has only reached its midpoint. Meaning that a Yellow person is still only far-fetched in a run-of-the-mill sense—no odder than a slightly nightmarish garden gnome from a yard sale.

Then Bob brings up Purple people.

Until now, the genre of Bob's story had seemed to be creative nonfiction, or maybe memoir. But the moment a Purple person appears, the truth is revealed:

Bob had planned to write *science fiction* all along.

When Bob says, "I don't care if you're black, white, yellow, or purple," one thing is clear: Yellow and Purple people are united in their function. Our jobs are to be improbably-colored humans.

On top of that, we are proximate in our positions. Considering how frequently we appear side by side in Bob's list, one might reasonably conclude that Yellow people are not merely white-adjacent. It would be rational to suppose we are purple-adjacent as well.

This is just not true.

Based on hundreds of years of color theory, everyone knows that yellow and purple are actually complementary hues. Yellow people and Purple people are—in fact—oppositely-colored people.

Earlier this year, our opposed positions were confirmed in the form of a *New York Times* best-selling book. Its title? *The World Needs More Purple People*.

I will confess that I have not read this children's book by actress Kristen Bell and creative director Benjamin Hart. Why read it, when one can glean so much intent from its title alone? *The World Needs More Purple People* is clearly an invitation for Purple people to procreate. Needless to say, this invitation is hardly ever extended to Yellow people, who are so often seen as existing in a state of perpetual overpopulation.

And yet, if we are truly, truly opposites, and if Purple people signify a state of outlandish nonexistence, then does it not therefore follow that Yellow people, conversely, become default markers of quotidian existence? If this is the case, all real people—whether black, brown, red, white—are rendered yellow. Default-yellow emoji faces lend credence to this hypothesis.

So what is it like for us, the Yellow people, to find ourselves serving as symbols of the real? I think it is not the worst place to be.

But, for a moment, let us compare that to the privileges afforded you in your subject position as a Purple person. You are allowed to be a cipher. You live your days unscathed by the shameful arrows of specificity. You exist free of vexatious stereotypes that never seem to die.

But what if social media rhetoricians knew more about you? Would they remain just as indifferent whenever you appeared on the scene?

Would they still be so welcoming of Purple people if they knew you ate fried sea snails? Or if you sometimes get a tad loud in public places?

So let me ask you:

Do you fry sea snails? Do you speak freely in public places?

How spicy is your cuisine?

Do your elderly tend to struggle with any specific kinds of chronic diseases? Do you battle any addictions to substances that were once brought to your shores by people with other colors of skin?

How many words do you have for snow?

What types of dance and/or exercise do you do in courtyards at night? What rewards do your children get when they're good? How are they punished when they're bad? What fruits do they consider the most refreshing summer treats?

Which of your movie stars are most celebrated for their beauty? Have any progressive denominations of your major faiths evolved to expunge earlier, homophobic beliefs?

Do your tabloids use puns in their headlines? Where do your grandparents go when they cannot live on their own? How often do your office workers take naps? How often do they break for tea?

What do you fear? How do you mark the passing of time? Whom do you consider family?

JESSE CHUN

October 16, 2020
U.S. Department of Homeland Security
United States Citizenship and Immigration Services (USCIS)

Dear USCIS,

It's been a year since I've written to you.

A year and 592 pages of evidence, petitions, photos, clippings, medical records, criminal records from South Korea, Hong Kong and Canada, biometrics, itineraries, letters,university certificates, and a plastic card later, you'd be happy to know that I'm still keeping true to my last promise made to you as an *EB-1 Alien of Extraordinary Ability Visual Arts Category*. I am still a Visual Artist and am not stealing other American's jobs -- at least, not yet.

Although we have been writing to each other for over a decade, there's still a lot you don't know about me. Maybe it's finally time that we dig a bit deeper -- 1678 pages, 67 letters, over 80 stamps, and 18 years later.

I want to tell you about my grandmother. 이옥선 Lee Oak Sun was her name. Lee Oak Sun was a professional Korean traditional dancer, Gayageum player, and a dedicated Buddhist. She lived in two temples in Seoul and on Jeju Isiland. She wrote out Buddhist scripts every day for hours, days, and decades. Every time I visited her, we ate soybean sprouts with metal spoons. Her last words to me were "you are gold president". She loved to make up words that made no sense to anyone but her. I didn't get to attend her funeral because I was landlocked waiting for my green card. To this day I think about all the strange words I missed out on, all the losses I'm still carrying from faraway, and the taste of soybean sprouts that I can never emulate no matter how many trips I take to H mart.

I still think of her oversized grey linen outfits, and the fuschia cushion that she used for her knees after daily 108 bows and chants. I still think of the garden balsams that she crushed and stained my nails with. I still think of the time when I only spoke one language, and that language was whole.

Who do you think of when you are reading these documents?
Is it me, is it you, or is it us?

Warm regards,

Jesse Chun
Gold President
천경아

CHUN I-140-4

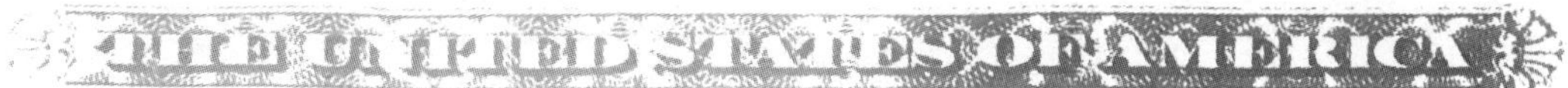

I-797 | NOTICE OF ACTION | DEPARTMENT OF HOMELAND SECURITY U.S. CITIZENSHIP AND IMMIGRATION SERVICES

		A A A A A
a	a	A a A AH
a	a	a A AH

AH A	A a : A , A:

a a a a a . a a a (
a). a a a a a a a a
a , a a a a
a a a a a a a , a a
a
: A a a a a , a a a
a a / a a a a a a a a a a , , a , a
a a a a a . a a a
a a a a
a a a a (a a a
) a a a a a a a a a .

a a a a a . aa a a a

National Benefits Center
U. S. CITIZENSHIP & IMMIGRATION SVC
P.O. Box 648003
Lee's Summit MO 64002
USCIS Contact Center: www.uscis.gov/contactcenter

FORM I-797 [REV. 08/01/16]

ARUNA D'SOUZA

July 27, 2020

To Whom It May Concern:

A funny way to start a letter, if you think about it—but I do wonder who will find this of concern. Still, I would like to take this opportunity to bring to the attention of my Asian, and especially South Asian, friends and family some of the lessons I've learned in my life as an Indian Canadian living in the US and working in the loosely defined "art world."

I grew up in Canada—southern Alberta, if you must know, which is the Texas of Canada (oil and cattle) but with socialized medicine—to parents who had answered the call in the late 1960s for doctors to immigrate to North America. They showed up, and after the medical licensing authority made them complete a third residency (after India and in England), they were dispatched to a remote town in northern Manitoba, and then, after my mother put her foot down at the idea of spending too many years in a place so cold, they moved to the place where I spent most of my youth: Lethbridge.

At the time, Lethbridge was very White. We were befriended by other Brown families—mostly people from Goa by way of East Africa—who found us because one of the uncles would scan the newly printed phone books each year to find out if any other Brown people had moved to town. My dad's best friend was a Black doctor—African American; he had fled the US to avoid the Vietnam War. Feeling some sort of kinship, my dad would stop to converse with every Indigenous man he saw on the streets, and pick up every Indigenous hitchhiker, no matter how much my mom worried about safety. We clung to the only spots of melanin in a sea of White.

In this context, not recognizing racism was a survival skill. Better not to understand. When, on the first day of school, the kids at the bus stop danced around me singing "manure, manure"—a word I didn't know, having spent my earliest years in a coal-mining town, not a farm community—I was thrilled at the joyousness of the song and dance, rather than hurt by the insult. As I grew older, because I didn't understand where they were coming from, I internalized the slights—when my best friend never allowed me to meet her dad, for example, or when the boys with crushes on me were hesitant to be seen with me in public, or when I moved to a new school at the age of 10 and the whole class made a game of pretending I was invisible, not saying a word to me for months—imagining they were the result of my own unkindness or some other failure.

It was only when I moved to New York for grad school in art history that I came to understand what people had been saying to me, in word and deed, all those years.

When I arrived at the Institute of Fine Arts, a faux chateaux on Fifth Avenue near the Met, a professor I had hoped to work with looked shocked when I introduced myself. "YOU are Aruna D'Souza?" I was confused at the confusion. He explained, without a trace of irony, in the middle of a crowded room where I was the only melanated person, "We thought you were Portuguese. We admitted you hoping to get a bit of variety among the students." (My surname, the product of centuries-old colonial domination of parts of India by the Portuguese, is extremely common in India but uncommon enough in the US that not only am I consistently assumed to be Portuguese, but I am also—contradictorily, and mortifyingly—assumed to be the sister or daughter of famed asshole racist Dinesh D'Souza. One of the art history grad programs I applied for, in fact, denied my application based on that assumption. For the record, I am not.)

Another time, a well-known professor of South Asian art history—a White man—made a beeline for me at the reception after his talk; I was the only Brown face in the room. He was very chummy in a way that I now recognize clearly: he wanted to prove his desi cred to me—perhaps not only his credibility, but his superior ability to cut through all the Indian spiritual bullshit to understand what's really going on in Indian art. (You see this a lot with yoga instructors, too.) He began speaking with a parodic Indian accent and imitating what he thought was the trivial way old uncles explained temple sculpture, by focusing on the stories of the gods versus the formal and structural semiotics of the arrangement. Perhaps he thought I was as amused as he was; instead, I was ashamed for him. For the arrogance, and for the pointlessness of his life: Why devote your career to studying a culture you despise? How small a man must you be to want, every day, to reassure yourself of other peoples' inferiority?

I was told more than once by people who thought they were giving me great and original advice that I should consider studying Indian art instead of the 19th-century French modernism I had chosen to pursue. Never mind that I didn't speak or read any Indian languages—these self-appointed mentors hadn't thought past my name, the color of my skin, and my heritage.

Once, as I interviewed for an academic job, one of the members of the search committee started surmising about the ways I could pivot my career from Cézanne to India so as to solve their most urgent problem: on the one hand, they wanted to hire someone who wasn't White; on the other hand, most of the people at the time applying to teach non-Euro-American subjects were themselves Euro-American. In the middle of interviewing for a job I really needed, I was forced to say that I didn't think that solving that problem was my responsibility.

The last time I went to the College Art Association Conference—many years ago by now—someone came up to me and gushed in a completely sincere and passionate way about how much they admired my writings on South Asian art. I have never written about South Asian art. Imagine being so blinded by your assumptions that you make up a whole CV for me that doesn't actually exist.

It was only after one particularly awful experience—one that I am prevented from discussing thanks to a nondisclosure agreement—that I was able to see the many ways I had been instrumentalized in academia: in a time when *multiculturalism* was the word of the day, I, like so many of my Asian colleagues, was hired or included by institutions, by panel organizers, by museum public programmers, by committee chairs, to make sure diversity had been achieved—often at the expense of Black scholars and experts. If they had a model minority like me to achieve minimum melanin content (MMC), they wouldn't need anyone else. When I realized this, I could also see the painful truth that so much of the abuse that I experienced was because I had veered out of that lane that had been assigned to me—the "safe" representative of diversity who wasn't supposed to challenge the status quo in any meaningful way.

The light bulb moment was horrifying. I could see I was culpable, not only for the exclusion of Black people from institutional spaces, but for the continued marginalization of my own voice and freedom and even safety within those institutions. What I understood as being included or being granted a modicum of power within the institution was a privilege that was subject to severe limits. The trade-off I made (without even being conscious of it) had not done me any favors.

I know and admire many women of color who manage to remain in academia and genuinely make a difference in their institutions, who manage to write and make work that truly challenges the assumptions on which those institutions are built, who find ways to amass enough power so that they can act as a counterweight to the inertial sag of them, who use their model minority status to cut deep into the rotten heart of the matter. I was not up to such work—I have no political instincts, and I'm allergic to power; I am neither subtle nor canny. For me, the only way out of this conundrum was to leave academia entirely. To absent myself. And to become something like the inverse of the model minority—to become the pain-in-the-ass minority, the fuck-things-up minority, the make-people-uncomfortable minority. I didn't leave academia to become part of the art world—that would have been out of the frying pan and into the fire, as the saying goes. Rather, I took detours—into the world of freelancing, writing puff pieces for the *Wall Street Journal*, doing legal marketing writing, acting as a ghostwriter, doing social media marketing for small companies. Trying to divest myself of the influence that so many years as a professor had granted me. Doing this work at a distance—over the phone or email, never meeting my employers, having many of them assume I was Portuguese or some vaguely Hispanic person (the name has some advantages, I suppose), and being absolutely outside of the companies I was working for, meant I wasn't worth much to them beyond the paragraphs I wrote. I couldn't be instrumentalized in the way I allowed myself to be in the past.

When I did return to the art world as a writer and a critic, it was with my knowledge of past mistakes and naivetés in mind. Every invitation, every commission, I was asking different questions, most of which involved counting heads: Am I the only person of color on this panel? Are there Black or Indigenous voices included? Will I feel sufficiently empowered to say what I need to say— to criticize my hosts, to take them to task for their own institutional failures? Or will I be in a position where my own need for self-preservation precludes such pain-in-the-ass behavior?

I don't know if I've gotten there, or will—but once you become aware of how you've been put in the straightjacket of White supremacy, the only way to fight for your liberation is to claw and tear your way out of it. And there are no half-measures here. There is no staying in your own lane. Fighting on behalf of your community (or yourself alone) is not enough, because no matter how you slice it, White supremacy is rooted very fundamentally in anti-Blackness. The myth of the model minority is rooted in anti-Blackness. This is true, too, for the anti-Blackness that rots Indian and Indian diasporic culture—the British may have quit India in 1947, but it continues to rule the mindsets of privileged patriarchal culture in that country. The first person I ever heard say the n-word was an uncle of mine, despite the fact that the British had used that terrible slur against South Asians for centuries. For a people that managed to free themselves from the rule of the most powerful empire in the world, despite forced impoverishment and the threat and actuality of violence, Indians have, as a rule, been really bad at decolonizing their thinking. Part of my work, as I see it, is to be outspoken about the ways in which my position as a non-Black woman of color makes my experience distinct from that of a Black woman—and to elaborate the ways that, ultimately, my own freedom will be delimited as long as anti-Black racism is allowed to persist.

There is no liberation from White supremacy unless we work for our communities and for everyone else's.

When my dad turned 60, he took our whole family (including two White sons-in-law) to Las Vegas for the weekend. His friend had gotten us a special table for the Wayne Newton concert at Caesar's Palace and tipped off Mr. Newton that my dad was in the audience celebrating a milestone. Wayne Newton (who is Native American) made a big deal of my dad being in the audience—the guy is a true showman—and sang a song in his honor. My dad stood up and said, "Mr. Newton, from one Indian to another, I thank you." The audience and the performer roared with laughter. It was a moment of joy, in which one brown skin person claimed an imagined solidarity—and even love—with another.

Love,
Aruna

PAMELA M. LEE

Dear Karin,

A confession: when Christopher Ho and Daisy Nam invited me to contribute to their project, I admit that you were one of three candidates in the running to receive my letter. Rest assured you were in great company. I first thought about writing to Grace Lee Boggs (1915–2015) because, well, *Grace Lee Boggs*; but any letter to the pathbreaking philosopher and activist would be little more than a fangirl's valentine. Then I considered my friend Mel. But since I text Mel every day, a letter seemed redundant. Besides, no one wants to read our habitual musings about *The Joy Luck Club* and Amy Tan's jewelry collection. (Daughter: "NOTHING I CAN EVER DO CAN EVER PLEASE YOU." Mother: "… I SEE YOU … I SEE YOU …")

Truth be told, I've been composing letters to you in my head since you left us seven years ago. Letters about art, books, and writing. About fashion, travel, and hiking. About family, food, and friendship. About politics, culture, and community. And yes—even a little gossip. You would have so much to say to what Christopher and Daisy call this "moment of high visibility" for Asian Americans. Your achievements as a scholar and curator, your social worlds, family history, and personal experience all speak powerfully to the question, "What does it mean to be an Asian in the art world?"

This is to make a flat-footed point: I miss you. No secret in that. By the same token, this is also how I want to frame this letter: in terms of what is missed, or what has gone missing. And what might, in a cognate turn of phrase, be *misrecognized*.

I'll start with one version of misrecognition—the literal kind—because it's the most egregious and, for some, the most easily dismissed. I'm talking about those everyday encounters in both the mainstream art world and the academy, the ones we file under the rubric of microaggression. Once, you recounted bumping into Artist X at an opening in Los Angeles, where he enthusiastically hailed you by shouting "MAYA!" You told him that you were most definitely NOT Maya Lin. When the artist began tripping over his apologies, each mealier than the last, you flatly responded, “That’s OK … I know you’re a racist.” I almost spit when you told me this story. I could imagine the look on your face, your gaze level, and hear the coolness of your rebuke.

For my part, I think I’ve mentioned how often I’ve been mistaken for Miwon Kwon over the years. Absolutely nothing against Miwon—who wouldn’t want to be like the divine Miwon?—but still. The last time this happened was when I crossed paths with a blue-chip gallerist in Chelsea, whom I had met at least two times earlier. She said something like, “Oh, *Miwon*, of course … I just love your work on site-specificity!”

How come it seems that there’s only so much gray matter one can reserve for a female art historian, theorist, or critic of Asian descent? Goodness knows there are so many of us. I can give a quick shout-out, for example, to three of my former colleagues in my previous university department, all brilliant historians of art, film, and media (waves to Jean Ma, Marci Kwon, Usha Iyer). And yet the number of us on faculty, the sheer fact of our departmental *representation*, did little to mitigate the daily indignities of misrecognition. In fact, representation may be beside the point in my telling. Alas, it was not uncommon for one staff member to confuse me for Jean or Marci. Keep in mind this was a person I saw maybe three or four times a week, over the course of several years.

So, I’ve now been reduced to stating the painfully obvious: No, we *really* don’t look alike—not even remotely—let alone think alike; and the dozens of countries from which our respective diasporas launch are extremely different in their cultures, histories, languages, ethnicities, priorities, politics, immigration patterns, and outlooks. The fact that I just committed such words to paper would be embarrassing were it not so pathetic. How many times are we forced to repeat them?

Some might protest that these incidents are “no big deal,” claiming that such episodes can be chalked up to busyness or bad eyesight. Or maybe there are too many faces and names to store in an already overloaded brain bank; or maybe, just maybe, you do look a bit like Maya Lin, or I bear the faintest resemblance to Miwon Kwon. (We don’t.) “Get over it,” or “Lighten up,” is the tacit message underlying such responses, what some folks these days would call “gaslighting.” To counter these reactions, I’ll put on my academic hat for a moment. Let me describe two notions of misrecognition at work here:

Writing on systems of domination within education and the culture at large (as in the art world, for example), Pierre Bourdieu elaborated a concept of misrecognition that addressed the structural logic of power relations as they are crystallized within interpersonal settings and encounters. “When domination can only be exercised in its elementary forms, i.e. directly, between one person and another, it cannot take place overtly and must be disguised under the veil of enchanted relationships,” he writes. “In order to be socially recognized [domination] must get itself misrecognized."[1] Misrecognition, in other words, legitimizes and reproduces forms of social dominance at the scale of these banal and allegedly harmless exchanges. It masks the actual violence which historically informs and reproduces the systems in which we work, live, move, play. Instead, misrecognition exacts a kind of "symbolic violence," which Bourdieu and Jean-Claude Passeron elsewhere note is "exerted for the most part ... through the purely symbolic channels of communication and cognition ... recognition or even feeling."

Nancy Fraser, in critiquing the liberalism of identity politics and the wan ministrations of multiculturalism, renders an adjacent definition of misrecognition. "To be misrecognized ..." she writes, "is not simply to be thought ill of, looked down upon or devalued in others' attitudes, beliefs or representations. It is rather to be denied the status of a full partner in social interaction, as a consequence of institutionalized patterns of cultural value that constitute one as comparatively unworthy of respect or esteem."[2]

To be "denied the status of full partner in social interaction": is this not the logic of what it means to be an Asian in the art world? Fraser's formulation points to what is *missing* in those interactions, whether being accorded the privilege of your proper name, let alone your face; or the right to hold space within those worlds without apology or justification; or the freedom *not* to have to educate or correct your co-workers about Things That Are Most Definitely Not OK. Like that time when I was working at a famous museum on Fifth Avenue, and a senior curator, standing right next to me, was laughing about a colleague's dismal situation. "*He didn't stand a Chinaman's chance!*" she squealed. Or that meeting back in the early 1990s when you and I pitched an exhibition proposal at the Whitney. This was a show in which the overwhelming majority of artists were of color. Surely you remember, Karin, how one senior curator responded to our checklist, which included such formidable figures as James Luna, Renée Green, Fred Wilson, Tseng Kwong Chi, and Tomie Arai? He called it "the museum equivalent of busing."

Yes, while it's true these things took place a while ago, it's also true that the chronicles of such art-world occurrences keep getting longer, as dispiriting as they are exhausting. If you hop on social media these days, you'll read an endless, perpetual tally of misrecognition and the missing within the culture of museums, art galleries, and universities. No matter the recurrence of these events, this is not how I want to end this letter. Setting these things down for the record is critically important, but it's just as important to look forward. Of course, looking forward doesn't mean ignoring the past. Sometimes you need to go back ...

I'm thinking of the exhibitions you organized: on the art of the internment camps, for example; or the research on photography in LA's Little Tokyo you conducted; or the connections you drew for so many of us across different communities and spheres of influence. I'm thinking of the times you took me to Godzilla meetings and the collaborations you engaged with artists, critics, and curators, unfolding minor histories in the present that mean even more today than they did back then. These histories, indeed, accrue new layers of significance—new resonances and powerful vibrations—as we revisit them in the present.

For example, in the spirit of 2020, with the brutalizing continuance of White supremacy and the revolutions for Black Lives Matter underway, I especially think of the catalogue essay you wrote for Kellie Jones's brilliant exhibition *Now Dig This!* in 2013. You spoke to the mutual respect, collaboration, and exchange between African American and Asian American artists in the 1970s in Los Angeles, highlighting Robert A. Nakamura's beautiful portraits of artists such as Noah Purifoy, Betye Saar, and Charles White. The essay detailed an untold history of artistic communities of color working together in coalition, solidarity, and affirmation.

What gave this history its rare poignancy were the personal narratives of friendship and family that inspired such exchanges in the first place. Your father, Kazuo Higa, was instrumental in establishing these relationships in Los Angeles as an artist, educator, and director of the historic Da Vinci Art Gallery. And he modeled the kind of worlds that you would recreate, over and over, as curator, art historian, colleague, and friend.

When I think of these worlds, Karin, I can only correct my own assumptions about what it means to be an "Asian in *the* art world." Because what you've shown us is that we are *all* cocreators in the making of worlds—worlds we might anticipate and work towards, worlds we can envision on the horizon, beyond those I've outlined above.

In other words, following Nancy Fraser, we claim our shared status as full partners in these social interactions. And to this point, we can only recognize that *we* are missing nothing at all.

Miss you and love you, always,
Pam

1 Endnotes in a letter? Ugh. But let's give credit where it's due. The Bourdieu and Passeron quotes come from Pierre Bourdieu and Jean-Claude Passeron, *Reproduction in Education, Society and Culture* (London: Sage, 1977). They are cited in an instructive essay by Suruchi Thapar-Björket, Lotte Samelius, and Gurchathen S. Sanghera, "Exploring Symbolic Violence in the Everyday: Misrecognition, Condescension, Consent and Complicity," *Feminist Review* 112, 144–62, 2016.

2 Another endnote, sorry, but FWIW: Nancy Fraser, "Rethinking Recognition," *New Left Review* 3, May/June 2000.

AJAY KURIAN

Dear V,

There were so many things I felt certain of before sitting down to write you. When you're away from the screen, all these constant, swirling, miasmic thoughts feel like they hold the immediate possibility of solidity—as if everything you contain, contradiction and all, can somehow find its way out of you, and that in believing and trusting this miraculous conduit, it is all the more likely to take place. This is very far from the case.

The truth is that all these fluid ideas freeze up as soon as they face the screen, solidify into parts and shards, breaking into digestible-but-limited fragments that don't provide the holism that intuitive reflection first promised. I thought that by girding it to a single story, one that felt indicative of a way to understand diasporic existence, I would also ensure the safe passage of my shattered thoughts.

I thought about my grandfather in India, a botanist who studied orchids and spliced their genes. He wrote a book on them that I own but have never read. As a child I'd go to his house every other year, spending two months of the summer there. In the front of his house were several plots of scaffolded orchids. It was a model city of strangely rooting creatures, most of which would not be in bloom. I remember it as mostly a palette of opaque and vibrant greens. They grew out of coconut shells and husks, their roots shakily wrapped around wooden stakes and coconut parts looking only partially certain in their search for moisture. In America, orchids were considered difficult to cultivate, hard to manage and maintain, exoticized constantly, and prized when they blossomed. Here they felt ordinary. They weren't expected to perform, only to exist and thrive. And they did.

What was even more fascinating to me was that they didn't need to be in the ground. They could hang, float, and find odd homes outside of any conventional soil or earth. This felt constitutive of the diasporic experience to me, *to be rooted without ground*. I held onto this metaphor for quite some time, and still do, I suppose. But when I really think about it now, the problem of first-generation experience is precisely the problem of roots. The pithy image feels too neat, still too performative. If you can't find your roots, and you may not even recognize them, what does it even mean to say that you're rooted without ground?

I grew up largely around White men. I went to an all-boys private school for twelve years and was educated and groomed in such a way that both my sense of self and alterity were conditioned by Whiteness, by histories I was supposed to know yet weren't necessarily my own. This confusion was further instilled, unknowingly, by my immigrant parents, who wanted me to assimilate as well as possible, while also holding onto my cultural heritage, my roots. I was unclear what these roots might be. A sense of family, and sense of collectivity, "values"—all things general enough to be dismissed by a skeptical teen trying to find certainty by tearing things down. An ego struggling for space, brought up around ego-driven White boys, is an ego in distress. Developing criticality was meant to give me the tools to destroy the old ways and look to a new way of life. I didn't realize that in this act of destruction was the preservation of Whiteness and the preservation of a poison more potent than any my own culture could offer.

So then rely on your sense of "Indianness," one part of me would say. Even this identification was already split by our membership as Dravidians rather than Aryans. We are South Indian, categorically different from North Indians. We are darker, considered coarser—a working people, a rougher club. My father, in particular, reinforced the chip on my shoulder from being from the South. This might be part of the reason that when any Malayali or Keralite does something of note, my parents immediately become CNN correspondents reporting live, covering the story as it unfolds, as if they were breaking it to you and the rest of the world. Joyous because the careers of other scattered Malayalis are vicariously ours. I should say that it's an Indian trait regardless of regionality, but the specificity in reporting is absolutely regional. All in all, it was a further weight to tip the scales in our favor for a sense of approval from some unknown entity. Seeking approval feels as Indian as samosas to me.

Learn more about your culture, another me says. Okay sure, but then when is it mine? Does simply learning more about my ancestors necessarily make it my ancestral well? Learning about my cultural pasts has meant coming to terms with how much has not yet been written about my cultural pasts. Much of what has been written is shown through the lens of the British and distorted by the conqueror. Of course there is plenty of established and budding scholarship theorizing the postcolonial, but I'm more interested in learning about the precolonial. So much of what I see from ancient India through its temples and sculpture feels abundant, fluid, and full of desire. Perhaps I notice this because of how deeply felt desire was repressed in my upbringing. If kisses went on too long on television, there was a panicked scramble to change the channel. If there was nudity, we would all collectively sweat till the indiscretion ended.

My parents grew up in a liberated India, but it was newly liberated. They grew up with the heavy hangover of colonialism. They were left to sift through the colonial decisions of yesterday without much clarity and feeling an unnecessary sense of guilt and shame that follows them despite the fact that the people who instilled it are far gone. Those people never cared about their thriving, and yet they are still afforded psychic residence, inadvertently becoming apologists for their unrepentant squatters. They grew up with so many British values that they didn't understand what was before. Where is the matriarchy of Kerala? Where is the fluidity of gender, the unnamed multiplicity of desire? Where has it gone? And if I find it, will it be mine? Is my identity based on what I recover or what I experienced? Is there ever such a thing as an original root? Or are there constant revisions, reclamations—a psychological weeding, as well as replanting alongside so much that remains preserved and further cultivated?

I've wrestled with these anxieties since I was a kid, but it's only through making art that I've found ways of owning my shame, embarrassment, insecurities, and contradictions. There was a point where I finally stopped fearing the possibility of being wrong and instead embraced what I knew was simply the case for myself, which is, as it is for everyone in their own peculiar way, lived contradiction. In dwelling on my past experiences, retrospective feelings started to take shape, formed by intuition and sometimes faulty memory; but, I realized through close observation of these feelings, intuitions, and memories that they are not based purely in the individual. When you look closely enough, you start to notice the shimmer of history's web around all those seemingly inchoate feelings and thoughts.

The first figurative sculpture I ever made came to me first as an image-feeling, as if the thought itself was a glyph that represented a feeling—two White boys, one pissing into the mouth of another, both in a state of bliss, while a third Brown boy watches in confusion, horror, and simple observation. I had never actually witnessed this scene, but I knew it was true. I could later speak about complicity, White adjacency, cultural tautologies, and assimilation, but it started as cultivating that image-feeling. In its making, other things came to light, each decision sprouting the next. Fear is the act of cultivating an idea foreign to yourself, even if it means your own diminution. This was a different kind of cultivation, one that accepted what was in order to build what will be. These consistent acts of critical cultivation lead to an always emerging understanding of the moment as well as history, the individual, and the collective.

It is the event of realizing that we are always double, existing as garden and acting as gardener—both noun and verb. I have been shaped and molded by countless variables, too many to name, but I've tried to garden myself as best as I can, making what I believe in, and inevitably what will be—whether I or you like it or not—a first generation of Indian American Art.

My best,
Ajay

JOHN YAU

May 28, 2020

Dear Matsumi "Mike" Kanemitsu:

You were born ninety-eight years ago in Ogden, Utah, and died in Los Angeles, California, on May 1, 1992, a few weeks shy of your seventieth birthday. It will be my seventieth birthday in a week. Though we never met, you have been in my life ever since I read your name in "Personal Poem" by Frank O'Hara in the spring of 1971. I was a student at Bard College, a small, progressive liberal arts college in the Hudson Valley, two hours north of New York City.

"Personal Poem" was included in *The Collected Poems of Frank O'Hara* (Alfred A. Knopf, 1971). It was a big, thick book, and I was in my dorm room working my way through it when I read these lines:

> Now when I walk around at lunchtime
> I have only two charms in my pocket
> an old Roman coin Mike Kanemitsu gave me
> and a bolt-head that broke off a packing case
> when I was in Madrid the others never
> brought me too much luck though they did
> help keep me in New York against coercion
> but now I'm happy for a time and interested

I was jolted, as I experienced something I never had before: I had come across an Asian name in a poem by a contemporary American poet who happened to have lived in New York in the 1950s and first half of the 60s and worked at the Museum of Modern Art.

It would be like seeing a modern portrait of someone of Asian descent by an Asian American artist in the Museum of Modern Art or the Whitney Museum of American Art—something I have yet to experience.

Kanemitsu. Your name joined a small list that included Anna Wong, as well as Isamu Noguchi and Wifredo Lam, both of whom were biracial. I read about Noguchi and Lam when I was younger, most likely in a newspaper, and their names—and what I read about them—seared their way into me, as did seeing Wong upstage Marlene Dietrich in *Shanghai Express* (1932) when I was 16, and reading your name in a poem, which also mentioned LeRoi (Jones), Miles Davis, and BIRDLAND.

Did I tell you that I was the only Asian American student at Bard College (1969–72), and that there were none on the faculty or in the administration?

More than a decade would pass before I learned that you were a painter, from the painter Norman Bluhm, whom O'Hara dedicated poems to as well as wrote about. By then, I had moved to New York and had started reviewing art for *Art in America* in 1977 because John Ashbery told the head editor, Betsy Baker, that she should give me a chance, and she finally relented after he had pestered her for more than a year. So while I never met you, I met people in the early 1980s who knew you. This is how I learned that you were a painter and that Jackson Pollock had given you the nickname "Mike," which further Americanized you.

According to Bluhm, you hung out at the Cedar Bar, which is how you met Pollock. I also learned that you had grown up with your grandparents in Japan, in a suburb of Hiroshima; that you came back to America in 1940 and had been put in a Japanese detention camp, where you began drawing and working with pastels given to you by the American Red Cross; that you enlisted in the United States Army; that you studied with Fernand Léger in Paris after the war and then, in 1949, came to New York to study with the early American modernist Yasuo Kuniyoshi at the Art Students League. Within a short time, you were part of the downtown New York art world.

Your work was included in a Whitney Annual (1956) and *Recent Drawings USA* at the Museum of Modern Art (also 1956). In 1962, you participated in a group show at the Tanager Gallery, a 10th Street cooperative, and were one of the artists included in the traveling group show *Abstract Watercolors by 14 Americans* (1962), organized by the Museum of Modern Art. In the mid-1960s, you left New York and moved to Los Angeles.

You were at least two people: Mike and Matsumi.

Like Bluhm, you were considered part of the "second generation" of Abstract Expressionists. Despite all of this, your name remains almost completely absent from most histories of the New York art world in the 50s.

Forty years passed before I saw any of your work, and it was not in New York.

In the spring of 2008, while I was in Los Angeles, I learned that there was a small selection of your prints and lithographs, *Kanemitsu in California During the 1960s and 1970s*, at the Los Angeles County Museum of Art (February 23 – June 15, 2008). This is what Aya Yoshida, the curator of the exhibition, said:

> It's always amazed me that Kanemitsu is never hung in museums along with Rothko and Pollock, and the others, since he was such a part of that movement. But perhaps there is a hint of 20th-century racism. Kanemitsu is seen as an exotic "Asian" artist.

Although I did not know about Yoshida's observation when I went to the museum, I had had a similar thought. This is what I wrote in my review in the *Brooklyn Rail* (May 2008):

> I thought about [Kanemitsu's] erasure when I went to the Los Angeles County Museum, where I asked for the location of the exhibition and was directed to the Japanese Pavilion. The docent at the Pavilion brought my two friends and I by elevator to the second floor, saying that his work might be among the prints by Hiroshige and others, but that there was no show of his at the museum and she didn't know whom I was talking about. After returning to the ticket office and asking a number of people who tried to get me to become a member of the museum, I was directed to a small room segregated among large rooms of period furniture. There were no signs along the way to guide us. While there was a wall text, there wasn't even a modest brochure explaining whom Kanemitsu was to someone who might have accidentally stumbled into the exhibition.

In 2018, I was finally able to see a painting you had made while you were in New York, along with one you made more than a decade later, after you had moved to Los Angeles and made the prints that I saw at LACMA and wrote about.

This is part of what I wrote after I saw your work in the group show *Painting: Now and Forever, Part III* at the Matthew Marks Gallery and Greene Naftali (June 28 – August 17, 2018):

> Kanemitsu, who painted in Japanese sumi ink and brushes his entire life, recognized that he had multiple identities—something reflected in his work in multiple mediums, which he never tried to unite under a single style. This is why seeing paintings by Kanemitsu in this show was so important to me; they offered a glimpse into a side of him I did not know. *Untitled (A)* (1956) was done the year Kanemitsu was included in a Whitney Annual, and his other painting in the exhibition, *Untitled (C)* (ca. 1969) is from more than a decade later, and after he moved to Los Angeles.
>
> The bulbous blue shape hanging down from the painting's top edge in *Untitled (A)* anticipates a shape that Paul Feeley began using in 1957 in paintings such as *Kilroy* (1957). If the dates of Kanemitsu's paintings are

any indication, he was at the forefront of artists who rejected both the gestural and strict geometrical aspects of Abstract Expressionism in favor of rounded forms and solid planes of color. His work is right there in the mix with Feeley's classical forms and Nicholas Krushenick's Pop abstractions and yet remains neglected, at best. His absence from an art history that is just getting around to acknowledging its nonwhite artists is telling.

More than fifty years had passed between when I first read your name and the first time I saw one of your paintings. I was not disappointed. It was not derivative, and you were clearly moving along your own path.

During that half-century, I never saw your work in a New York museum, never saw a photo of you hanging out at the Cedar Tavern, and never read about you in any survey of paintings in the 50s in New York, nor saw something by you included in a group exhibition focusing on the "second generation" of Abstract Expressionists.

I have also learned that you did the cover for *Projective Verse* (1959) by Charles Olson, which was published by Totem Press and LeRoi Jones (Imamu Amiri Baraka). You knew Jack Kerouac, most likely through the painter Stanley Twardowicz, who had been introduced to Zen by Kenzo Okada, another neglected artist.

Between 1958 and 1962, you had four shows at the Dwan Gallery, Los Angeles. You also showed at the Stephen Radich Gallery in New York in 1960 and 1962. Despite being part of the New York and Los Angeles art scenes, you continue to be invisible.

In two years, it will be the centenary of your birth. Perhaps by the time you are 100 years old, you will not be invisible anymore, nor be seen as an "exotic" Asian artist. I have spent half a century looking for you, and I promise I won't stop looking. Until then, I will bring up your name every chance I can.

Sincerely yours,
John

CATHY PARK HONG

Dear Meret,

I want to capture a season for you, the summer of 2020 during the pandemic, when we escaped the city and lived as if the virus furred the edges of each day's film strip but never tore the day in half. We are surrounded by trees that I cannot name that surround our deck. One maple has been sundered by lightning and slopes to the left, offering a pleasing asymmetrical composition to a painter if she were to paint our backyard. The greenery of Vermont turns theatrical as the day wanes where the last strains of sun slit through the branches, turning our copse of oak into a cathedral of light. A wood thrush in the trees sings several ethereal notes to the faint, coppery chorus of crickets that curtains the forest. We hear shots, target practice for the fall, when the air will crisp and woodland creatures will be skinned and dressed, which scare the neighbor's white Pomeranian into fleeing their home for the woods, never to be seen again.

When you're not at camp, we head to the local pond. I swim when you're at camp, too. I search restlessly for the perfect spring-fed pond, a body of water that is clear and silvery and not fretted with the roots of lily pads or a map of algae scum. Your father doesn't want me to tell you that I've been sneaking into a pond that has closed for the season because of the pandemic. There is no barrier except for a gate that I can easily climb under. It is a man-made pond, ninety feet deep, used during the winter to churn out snow for the nearby ski slopes. From the aerial view of a drone, the pond is an eye, cleared of trees. When I swim, I never wear goggles because I don't want to see what is beneath me, just a hazy blue galaxy where I only see my thoughts. Sometimes there are other trespassers jogging or walking their dogs around the pond, all of whom, except for me, are White.

Darkness, your father is gathering wood to make a bonfire. You are climbing the pyramid of chopped wood, shouting that we will all toast marshmallows for s'mores. I become irrationally annoyed when your father begins to gather the wood to cultivate a fire, perhaps because I am pulled from the safety of the deck into the dark meadow, where I am attacked by bugs. You run up to me and beg to eat three s'mores, to which I assent, but then you demand that I go to the kitchen and deliver the marshmallows, which is your habit: to follow a met demand with a bigger demand. If that is what you want, I say, you bring down the marshmallows. I stay on the deck. Maybe I dislike bonfires because it reminds me of forced gatherings where we are required to sing songs. There are two friends visiting us from the city with proof they have recently tested for the virus. They migrate slowly towards the fire. Earlier that day, they had surrounded you like supplicants from a Baroque painting, each one of them taking turns trying to pluck a splinter from your toe that, in the end, refused to give. Now you dance among them around the fire, handing each one a sparkler.

The next month, another family with twin boys arrives from the city, with proof that they too have tested negative. A tent sprouts up like a mushroom in our backyard. The boys, who are seven, seem permanently spooked by the virus, afraid of anyone who is not kin, but after acclimating to our home and the woods, they become emboldened. By dusk, around the fire, they insist on telling ghost stories.

When there's a lull in the conversation, I gravitate toward my pet topic, UFOs. I saw an episode of *Unsolved Mysteries* about sightings in 1969, when dozens of families living in the Berkshires spotted an unidentified spacecraft that lingered in each small town as if the aliens were on a safari of small-town White America. I test out my theory that the UFOs might not be aliens but us, traveling back in time to study our evolutionary past. Since Egyptians and Ancient Greeks have spotted these spacecraft, witnesses have consistently described these aliens as humanoid, bipedal, and large-headed. Why would extraterrestrials from another galaxy look that humanoid? Why would they take such a keen interest in Earth when there are an infinite number of planets with possible life? And why would they take such care to only observe from afar, rather than wiping us out? I am met with amused expressions from our company, and your father tells them that I've been repeating this theory to him nonstop. As I turn to rebut something your father said, one of the twin boys begins to shriek that aliens will attack us, his increasingly loud wails piercing the dark bowels of the forest around us, stirring the wildlife within.

Your father admonishes me for not being aware of the audience to whom I was speaking before he departs for the house. The mother consoles her boy but when he won't stop crying, she turns stern, telling him she's had enough. UFOs are not real, just like ghosts and vampires aren't real. I am sheepish that I didn't take heed of the children around me, though you remained unperturbed and sanguine, perhaps because you are still unaware of the phenomena of UFOs.

Since the pandemic, I have become frustrated with the linearity of time, how it speeds past us like a bullet train without stopping for us as passengers. I want to halt this train. I want to believe that we will evolve into hairless, benevolent beings, with the advanced technology to loop back in time to tour our past selves, which we will implement for study and not for harm, with the caveat that I understand that our quest for knowledge can cause its own harm. If we from the future have been detected by our ancestors, they would only be able to fathom what is unfathomable as further proof of God.

Maybe I embrace this theory because I can't imagine too many generations after you, because of our human follies, and it's my way to reassure myself, and you, that we will find a way out. My theory makes me not a New Age crackpot but a depressingly pragmatic secularist because I'm thinking that it wasn't God or even aliens. It was us, all along. I am tempted to tell the boy my motives behind my theory. But instead, I echo his mother and tell him that none of what I said is real. The boy continues to weep unconvinced, protesting that I talked about UFOs as if they *were* real.

Just then, your father returns carrying a mason jar. Inside it is a toad. I found this little jerk trying to get in the basement, he says. A little water slides around the jar. What's that, you ask. Toad pee, your father says. The boy immediately stops crying and runs up to the jar, demanding to hold it, which sparks an argument between you and the boys over who gets to hold the jar first.

Mom

KENNETH TAM

Dear Dad,

How are you? Are you taking care of yourself? I worry about your health, your bad leg, how you and Mom will look after each other. Please try to stay home more. The baby is doing well, I think he looks like me, so it also means he will look like you. I hope you and Mom will get to spend more time with him. I worry he will grow up not being able to speak Cantonese. I remember how much I hated Chinese school growing up. I remember dreading being driven there early each Sunday morning, and then sitting in the cambling public school building where it was held. and not paying any attention in class. I remember constantly goofing off in class, in a way I never did in regular school. I thought it was a joke and didn't take it seriously, at all. I remember one day even doing something terrible. I squeezed an entire bottle of Elmer's glue into the desk where I was sitting, and in the process destroyed the contents of whoever's possessions were inside. I remember having to talk to the principal the following week, not the principal of the Chinese school,

wishing you
ALL GOOD THINGS
this year

but of the regular school, who was an older white man. I remember denying the whole incident, and I'm sure I didn't tell you or Mom. I probably put our entire school at risk, as we were only renting weekend use of the building from the city. I think you stopped taking me shortly thereafter. I hope this isn't upsetting news. I wonder what we'll do with our son.

Have a happy birthday, I hope we can get together again soon.

Love, 勁軒

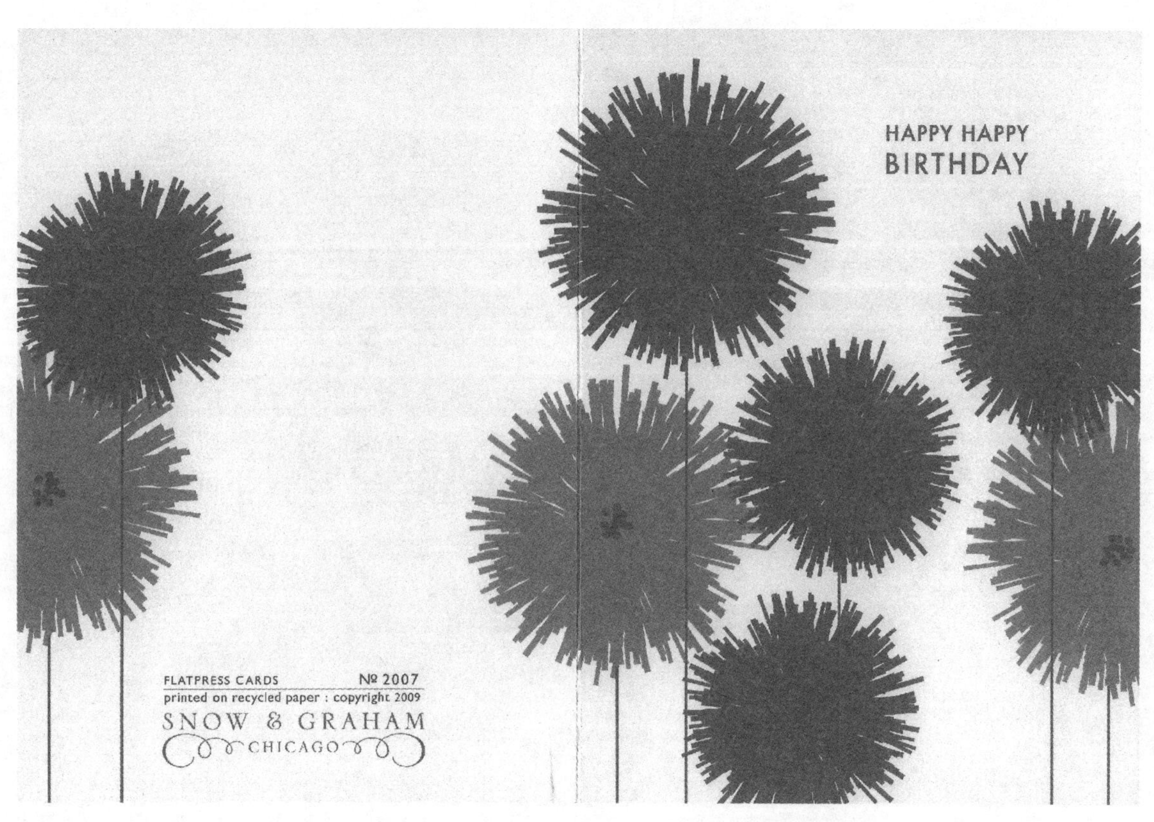
HAPPY HAPPY
BIRTHDAY
FLATPRESS CARDS № 2007
printed on recycled paper : copyright 2009
SNOW & GRAHAM
CHICAGO

MARC HANDELMAN

Dear Mika,

Looking back on our childhood, it's curious that I hadn't really recognized the fact that you didn't pass. I've been increasingly wondering about how our shared biraciality has meant different things for us, and also why it has taken us so long to start exploring it together. What factors in the world and in our lives have made this more or less urgent, and more or less possible? I wonder about this space that sits between the desire for, and impossibility of, certain forms of cultural ownership. I grapple with the inheritances we do and don't get to choose as things that are passed on or passed over between generations. There's too much that feels too convenient to merely own or disavow. I've wondered about how each of us moves in and around these spaces of non-belonging and in-betweenness, which still remains so inarticulate for me.

Do you remember those Asian American cultural pride commercials on KQED? You might have been too young. This was the Bay Area in the mid-80s. For me, the problem wasn't in trying to be more White, though I struggled with that too, but in trying to feel more Asian, which became acute during the years I was in an Asian American Little League. There is also a lot here that's bound up with ideas about masculinity and what that was supposed to look like. By the time I was a little older, I think I understood the value of pride in one's cultural heritage in an abstract way, but I was confused by what that was supposed to mean. Having White-Jewish and Japanese parents touches these strange, entangled dialectics of cultural and racial power: oppressor and oppressed, White and Other, imperialism and colonialism, passing and not passing, Japanese shame and Jewish guilt, with parallel doses of historical assimilation and identification with victimization—all the while being privileged in the proximity to and even surrogacy for Whiteness.

In passing, I wonder about all of the things I will probably never be forced to be in proximity to. I remember the story from before we were born, where mom was disinvited to a family Seder "because there weren't enough chairs." Mom was immediately sickened. She actually *became sick* as if to preempt or repossess her pending absence, wresting away the family's accountability and substituting this rejection with her refusal. I've wondered about the internalized violence of this gentle relinquishment—gentle because, in becoming sick, she let the family believe her absence was inevitable. I've wondered if this relinquishment wasn't accommodation—as an internalization of what Asian Americans are expected to do, as if to account for their own negation, as if passing for passivity? Is Asian American invisibility the instrumentalization of one's quietude or forced withdrawal? I've thought about how this manifestation of mom's sickness, unconscious or willed, was also a form of protection from what it would have felt like to insist on being at that table, knowing she was not wanted. When I recall these stories, I understand another level to mom's overcompensation and assimilation ... her beautiful daily handwritten letters to Nana about our infancy, or why there wasn't any Japanese culture, food, or art in the house for many years.

I just learned that Grandfather took a photo of the Nagasaki mushroom cloud from across the bay in Uto, Kumamoto Prefecture, where the family had relocated. Dad is still convinced that radiation exposure there led to his leukemia. It's interesting that after the war, the extended family wanted to leave the past behind. They apparently sold all of the samurai armor at a garage sale. I continue to question what it means to take pride in and identify with our Japanese heritage, as if doing so would be to locate a solidarity in being Asian American, or to celebrate a space of identity that, in its difference, implicitly stands against or resists forces of ethnic or racial subjugation. How does one account for the violence of an imperial past aligned with Hitler and Mussolini in the Triple Alliance? What does it mean to feel or be Asian American when the Japanese were the most brutal and horrific of colonizers in Asia? In that is another dialectic of oppressor and oppressed. How were we to square these forces of brutality with our pilgrimage to Hiroshima? As Americans, where was our empathy aligned? How were we to trade victimization for shame in the gravity of our visit to Dachau? And even today, how can we ignore the unceasing patriarchy and misogyny of Japan? As Japanese Americans, as biracial Asians, where does identification (or even solidarity) emerge from, and with whom—without the comfort of merely cherry-picking our past?

I wonder about the desire to belong, as well as the desire to refuse this destination, which inherently necessitates borders. What would it be to reject the call for essences and natures, for selfsameness and coherence? Maybe the feeling of longing, even loss, might be experienced less as something contradictory than as a necessary phase of mourning? I am trying to imagine this beautiful, consensual dispossession of belonging. I am trying to think about non-belonging as a place and feeling that is actually a sought displacement, an allegiance to un-rootedness. I want to imagine this ever-receding opacity, this "infinite alterity," that trembles at the core of any identity. I want to imagine an identity always fugitive to itself. Of course, it's much easier to intellectualize some rejection of essentialization than it is to live there and hold that space. Then again, a refusal of reduced identity is quite another thing from owning the privilege and identity that comes into focus through passing.

I can barely remember the Otanis' farm in Lodi. I recall the searing dry heat and the tomato caterpillars, which always terrified me. I remember the ground was always so baked and dusty. Just before Aunt Karen's parents were taken away to the Rohwer Internment Camp, their Jewish neighbors offered to watch over their farm, promising to return it if they came home. Miraculously, it was a promise they kept. I've wondered if the fact that they were Jewish had anything to do with their empathy? If they somehow identified in the fate of the Otanis' their own boundedness to forms of ethnic persecution? Over the years, I'd thought of the gesture of these neighbors in more simplistic terms as an isolated act of compassion, an image of solidarity. But I've wondered about the contingency and precariousness of empathy too. How this story, however beautiful, betrays the broader contours of a "tolerance" of Asian Americans by White society more generally. For all the violence, racism, and discrimination so many Japanese and Asian Americans have experienced, it pales in comparison to the ongoing subjugation and dispossession of everyone darker. In 1966, shortly after the elimination of exclusionary immigration laws against Asians, the *New York Times* ran an article by William Peterson lauding the "success story" of Japanese Americans rebuilding their lives into model citizens after internment. Using a false equivalence of histories of oppression and racism, the article directly weaponized this myth against Black Americans. It's the discursive origin of the myth of the "model minority." This myth has been internalized so deeply by a lot of Asian Americans, not least Uncle, as the basis for his own anti-Blackness. His resentments cling so dearly to this lie ... *I worked hard, I kept my head down, we've suffered too, we've succeeded* ... I've tried to talk to him, but I've failed, pushing only so far, so as not to ruin the few moments we've had together over the years. *So eager to connect with my Japanese roots* ... I've wanted to remind him of the Otanis' neighbors. I've wanted to say, *you have to understand there are different conditions and different histories of theft!*

I was surprised to see those anti-Chinese posters in Brooklyn, let alone down the street from my house. It is perhaps telling, even naive, that this surprises me. In other ways, it is increasingly hard to sustain the ability to be surprised. Did you see Kayleigh McEnany's press briefing gymnastics while trying to defend Trump's use of "Kung flu"? There have been so many recent attacks on Asian Americans across the country ginned up in this backlash, which of course is tethered to a deeper form of xenophobia. One of the things that being Asian American means right now is experiencing a special dis-articulation in identity—a cultural dysphoria that erupts into being or is suspended as a kind of paranoia and internalized gaze as these attacks are leveled across Asian ethnicities. But this conflation and flattening of Asian Americans also produces in response a strange porousness in identity—a space of relation in the common grounds of that violence and fear. Being Asian American right now means there is a salient and practical need for solidarity in orbiting this abstract and impossible reduction, even in the very process of trying to disentangle it.

I've wondered about the things that are said to me in passing, and maybe because of my passing. Proximity to Whiteness is a space that seems to orient others, that can call forth assumptions as if they were agreements.

Recently, after a difficult year of struggling to increase the diversity of the department, a White colleague said to me, "If you want us to advocate hiring a person of color the way you are, we wouldn't have even hired you." She said this all smiling, as if she had found a loophole in my exhaustion. What she said betrayed and exposed the way different identities might be moved to labor for certain things, and what they come up against: if we had known what you'd be fighting for, we would never have hired you. My colleague's comment haunts me as a uniquely perverse experience of erasure and essentialization, holding me accountable to a false and impossible set of equivalencies about representation: *You're not Asian enough to meet your own criteria for diversity, but you are ethnic enough that what you're doing is "reverse racism."* I pushed back, but ultimately, I protected this person from my rage. *I'm going to be patient and help this person understand ...* I performed the role of the good colleague, the model minority. The very presence of my body already allays White discomfort. One of the things that happens in passing is that people constantly say and share things they wouldn't otherwise if they didn't think of you as White.

When I first joined the department, there was a senior faculty member of color who didn't speak to me for four years, confiding to a colleague that "Asians aren't true minorities." I've grappled with this on many levels over the years ... my profound disappointment and frustration, my desire to be close and seen as an ally, but also the acknowledgment of what Asian identity has so often meant with regard to Whiteness. I have wondered about this professor's experience, perhaps their own profound disappointment and frustration with the absence of support or solidarity from other Asian Americans, in life, in the art world, in our department. For all of my indignation and pain at being invisible to this person for so many years, there was admittedly a kind of recognition, an understanding that aligned with my own fraught perception of political alienation from other Asian Americans. I was recently at a university-wide diversity, equity, and inclusion leadership event, and out of a hundred fifty or so people, I counted *four* Asians, including myself. I had decided to walk around the room for a head count. Maybe others were passing too! But in a school with so many Asian faculty and staff, where were they? And this was where I was able to fully see my own internalized racism—as I imagined these ostensible *missing Asians* in passive diligence, lost in study, focused on their engineering and medical degrees, holed up in their research labs ... These deep-seated stereotypes are so pervasive. And yet, the glaring absence of other Asians in this room felt symptomatic of one of the things the model minority myth helps to obfuscate: the violence of racial capitalism and Asian American complicity within these systems of oppression. There is a powerful wager that a lot of Asians accept, willingly or unwittingly, because White supremacy *simply works well enough for us*. Or so it seems.

I've often wondered about the moments when I've been prompted to situate my identity. I remember the year I joined my New York gallery and was asked if I wanted to be a listed artist during Asian Art Week. After much deliberation, I said no. I remember thinking that to claim that identity would be to betray all the privilege of my passing, potentially benefiting from a visibility that was not quite meant for me. The other reason for saying no was an anxiety that my work couldn't meet the representative expectations that are so often put on artists. And I was probably right. Some months later, I had the curious experience of having closely scheduled studio visits—one with a curator from the Jewish Museum, the other from an independent Asian curator and writer. Each was seeking cultural references in my work: Jewish symbols and Japanese iconography, respectively. Of course, none of this was explicitly available in my paintings, and those were the last visits I had with them. I felt I had failed my own identity test, and yet so much of my work has developed out of these complex and fraught assemblies of identity and history. I still wonder if these identitarian criteria are different forms of assimilation in their grasping for transparency and legibility.

In 2019, there was a controversial painting exhibition by Kai Althoff at Tramps, a gallery in Chinatown. The criticism of the show had to do with gentrification and cultural appropriation, cultural-working-class tourism, and modernist exoticization—a kind of neo-Japonisme for the 21st century. Two critics, Jamie Chan and Leah Pires, wrote a piercing review in 4Columns characterizing the show as, among other things, "a freewheeling pastiche of 'Asian' culture writ large." What was amazing to me and I'm still processing is that a lot of the proto-Edo period imagery in that show—imagery which, of course, we ended up growing up with and loving—feels *untouchable* to me ... It's a very complicated and contradictory thing. I'm still trying to disentangle it. I don't believe in a litmus test to use certain kinds of imagery or cultural forms, but the contingencies of appropriation have profoundly fraught and nuanced ethics. On a super uncomfortable level, the atmosphere of nostalgia within the paintings themselves, however vague, performative, aestheticized, and questionably appropriative, struck a deep nerve. As a biracial Asian, I found that it triggered an almost parallel and yet impossible nostalgia, an *inauthentic nostalgia*—a displaced longing for my own sense of cultural connection to our past. And maybe it is that feeling of my own displacement, and the impossibility of something like cultural ownership of that past, that stings in seeing this work, that registers confusion and shame. Maybe it's why I feel I could never draw on this kind of imagery, or, draw on it without having to confront the transparency and overcompensation of my desire for belonging. What is astounding to me is imagining this artist's sense of uncomplicatedness and dandyism, his pitch-perfect balancing act of irony and aesthetic elegance, working from a space of coherence—a confidence and insatiable motility of thought claimed and enacted as artistic freedom. There was a vestigial, embarrassing *jealousy of Whiteness*, of what it would feel like to paint, unburdened by all these minor feelings.

A couple of years ago, I brought homemade furikake with shiso from our backyard to a Roots and Community Dinner at Nora's school. The Japanese parents at the table were so impressed, sweetly teasing me about how authentic it was. They, of course, bought theirs at the store. But somehow my overcompensation, and I'm actually not sure if it was that, felt unburdened. For whatever reason, Japanese cooking maintains a space of levity.

To be continued! In the meantime, I'm finally sharing this obanyaki batter recipe Nora and I have been honing:

2 cups cake flour
2 tablespoons baking powder
1 cup milk
2 large eggs
4 tablespoons white sugar
2 tablespoons honey
1 tablespoon vanilla extract
1 teaspoon vegetable oil
Pinch of cinnamon

Mix the sugar, honey, eggs, and vanilla extract together until the sugar is dissolved before adding milk. Then add the flour, baking powder, cinnamon, and finally, the vegetable oil, stirring to an even consistency. You gotta put the batter in a container in the fridge for at least a couple of hours. And remember—don't overmix, or it won't rise properly!

Love,
Marc

1 Jamie Chan and Leah Pires, review of Kai Althoff, "Häuptling Klapperndes Geschirr," Tramps, 75 East Broadway, New York, October 24, 2018 – January 20, 2019, *4Columns*, November 30, 2018.

2 "Press Briefing by Press Secretary Kayleigh McEnany," The White House, June 22, 2020.

CFGNY

Dear CFGNY2,

When I first got a seat at the table, it was at the kids' table. The hierarchy of a seating arrangement wasn't lost on me.

Alongside the humbling sting of being publicly marked as insignificant, I have come to appreciate the kids' table as a safe zone. There is no one to impress at the kids' table. Your neighbor is random, without premise of vertical opportunity. No one at the kids' table has been around long enough to accrue social capital or the accompanying baggage.

Occasionally, someone breaks off from the central tables to crouch beside the kids' table, a well-intentioned gesture meant to level our eye contact.

Here, they are a tourist regardless of their place in the outside social hierarchy: the unknown quotient of a guest assigned to the kids' table can make for an attractive accessory, or a cause for dismissal. They never sit during this visit, in case their ass falls through a socially demoting trap door. I feel comfortable talking to them with my mouth full.

Best,
xxx

Dear CFGNY2,

I don't like to use people as tools for my own personal gain ... especially while I'm eating. I'm here for the free food, and I hope no one hits on me.

Late capitalism is so crazy. This entire table of adults is infantilized by a seating arrangement and a hierarchy that radiates downward from the seat of power at the center. Everyone is asked to play their part for this center in perfectly calibrated roles, the whole dinner a portion of the cost of one sale. They get their food first, of course.

The person sitting next to me asked, "So, what do you think of the show?" and I said, "I want to go back and see it when it's not crowded and full of people."

I'm not going back.

Sincerely,
XXX

P.S. Did you know that lack of empathy is one of the defining characteristics of a sociopath?

Dear CFGNY2,

To have a seat at the table means that you might be somebody. Occasionally, one of these somebodies breaks off from the central table to crouch beside ours, a well-intentioned gesture meant to level our eye contact. They lower their body close to the ground, bending their knees at different angles and using their toes to balance on one foot. This position takes endurance, and one can soil their clothes if they can't do it for long and lose balance.

Different crops grown from the same soil are rotated annually, as their combined diversity reduces reliance on one set of nutrients while maintaining a resistance to the development of pests and weeds. This resistance is an invisible strength that collectively grows through time, the shared ground being able to supply each of the seasonal plant's individual needs. The crops live in better harmony this way, using one another's byproducts as fuel for growth.

Although monoculture crops are able to produce in large quantities, they rely heavily on external input—namely pesticides—to be sustained.

You are what you eat.

Forever,
XXX

Dear CFGNY2,

What we offer is unscalable.

What do I mean when I say "we"? Not the monolith "we" that is often used in the context of speaking about race, but a "we" in the sense of the many, a specific number of others that surround me. A "we" that encompasses an "I" that comes with the understanding that I can only find my true expression in relation to others. An "I" that grants the opacity that Glissant describes: "it does not disturb me to accept that there are places where my identity is obscure to me, and the fact that it amazes me does not mean I relinquish it."[1] I can see myself in others, perceive the "we," but only in glimpses. A glimpse of recognition that becomes powerfully binding and one that opens up unknown parts of myself. A deliberate confusion of "we" and "I" in which to get lost and start feeling the contours of a self.

What's allowed at the kids' table?

A playful reordering of chairs. The passing around of dishes (sometimes twice!) until all the plates are empty. The co-mingling of energies that nurture. Gossip. Carmel, Popsy, Tamara, Doggy, Flopsie, Pierre, Teddy. Taking the left-overs from the other table, that no one else dares touch, and eating them for a week. A plea for karaoke and the first one up to sing. A Disney song that is modeled on a Broadway hit. The nervous energy of someone seemingly mis-placed and looking to dart out; furtive glances elsewhere. A mode of study where everyone learns through a shared experience. Queer reckoning with above and below. Looking side to side. A shared presence with each other. Presents. A gift.

Best,	Sincerely,	Warmly,	Cooly,	Obsessed,	Never,	Love,	Always,	Forever,
XXX	XXX	XXX	XXX	XXX	XXX	XXX	XXX	XXX

1 Éduoard Glissant, *Poetics of Relation*, translated from French by Betsy Wing (Ann Arbor: University of Michigan Press, 1997).

PHILIP POON

MARKET STREET
FORSYTH STREET
EAST BROADWAY
2nd Floor
202A 千枝童裝精品屋
202B 蘭桂坊
202C 日月星時裝屋
203A 卡妮娜時裝
203B 東方牙室
203C 羽西護膚化妝品店
205 非凡地帶男女服飾
206 ECKHAUS LATTA
207 心地帶男女裝飾
208 雪兒服裝店
209 姐妹花睡衣專門店
210 東方旅行社
211 華麗睡衣店
12 好旺角童裝
電梯請按B
215 倩影時裝屋
216 甜甜服飾
217 鴻運時裝店
218 涵平服裝店
221 絢麗時裝店
222 伊人坊女仕服飾用品
225 星月屋(服飾&天然水晶)
226 麗穎百貨店
227 女友化妝品屋
228 利利工藝精品屋
229 雅秀服飾坊
230
231

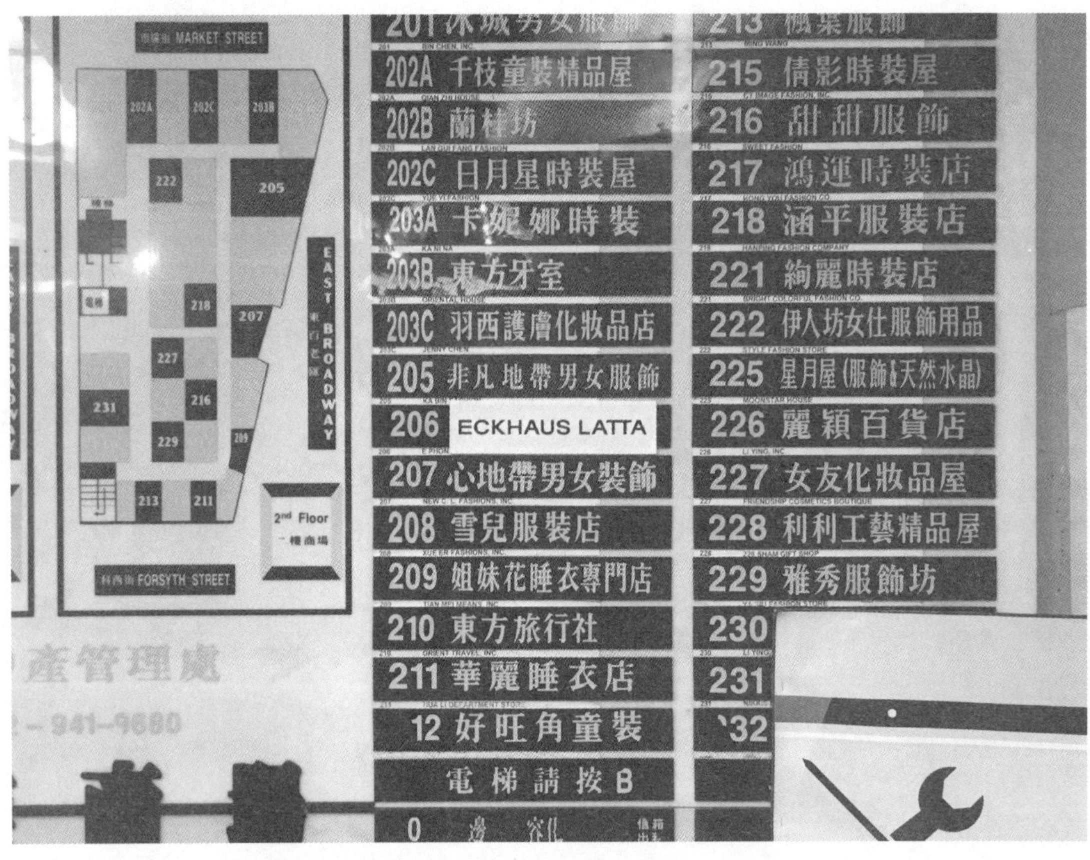

Dear Mike Eckhaus and Zoe Latta,

As an art-adjacent millennial who lives in Brooklyn, it's not a surprise that I admire your work. I like how your projects question assumptions about beauty, gender, and art—they're exciting because they transcend expectations and trends.

It is for this reason that I'm disappointed in your retail stores in New York and Los Angeles. Unlike your clothing, the aesthetic fetishization of both Chinatown locations is unoriginal, and worse, unintentionally cliché. Not only is there a tired history of the Western gaze exploiting racialized eccentricities of Asian cultures for cheap inspiration, but also the trend of opening experimental art galleries and high-end stores in hyper-local Chinatowns is so ubiquitous today that it's beyond boring. A few years ago, places were cool if they didn't have a sign and you needed a password—today's cool is deliberately contrasting high culture against a backdrop of Chineseness, like using kitsch neon signage and displaying high fashion or art in a Chinatown mall that sells underwear and other essentials to working-class immigrants.

You must know this already. All the neighbors of your New York store are either art galleries or high fashion boutiques—you're actually one of the later additions to the mall. Restaurants and bars in that part of Chinatown that cater to the young, White, millennial art crowd are equally ubiquitous. The aesthetics of these places are remarkably similar, if not identical—gender-ambiguous clothing, meta art, and well-plated small dishes photograph nicely against backdrops of tacky decaying remnants of immigrant Chinese culture. (The Chinese hawker in the background adds a certain *je ne sais quoi.*) Whether it's Kiki's, a Greek restaurant keeping the Chinese sign of the joss-paper shop that preceded it and making a second awning with Chinese characters, or the cocktail bar Apotheke designing a classy, retro speakeasy interior while leaving the old Chinese sign outside, it's all the same. Also, Lalito, Dah Shop, The Hunt, Reena Spaulings, Alden Projects, Pablo's Birthday, Jeffrey Stark, Super Dutchess, Vacation ... the list goes on and on. Happy Ending, a nightclub on Broome, kept the Chinese signage of Xie He Health Club and gut-renovated the interior into a neon-lit cocktail bar ... it's a cool name for a club because we all know that immigrant Chinese women are good at assembling iPhones and tug jobs! (I heard if you go to the spa on Eldridge, you can get a blowjob for $20, lol.) But yeah, associating sex work with working-class immigrants is funny and profitable, even today.

I mean, we *get* it right? The contrast between high and low, edgy and basic, cool and Chinese ... *I* get it.

When Omer Fast transformed James Cohan Gallery in Chinatown into a dilapidated Chinese storefront as a gesture to what he imagined the space to have been before, there were protests. Danielle Wu in *Hyperallergic* and Holland Cotter at the *New York Times* called him out. You're not exhibiting overflowing trash cans as representations of a Chinatown past, but the Eckhaus Latta flag staked indiscriminately into the pagoda-style storefront of your LA store is a bit aggressive, no? High fashion has colonized the cheap kitsch of the Chinese!

As Pei-Ru Keh put it in the *Wallpaper* write-up of the New York store, the hyper-local Chinese setting is interesting because it provides an "installation-like environment" to buy your clothes in. But those people—the fishmonger in the market below, the store clerk selling shoes, the Chinese American child helping his parents in the shop—they're not art, or worse, background props for expensive clothes. They're people, and their lives are complex, valuable, and beautiful just as they are.

Maybe the adjacency to minority cultures, something that isn't afforded by a SoHo or East Village storefront, is desirable for you. I know the rent in Chinatown is cheaper too. For these reasons, perhaps I could suggest relocating to Harlem? Bodegas and local clothing stores are going out of business as a younger, White, population is moving in. Perhaps 2 Bridges Music Arts could open up next to you and graffiti their name onto their window?

I jest, haha lol smfh. We all know that Diet Prada would call out an Eckhaus Latta store in Harlem or Bed-Stuy the next day. It'd be an offensive juxtaposition of class, wealth, and privilege. It'd be racist. We all know the fashion photography trope of slender blonde models posing exuberantly in front of African children and straw huts, and we all know that it's wrong. Which is why it's so frustrating to see you partake in this trend so uncritically, with Yellow instead of Black and a gender-ambiguous model posing in front of someone who reminds me of my grandma.

Why is it that the *only* ethnic culture you engage with is Chinese? It's like a weird Asian fetish where you're deliberately seeking out the most stereotyped and exaggerated aspects of immigrant Chinese culture. You do know that Chinese immigrants aren't that different from your parents, your aunts and uncles, your grandparents, right? Of all the films you made with Alexa Karolinski, only one features older people of color and it's of Chinese women in Seward Park who don't speak English, doing an exercise routine that we all know looks comical to an American viewer. When you filmed Melony Matthews, a Black female opera singer, you did so in a refined setting with a curated selection of expensive plants—she's dignified, and her artistic expression is taken seriously. The Chinese women aren't—they're quirky, funny, and their unusual exercise deliberately contrasts the refinement of your clothes on their aged bodies. Can you imagine what the film would look like if you understood that these women were as beautiful and interesting and complex as Hari Nef? Not in a cheeky way but in a serious one—if you saw their full humanity. Despite being the only people in your first film, these women are noticeably absent from all your subsequent ones with your friends and collaborators—Black and White millennials who are entitled to artistic and complex expressions of their beauty. Why didn't you ask these Chinese women to describe the first time they fell in love, as you did to the White and Black millenials in another film? Unlike them, these Chinese women would never step foot in an Eckhaus Latta store—despite being in their neighborhood, the store's not meant for them. It's a funny thought though, right? The image of an older Chinese person asking the 25-year-old clerk to try on the latest Come Tees collab? Or is it more serious?

Do you know that the part of Chinatown where your store is has a poverty rate of more than 30 percent? Perhaps that's what you were referring to in your interview for Mykita when you said, "nothing is nice" in the part of Chinatown where you live. Is poverty the appeal? But in all seriousness, what would an Eckhuas Latta store in a part of Brooklyn with a high poverty rate look like? Would you describe that neighborhood using the same words? Would that be nice?

Do you speak to your Chinese neighbors? The woman selling socks downstairs, or the dumpling maker down the street? Do you want to? Do they like your clothing? Do they follow you on Instagram? Did they like the Whitney show? Does it even matter?

Donald Trump and his supporters probably view working-class Chinese immigrants who don't speak English in a similar manner to how you do, as comically eccentric, foreign, and un-American. How would a bro in a MAGA hat describe Chinese immigrants in Chinatown? What would the *opposite* of that be? Trump benefits from the othering of minorities because it animates his pro-White base. Locating both of your stores in immigrant Chinatown malls must also be financially profitable.

This criticism may come as a surprise because we're all liberal progressives who support racial justice. Internalized racism is supposed to be something that others need to grapple with—Republican bigots in the Deep South, or White men without college degrees. It's difficult work to truly understand perspectives that are not one's own and to confront our own prejudices. Trump is a prime example. Our president has said that he is "the least racist person there is anywhere in the world." When Bob Woodward asked him whether White privilege prevented him from empathizing with the anger and pain of Black Americans, the President simply said "no," and laughed at the idea. I'm hoping you won't be as dismissive as Trump was about your relative (White) privilege in Chinatown.

Today, most people in progressive communities recognize that systemic racism, sexism, and economic injustice are real. It's both morally right and even "cool" to support those who have been historically marginalized.

This is why your choice of models is commendable—you frequently cast people of diverse ages, races, and body types who are typically excluded from traditional conceptions of beauty. Can it be cool to elevate the lives of working-class Chinese immigrants in Chinatown, to forefront their humanity rather than pose in front of them?

In today's polarized, segregated, sexist, homophobic, transphobic, ableist, racist society, let's not capitalize on negative stereotypes of Chinese American culture as dirty, cheap, weird, foreign, *otherworldly*. Given the racism and xenophobia championed by Trump and revealed in the coronavirus-inspired attacks against Asian Americans, let's elevate those who work in low-paying jobs, those without voices, those in the background of your Instagram posts ... your Chinese American brothers and sisters.

I would love to see what the true expression of progressive, inclusive, and *unique* fashion can be.

最好!
Philip Poon

PREM KRISHNAMURTHY

Dear dear Zia,

How lovely to hear that you're moving to Ireland! Bet you'll find it a welcome change from London. I've only been twice, but I feel an odd sense of kinship with the Irish. Perhaps it's a sense of shared or at least sympathetic colonial history, the idea that "we" were all against the same enemy. I remember what my dad used to say: "The British: they'll shake your hand with one hand and stab you in the back with the other!" Delivered in a comedic mode, but it definitely left an impression on me.

I can't believe it's been only (already?) six years since we first met. Or rather, I should say since I "met" your novel—because we actually met IRL later on.

On August 9, 2014, as I was reading *In the Light of What We Know*, Michael Brown was being murdered by police in Ferguson, Missouri. What a brutal and senseless juxtaposition of verbs. His murder sparked a collective uprising against racism and police violence, which I followed from afar. In New York, I happened to be hosting Mitch McEwen, a member of the Black art collective HOWDOYOUSAYYAMINAFRICAN?, for a residency at my gallery P!. It's now a bit of a blur, but within days the entire residency pivoted, and the group responded in their own, all-in kind of way. Over the remaining weeks of August, they created a total installation at P! that featured a 24-channel video piece, *thewayblackmachine*, put together by Richie Adomako. It collected and presented social media from the BLM protests, transformed visually by algorithmic scripts. It also transformed the entire gallery space, and my life.

Since no one will read this letter but you, I can safely admit a sorry truth: I never really began to think consciously about race, especially my own, until I was a lot older than most folks. In high school, my own upper-middle-class upbringing and assimilation into mainstream American culture meant I took it for granted that I belonged to the same category as the other folks in my small, WASP-y Connecticut town. Were there ever moments of discomfort? Sure. Did I feel like I fit in completely? Never. But I didn't make too much of it, and anyway, I had enough support on other fronts to make it work.

That feeling of slumbering safety and oblivious ease continued through my college years. Wasn't I just so *lucky* that I never had to think about race? As a high-achieving Indian American, I felt impervious to most of the discourse around postcolonialism and stuck to the things I loved most: my postmodern American novels and continental philosophy. By the time I was in university, there were enough Black and Brown folks around me to make me feel even more like a good model minority. Maybe it was moving to Germany that triggered something; I remember the moment on a train platform in Berlin when I realized that someone might actually flirt with me *because* of my skin color. The first time, it was thrilling. After a couple more references to *Siddhartha* and Germans looking for Kama Sutra enlightenment, I had a less rosy picture.

But I really don't need to tell you my entire life story, Zia! I've been tending too much to shaggy dog tales these days. Maybe I just need to sit down and finally pen some sort of sprawling memoir or fiction (or combination of both) that can capture these ideas adequately. I suppose that's what you did—though much better than I'll ever be able to do—with *In the Light of What We Know*!

When I first read your novel that summer and fall of 2014, one particular passage struck me: your itinerant and mysterious protagonist, Zafar, is queried about his penchant for wearing dark suits at all times while navigating in Afghanistan, Bangladesh, and Pakistan. His response is telling, though now flipping through the book I realize that I can't find the exact words I remember. Did I make it up or extrapolate from the text? You once told me that there are lots of things that people recall from your books that you never explicitly wrote, but that you actually did intend to imply.

In any case, Zafar tells his friend that his generic but formal clothing choice helps him to avoid certain kinds of attention, to unmark himself. That fall, in the wake of Michael Brown's murder, in the wake of Ferguson, in the wake of *thewayblackmachine*, in the wake of *In the Light of What We Know*, I traveled around the US, moving through the international art world like a fish out of water. Wherever I landed, I would insist, even more forcefully than in the past, on wearing a dark suit or at least a blazer at all times, regardless of temperature or context. From steamy gallery openings to museum dinners to art fair previews to friends' birthday parties, I would answer queries about taking off my jacket with a paean to your book and a line that I guess I invented: "I always wear a dark suit when traveling in a war-torn country."

Until reading your book, I had never thought too carefully about how I dressed, but that passage (even if I invented part of it!), made me realize how my particular garb has served as a shield. In the several years leading up to 2014, as I had started to spend more and more time embedded within the art world, chatting with folks whose skin color was a lot lighter and whose net worth might be a hundredfold or a thousandfold my own, I felt an even greater need for protection: a distinctive layer of clothing that would mark me as belonging to the class of people allowed to frequent these hallowed white cubes of White culture.

Clothing has always been a strong signifier of identity and aspiration. My dear friend Roger, a founder of the art journal and publisher I was telling you about, wrote a trenchant yet humorous essay about clothing and etiquette in the art world for our first book. But beyond signifying belonging to a particular creative class or profession (for example, that of the artist), having uniforms for certain roles and classes also represents an attempt on the part of the wearer to conform, to fit in, to stand out less—and thus to make the experience of social interaction between folks from different contexts smoother.

I'm sure that Erving Goffman must have said something about this, but it's been a couple decades since I read him. The jacket and boat shoes required at a country club (a type of place I've been exactly once, with the upstate New York grandparents of my stepdaughter's close friend, where I suspected, correctly, that I might be the only person with tawny skin not working the service); the basic shirt and shoes required for more modest spaces. I often think of the historical anecdote, hopefully not apocryphal, that a friend once told me about the characteristic garb of the Hasidim. Apparently, they originally donned black suits and hats in order to imitate the Polish or Russian nobility, and therefore blend in better. Except that, in continuing the style for centuries after, their attempt at assimilation, ironically enough, became a highly visible marker of otherness and *not* belonging.

Eventually, my own habit of wearing a blazer to every art-world event or meeting started to seem more like a forced gesture, one I imposed on myself in order to feel a sense of fitting in. Although, come to think of it, sometimes I also took the opposite tack: one day many years ago, I was meant to gather my then-girlfriend from Tempelhof Airport in Berlin. Her flight had been scheduled for September 12, 2001, and so it was delayed for a week or so by the World Trade Center attacks. I was nervous about being picked up as a suspicious individual in the airport, so I decided to make myself *really* conspicuous: I headed to the airport wearing safety orange pants, a safety orange jacket, and a safety orange hat. Plus, I whistled the whole way into the airport, just to make it clear that I was no threat. The security personnel probably thought I was insane rather than scared.

Although America and Germany are the only countries I've known as a resident, I can feel with clarity the powerful connections between class, race, and clothing in the home country of my parents, India. As Tamil-speaking, highly educated Brahmins, my parents belong to the elite of their own context. Even though they left that context for the USA and arrived as dark-skinned, ill-fitted immigrants with funny accents who lived off of food stamps for the first few years, what they left behind was privilege: as Brahmins, belonging to the highest caste, they could make good use of education, capital, advancement, and social networks, resources withheld from others around them. And this shows in their garb, in the veshtis and dhothis my father might wear to the temple, lined with gold filigree; in my mother and grandmother's nine-yard saris, equally resplendent with precious metals. Those clothes allowed them to lord it over those of lower castes. How was it read by their colonial masters?

It's hard for me to say, since my father was born only four years before Indian independence and my mother three years after—and I, born and raised only on the East Coast, in the US, have little access to the sartorial codes of their native country. Yet within the context of our transplanted Hindu community, I started wearing my black and gray blazers as a badge of pride on the rare occasions that I went to the temple after college. There, it was a nearly aggressive sign of deliberate Otherness, an attempt to represent power from another context in one that was foreign even to me.

Of course, I owe my mother even this badge of honor, this suit of armor (is it a coincidence or a fact of etymological clarity that we call it a "suit"?). For it was my mother, who, if I remember correctly, first took me when I was 14 or 15 to a Macy's department store in our local shopping mall to buy me my first blazer: a navy blue Brooks Brothers jacket with fake gold buttons sewn on the outside of the sleeves, which marked me as a Connecticut man. This blazer, which was probably acquired in preparation for my first serious debate meet, would be the one I carried through college and into my first years afterward in Germany. In my twenties, after having sneered at the extreme privilege and opportunity that allowed me to study, debt-free, at an Ivy League college, receiving an undergraduate degree in fine art (of all possible subjects! For an Asian child to pursue art at an expensive college instead of something more practical! It is a testament to the love and care my parents have for me, something it took me decades to realize, that they even allowed this. A whole other letter to send one day!), that I realized the truth: I owed my parents the fact that they first tried to armor me. They gave me a garment to protect me from the hostile White world that had made a smaller man of my father and worse of too many others.

So today, despite the baggage of a blazer, I can wear it more lightly, thanks to your fantastic book and the journey it began in me. I can wear a blazer to openings, even in the Miami heat (the worst kind of openings, let me tell you! And the place from which I first called you after a raging all-nighter to talk about doing a show together); sometimes, rarely, I even trust myself enough to wear shorts to openings, the way other folks around me seem to do with relative ease.

On that note: a couple of months ago, my dear stepdaughter, who had helped assist a major German artist install a museum show, took me and her mother as *her* guests to the private opening. It was an unusually hot day, and my wife suggested that it was *just fine* for me to wear shorts. As I walked out towards the door, I asked my very stylish stepdaughter if it was an appropriate choice. She looked me up and down, and told me that it would probably be better if I at least went in pants. I ended up throwing on a blazer—not the worst decision I've ever made.

Big hugs,
Prem

August 9, 2020, Berlin

ANNE ANLIN CHENG
TO LIN TSU-AI, MY GRANDMOTHER

July 10, 2020

You were named after Love, but you did not love me. Everyone knew and seemed to understand that you preferred boys. Boys meant worth and futurity; girls were disposable (you raise girls for other people). You found me too skinny, too mouthy, too smart for my own good. Naturally, I became your husband's, my Agon's, favorite—because we were both born in the Year of the Tiger, because he thought I took after his brains, and I suspect, if he were honest, because he wanted to tweak you a little.

You tried your best: the awkward hand on my cheek in one photo, the many dresses to tame me, the way you always explained why my brother needed the bigger slice of cake or the extra bun. But I could see the softening of your gaze when you looked at him, the way he could make you smile in ways that no one could coax you to do in a photograph.

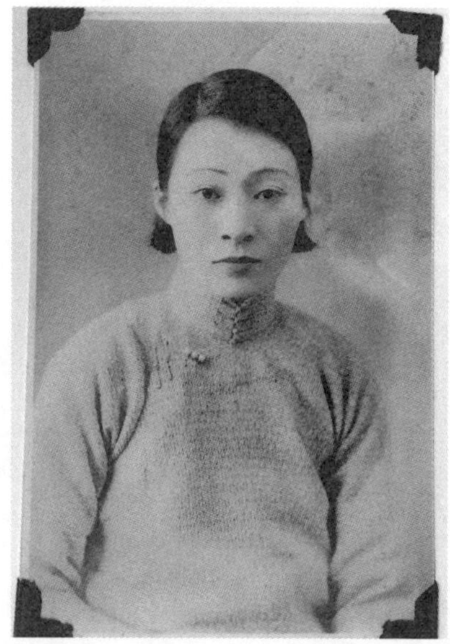

It's odd then that years after we moved to America, my most vivid memories of my childhood revolved not around our life in Taipei, but around the summers we spent in your house in Tainan. Maybe summers are always more memorable for kids. Maybe it is because your house was so extraordinary, the stuff of exploration: a white stone building standing three stories high, with balconies, a rooftop terrace, three interior courtyard gardens (one with a real well)—complete with a mysterious and slightly scary, vacant back compound where servants used to live—and the long-unused water gully set along the perimeter that bred mosquitoes and made the best running guide.

Every summer, you would summon your daughter home. My mother would pack up my brother and me, leave my father behind, and take the train southward. That ride (now two and a half hours) used to take six to seven hours, but my brother and I loved it. We knew all the landmarks by heart: the wet, tiered rice paddy fields that would appear the moment the city receded, the Eagle Rock that anticipated Taichung, the midway point. Trains in those days boasted dining cars with crisp, white tablecloths, a vase on each table, and such great food that reputedly people would take the train just to eat. Even the bento boxes that came by on steel carriers were delicious, especially the grilled pork chops with pickled vegetables. To my mother's frustration every time, my brother and I would bounce off our seats, only to wilt just before the train pulled into Tainan, and then she would have to contend with luggage and two half-asleep kids.

By the time we got to your house, we would be totally awake again. While you fussed over mom and my brother, I would rush upstairs to mom's old room. First, I checked on my friends in the glass bookshelf: the little wooden Dutch milkmaid whose butter stick is really an hourglass, the neat queue of kokeshi dolls, the kissing Dresden salt-and-pepper bride and groom, the miniature purple mandarin duck whose back sported tiny holes for a jasmine flower or two. The bookshelf smelled of strange and faraway places. Then I would, at last, turn to the doll that hung next to the bookshelf—not really a doll, but a ceramic face of a foreign little girl with big, flat blue eyes, cherry red lips, and a headful of yellow curls. Years later, in America, I would learn that it was Shirley Temple, whose likenesses were sold to adoring mothers and daughters all over the world.

Back then, I found her shiny, anonymous face, with its stark colors, slightly repulsive but fascinating. I would carefully take it down, turn it over, and trace with my fingers the white, hollow backside that looked like a concave face; the contact made me inexplicably queasy. My mom told me that she wanted nothing more than to look like that girl. Once, she sat patiently for hours while you curled her hair with a heated rod. The results, according to mom anyway, were disappointing.

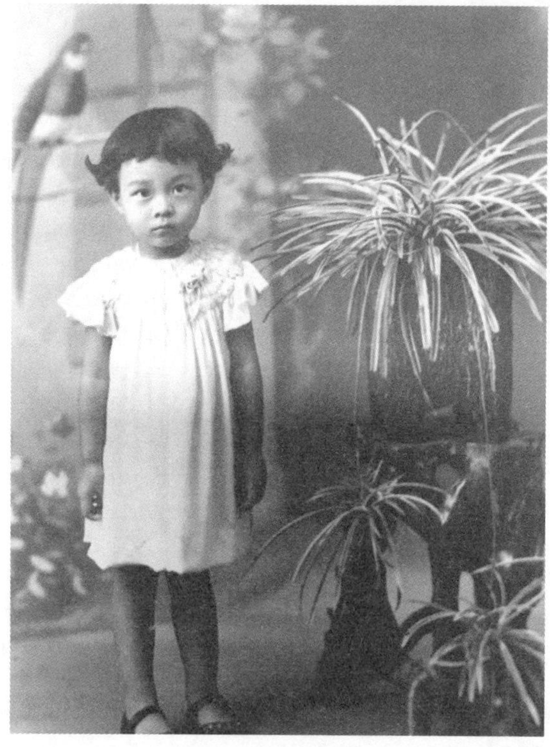

Those days felt long and luxurious, cloistered in time, imprinted with sun and moisture. The hours were mostly marked by our stomachs: the small eel-fish that one can only buy in Tainan, poached with ginger to delicate perfection for a special afternoon treat; the sweet tofu bought from the vendor whom you paid extra to add an additional spoonful of brown sugar to the soup; the six-course meal every night; your homemade vanilla ice cream served between square monaka shells that melt in the mouth. You did not like me in the kitchen, but you did teach me to sew. I think I got some of my unforgiving perfectionism from those lessons. Once, I rushed through a dress I was eager to wear, proud of my own speed. You came along, turned the dress inside out, inspected the workmanship, and calmly ripped the seams apart. The stitches were uneven and the seam allowances inconsistent. Do it over, you said. Your eye and your hand for precision and detail were the stuff that family legends are made of: the inch-tall, faceless, silk clown dolls that you made in a rainbow of colors and placed in miniature glass jars; the dark red velvet baby shoes with the kitten lining inside and backing whose rows of hand stitches looked machine-made.

Although it was never overt, you and I butted heads all the time. Like how, in those Tainan summers, in spite of my begging, you would not allow my mother to wake me up from naps; I would always wake up sweaty and alone behind the mosquito netting, while I could hear the rest of the family downstairs talking and laughing, already having had midafternoon snacks together. Or, how you kept asking Agon not to let me follow him around the house while he fixed things—because girls don't mess with tools. Or, later, after we moved to the United States, how you complained to my mom about my skin darkening under the Georgia sun: "Why do you allow her to go to the beach? How can you let her run around looking like that, like a peasant?" I remember being embarrassed by your outdated notions, but also feeling shame behind my defiance.

As a teenage immigrant, I could barely find my place among American ideas of femininity, and I had already bungled Chinese girlhood. In Tainan, you, your sisters, and my mother were all known, both inside and outside of the family, as great beauties. I can say this because I looked nothing like you. In this, too, I failed you. You always had to explain to people that I took after my father. One time, my mother took me aside to tell me, "You know, you don't have beauty, but you have likability, and that is more important." (The Taiwanese word for "likable" means, literally, "not deserving of hate.") Well, maybe—but not what a 6 year-old girl wants to hear from her mother.

We fought to the bitter end. After your stroke, I went back to see you. (Were you disappointed that it was not my brother?) When your jaw first relinquished its hold, you stopped eating and talking. You would rather commit to silence and hunger than dribble words or food. It must have been cruel for someone who used to iron her handkerchiefs and bed linens to find herself drooling, unable even to bathe herself. Wiping down your loose skin and jutting bones, I would feel the air being squeezed out of my lungs. (*This* belonged to someone who believed that being plump is a sign of fortune.) Even then, you remained sharp, asking after the mailman's timely arrival, noting the exact day of the week without the help of a calendar. Your handwriting on the small, white pads was distinct and elegant, like hawks thrusting through air, demanding their wild fields. You did not understand why we were fighting to keep you. You wanted so much to be released, and we could not allow it. During the force-feedings, your fingers gripped my wrists like small, angry ferrets—anger, for love's severity. Anger, for the body that continues to need tending.

At night, in the other room, I counted your ragged breaths. One evening, I found you crying. I sat down to cry with you. You wrote something on your pad. I thought you wanted to comfort me. Instead, you wrote, "I am glad you are crying. I do not want to be alone."

*

Now I'm the one facing the ends of time. Disease (cancer, a global health crisis, racism) makes and unmakes my days. Although I continue to do all I can,

I understand something of your refusal. When chemo was erasing me with its indifferent and brutal malaise, there were days when, in the silent recesses of my mind, I wished I could just stop being. This is something I could never fully admit, even to myself—because it feels deeply ungrateful, because it feels like a betrayal of my job as parent and partner.

In chemo time, everything falls away except the barest love.

At the same time, the world outside is showing me that love is not enough. In 1920, W. E. B. Du Bois wrote a short story called "The Comet," a dystopic vision of the end of the world where, at long last, interracial love (between the last White woman and the last Black man) could be redeemed. Only with the end of the world and the breakdown of all societal rules, according to Du Bois, can love between the races be imaginable. And, indeed, in the story, her family returned in the end—and all that was between the lovers was dashed, erased as if it had never been. No, love is not enough. Here we are: in this extraordinary moment when *everyone on earth faces the same threat*, and we are still besieged by old hates. Anti-Black racism in America is as bold, as virulent, as ever. Anti-Asian sentiments, which have been around since the 19th century, have surged with frightening ease (perhaps because they never fully went away). They have gained traction along with the pandemic, itself formulated as a racialized contagion, what our president calls the "Chinese virus." I feel my vulnerability every day. And I fear the multiple toxicities (viral, political, cultural, environmental) that threaten the future of my children.

Years ago, I wrote that America suffered from a racial melancholia it could neither swallow nor digest, that unprocessed grief hidden behind grievances continues to haunt our social relations, that the discourse of racial *identity* has obscured the history of American racial *entanglements*. More and more, I think there is no getting over three centuries of American racial strife, and the enduring and knotted legacy of systemic and cultural racism. But I still need to ask: in the absence of love, what is possible? What are relations that accommodate fissures?

*

Amah, my world is so different from yours in a thousand ways. And in real life, we would never be having this conversation. You did not live in a world where people talked about race or racism, or even about love. You would be mystified by my work and what I do. The truth is, I do not remember ever having had a conversation with you beyond passing, quotidian exchanges. But, once, the day before I left you to return to the States, you sat up in bed and allowed me to brush your hair, undyed and brittle, though still startlingly thick, each strand seemingly alive with its own will. I managed to twist it into a neat bun.

I powdered your face, put on some light blush and a thin coat of lipstick. You looked up at me with those huge, dark lynx eyes of yours, made even more preternatural by weight loss, and I thought I saw something like pleasure.

Weeks after the news, here in America, I found myself confessing your passing to almost everyone I saw—the mail carrier, the gas attendant, the fruit stand checker. I knew they were strangers; I knew it was TMI. Something in the recitation made your vanishing, halfway across the world, less ephemeral. People offered sympathy. Some shared their own losses. Looking back, I was too young then, even in my early thirties, to grasp all the ways in which suffering and loss can create company, how intimacy can be forged between strangers, and that just because something is provisional does not mean it is not doing some work.

Amah, I want to be able to say, in the common grief of strangers, I have not left you alone.

JOSH KLINE
WHAT ARE YOU?

To whom it may concern:

My name is Josh Kline.

Am I Asian? Or Asian American? Am I American? Am I one of you?

When people—of all backgrounds—see my name on paper, they assume I'm a White Jew. Perhaps you're wondering to yourself right now why someone with a name like mine is even in this book. Or asking whether it's problematic for someone with a name like mine to claim certain identities. Or to speak out about certain subjects. Or maybe you live in the kind of utopian majority-minority future America I've fantasized about living in for decades, and this letter is completely banal, my concerns obsolete.

If only I were there with you now in the year 2121, instead of living in Donald Trump's America in 2020.

Meeting people in person for the first time, before my background gets unpacked, I frequently get told I must be Mexican. Or Colombian or Ecuadorian. Once, in the immediate aftermath of 9/11, when I still lived in Philly, I was waiting for the bus, and a teenage White girl called me an "Ay-rab" before she flicked her cigarette at my face. A few years ago at a bar in the East Village, a well-regarded Japanese performance artist with an expensive MFA from Bard College asked me: "Do you think you're Asian?" I asked him in response if *he* thought I was Asian. In his slippery awkward-cool way, he very slowly and very briefly gestured to the sides of his eyes and their epicanthal folds, and almost under his breath, said: "You ... look ... Hispanic." In response, I asked him if Filipinos are Asian. And if the Philippines, where my mother and her family come from, is in Asia? He demurred, and the conversation slithered elsewhere. I decided not to share with him how, when she was a little girl, my mother and her family—my grandparents, my aunts, my uncles—had to flee into the forest after the Japanese Imperial Army burned down their home. I decided not to ask him if that took place in "Asia."

My whole life, I have often had to muster long arguments with you about family, heredity, or the nuances of my upbringing when I attempt in conversation to casually embrace the identities I claim or am connected to—in the casual, thoughtless way that White people or people from less complicated family backgrounds are allowed to in our society's racist hierarchy. Questions along the lines of "What are you?" or "Where do you really come from?" follow people like me through our entire lives like aggressively ignorant stalkers. Even worse are the moments when people take it upon themselves to play a game of ethnicity jury or race court and assign mixed-race people an identity. *Half-this, half-that, he's not really, that name, that doesn't sound, you don't look, the shape of your eyes, you're like a Seinfeld character*, etc. So, before I come to my point, I am going to write this all down for you now. For you, my friends and frenemies, casual acquaintances and interested strangers, colleagues and random art historians of the future. You can decide for yourself what racial and ethnic taxonomies are appropriate for me to claim. I decided for myself long ago.

Mixed-race identities are complicated ... for people who carry or cling to certain ideas, assumptions, or theories about racial and cultural purity. And for Americans. Whiteness has long been an imagined absolute in the United States. For generations, it was a legal absolute. "One drop" of African ancestry and you are Black. But what if your "drop" of blood contains DNA from this immense region Europeans decided to call "Asia"? Does one drop make you Asian? What about close to 50 percent of your genetic inheritance? Sometimes when I talk about race with my White friends, some of them will get uncomfortable and declare "you're half-White" to try and neutralize my arguments. As if reminding me that I have a White father somehow neutralizes everything in my past that has led to a non-White perspective inside my skull. If Whiteness is an absolute—the absence of melanin—and you have brown skin—even light-brown skin like me—can you be "half-White"? Does Crayola make a "half-White" crayon? And what does that color look like? Along with being Filipino and American, I can "claim" Jewish, Russian, Austrian, and Hungarian descent through my father, but like so many other Americans with complicated roots, I am not White. I have never been and will never be White. Or be allowed to be White ... if for some reason as an adult I even desired that.

Some background testimony for my what-are-you?-conversation trial:

My mother was a Filipino woman with dark brown skin who was brain-drained out of Manila in the late 1960s along with many of her classmates from the University of the Philippines. She arrived in New York City two years after *Loving v. Virginia* ended all the laws criminalizing interracial marriages. My father is Jewish and White with pale skin and reddish-brown hair. In the late 19th century, his parents' families fled antisemitism and poverty in Central and Eastern Europe for America, settling in Philadelphia. I was born twelve years after what used to be called "miscegenation" was legalized across the USA.

As a child, I had dark blond hair, my nose didn't have a pronounced bridge, and my eyes had epicanthal folds. Over the summers of my 80s and 90s youth, my skin would get very brown in the sun. As I've grown older, my hair has gotten darker. During puberty, the shapes of my eyes and nose changed. Before that, in elementary school in the 80s, my White and Black classmates would ask me if I was Japanese or Chinese and pull the sides of their eyes with their fingers and make slanted eyes at me. I grew up in a neighborhood that is now Philadelphia's equivalent of Queens, but at a point when the non-European immigrants were just starting to arrive en masse. The Catholic and Jewish White children that dominated the public school classes I was interned in didn't know what to make of the young Korean immigrants in our classes, but they had sort of heard about Korea because of the American war there three decades earlier. There was a TV sitcom on the air in syndication set in the Korean War (which didn't feature any Korean characters). The Philippines, though ... might as well have been somewhere in outer space. There were no significant American films or TV shows set in the Philippines.

My early birthday parties were basically Filipino fiestas. I would fall asleep on the couch at some point to the clacking of mahjong tiles in the middle of the night. Thanksgivings with my mom's friends in the Jersey suburbs involved a buffet table with an untouched turkey that sat next to the real celebration—lechon—a whole roast suckling pig. My childhood, like the life that's followed it, has been entirely unkosher. Every meal my mother cooked, except spaghetti, tacos, and pancakes, was accompanied by rice. Breakfast on the weekend was often turon or suman steamed in banana leaves. Weeknight dinners would involve dishes like chicken adobo or beef kaldereta. The den in my parents' house had 1970s landscape paintings of rice paddies and decorative cooly hats on the wall. There were shelves full of canned lychees, bagoong, Spam, and fish sauce in the storage room downstairs. My mother's Filipino friends and their first-generation American children were a constant presence in my childhood. And of course, I was raised by a Filipina immigrant—who lived the first three decades of her life there, and not here. Have I established my Filipino American credentials yet? Is it possible for someone named Josh Kline to be Filipino American? Am I a Fil-Am? Or perhaps Filipinx? And if so, does that make me "Asian"?

All of you who either openly or deep down have trouble with mixed-race people claiming multiple and supposedly contradictory identities—I wish you were familiar enough with the Philippines to understand the possibilities that lie in abandoning cultural or racial purity as values and embracing hybridity. Or the freedom that comes when hybridity becomes banal and ubiquitous.

I wish you could understand that these apparent contradictions many of you get hung up on are artificial constructs, like the ideas of racial and cultural purity that people who are in love with sick racial myths rooted in colonial imperialism and slavery cling to.

The many sides of the Eurasian and African continents are a vast pool of cultures and genes that have been in slow contact since our species first ventured out of Africa tens of thousands of years ago. In a world where you can fly around the world in a matter of hours, contact has sped up. What would happen in our own country if race-mixing among our country's different racial groups lost all stigma? If it really lost all stigma? Or if it was embraced? Can Americans learn to love and celebrate "The Great Replacement"? No one is going anywhere or being violently disappeared; there are just more beautiful, lovable, mixed-race babies being born with American passports.

Assuming you accept that someone like me could maybe be "sort of" or "vaguely" Filipino—or at least Filipino American or Filipinx, you can open up any number of questions regarding the larger cultural taxonomic status of Filipinos. For instance, my question to the performance artist from Fukushima: "Are Filipinos Asian?" And then the larger question of what defines a Filipino? A job as a nurse? Relatives cleaning homes in Dubai or Hong Kong or working in a Manila call center? An obsession with pork and a longing for tropical humidity? Exposure to bad dad jokes involving puns?

Assuming they even know that the Philippines exists—an official, on-paper American colony for half a century, and within living memory—Americans of any background with any familiarity with Filipino culture have difficulties with the Filipino/Asian dichotomy. It hurts their heads. *You don't look Asian. You don't look Asian Asian. You're so brown. You look Mexican. They're Catholic. She has a Spanish last name. Flan is not an Asian food. The three words I've heard in "Tagalong" sound Spanish. Everyone speaks English there.*

Allow me to read between your lines and translate for everyone else: What you're talking about is racial and cultural purity, and GDP.

My mother's family, the Jesalvas (I'm fairly certain the name is shorthand for "Jesus saves" or "Jesus is Salvation"), comes from Sorsogon in Bicol, near the southern tip of Luzon, the largest island in the Philippines. According to my mom, there might have been one or two Spanish ancestors four or five generations back—she wasn't certain—but everyone else has Native ancestry and has lived in villages on this small peninsula for countless generations, harvesting coconuts and planting rice. Luzon is located in the Pacific Ocean immediately to the south of Taiwan and to the east of Vietnam and southern China. Further south, past the other Philippine islands, lies Indonesia. Prior to the arrival of the Spanish, there was no "Philippines," and there were no

"Filipinos." Luzon was just another island in a vast geographic and cultural archipelago that includes Mindanao, Java, Sumatra, and Borneo—and thousands of other islands—all peoples with related cultures speaking related languages. The Spanish arrived on one of these islands and forced their religion, some of their language, and much of their culture on the peoples there—including my maternal ancestors. In what is now Indonesia, it was the Dutch. In Malaysia, the British. But before the Europeans arrived with their crosses and their cannons, those ancestors of the Filipinos, Indonesians, and Malaysians were already under the cultural influence of India, the Islamic world, and China. But they were not directly colonized or conquered by these cultures. The Chinese had come to the Philippines centuries before the Spanish as traders, not as colonists. Out of the influences that these immigrants brought, what the pre-Filipino people liked, they adopted as their own. One lens to look at Filipino culture through is its capacity for cultural absorption. And through the unrestrained, guiltless pleasure Filipinos take in sampling from other cultures, adapting newly discovered foreign novelty for native tastes.

Filipinos are a mestizo people by definition. The majority of Filipinos descend from the pre-colonial Native population of the islands—the result of multiple waves of migration stretching back thousands of years. Many can also claim descent from more recent waves of Chinese settlers and/or the relatively small population of Spanish colonists. Like many mixed-race/mixed-culture peoples who have emerged, are emerging, or perhaps yearn to emerge from a colonial legacy, most Filipinos see no contradiction in this racial, ethnic, and cultural mix. It is not a problem or a source of confusion to the people in that mix. I want to be clear that I am not suggesting ignoring the very real class-based, economic, and political divisions that emerge from the country's troubled history. I am in no way trying to hide the skin-lightening creams and the Ayala family and Rodrigo Duterte. I want to draw your attention to one part of a complex postcolonial reality. Something profoundly inspiring rising out of centuries of colonial and postcolonial abuse.

In the Philippines—which has a population of 107 million people—there are tens of millions of people with Spanish family names who have no Spanish ancestry. There are thousands of places with Spanish names. The non-Western languages of the Philippines are full of Western words. Foods that have been cherished in the Philippines for untold millennia have ended up with new names in Spanish and English. *Adobo. Beta Max. Bicol Express.* The Philippines has no L'Académie française that hovers over its languages and mass media, attempting to freeze some linguistic golden age in place in eternal ice. There is no popular mass movement trying to decolonize adobo. Filipinos are gleefully drowning the English language in tangy vinegar. Perhaps someday

Duterte or one of his successors will rename the country Maharlika, but it hasn't happened yet. If Filipinos like something or like the sound of a word for something, they will adopt it. They will absorb it. They will make it their own, adapting it to native tastes. Few Filipinos give much thought to whether European words are polluting their culture or whether their Catholic religion (or Islam) makes them less "Asian." Or, for that matter, whether Chinese influence in the last thousand years has tainted some primordial Pinoy culture. A past rooted in racist, exploitative colonization has left many tragic legacies and injustices in the country, but a national mass obsession with cultural purity is, fortunately, not one of them.

All this absorption doesn't make Filipinos any less Filipino, any less themselves. Their culture is the opposite of stasis: it is defined by constant metamorphosis. As America's culture has been, in many ways.

America counts many characteristics in common with its former colony and current client state. Both the Philippines and America are racial and cultural melting pots, and both constantly reinvent and renew themselves by embracing outside influences to trigger internal innovation. America is a larger, wealthier, and more complicated melting pot and comes with a more problematic history rooted in its specific history of genocide, slavery, Jim Crow apartheid, and overseas imperial misadventure. The word *appropriation* is appropriate in the American context in a way that it isn't in the Philippines. In spite of this history—as well as because of the affluent, bourgeois society built on and financed through its original sins—people from all corners of the Earth and their descendants, numbering in the hundreds of millions, have come to call the USA home. Even in 2020, the interracial, multiracial, and multicultural realities and possibilities in this country are awe-inspiring—even if *Fox & Friends* tries to pretend they aren't real. The inspiration catalyzed through the juxtaposition of, conflict and collaboration among, and possible consensus within so many different perspectives and histories remains a source of hope for those of us dreaming of a different and more just—not to mention more interesting—future on this continent.

The blurring or transgression of racial boundaries remains radical in America's race-based hierarchy, especially outside the racist order established by America's British founders. The choice to partner and have children outside your lane remains subversive because it carries with it the possibility of dissolving the categories America's racial hierarchies are based on—as well as the racially demarcated economic boundaries that have defined class inclusion here. As more and more non-Western immigrants settle in the United States—and as their descendants mix with the people already present here, another family of questions comes into focus. Especially in those parts of the country—especially in the cities—with majority-minority populations.

Are all of the immigrants here and all their multiracial descendants Westerners? Is "the West" really just code for White people? Is "Westerner" even a relevant category for discussion in a globalized world increasingly defined by disparities between the rich North and the impoverished, looted South? If America can't escape categorization as a Western culture in 2020, is there the possibility that it is undergoing a process of metamorphosis and becoming something else? Assuming the country still exists in 2050 or 2150, will a majority of Americans even want to consider themselves Westerners? Or will they see themselves and their even more hybrid culture as something else? Perhaps America is in denial about something that's already happened.

Here is where the example set by the Philippines and Filipinos—their attitudes toward cultural and racial purity, their nonchalance around their culture's complicated roots in the East and West—is so revelatory. These binary categories melt down in a place like the Philippines. American culture can also be described as highly absorbent—augmenting itself with the cultural achievements of all the immigrants drawn to the myth of the American Dream and, of course, through the achievements of African Americans, who have created much of what we think of as American culture while being assaulted by this country and denied that Dream for centuries. American culture has been a hybrid culture from the beginning, combining elements of Western European, West African, and Indigenous cultures. White American conservatives—and many liberals too—are seriously uncomfortable with just how much of their culture's foundations are non-Western. African. Native. And now increasingly Latin American and Asian. A large percentage of White Americans—71 million people voted for Trump in 2020—appear to be totally terrified of this truth. They are scared shitless of the culture growing in America's majority-minority cities—and of the future those cities, and now their suburbs, are ushering into being across the country. As of 2016, the majority of babies born in the USA are now non-White. It is predicted that America will cease to have a White majority at some point in the mid-2040s, two decades from now. Today around 7 percent of Americans identify as mixed-race/multiracial. In 2050, that number could be 20 percent, or one out of every five people here. How do these demographics make you feel?

The deeper changes brought by this growing population of multiracial and multicultural people will extend beyond radical new mixtures of facial features and endless ignorant questions about family names and identity. They are cultural. They will be political. No bureaucratic checkmark box labeled "Other" will contain them forever. Regardless of what languages are coming out of our mouths, and what European names appear on our government documents, non-Western cultural perspectives and non-Western family histories remain as part of the mix in the descendants of all the immigrants coming from Asia,

Africa, and Latin America, and they can't help but rearrange and reshape this fucked-up place.

Ingat,
Josh

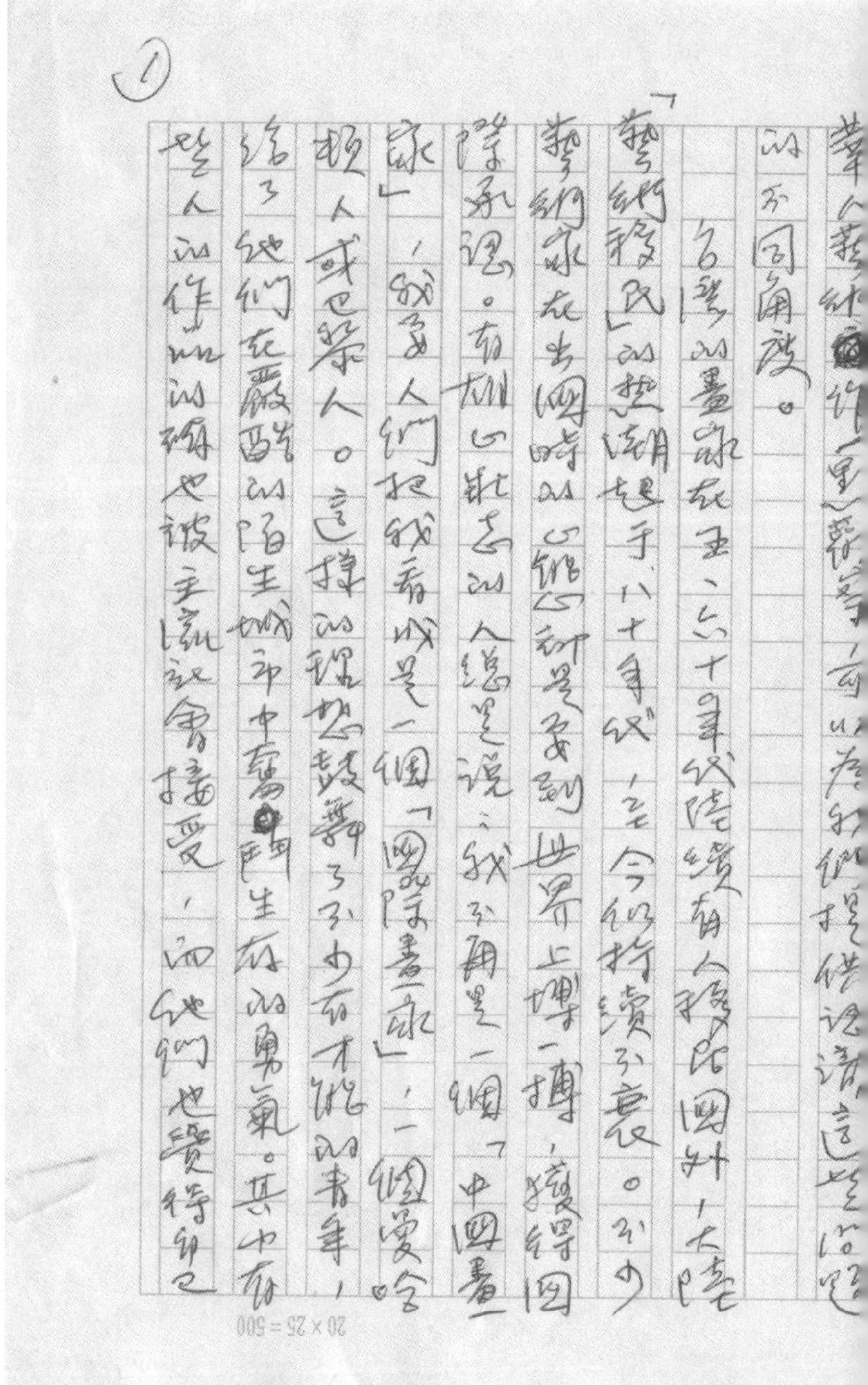
①

華人藝術家作[illegible]……

的不同角度。

台灣的畫家在五、六十年代陸續有人移民國外,大陸「藝術移民」的熱潮起于八十年代,至今仍持續不衰。不少藝術家在出國時的心態都是要到世界上搏一搏,獲得國際承認。有雄心壯志的人總是說:我不再是一個「中國畫家」,我要人們把我看成是一個「國際畫家」,一個優秀[illegible]人或世界人。這樣的理想鼓舞了不少有才能的青年,給了他們在嚴酷的陌生城市中奮鬥生存的勇氣。其中有些人的作品的確也被主流社會接受,而他們也覺得自己

20 × 25 = 500

燦鑫兄：

和林、劉二位在灣仔的酒店談話彷彿就是昨天的事，實際上時空交逝，已飛快地過去了三個月。現在我又在由香港去華盛頓的飛機上，着手寫完這段可算結語的結語。下周第一個「國際新興藝術博覽會」又要在香港開幕了。亞洲的藝術脈搏已經越跳越快。

我想補充的是，在這樣一個被噴射機和傳真機聯結起來的世界上，「本土化」和「國際化」這兩個名詞聽起來都有點古色古香。那天晚上我們沒有來得及談到海外的華人藝術家，也許恰恰是對散居全球的

②

而是如我在談話中所說的，是一種文化現象，而文化是社會現實的反映。一些西方評論家也意識到這一點，使他們反而對海外的華人藝術重視了起來。美國人所稱的「少數民族藝術家」（包括華人在內）的重新認同自身文化的趨勢，是八十年代以來多元文化主張逐漸被接受的必然結果。

我想到學界幾件很有意思的活動：有個組織的一位美國學者一直在倡導成立一個學術機構，並組織各國專家撰寫自己的美術史，再譯成國際通行的文字，成為目前在大學院校使用的歐美著者的教材；我的一位印第安藝術家朋

20×25＝500

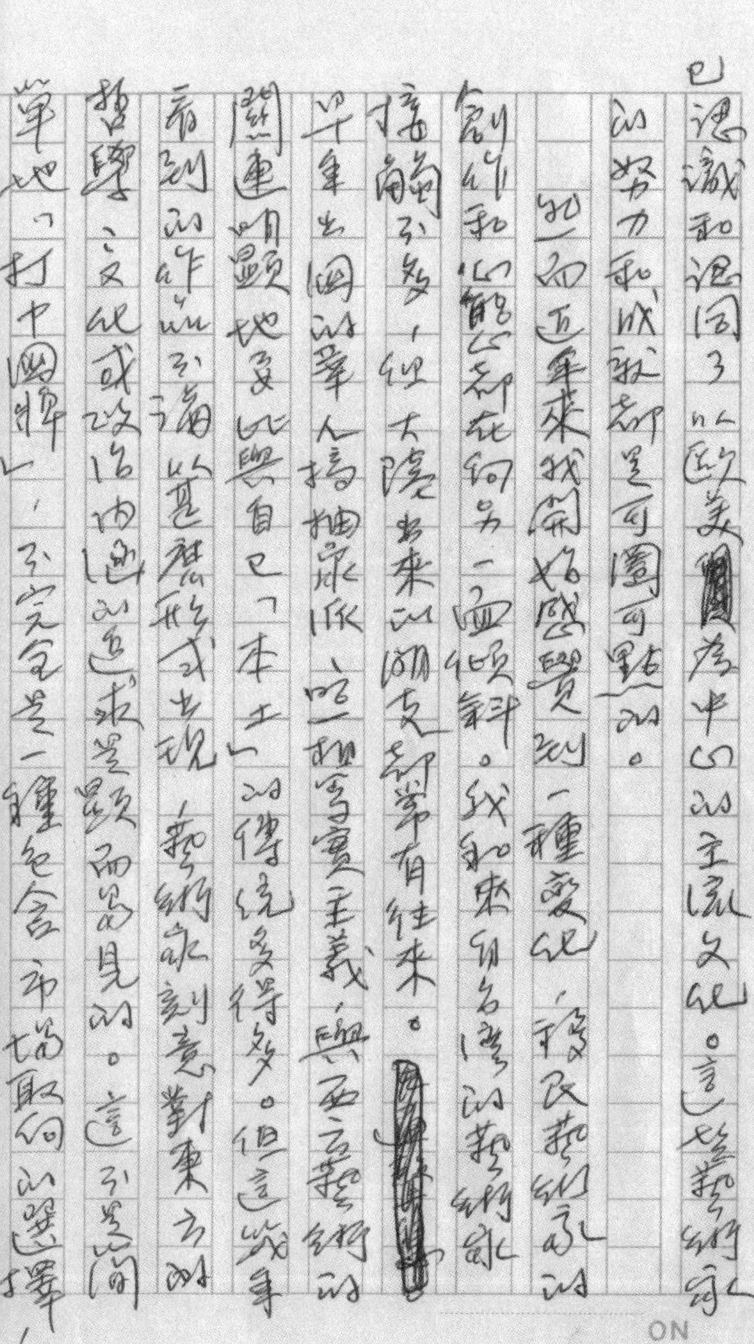

已認識和認同了以歐美國家為中心的主流文化。這些藝術家的努力和成就都是可圈可點的。

然而近年來我開始感覺到一種變化，移民藝術家的創作和他們卻在向另一面傾斜。我和來自台灣的藝術家接觸不多，但大陸出來的朋友卻常有往來。早年出國的華人搞抽象派、照相寫實主義，與西方藝術的關連明顯地要比與自己「本土」的傳統多得多。但這幾年看到的作品不論以甚麼形式出現，藝術家刻意對東方的哲學、文化或政治內涵的追求是顯而易見的。這不是簡單地「打中國牌」，不完全是一種包含市場取向的選擇，追求洋化，西方人對所謂的「邊緣文化」也習以為常，不至於完全無動於衷或大驚小怪。在這種比較健康的文化社會氛圍中，最明智也最可能成功的終究恐怕就是西方人常說的一句話：To Be Yourself。

自我肯定和自我尊重，才能在人際交往中瀟灑自如，也才能顯出個人本色，這是做人的道理，也是做藝術的道理。我個人以為，無論是台灣的、香港的、大陸的藝術家，這幾年的自信心都愈來愈強了，不再只是東張西望，這樣別人也對你刮目相看。藝術終究是個人的，怎樣的標籤並不太重要。

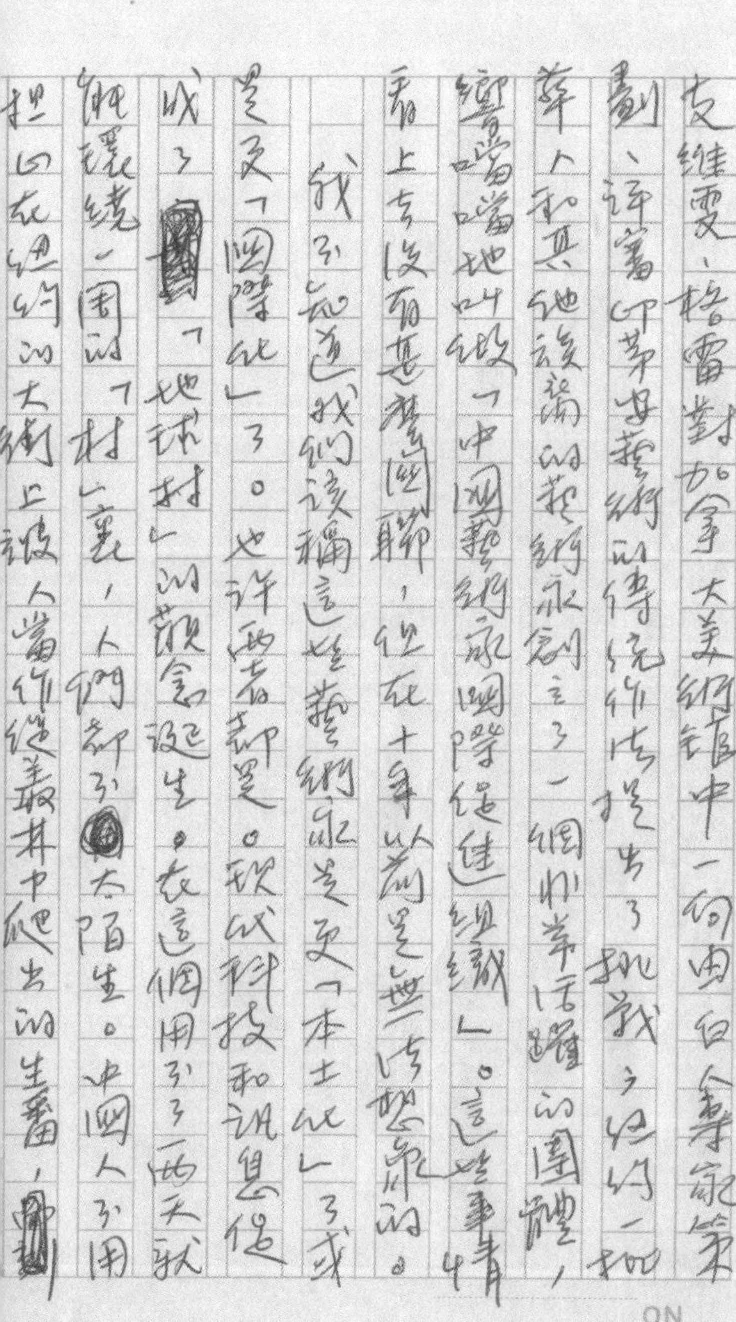
克維雯、格雷對加拿大美術館中一件由白人專家策劃、評審印第安藝術的傳統作法提出了挑戰；紐約一批華人和其他族裔的藝術家創立了一個非常活躍的團體，響噹噹地叫做「中國藝術家國際促進組織」。這些事情看上去沒有甚麼關聯，但在十年以前是無法想像的。

我不知道我們該稱這些藝術家是更「本土化」了或是更「國際化」了。也許兩者都是。現代科技和訊息促成了「地球村」的觀念誕生。在這個用不了一兩天就能環繞一周的「村」裏，人們都不太陌生。中國人不用擔心在紐約的大街上被人當作從叢林中爬出的生番，

ON

55-4586 共4頁

④

藝術家需要去極端，而藝術的欣賞者卻不妨寬容一些。一切存在的事物都有它的理由。台灣和大陸都處在不同的開放轉型的過程中，文化藝術的定位可能搖擺，但下一個世紀會更成熟，這是絕對沒有疑義的。

鄭濤天

九四年三月于太平洋上

This letter was sent on March 3, 1994, to Taiwanese artist Lin Hsin-yueh「林惺嶽」via Charles Liu「劉昌漢」, a Taiwan-born American artist and writer. The year before, Liu interviewed Lin and Zheng in Hong Kong during Fine Art Asia. This letter is Zheng's response to that interview, which was subsequently published in the May 1994 issue of *Artist* magazine in Taiwan. The interview was titled "Localism and Internationalism."

ALEXANDER LAU
TO MY COMRADES WHO EXPLOIT THEIR EURO-AMERICAN CULTURAL CAPITAL IN THEIR HOME COUNTRIES (OF WHICH I MYSELF AM ONE), OR ON RETURNING TO ASIA

The flow of discursive commerce between the Asian diaspora and Asian nations active in the field of contemporary art increases every day. Although perhaps slightly late to the game, these nations now realize that visibility on the global art stage is a highly desirable (if not strictly necessary) element of their strategies concerning soft power, diplomacy, and the self-imaging of a sophisticated capitalist modernity. The galleries, museums, cultural districts—it should be noted that any place referred to as a cultural district is fated not to produce any significant culture—and coffee shops come breathtakingly quickly; in fact, they are erected seemingly overnight. However, these emerging ecosystems crucially and fundamentally lack artists, curators, and other cultural managers—specifically those of sufficient skill and sophistication to operate in what might be called an international context. There is a colossal and ravenous infrastructure waiting to process material into content, but only trimmings to feed through the grinder.

Initially, and for a long time afterward, all the senior positions of note are filled by White men (and the occasional White woman): underqualified but more or less well-meaning people who were in the right place at the right time and shared drinks with the right people. In China, this tends to mean former journalists. Somewhere down the line, this state of affairs is privately deemed egregious. It uncomfortably calls to mind bygone episodes of foreign domination which linger in the collective consciousness. Someone with the *right* ethnicity, a similar skill set, and a certain degree of ethical pliability (sometimes known as discretion) must be found.

In this system, the diasporic Asian artist, curator, or cultural worker occupies a position of privilege—as an actor who is called back to their "homeland" to fulfill a symbolic duty. Like the engineers, scientists, and statisticians who came before us, we are wooed and fawned over, objects of an attempted seduction by our would-be countrymen. The financial rewards for returning are not inconsiderable, and that will be enough for some people; but it is the emotional and existential ones that really get us.

To say that the diasporic experience is one defined by displacement and loss, exile, and alienation is by now so trite a statement that it barely merits repeating. However, sometimes these mundane truths can be everything. Visiting our ancestral homelands, we enter a state of precarity and vulnerability precisely because of these experiences. It is difficult to stem the tide of emotions because what is on offer is not just money. It is solidarity and belonging, an escape from the constant tension and anxiety of a split consciousness, and a chance to incorporate ourselves into a stronger and ostensibly purer body—regardless of which side of our hyphenated personhood we choose to identify with. One prominent Chinese American who had returned to China in order to build a life and business there told me that he had heard the "call of the blood," perhaps not registering the historical associations such a turn of phrase might call to mind. The idea of "returning home," however relatable, can thus become a treacherous fantasy, one which is often instrumentalized for political ends.

Encountering the foreign substance that is supposed to constitute both our origin and essence, our status as hyphenated beings seems to collapse under the pressure. We tend to become either apologists and zealots for the country in question, or else arrogant Americans making the best of our privilege. Whether we decide to play the localist or the imperialist, both choices lead to the same outcome: the circulation of bad art and the impoverishment of the cultural sphere. Artists vaunted for their integrity end up producing installations for shopping malls. Critical investigations of race relations and the history of colonialism are weaponized as ethno-nationalist propaganda. Fourth-rate Rauschenbergs are sold under the guise of imparting cultural knowledge. After all, what we do *over there* (much like what happens in Vegas) doesn't need to follow us *back here*.

It might seem pertinent here to ask whether our professional presence in our homelands might actually be a symptom of some type of systemic moral bankruptcy. Even if the answer is yes, it still doesn't absolve us of our agency and responsibility as individual actors. Those who are privileged to move freely between different cultural spheres in this moment of increasing nationalism and bigotry might still have some mildly helpful role to play. This means resisting the temptation to identify with either side of our cultural heritage and insisting on our own hybridity—realizing that regardless of whichever ethnocultural mask it dons, power operates in the same way on both sides of the ocean. By preserving a sense of tension between opposites, and accepting the uncomfortable but clarifying distance which is part and parcel of the passage between cultures, we can perhaps move beyond the current impasse that characterizes the relationship between the Eastern and Western art worlds.

After all, there are still many things that the Asian art world lacks (a sense of genuine bohemianism and respect for critique, to name two). We may as well dispense with the false oppositions and set about giving them what they never asked for.

J FAN

Dear Diaspora,

You are an incredibly difficult word to pronounce. I've practiced you many times but never really know how long to stress your "i," or if the pitch of the "a" should arc upwards or stay flat.

I think it's funny that a word like you, meant to describe displaced folks like me, is such a tricky English word to pronounce. You trip me up every time.

I left Hong Kong for the US ten years ago. What was meant as a four-year stint at art school ended up being a ten-year stay. Six or seven years ago, I stopped writing in Chinese, and am now thinking in English. This is new.

I have come to understand language as materialized thought, and so I wonder: What is happening in the space between my left brain and my tongue when I think in Chinese and speak in English? What is happening as my thoughts materialize and also undergo translation? Do the contents and emphases of my thoughts change when their linguistic framing differs?

Di-*ass*-spora ... *Dai-ya*-spore-rah. ... There's no Chinese word for either.

I just broke up with a person I was seeing. She was White and American and cisgender. She had never lived in a country in which she didn't speak the language and never had the experience of being dysphoric in her own body. It is what drew me to her, and also why we parted ways. Being with her forfeited a sense of belonging in a land (and in a body) in which I am increasingly feeling foreign. But it was also alienating to be with someone whose home excluded my existence, in its reality and its imaginary. We parted ways because I came to understand that she was incapable of feeling the experience of being an outsider, of being in the minority and perpetually looking in, and of not belonging. This feeling sits at my core, and I am learning that it is impossible to offer someone a feeling. A feeling, unlike a thought, cannot be translated.

I wonder what language I feel in.

In Chinese, the words *feeling*「感覺」and *thought*「想法」can both be expressed by the same verb: 覺得.

Right now, I feel trapped in America.

With warmth,
J

HOLLY SHEN

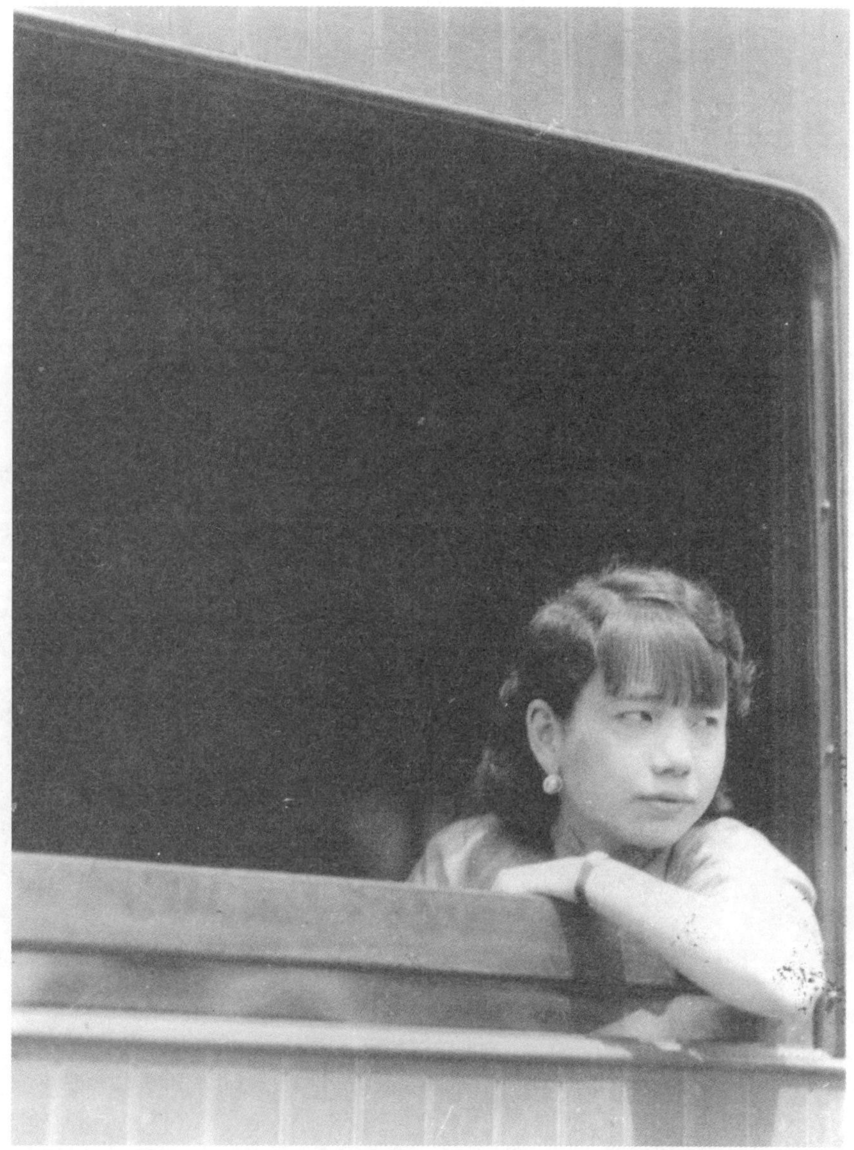

My paternal grandmother, whose English name was Cecilia, on a train to visit her new in-laws shortly after marriage, ca. 1930.

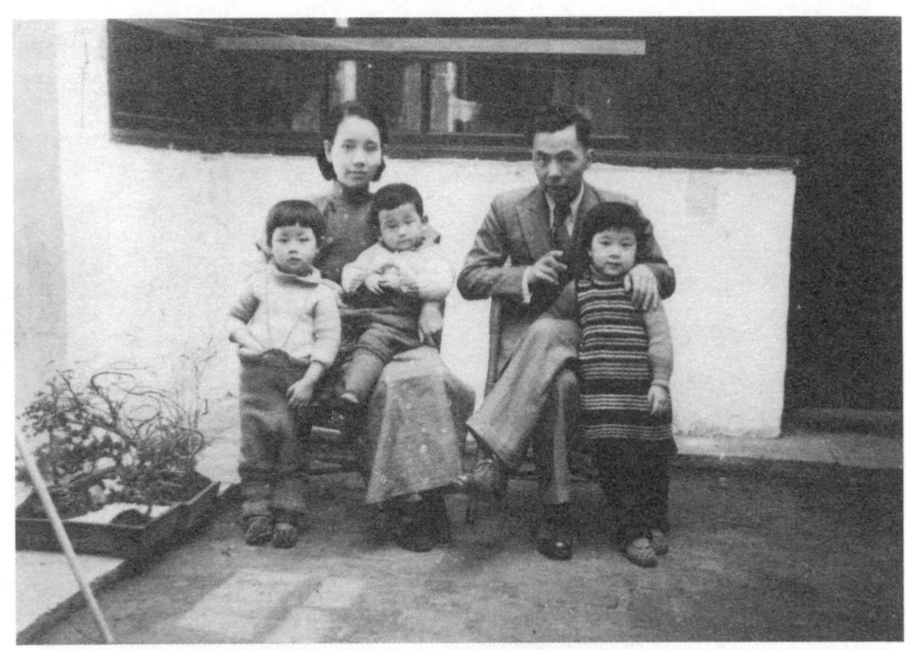

My dad seated on his mother's lap, with his father and two older sisters, at their home in Shanghai, ca. 1936. The family portrait was taken with one of the many Leica cameras my grandfather, an amateur photographer, had acquired while traveling.

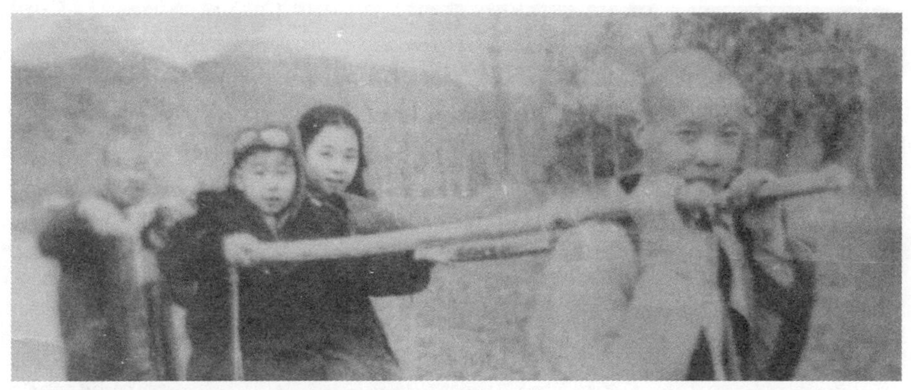

My dad and his older sister Margaret fleeing Shanghai on foot during the Sino-Japanese War, ca. 1944.

Year 2020, Day 183+ of Shelter in Place

Dear H,

It would be an understatement to say that our time together in quarantine is a gift. You have, in many ways, saved me from self-destruction during this objectively stressful time. Yet this abeyance of normalcy is marked by the trauma of a global pandemic, national protests against systemic racism and police brutality, extreme fire and weather caused by climate change, the din of the 24/7 election-year news cycle, your grandpa's indomitable mind despite flagging health, a punishing sense of the unknown, and a crippling suspicion that there are no answers and never will be. Marshaling the discipline to write a deeply personal missive on a heady topic like Asian American identity against this freefall was daunting, and the task has been arduous.

But I agreed to write this letter because you, like me, are Asian American—colloquially, an American of Asian descent. Yet the term "Asian American" belies the complex, heterogeneous social and political histories of—and interethnic, global relationships among—East, Southeast, and South Asia, the Pacific Islands, and the Americas. It condenses a range of experiences into a monolithic identity; reduces details of distinct and at times opposing immigration and migration histories, diasporas, and displacement narratives; perpetuates evolving stereotypes; and enforces noxious biases. The history of visual representation is equally riddled with problems—from colonialism, capitalism, and single-point linear perspective (the breeding ground for racial and religious propaganda) to the deleterious effects of pop culture representations of Asian Americans in film and literature in the last century.

I agreed because representation operates inversely, too. It splinters the universal into immeasurable fragments. It refutes existing narratives while at the same time strengthening collective resonance. Representation via the heterogenous Asian American voices in this collection of letters, in mine to yours, is one gesture towards the capacity of the term to hold the expansiveness and nuance of our experiences.

I agreed because the only thing I believe with my whole heart and mind about identity is that dialogue is irrefutably necessary for its creation. Thus, here is my dispatch to you, nestled within grandpa's story: a seed of a conversation stretching back more than a dozen generations. I'm tending to it now in the hope that we can cultivate it together and share in its bounty; that grounding your self-perception in these exchanges might lessen what pain arises as a result; that in trying to show you the path to find the answers, I might uncover them myself.

//////////

The genealogy of the Shěn clan, commissioned in 1916 by my great-great-grandfather Zhì Xián「志賢」begins with the following reflection:

> Alas, preparing a family genealogy is like writing a country's history, the purpose of which is to record praiseworthy virtues and laudable achievements, so as to encourage and guide posterity for their betterment. Our ancestors were fishermen of obscure origins and of no particular fame or entitlement. For generations, they were simple, honest, hardworking people whose family interrelationships and individual endeavors and exploits are difficult to trace and arrange in proper order and time sequence.[1]

My dad was born in Shanghai in January 1935, the first son and third child of Hè Fǔ「鶴甫」, one of dozens of grandchildren of Zhì Xián「志賢」, a wealthy and powerful businessman in late 19th-century China. The genealogy traces the first generation back to the late 1600s, and our specific line is descended from the third-generation adopted son Yún Gāo「雲高」. My dad represents the tenth generation, making me the eleventh and you the twelfth.

The Shěn compound built by Zhì Xián「志賢」—representative of the seventh generation—on the northeast side of the city was expansive and featured many ostentatious displays of prosperity, such as a billiards house, a chapel, and professionally maintained gardens. It also included a row of homes for his twenty-four children, which he fathered by two wives. Around the time my dad was born, his father—a civil engineer trained in Paris—ran a successful architectural firm and loved dogs, owning six of them. They lived in a well-appointed French-style home in the southeast end of Shanghai. He had two older sisters and a loving mother, Cecilia「顧敏恆」, who cared well for him as a toddler.

But their privileged world was short-lived, ending when the Japanese took control of parts of the city during the Second Sino-Japanese War. The lavish estate of his great-grandfather was ransacked and destroyed in 1937 by invading Japanese troops. During the occupation, my dad's father left for the interior of China to assist the nationalist military. He also left his three small children and wife behind in an apartment in the French Quarter—part of the so-called Solitary Island, an area of foreign concessions that remained intact after the Battle of Shanghai in 1937, surrounded by war zones and providing refuge for some of the 400,000 displaced Chinese for several early years of the war. Without access to adequate resources or support, my dad's middle sister fell sick and died toward the end of 1941. A little over a year later, his mother suffered a fatal stroke, passing in early 1943.

Though we've lived less than a mile apart for most of my life, my aunt Margaret—my dad's surviving older sister—has rarely spoken about this part of the family's history. This summer, as the pandemic wore on in Santa Clara, where we both currently live, we adhered to social distancing guidelines and spoke by phone. In a short and anomalous reflection, my aunt told me that she knows the date of her sister's death because it was three days before Pearl Harbor was bombed. She recounted with a tinge of urgency in her voice how she had been very close with her younger sister and that her death is still a painful memory. She can still conjure an image of her little sister being carried away down the stairs of their cramped apartment, too weak to be saved, but nonetheless crying and calling out Margaret's name while she stood helpless, horrified at the top of the stairs. The real shame, my aunt noted, is in never knowing where—or even if—her sister's body was buried: no grave exists; none had existed.

After his mother and sister were gone, my dad's father returned to Shanghai in 1943, becoming severely ill before recovering enough strength to organize their clandestine departure. In 1944, they left at night on foot, though at 9 and 11 years old, my dad and Aunt Margaret were carried by rickshaw. They traveled to Chongqing by way of Quanzhou, not returning to Shanghai until the war ended two years later.

//////////

Minor Feelings: An Asian American Reckoning, a collection of seven essays released this spring by poet and Korean American author Cathy Park Hong, develops the titular phrase to describe "the racialized range of emotions that are negative, dysphoric, and therefore untelegenic, built from the sediments of everyday racial experience and the irritant of having one's perception of reality constantly questioned or dismissed."[2] *Minor feelings*, Hong concludes, are the result of unopposed, reoccurring microaggressions of race—what author Viet Thanh Nguyen has also termed "low-level racism"—towards Asian Americans and other non-Black minorities, compounded over time to create dissonance between one's perception and reality.

In a *New Yorker* review, staff writer and Asian American author Jia Tolentino uses a clinical metaphor—apropos of the times, if a tad macabre—to describe the impact of reading Hong's memoir on racial identity: "It bled a dormant discomfort out of me with surgical precision." Following in this vein (no pun intended), for me, *Minor Feelings* hacked away mercilessly at an aged, congenital scar with such guttural force that it unleashed a mystifying combination of rage, satisfaction, and melancholy. The pleasurable yet painful orgasm of validation perpetually shy of vindication. I read it with a strange, delusional excitement—finally, words to describe feelings and ideas I had laid to rest with neither the language nor emotional confidence to codify them within a known hierarchy.

Unmoored by the multiplicities of location and diasporic imagination, and complicated by notions of nationality and nationhood, Asian American identity is a mosaic of dissimilar places and histories. Growing up, I was—usually in this order—from Shaker Heights, Catholic, American, Midwestern, half-Chinese and half-Caucasian, mixed or biracial, part Jewish. So, not at all like Hong. Why, then, did reading *Minor Feelings* so resonate with me? It's hard to reconcile the term *Asian American* with its paradoxical connotations: extreme disparity here acts as a unifying foundation.[3]

In "The Indebted," the concluding essay of *Minor Feelings*, Hong describes an early racialized encounter at a pool in her aunt's apartment complex while she was babysitting her young cousins. A White man yells at them for trespassing in the pool, overruling Hong's logical explanation and muttering *They're everywhere now* as she obediently leaves. Hong carefully prefaces this reflection with a disclaimer: "The public pool is such a stark example of how much this country has been hellbent on keeping black and white bodies apart that I became unsure if it was my history to retell."

Could it be, I wondered, mere coincidence that one of my earliest memories with racialized emotions also happened at a pool? I was 5 or 6 years old, watching my older brother jump off the diving board at Thornton Park, the community rec center in Shaker Heights, Ohio, where I spent a good chunk of my childhood schlepping between the pool, tennis courts, and ice rink. I stood on the concrete deck of the deep end, dripping wet, squinting in the sun to catch a glimpse of his bravery and unaware I was blocking the line for other eager divers.

Behind me, a group of Black children started snickering, and I turned around to confounding jeers and gestures. They pulled back the corners of their eyes, joined their hands in prayer, bowing. *Chink! A Konnichiwa! She can't see the line because of her slitty eyes!* they taunted. Each insult elicited hysterical giggling, which fueled more teasing. I turned back around, pretending I couldn't hear them. In fact, I was frozen with bewilderment.

By this age, I generally understood the concept of racism towards Black people. But I wasn't Black, and I couldn't figure out what the insults meant. I asked my mom about the incident later, though it occurs to me now that I don't remember exactly what she said. I carried forward only the takeaway: my dad was Chinese and she wasn't, so I was half-Chinese. There weren't a lot of Chinese or half-Chinese families in our town, so I looked different than other kids. Even more tellingly, I'm nearly positive my mom did not use the term Asian American.

My story differed significantly from Hong's: the offenders were children rather than an adult, Black instead of White, and the location was public, not private. Nonetheless, it substantiates the damning and recursive logic of racism. It's also hard not to draw a connection between my low-level racist incident at the pool and the model minority myth's perpetuation of anti-Black racism, though playing out here inversely. Shaker Heights residents love to tout the fact that their community was one of the first suburbs to racially integrate, and in 1986, the city began a "Fund for the Future of Shaker Heights," offering loans for down payments for residents buying homes in segregated neighborhoods to promote multiethnic neighborhoods. But the enduring legacies of colonialism and capitalism rely on and desire to identify the other. Progressive housing tactics helped avoid some of the pitfalls of White flight, but they also unwittingly promote a White savior mentality that can be as harmful as outright racial bias.

Celeste Ng's 2017 novel *Little Fires Everywhere*, centered on the travails of an upper-middle-class family led by matriarch Elena Richardson, is set in Shaker Heights in 1997. I would have been in eighth grade that year. The story begins when Elena, a third-generation Shaker Heights resident married to a prominent lawyer, rents a home to single mother and artist, Mia, and her daughter, Pearl. She takes them under her wing in the same misguided manner that Cher adopts Tai in *Clueless*. Ultimately, Elena turns against Mia when she finds out that Mia has befriended the mother of a Chinese American baby whose custody is in dispute. Close family friends of the Richardsons claim rightful adoption of the baby, while Mia sympathizes with the child's immigrant mother, with whom she works at the only Chinese restaurant in town.

Ng, who drew upon her memories of growing up in Shaker Heights to write the novel (it's sadly true there was only one Chinese takeout restaurant in town, Pearl of the Orient, across from the apartment where my aunt Margaret lived for nearly thirty years), cleverly reveals how racialized power dynamics converge with economic and social hierarchies. The opportunity for this story to serve as a stage for a deeper probe of race relations became evident when Hulu optioned the novel as a miniseries, casting Mia as a Black woman played by Kerry Washington. (In the book, Mia is presumably White.)

Would a baby have a better life with an adopted family who doesn't understand the culture of her biological race, or a single mother who does? Should a biracial family in late 20th-century Ohio celebrate their Chinese culture or embrace the new "American" identity? My parents chose assimilation wholeheartedly. We spoke only English in the house and were raised to believe we were no different than anyone else. But in the racial hierarchies of Shaker Heights, being Asian American *was* different.

//////////

The honorable Ren Xian, a fisherman plying his business in Lake Tai Hu near Zhang Sha Island, and his eminent wife from the Wang Family were the first ones to convert, he assuming the name John, she Cecilia. There are no records prior to that time. There have been two-hundred-sixty-some years and ten generations since the time of the conversion to the holy church of the honorable Ren Xian Gong. The family was in Zhejiang, then moved to Qingxi and eventually to Dongjiadu, Shanghai. Simplicity and diligence in raising family, honesty and loyalty in dealings in the world: these are the ways our forebears conducted their lives and hoped to pass on to their progeny.

Consequently, without a genealogy, the descendants will not remember the past achievements, observe the law, and continue the family tradition. So under uncle Reverend Jin Biao's kindly urging, the other uncles and my father strongly felt that a genealogy must be undertaken. They raised large sums of money for this purpose, but then uncle Jin Biao was transferred to a different location for his priestly duties, so he could not contribute to or be responsible for this undertaking. Fortunately, my older cousin Reverend Liang Neng happened to be transferred to pastoral duties at the church at Xujiahui, and he took over the genealogy task.

The influence of Catholicism, specifically Jesuit ideology, upon the Shěn clan (and thus on the genealogy) is indisputable and seeps into nearly every aspect of my father's life. When he returned to Shanghai in 1946 with his father and surviving sister after the war was over, my dad enrolled in high school at St. Ignatius College, a well-known Jesuit prep school in the French Quarter where his paternal grandmother's family had achieved scholarly renown; a monumental bust of his grandmother's uncle still sits on the sprawling campus. During this short spell of pseudo-normalcy, my dad's father remarried and had two more children with his second wife, Lily.

In 1948, the Communists took control of Shanghai, and by 1949, the political situation had worsened; my dad's father received word that his name had turned up on a list of political undesirables. He hastily departed to Hong Kong while my dad stayed with his new stepmom and half-siblings, my aunt Maria and uncle Larry. But dreading the looming reality, he arranged for his new family to join him not long after arriving. With his older sister in boarding school, my dad was left alone in the family's apartment; he was 14. Eventually, his father sent word to shut down their life in Shanghai. My dad was instructed to make all arrangements: settle accounts, disperse furniture and belongings among family and friends, call Margaret back from boarding school, purchase train tickets, and make their way to Hong Kong, all as quickly as possible. A risky encounter at the train station rattled their sense of safety, and out of caution, my dad and his sister destroyed any family photo albums showing evidence of their father's military record. For this reason, there are few extant photos of my dad's nuclear family.

Once settled in Hong Kong, my dad enrolled in another Jesuit prep school and resumed his studies. There, despite the frequent upheaval, trauma, and loss he experienced as a youth, he forged a strong bond with one of his teachers. After graduating in 1954, he enrolled in a Jesuit seminary college in Manila in the Philippines. He was following in the path of his mentor, as well as that of many of his forebears.

//////////

Catholic doctrine is founded on the idea that God's love is universal (the word *catholic* stems from its late Roman antecedent *catholicus*, derived from the Greek adjective *katholikos* meaning "universal"). It is available to all, blind to worldly distinctions like race or socioeconomic status or whether your parents were Catholic. All God's children can and will be saved. Confucian ideology, which places importance on adherence to a higher order, was well suited to reinforce Catholicism's emphasis on the inclusive whole over the individual. Both ideologies fetishize sacrifice and encourage a reverent fealty to power hierarchies.

I can't talk about my identity without addressing the outsize impact of Catholicism: being raised Catholic, attending Catholic elementary and high school, and not one but two Catholic universities—first Notre Dame, and then Georgetown, where I transferred after one year; even the "Catholic Disneyland" in Bend, Indiana, which was too much for even someone like me, indoctrinated at birth. I attended mass twice every week (more or less) until age 18, and I have earned five of the seven sacraments: baptism, confirmation, Eucharist, penance, and marriage (only for my first, which lasted just over two years). Until adulthood, I was pro-life by default. During my freshman year of high school, I participated in the so-called "life-altering" Kairos retreat—a multiday program rooted in Ignatian spirituality where teenage attendees are offered the chance to reflect upon God's role in their lives. Upon returning, I made a faith journal (an inconveniently oversized scrapbook decorated with a candle fashioned from colored construction paper) and filled it with cringeworthy notes about the important figures in my life who strengthened my faith: my Irish Catholic boyfriend at the time, whom I followed to Notre Dame (hence transferring to another Catholic university when we broke up), teachers, and classmates. In college, I studied art history, becoming obsessed with revealing the multitude of ways Catholic imagery in the late gothic and early Medieval period was developed and disseminated to educate, convert, and dominate existing populations and newly discovered colonies.

Sometimes when I'm fretting indiscriminately, I noodle the idea that Catholicism gave me a foundational moral core—or maybe more like a strong fulcrum from which to build sound judgment. Or at the very least, a guilt complex that propels me towards smart choices. I worry that without a starting point, finding your way may be unnecessarily arduous. I'm not sure if you know who Jesus is, a concern that occasionally makes an appearance in these quasi-subconscious speculations. The Catholic guilt of not raising you Catholic is impossible to eschew, but, for better or worse, the dictums of universal love and deferential obedience never fully took root in my mind.

The recollection of that encounter at our local pool, which is now reminiscent of a kind of impersonalized, racialized heckling that I've grown adept at ignoring, is less painful to recall than the racially tinged bullying directed at me at Gesu—a tight-knit and predominantly White Catholic church adjacent to a K–8 elementary school where I spent the bulk of my youth, if I wasn't at home or Thornton.

In first grade, several new students joined our kindergarten cohort, among them a charming, bright boy with blond hair and blue eyes who was popular with students and teachers. I reveled in being one of the top students in school, blissfully unaware of the unflinching way I lived up to the brownnosing Asian stereotype. I hardly cared about what had happened the previous summer—it was, after all, a relatively *minor* incident and still, then, a one-off. So, although I was one of only a handful of Asian American students at the entire school, I was a stubbornly precocious perfectionist. This likely irritated my teacher, who from the start seemed to delight in pitting me and this new boy against each other in performative competitions of wit.

We were both assigned to a small reading group for gifted students and quickly fell into a pattern of sparring for kudos. My exceedingly competitive nature was piqued for the first time. But I was smarter, regardless of ego or attitude. I won the class spelling bee. I could read aloud without fumbling over new words or being chided to sound them out. I could finish the hardest math worksheets first, conspicuously flashing a smug glance in his direction each time I proved this point. He was more likable than I (see: overly competitive), and for a while the two of us were a formidable yet balanced pair of teacher's pets.

Maybe a third of the way into the year, an organic rift between boys and girls began to swell in our class—this being the natural age when gender roles, groomed and stoked by Christian patriarchal rhetoric, began to take on sharp distinctions. By the middle of first grade in my parochial learning environment, boys had cooties and girls paired off in twos and threes on the playground to administer a special handshake that would ostensibly protect us from male infection. The bullying began as an innocent extension of this. On the paved lot at recess after lunch, when our teachers vanished and volunteer monitors were left in charge, my rival would hurl racially tinged insults at me. *Foreigner! Chink! Go back to your own country!*

Of all the off-color nicknames, "foreigner" stuck. Lining up in two parallel single-file lines—boys and girls—for recess, lunch, gym, music lessons, or dismissal, we were usually across from each other because our last names fell in the last quarter of the alphabet. He'd whisper "foreigner" under his breath, flitting a smarmy gaze in my direction—much like I had done to him when triumphantly yet discreetly noting my superior intellectual acuity. His message was unequivocal: I may be smart, but I was manifestly different from the rest of our classmates; I was Other. The gist of the earlier minor encounter came barreling back, and I finally understood that identity was largely governed, it seemed, by my physical appearance.

I don't know for how long this went on—maybe a few days? a week?—but one day, filled with indignation, I retaliated with enough boorishness to warrant a trip to the principal's office. Conveniently, I have no memory of what I did. Legs dangling, I sobbed in detail my side of the story to Sister Mary So and So, concentrating my gaze on her taut forehead as I relayed how this new boy was not only mean, but wrong. I was born and raised in Shaker Heights; just because my father was Chinese didn't mean I wasn't American; I had a right to be here as much as anyone else. My undeniable penchant to argue a point that I'm positive I am right about—defying authority to defend it because surely everyone else is as flabbergasted as me—had been unleashed. I waited anxiously, expecting to be marched out of the office with the principal's arm around my shoulder to signal the sorted misunderstanding.

Instead, I was stunned when I was admonished with a harsh warning and told that I'd be expelled if something like this happened again. Not an utterance addressing the racialized insults, not an iota of concern for the nature of this boy's ostracizing taunts. I ever so faintly recall being fed a platitude of the *sticks and stones may break my bones*–variety, but not even a nominal reprimand for his choice of language. It was crystal clear: this racial mockery was not the type of complaint that would be taken seriously. I was not physically harmed. We are not different; love is blind; we are all the same because of God's love.

//////////

《吳興五族家庭懇親會攝影紀念序》

Photographs for Remembrance of the Fond Reunion of the Five Branches of the Wú Xìng「吳興」*Family*

Introduction
by Zhòng Fāng「仲芳」and Yín Fāng「吟芳」, eighth-generation Shěns

鶺鴒在原，兄弟急難
凡今之人，莫如兄弟
Cranes and doves in the fields, brothers in urgent need
Men of today, not like those as brothers.

As one reads the pages of Chang Di《常棣》*in the* Book of Odes《詩經》, *it is hard not to clap shut the folios, sigh three times over, and wonder if—given it is said that people nowadays are not like people of old—it is possible nevertheless for people today to match people in the past? Our folks from Wú Xìng*「吳興」*have grown to such a great lot and have always shown friendliness and love towards each other from all generations in the past up to our own, where we are reaching into the fifties in ages in our lives, and as the ancient sage Boyu*「伯玉」*says, "one can then see things in better perspectives and make amends for previous misgivings."*

From 1955 to 1965, my dad remained in Manila and diligently pursued Jesuit formation. He was sent to Toronto to complete the final stages of his candidacy, and in 1968, he was ordained a Catholic priest in the order of the Jesuits. With Jesuit sponsorship, he enrolled in a Ph.D. program at the University of South Carolina, graduating in 1972 and thereafter completing a yearlong internship in Birmingham, Alabama. After certification, my dad applied to jobs in the US and Hong Kong. The Jesuits arranged a job for him in Hong Kong, urging him to return, but to their consternation, he accepted a position at Metro General Hospital in Cleveland, Ohio—the teaching hospital affiliated with Case Western Reserve University. Part of his job included supervising medical students, and before long, he became familiar with the CWRU campus and its Catholic Center. In 1975, he left the Jesuit order, pivoting more fully into his new life in the US, which came with a strong desire to start a family.

When my parents met in 1978 at the Catholic Center at CWRU, my dad was 42—a full twenty years older than my mom, who had just completed her first year at Case's law school. They married in the spring of 1979 after dating for less than a year. As we liked to tease her growing up, my mom's last year of law school was free because her husband was still teaching there. My older brother—also John Thomas—was born in January 1980, followed by my sister, Mary Kathryn, in 1981; me, Frances Holly, in December 1983; Andrew Nathaniel, the youngest, was born in the fall of 1985. Though my parents loved the name Holly—my mom thought it was fitting for a baby girl born in

December, reminiscent of the boughs of greenery that signal Christmastime—Catholicism requires a child to be named after a canonized saint, so Frances was put first on my birth certificate, after my dad's father's Catholic English name, Francis.

My maternal grandfather, born in Prague to Moravian Jews, narrowly escaped the Nazis, eventually landing in New Jersey. His blue eyes were as much an asset then as they are today. These blue eyes were passed to my mom, but all four of her children arrived with dark eyes and dark hair. Thus, my relationship with Whiteness is complicated by the simple fact that my father isn't White, but my mother is. Very White, as I learned to say when asked by new friends or acquaintances; very White as in blue eyes, fair skin, and hair. This explanation became necessary because my physical traits are predominantly East Asian to the point that I can usually pass as 100 percent Chinese. If my mom and I were shopping or dining out by ourselves, I was often mistaken for an adopted Chinese child—an undesired but extraordinarily lucky baby girl born in China, spared death via adoption by Westerners, as was sometimes inferred, or even directly asked, especially in the mid-1990s after *The Joy Luck Club* became a movie.

//////////

The convention of assigning racial percentages to individuals is absurd yet crucial to the understanding of contemporary identity; the practice defines an individual with irrevocable, often violent force. Poet and author Caroline Randall Williams recently noted in a *New York Times* opinion piece that the rule of hypodescent—or the practice of assigning the child of a mixed-race union to the socially subordinate group—has upheld confederate ideals in the South, which deny the truth of plantation rape and the mixed-race children abandoned and exploited by their White fathers.

Before now, I probably wouldn't have allowed myself the exercise of thinking about how this concept might apply to me. So, like Hong, I preface this rumination with the full acknowledgment that there is no comparison in the detrimental effects of hypodescent when considering Blacks and Asian Americans. Yet I can't deny the urge to wonder: Do I have more to gain with a 100-percent Asian face now than I did over three decades ago, when I was born? What do I lose by never being mistaken for 100 percent White—or at least partially White like my sister? Conversely, White people regularly mistake me for all stripes of Asian—Korean, Japanese, and less often, Southeast Asian. I think about how this objective fact makes me at once analogous to and discrete from 100-percent Asian Americans. Am I "more White" than Asian because I was raised in the US with one White parent, and under the conditions of assimilation?

Reading *Minor Feelings* the first time, while marveling at the brilliance and utility of the term "minor feelings," I told myself that I, like Hong, avoided identity politics in my chosen field—art history, museums, and cultural production—because I was enraptured with modernism. I wanted to understand the nuanced relationship between representation and objecthood. I was uninterested in leveraging or exploring identity because I considered it juvenile, already passé by the time I was in graduate school in 2010.

The truth is so base that I must nearly force myself to write these words. The truth is, I was ashamed of my Asianness, both physically and culturally. I just wanted to be normal. I hated that I would always be the Asian in a group of friends. In her recent book *Trick Mirror,* Jia Tolentino describes the moment she realized that identity is determined by external factors. During a game of Power Rangers, she was told by a friend that she *had* to play the Yellow Ranger; the game could not proceed otherwise. This revelation was made all the worse by understanding that her friend would never desire to be the Yellow Ranger because, by definition, no one desires to be her. I was determined not to be Other, to avoid letting my physical appearance define me. The truth is, I wasn't interested in identity politics because it meant having to engage in my Asian Otherness.

Despite the fact that my small world was mostly White as a child, I wasn't completely alone in my strange half-Chinese otherness. There were Asian American families at the Cleveland Institute of Music, where I took piano and violin lessons, yet I didn't feel totally comfortable in these surroundings, where most children had two Chinese parents or two Korean parents. When I was in preschool, my dad and mom forged a friendship with another biracial half-Chinese/half-White family in our neighborhood. They also had four children, one of whom was my age. Though we did not attend the same schools—Alison went to Shaker Heights High School, the objectively cooler and equally academically rigorous public school in our town, while I was forced to attend Beaumont School for Girls—we became very close during the two summers we spent as lifeguards (ironically, at Thornton Park).

Flipping through old boxes of my childhood belongings recently, I stumbled across a homemade scrapbook Alison made for my seventeenth birthday. I laughed intensely at the intentionally random Britney Spears references, the yearbook photos of crushes, and the enumerated lists of high, hilarious times. But I had completely forgotten that she devoted an entire section to the racism we experienced as teenagers. In addition to the lyrics of "Got Rice?"—a parody song about Asian pride set to Tupac's "Changes"—one page was titled "AP: What Does This Stand For." It describes in detail how we were often referred to as the "double Asian Persuasion," a double entendre for "Advancement Placement" because we were also smart. Another page reads, "Do you remember our conversation about all those RACISTS? Glad we're in the same boat." I hadn't forgotten so much as repressed these things; seeing them, the memory came thrusting back.

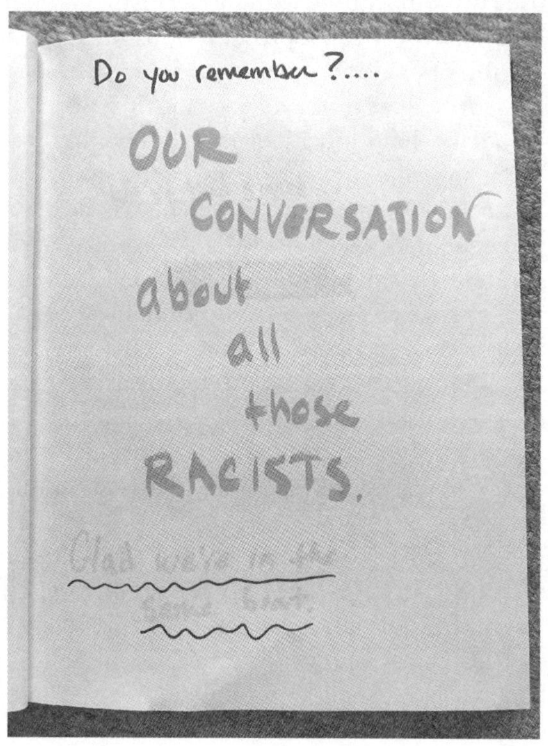

A page from the scrapbook Alison made me for my seventeenth birthday.

Bored and looking for something to do one night in our junior year of high school, Alison and I drove to a house party at the home of the little blond boy from first grade, the one from Gesu who called me "foreigner." He was now a popular high school student at St. Ignatius, the all-boys Catholic prep school on the west side of Cleveland that both my brothers attended. (To be factually accurate and as a point of pride, my little brother Andrew never lets me forget that while he may have *attended* St. Ignatius, he *graduated* from Shaker after being suspended from private school—enjoying his senior year smug as a motherfucker for figuring out what I never could.) Either surprisingly or unsurprisingly, I had been friends with the little blond boy on and off through the years, the result of the inevitable bonds forged between those who spend elementary years together. The teasing on the playground an ancient memory, we had even hooked up once in my friend's basement during my freshman year of high school.

As usual, his parents were out of town. I can't remember verbatim what was said, only that upon our arrival, he began drunkenly harassing us, calling us exotic Asians and asking if we would strip for the party. Alison recalls the racial epithet "Chink." But what I remember most vividly was our disgust at the way these boys—gleefully and with shameless pride—fulfilled their base stereotypical potential by reading Asian American identity as a fetish object of White male desire.

A few racially tinged epithets later, we left laughing, but also embarrassed and angry. On the way home and for the rest of the night, we talked about our racist experiences. I could feel the anger morph into rage, as we shared story after story of microaggressions of all stripe and scope.

But what could we do about it? We felt powerless. I don't know who suggested it first—probably me—but the idea to call the cops was floated. It was an underage party, and we had learned through the vulgar exchange that these boys *had* in fact hired strippers for the party. Both were major infractions at St. Ignatius and would certainly be a burden for whoever got swept up in a raid. It didn't take us long to decide, and one of us made a quick, anonymous phone call to the police department in Orange, the affluent eastern suburb where the little blond boy lived. Hence the scrapbook reference.

//////////

Memories fade, families disperse, before long there will be a gathering of passersby and strangers rather than a closely-knit, supportively bonded large family.

When I first approached your grandpa about this letter, I was consumed by the precarity caused by the global pandemic. I was also intensely aware that President Trump's intentionally racialized rhetoric (constantly focusing on China as the initial source of the virus) would resuscitate Asian and Asian American stereotypes across the US and beyond. Guardedly, I asked him to share his reflections on being both Chinese and Asian American—especially with a background as varied and complex as his. But in his typically vexing manner, he demurred by means of a conditional. First, he wanted to hear *my* evaluation of growing up as a second-generation Asian American. Already anxious at gauging the emotional capacity required to provide him with a sufficient response, I—lazily?—told him to read *Minor Feelings*. It'll give you a good primer into some of my feelings, I said. Send me the name and title later, he relented.

When I saw him in person a few days later, your grandpa wanted to know if I really felt singled out or treated differently during my childhood or adolescence. He seemed genuinely surprised when I responded, *of course I did*. I knew a long soliloquy, protracted by his recent brain injury, was coming. But when you are in the middle of a months-long lockdown caused by a global pandemic, what else is there to do?

I think we started by bickering about whether or not America has a racist past with regards to slavery—at least in comparison to pre- or post-Communist China. Eventually, he carefully pointed out that some of Hong's perspective is at least colored by the physical abuse she suffered at the hands of her Korean parents, a fact alluded to obliquely in *Minor Feelings*. He explained that he never really felt discriminated against because of various factors, chief among them his unwavering faith and participation in the Jesuit order, which he noted, is an elitist rank among Catholics (because they're highly educated). And because his mother always reminded him, in the years he remembers before she died, that he was descended from a noble clan.

When I was leaving his house later that day, he handed me a piece of paper with a short, numbered list scrawled hastily on the back of a medication print-out folded in half:

three incidents of
racially tinged
① a border custom officer
② a bunch of rowdy kids in a car on Laurel St. in San Carlos
③ a fellow graduate student at University of South Carolina a New Yorker, likely Jewish

Birth/Mo's influence
Jesuit education/Persistence
Ph.D.
Licensing
Acceptance by Americans in general, Catholics in particular
My language ability
4 Jesuits that impacted my life
1. a Hungarian/scholarship
2. an Irish, English
3. a Philipino, Psychology!!
4. an Irish American, En
5. a Jesuit psychologist

The left column noted "three racially tinged incidents" (he had originally written down "three incidents" and then gone back and added the modifier with a caret). On the right was a short list of major life events, untitled, but presumably referencing what he had previously expressed about the factors that had made him resilient to racism.

A few days later, your grandpa sent the following email:

> Thank you very much, Hol, for the visit yesterday and for the conversation on our individual experiences as an American of Asian origin. I have felt regrets since coming to California and learning that all four of you felt unease about being Asian amidst a majority of Americans. It was naiveté on my part to assume that my self-confidence would automatically transfer to my children. Hopefully yesterday's conversation will lead you to some kind of resolution on the issue of self-identity. Hopefully too my story will provide a broadened perspective in assessing the experiences and reactions of other people of Asian origin.

//////////

Nuance—I'm obsessed with it lately because I feel like it's slipping away from me. No matter how carefully I move from one thought to another, one moment to the next, I can't avoid extremes. I crave simple binaries like forbidden food, like the innocent themes and effortless melodies of a pop song. Love and loss, good and evil. Sometimes, locating myself within these emotionally charged clichés satiates a primal desire; I rationalize this penchant as an outlet for my natural "energy." At the same time, I worry that crusading for a cause is a harmful denial of powerlessness. Or that my desire for extremes is fueled by inertia—that it is a way to default to a certain moral (Catholic) code of behavior.

Is it part of the reason why I didn't turn down the unplanned opportunity to bring you into this world? Understanding and acknowledging every fragment of our family history, every layer of my perspective on Asian American identity, how it's colored by my experience and how it differs from those who have come before me, is tedious and exhausting. I'm embarrassed at how much attitudes about Asian American identity tend to shift, both in the short term and long term. Those who have the emotional and mental endurance to keep pace with the glut of information and perspectives—to parse it, understand it, reveal nuances, note contradictions, internalize perspectives, and learn from the discrepancies—thrive. Those who are lazy choose a side and stick to it. I'm tired.

On my best days, I summon the assuredness of the vibrant Asian American voices and positive examples I hear around me. This enables me to ruminate on my own success as due, in part, to my resolve to *not* be defined by my Asian American identity. On my worst, I'm the self-hating, dreadfully egotistical version of myself, the same ghost that tortured Hong. Somewhere between these two spaces, I start to approximate my own definition of Asian American.

But I am nowhere close to having this all figured out. My mind is plagued by abstract questions—Are words nonviolent by definition? Is representation more important than de-normalizing the use of racialized language? Or are we shaped most by the physical spaces and tangible realities of bodily harm that surround us at any given moment?—as well as concrete ones: Why am I so angry?

I try to tell myself (or remind myself?) that emotions can be simultaneous as well as discrete. But if non-cathartic states of feeling are associated with situations in which action is blocked or suspended, then shouldn't my anger displace envy, paranoia, and irritation? "I always thought my physical identity was the problem but writing made me realize that even without myself present, I still couldn't rise above myself, which pitched me into a kind of despair."[4] Reading this was like watching the evolution of my emotions sped up and played back for me. I had a pretty good run at fooling myself, believing that I had somehow risen above myself or beyond my racialized perspective.

I wish I could tell you that I live in hopeful patience, that love triumphs hate, or that God will save us all. My own experience has revealed the paradox of deception: when it is so blatant it becomes thick like a fog, hard to identify because it is so normal. Sometimes the last people and things on earth you'd ever suspect are complicit in systems of hegemony designed to differentiate us according to arbitrary hierarchies, deny us our personhood, and harm the individual at the expense of the collective.

It is impossible to enumerate all that I fear or don't know. Today I'm hopeful enough to start by offering this letter and in it, this message:

Love is ubiquitous, not universal. If we are one, the well-being of the fragment is essential to the success of the whole. The way you come to love someone is learned over time and yet inexplicably inherent.

I love you the most and I worry about you the most because you are the first me and I am the first you. I'm tired and sad, but not nearly complete. You and I will be OK, or as Grandpa likes to say these days when I ask him how he's doing, *my kind of OK.*

Love,
H

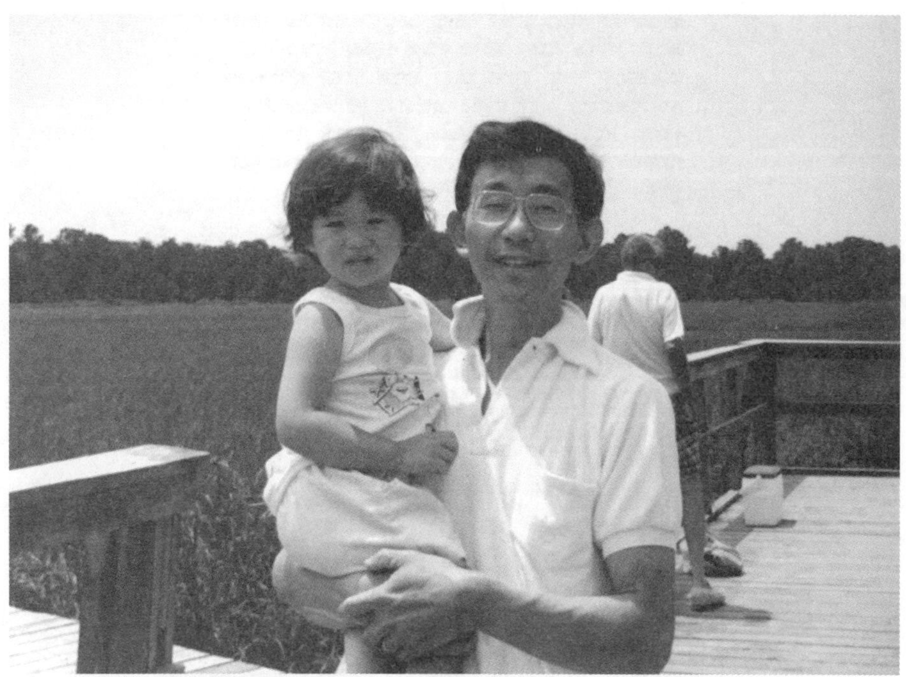

Me and my dad on vacation in South Carolina, ca. 1986.

1 *Shěn Clan Genealogy* as translated by the author's father.
2 Cathy Park Hong, *Minor Feelings: An Asian American Reckoning* (New York: One World, 2020).
3 Many recent articles on Asian American identity in the last few years have noted how the term *Asian American* was developed in the late 1960s as a political tactic to create a unified coalition of various immigrant communities.
4 Hong, *Minor Feelings*, 42.

ANOKA FARUQEE

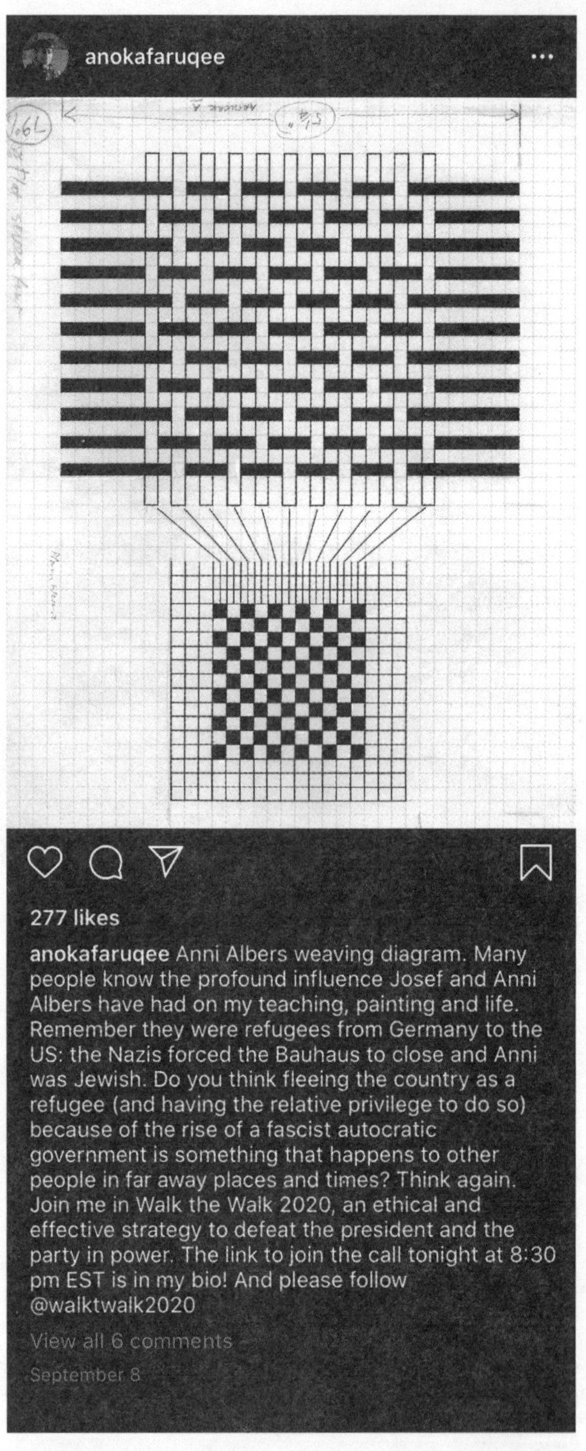

PATRICK JAOJOCO

from a Filipino/American
living on Canarsie land
born on Ramaytush land

to the building on Nacotchtank land
currently known as
1600 Pennsylvania Avenue NW
Washington, DC 20500

I wish I could burn this letter and bury the ash in your walls

"White House":

I wonder what you think of the people inside you
The people who have
kept on killing other people for the last
200 or so years from the offices within you

and the people who for the last 500 or so years
kept recreating the systems made by
the people
who killed people
to clear way for your foundation

I wonder who you are

I wonder if your grounds, your walls, your roof are tainted
by the work of murderers
whose blood
you run on

and from
and to

I wonder if by addressing this letter to you
I am speaking to all of the people who have been
displaced and taken and killed by
the people inside you

I want to assume so

I want to address this to you, the Nacotchtank community,
who were visited by a man named S*ith
whose land was taken to build you
and 18 of you were massacred by White forces in 1622.

I know you were forced to move from where this White House stands
to a small island nearby where you
maintained a community at least until
a virus killed many of you,
cleared the way so White people could come again and
claim that land in 1682
"patented" as Anacostine Island under White laws
so that some White man named R*ndolph Br*ndt
and his daughter M*rgaret H*mmersley
could live
happily ever after, as owners of that land
so that later in 1931
other White folks could monumentalize it
in T*ddy R*osevelt's White name

I know this: these White laws evolved
to be upheld by the people inside you

and about 100 years later you were built
and that the White people that created you envisioned a
"White House"
but is it really that important to you
to be so blank?

I know that the stone of your walls came
from Aquia Creek, some unique sandstone extracted from

down South on Patawomeck land where
today, a couple thousand of you live.

I know that you were built by enslaved Black folx,
who went by the names of

Abraham, Abram, Adam, Alexander, Amos, Anthony, Bard, Basil, Ben, Bob, Catherine Green, Cato, Charles, Clinton, Daniel, Dave, David, Davy, Davenport, Dick, Edward, Emanuel, Fielder, Frank, Francis, Gabe, George, Girard, Gus, Harry, Henly, Henry, Ignatius, Isaac, Jack, Jacob, James, Jarrot, Jerry, Jess, Jim, Joe, John, Joseph, Josias, Kit, Lewis, Lin, Liverpool, Luke, Manuel, Mich, Mike, Miles, Moses, Nace, Nathaniel, Ned, Nero, Newton, Oliver, Orston, Osten, Peter, Pompey, Ralph, Randall or Randolph, Richard, Robert, Salisbury, Sandy, Sam, Silvester, Solomon, Stephen, Thomas, Tom, Tony, Walter, Will, William

and maybe others.

I know that your stone cracked after you were set ablaze
by other White people in 1814

and I wonder if
maybe then in the fire with your
White skin melting away
you were beginning
to show your truth

but your sand-colored stone was repainted White
as your land kept getting mined, bought and sold again and again according
to a law that was not meant for you.

I know that less than 100 years later
some White people residing within you had a mind
to capture again others like you
and came to the islands of my ancestors
to claim our land and
exploit our labor and
import our goods
to uphold this White agenda that
was not meant for us

Southern Filipinos were named Négros and Moros by
other White folks when the
White folks you house came over
and killed us too

that's when your residents named M*Kinley and R*osevelt
sent their gang of murderers named D*wey and S*ith and O*is and M*cArthur
and M*rritt and W*eaton
to the islands of my ancestors under the guise of
liberation

And when that S*ith man said

"I want no prisoners. I wish you to kill and burn, the more you kill and burn
the better it will please me. I want all persons killed who are capable of
bearing arms in actual hostilities against the United States ... "

and when some White soldier said

"I am in my glory when I can sight my gun on some dark skin and pull the
trigger"

and when that great Black man named David Fagen
and some of his beautiful peers named Buffalo Soldiers
called bullshit on the situation and
joined to fight

for Bonifacio, for Luna, for the bayan and revolution,

(Makibaka! Huwag matakot!)

for Gabriela Silang, for Lapu-Lapu

(Makibaka! Huwag matakot!)

for Joma Sison, for Lorena Barros, for Randy Echanis

(Makibaka! Huwag matakot!)

for Larry Itliong, for Al Robles, for Brandon Lee,

(Makibaka! Huwag matakot!)

that's when we got to know
your murderers as ours

I wonder when you heard the word liberation
for the first time and if you knew then what those White men were saying
I wonder if you knew then that more than 200,000 of my ancestors
would be massacred for that word but

of course you know when
I address this letter to you
"White House"
you hold my ancestors too

and of course I know
when we, our people
say liberation we
mean it

I wonder if you think about that
I wonder if when they report on
more White laws
"coming from the White House"
Do you want that to be you? What's underneath
all that White shit?

I wonder what your Whiteness hides
the mix of skins betrayed from inside you
your walls a cold, systemic White when
your insides red Black with blood browning

from the trauma of the victims of your residents' transgressions
from the projects to the Philippines,
from Turtle Island to Palestine,
from Puerto Rico to Iraq

you, "America," you "melting pot"
you imperial crucible for stolen gold
set fire to your people and the global poor
our ancestors', heat for a liberatory boil

and in your history books one thing you teach us:
White paint melts easy

I want you to know
you are not alone,
you are our multitudes,
and we will liberate you from your painted skin

screaming

Say their names
and
Fuck the police
and
Palestine will be free
and
Makibaka! Makibaka! Makibaka! Makibaka!

Until then,
Patrick Jaojoco

PAUL PFEIFFER

Dear Cady,

I've been thinking a lot about your work lately, especially about the use of found objects in your sculptures and installations. There's something so particular and precise about the way you sample materials from the real world in your work. It's a meticulous process of selecting, arranging, and editing so finely calibrated to the psychic wiring of commodity culture that it makes me connect certain aspects of your work to the current cultural/political crisis we're facing. I'm writing this letter to start a conversation.

Society today is a stadium, a circus, and a hall of mirrors. Everything can be turned into wallpaper, from the most prosaic customs and routines to human and environmental tragedy, to political discourse, to intimate encounter. This doesn't make violence or pleasure less real. We are in a state of war conducted through images. If data-driven algorithms can interpret personal preference from clicks and eye movements and then customize a feed predicting our appetites as consumers, how, then, to discern free will from manufactured habit? If AI sets the ontological horizon beyond the limits of human perception, how can we be sure that what we see is real and not a customized projection? Can we discuss this as we tumble down the rabbit hole of 2020 together?

There's an affective quality that pervades your sculptures, that gets under my skin and that I can't get out of my head. Your found object sculptures radiate an intense aesthetic presence when encountered in a room and resonate strongly with a strange and current sense of all things familiar rendered vacant. It's a quality of unrealness or hollowness that I associate with this historical juncture. Your works convey a warning message for the world. Deep down, we understand it's the end of the world. The old world is dying, and a new world is struggling to be born.

The voyage we're on, as we navigate the perverse spaces and temporalities of global capitalism, is the ontological Exodus. The technologies are new, but the state of cognitive dissonance is not. The uncanny has been fundamental to human experience from the very beginning. In the current moment of sensory overload, we are reminded that the Exodus was never simply a geographic journey: it was always ontological—a journey to liberate human consciousness—and has been ongoing for millennia.

Though we haven't met in person, I feel I know you in some way because of a strong affinity I feel toward the objects you make. There are so many more things I wish I could talk to you about: reification, the opening scene of Paolo Pasolini's *Salo*, predatory camouflage. Can we do that one day soon?

Paul Pfeiffer

FUREN DAI

Dear Fellow American:

~~On behalf of the people of the United States, congratulations on becoming a citizen of this magnificent land.~~ Thank you for deciding to join us in becoming a significant part of our national identity. **No matter where you come from,** ~~or what faith you practice,~~ **you are now an American citizen.** You will contribute to the cultural value of diversity, **and you share the** ~~sacred~~ **rights, responsibilities, and duties that unite us as one** ~~people~~ Nation.

(Currently), **our** ~~Nation has always welcomed newcomers who embrace our values, assimilate into our society, and pledge allegiance to our country~~ government adopts an immigration system that serves the Nation's interest. However, even though you are officially an American citizen, when there comes a conflict of national interest, you might still be considered an Other. ~~In turn, America embraces you and ushers you into a fraternity defined by mutual kinship and affection.~~ Unfortunately, this biased perception is embedded in the foundation of this country. We believe **our** ~~patriotism~~ joint commitment to equality, equity, and justice will be ~~is~~ **the bond that holds us all tightly together.**

Although you and your fellow naturalized citizens hail from many places and come from many backgrounds, as Americans, you all now bear the torch of American history—inheriting a legacy of ~~common heroes, values, traditions,~~ achievements, and recognizing and expiating centuries-long pain and struggle **that stretches back through the centuries. This American legacy is now your legacy. This history is now your history.** This struggle is now your struggle. ~~Our traditions are now your traditions.~~ **You now share the duty to pass the legacy of liberty, history, and tradition to the next generation** ~~of Americans~~**.** At the same time, you will join us in reflecting upon the errors that we committed in the past, and share the obligation and responsibilities to identify and correct the systematic faults of the present day.

The United States is now your homeland ~~and all Americans are now your brothers and sisters~~**.** You might, for the first time, experience your "new" identity through interaction with "other" racial communities. Because of the diversity in this land, you will be confronted with the nonbinary complexity that exists everywhere. ~~You have pledged your heart to America. And when you give your love and loyalty to America, she returns her love and loyalty to you.~~ On top of all the daily duties that you were performing in your home country, you will now continuously be battling those whom you represent, and are represented by, in your new homeland.

We celebrate this special day. We welcome you into our national family. We applaud your devotion to America. ~~And we embrace the wonderful future we will have together.~~ Due to several issues, we might not be able to see a solution to these national problems within our lifetime, and we will have to figure out a way of cohabitating with them while simultaneously trying to fix them. Nothing is guaranteed. Therefore, it is essential to let your voice be heard; the power is now in your hands. Go and make active choices and decisions to protect and defend not only the equality, equity, and justice of this Nation, but the indigenous lands and water of this planet.

~~Congratulations and~~ **Welcome**, and it is a great honor to have you join us. ~~May God bless you and may God continue to bless America.~~

Sincerely,

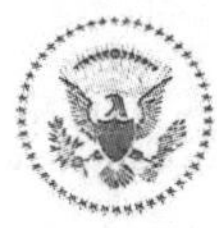

THE WHITE HOUSE

WASHINGTON

Dear Fellow American:

On behalf of the people of the United States, congratulations on becoming a citizen of this magnificent land. No matter where you come from, or what faith you practice, you are now an American citizen, and you share the sacred rights, responsibilities, and duties that unite us as one people.

Our Nation has always welcomed newcomers who embrace our values, assimilate into our society, and pledge allegiance to our country. In turn, America embraces you and ushers you into a fraternity defined by mutual kinship and affection. Our patriotism is the bond that holds us all tightly together.

Although you and your fellow naturalized citizens hail from many places and come from many backgrounds, as Americans, you all now bear the torch of American history—inheriting a legacy of common heroes, values, and traditions that stretches back through the centuries. This American legacy is now your legacy. This history is now your history. Our traditions are now your traditions. You now share the duty to pass the legacy of liberty, history, and tradition to the next generation of Americans.

The United States is now your homeland, and all Americans are now your brothers and sisters. You have pledged your heart to America. And when you give your love and loyalty to America, she returns her love and loyalty to you.

We celebrate this special day. We welcome you into our national family. We applaud your devotion to America. And we embrace the wonderful future we will have together.

Congratulations and welcome. May God bless you and may God continue to bless America.

Sincerely,

SRESHTA RIT PREMNATH

July 13, 2020

Dear José,

It was a real pleasure to see you again, although under difficult circumstances. Has it already been three months since you stopped by my place? I apologize again for the hurried exchange at the door. The pandemic has made us put aside basic courtesies. Still, I wish we had taken the time to sit on the stoop and speak.

When we first met, two winters back, you were waiting for work at the corner of McDonald Avenue near 36th. It's five minutes from my apartment and on the way to my old studio. I had walked that route for several years, passing the many day laborers waiting at the intersection. Men leaning against the cemetery's dark, metal fence or seated on milk crates in the scant shade of trees. Backpacks, work boots, and gloves on, ready to face whatever the day may bring.

Years before we met, a black SUV pulled up as I approached the intersection one day. The driver, a Hasidic gentleman, rolled down his window and asked me if I wanted work. Indeed, I am a dark-skinned man, and I too wore a backpack and work boots—so the confusion was not surprising. I declined, and he drove on. This is an insignificant incident, I know, but it made me curious about the people for whom I had been mistaken.

When we spoke, you told me that you hadn't seen your wife and children in a long time. You spoke of your life as *una doble vida*—a double life. You work here afraid of being cheated out of payment on the one hand and fearing deportation on the other. You wait every morning for work and risk everything for three people in El Salvador, half a world away.

You wouldn't know this, but I grew up in South India and came here as an undergraduate student. We are both immigrants to the US, but your path here was a harder one. I know you crossed the southern border, but we didn't discuss how. It's not my place to ask, and you made it clear from the very beginning that your past was difficult and you don't like to dwell on it.

Another man—perhaps you know him—whom I interviewed the same day spoke of crossing the river that divides our countries as a child. One day at dawn, he almost drowned. He remembered it as death and resurrection. A crossing not only of political boundaries, but also of the liminal boundary between life and death, which, like the surface of water, is invisible from certain angles. These are traumas I cannot fully comprehend.

I bring this up because we have crossed different borders to come to the same place. Yet we live in different worlds. I have been reading a book that warns us of fixating on the wall as a metaphor for the border. It is so solid and fixed as an image that it gives us a false notion of an equally solid and fixed nation. The author argues that the border is not a place, but rather a method: a means of regulating and controlling the movement of people—people like you and me.

I had it easier than you, but still, coming from a poor country meant innumerable documents, long lines at consulates, proofs of solvency and responsibility each time I crossed a border. The poor are regulated—and only the desirable few from poor countries are allowed to move. Desirable because we bring privilege, or conversely because we will do the dirty work. Some move quickly, some move through molasses, while others—like you—wait.

I hope you get a US passport one day. It is a magical thing that allows me—the same person who was once looked at with suspicion and pulled into "secondary inspection" in airports— to go anywhere. Can you believe it? I have acquired a sense of entitlement to match my new status. I have almost lost my irrational fear of immigration officers. I walk up to the counter, look the officer in the eye, and present my identification. And just like that, they let me through.

Perhaps we had even crossed paths before, but it took a misrecognition for us to meet. Borders are learned, internalized, and enacted in every interaction. They are spatial concepts that keep us in our designated place: you at the corner of McDonald and 36th, me just passing through, and another man—acting on his understanding of who looks like a laborer and who does not—mistaking me for *someone like you*. Yet, when we spoke, you seemed to trust me. You were eager to tell me your story, which is now a part of me and directs so many of my thoughts and actions. How else do I say it? You are now a part of me.

We have a new visitor, traveling with us on planes, on the road, and in the air, with no conception of political boundaries. A pathogen that has brought the world to its knees and put all our lives on hold. When the city shut down, I thought immediately of you. There is no country that protects you, and no family here for you to return to. Must I not care for you? You might say that my identification with you is false—imposed by someone else—but what kind of society places the abstract laws of citizenship above the familial law of care or, dare I say, love?

The word *love* is seen as weak. In it, we sense our eventual betrayal. When we love, we give a part of ourselves and become incomplete. We know this from every generic love song, but there is some truth to it. A social bond is one that is freely given, and the resulting incompletion is filled by the giving of another. When you spoke so openly with me that day, and entrusted your story to me, the abundance of your generosity was enough to share with many others.

I know you were surprised to hear from me, and as I said at the outset, I wish we had talked more when you came to collect the money. My gesture felt transactional in comparison with what you had shared with me, and I felt awkward in the moment. I would like to have a beer together sometime—perhaps a more convivial gesture than a letter. I don't know if I will send this after all.

I hope you are well, José.

With love,
Rit Premnath

P.S. I appreciate your offer to repay me with work, but as I have explained, you don't owe me anything.

MEGHA RALAPATI

July 10, 2020

Dear Mom and Aunties Veena, Sunila, Surekha, and Neetu,

I reach out to you to share some thoughts and invite you to join me in considering an urgent problem.

I was recently reflecting on how you all met, in 1988. By then, it had been over a decade since you had each arrived in the US, as students or recent graduates. You were married and you had children; you were excited to raise families and live good, comfortable, and independent lives.

We, your children, were so little then—and you did everything for us. You organized our birthday parties and made us delicious cakes using instant box mixes. You bundled us up in the cold Chicago winters to tromp around in the snow, something you never did growing up in India. You dressed us up for picture day (when you remembered it was happening) and packed us lunches for school: tasty leftovers from dinner the night before, turkey sandwiches when we begged for something less fragrant, homemade soup, fresh fruit, and little rectangular juice boxes with tiny straws (or Capri Suns, if we were lucky).

By 1988 we were 6 or so, and you each decided to enroll us in Bharatanatyam—classical dance lessons. And that's where we all met. Every Saturday morning, we woke up earlier than we wanted and reluctantly dressed up in salwar kameez with dupattas tied around our little waists so we could get to class on time. Rubbing the tired out of our eyes and longing for a break to sip our rationed water, we did our basic steps and postures. The most challenging was aramandi, or "half-sitting"; when performed correctly, it would light a fire inside our tiny legs. We would look out at you all, hilariously miming the steps and motioning for us to sit more deeply ("Sit! Sit!"). You whispered jokes to each other, laughing too loudly, then giggling into your hands when Hema Aunty threw you a sharp look.

Back then, you were younger than we are today, which is nearly unimaginable to me. You seemed to have it all together. Not only were you balancing careers with children and marriage, but you were doing it in an entirely foreign cultural context. Some of you were happily married, and some were survivors of marital trauma and divorce. Some of you came from big cities in India, while others were from small villages. Despite your differences, 1988 found you together.

I honor your courage and independence, and all the sacrifices you had to make. I'm grateful for your individual journeys as women and mothers, as you modeled for us how to live and struggle, to find joy and humor, to leave a toxic marriage, to rebuild yourselves, to forge community, to nurture your children and family, and to never feel entitled to anything. Thank you for all you've done for us.

Today, I want to talk with you about something difficult. Since 2016 and especially over this past year, I have become increasingly alarmed by what I see evolving, slowly and steadily, inside the Indian American community—a community I feel proudly and deeply connected to. Like you, I am not a member of the Republican Party, nor have I ever felt fully aligned with the Democrats. And, like me, a large percentage of Indian Americans voted against our current administration in 2016. In fact, it was widely understood until recently that Indian Americans were not a segment of the population that would ever favor Trump's reelection.

It's now 2020, and things have changed. And, I am concerned about the direction I have observed some in our community moving, ideologically. To complicate things further, the Trump campaign has allocated considerable funding to buy ads that specifically target Indian Americans leading up to the election. I am asking you to join me in making sure our community doesn't fall prey to such transparent persuasion.

Do you remember last year's "Howdy Modi!" rally in Houston? It seemed kind of ridiculous to us at the time. But I believe this event helped cement the mutually advantageous relationship between Trump and India's prime minister, and started a powerful chemical reaction. It transformed many Indian Americans' generally favorable feelings about India into vociferous support for the ethnonationalist surge we're seeing there today—including the burgeoning state-sanctioned pogrom against India's Muslim population. Simultaneously, it catalyzed those favorable feelings into approval of the American president: if large populations of Indian Americans support Modi, and Modi is cozy with Trump, I'm afraid that their support will transfer directly from one to the other.

While seemingly contradictory and nonsensical, increasing support for Trump in the Indian American community is the result of factors rooted in the experiences of many in your generation.

In the decades that followed your immigration, social structures demanded that Indian American families be successful, productive, hardworking, silent, nonthreatening, complicit, harmless—and most importantly, distinct from other immigrant groups seen as dangerous, underemployed, undocumented. For many Indian Americans, assimilation to the United States meant moving to safe and cloistered suburban areas, and being surrounded by like-minded people of similar socioeconomic status. It has often meant being cocooned within American Whiteness—further reinforcing Whiteness as the norm. In meeting and often exceeding these conditions, Indian Americans successfully performed the role of "good immigrants."

I believe this notion of a model minority is a trick—a mirage that seems to reward those of us who can successfully perform model behavior. It drives a deep wedge between our distinct immigrant and ethnic American communities, and has encouraged an idea shared by more and more Indian Americans now: that their survival is tied to the ability to distance our community from the immigrants actively targeted by our current administration. While I understand how it can feel like a matter of life and death to protect the assets you have worked hard to accumulate, I sometimes wonder if our community will be able to see clearly out of such a complex and illusory maze.

Fortunately, there are paths out. Reflections on India's journey towards liberation can lead us to find common ground with Americans of other backgrounds. Family stories, like when your grandparents participated in Gandhi's Salt March, have been seared into our memories. That your parents' generation not only supported but participated in protest can help us connect our heritage of anti-colonialist struggle with the battle for civil rights still unfolding in the United States today.

I am proudly part of the first generation of Americans born in the US as a result of the US Immigration and Nationality Act of 1965, which eased visa restrictions and made it possible for immigrants like you—those with "in-demand skills"—to enter the country and build a life. This policy benefited so many of our families, yet few of us recognize how instrumental it was. Did you know that this important policy was a direct result of the US civil rights movement?

Over the past year, I have come to understand and appreciate how many people in your generation believe deeply in the fantasy of individual achievement, of being solely responsible for one's success and well-being. I believe we are each connected to many who are living that cloistered existence. I am trying to understand how together we might slow the momentum of our community's support for the Trump Administration. Let us talk with each other more, expand our understanding of US history, the electoral process, and our role in this democracy. Let us consider our responsibilities to the collective in exchange for the comforts we enjoy.

This is a crucial time in the continued formation of our community in the US: not simply because of the upcoming election, but because we need to consider the legacy we are creating for our children, your grandchildren.

I invite you to join me in learning more, discussing honestly, and voting in November as informed, empowered citizens.

With my deepest respect, gratitude, and love,
Your daughter,
Megha

MEL CHIN

November 2, 2020

Dear Sunny, Ken, Yvonne, Wayne, Warren:

I wanted to call and tell each of you: this is an OUTRAGE! How did this happen? How did we reach these advanced ages so quickly? But my calmer side ordered me to write a letter, which is probably strange to you since I normally use the horn; but each time I call, recently, it seems one of us is modeling a hospital gown. It is probably healthier to send you this note.

Okay, gotta tell you: your kids are following me! No worries, it's not freaking me out or anything, but I thought you should know. It was actually a humbling experience when I started to notice they were "following" me, as it's called on Instagram. I don't feel like I'm telling on them (as they are full-grown), but you might be pleased to know they are influencing me as opposed to me influencing them. When they were children, I might have related a few exaggerated stories while drinking and smoking, living in broken-glass, beer-bottle-strewn squalid conditions (full transparency ... a few of those squattings were my "movie sets" ... honest!). Since no one is serving time now, we can all be grateful they steered clear of drinking and driving and emulating some of my more colorful and "panic-ramic" antics back then. Have to say I think you all have done excellent jobs. When I do convo with them, they are articulate and fun. They force me to shake off some of my pessimism ... that the world will be forever stuck in the bad shape our generation is leaving it in.

When I draft some of my mini social media essays, I often think of them.

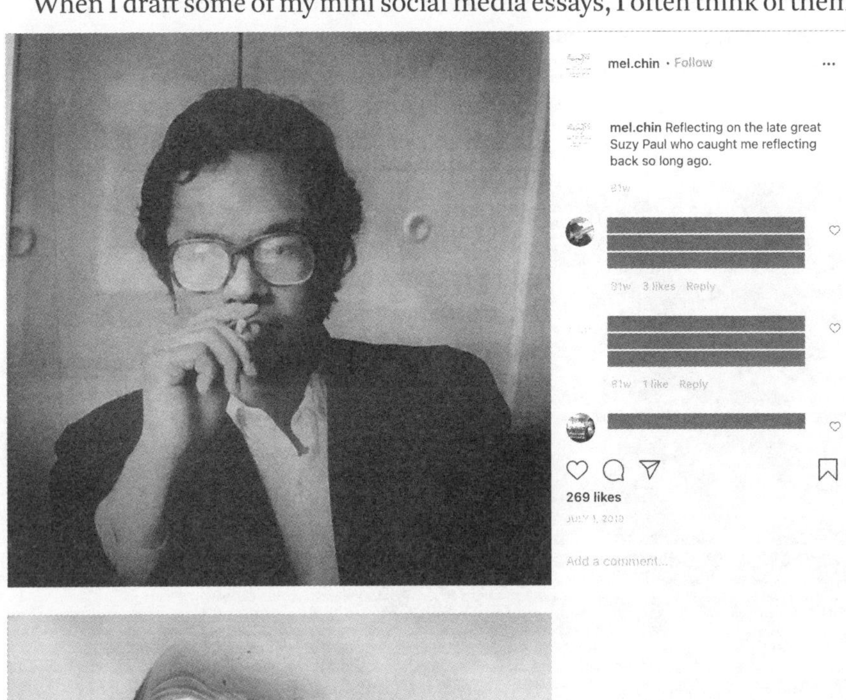

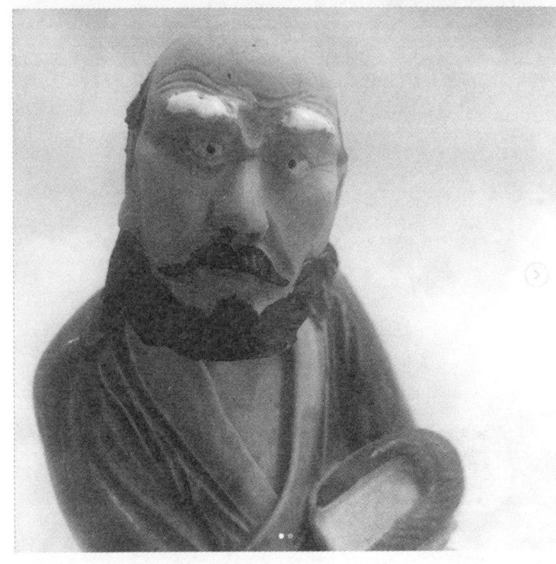

During these months of COVID-19 quarantine and self-imposed isolation, I've been using social media to share thoughts. Ruminations of our youth have invariably come up. I'm sharing with you the posts that your children have reacted to ... they might reveal some special effects of being raised Chinese in Texas!

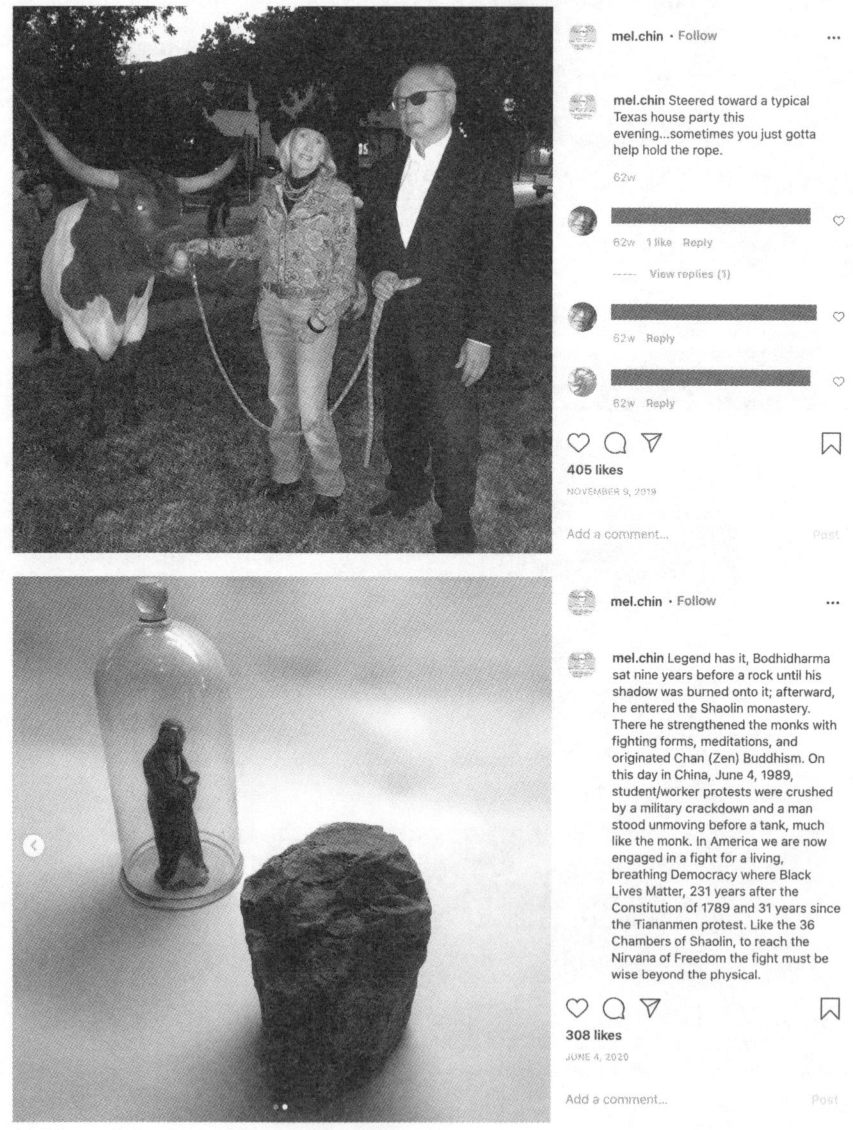

Here's a post of Mom with Sunny, Ken, and me in self-absorption. And here is one of her with Yvonne, Wayne, Warren, and me on a visit to DC in 1964, just before my mysterious breakdown.

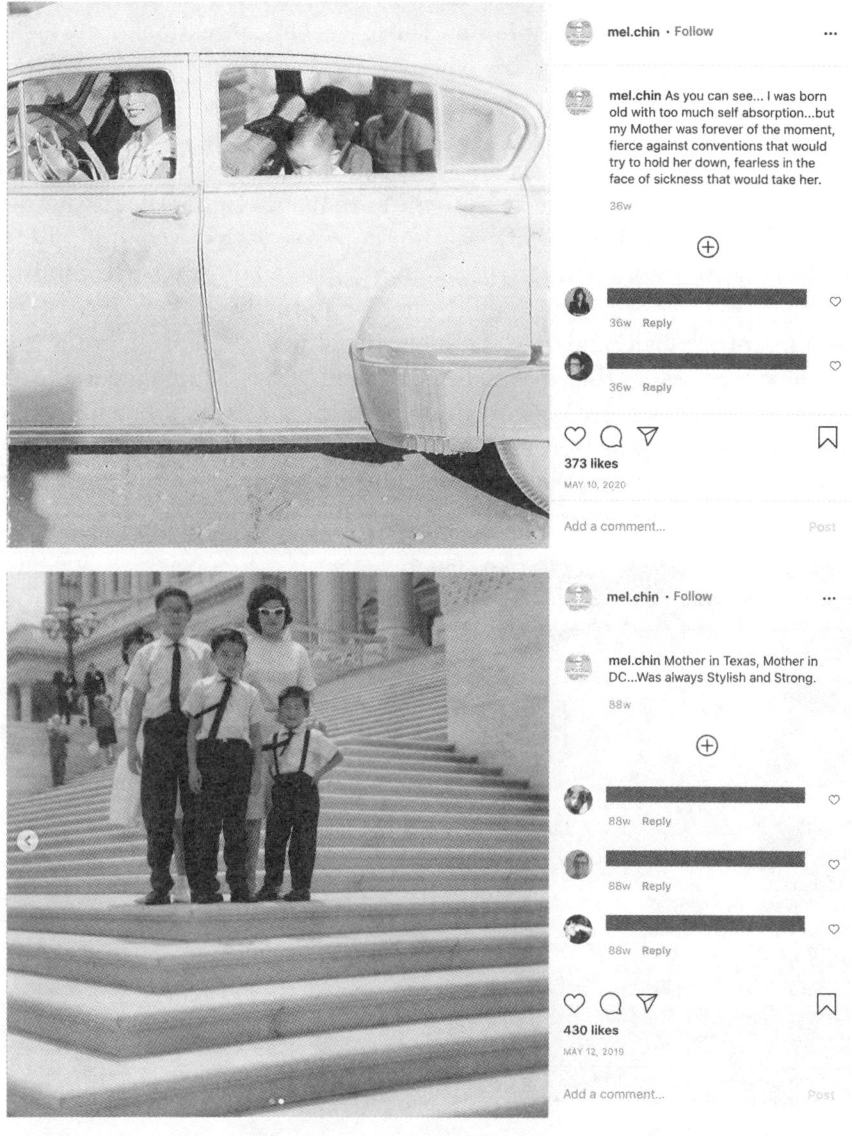

When I took sick for that year and half when I was 13, you all pitched in. Damn, you were just kids, leaving school to work in the store, while Mom and Dad took me to a stream of hospitals, clinics, and specialists; and you helped tend to me in my catatonic state when they decided to do away with medical advisement and to keep me at home. Those 60s shock treatments erased all memories of that time for me, but when I woke, there you all were: I was surrounded by your sibling solidarity. You are the family that gave me the love and time to recover.

The times together I do recall inspire, inform, and sensitize me to this day, and compelled me to return recently to the Fifth Ward neighborhood where we started, when I was asked to work on some concepts with the community. We have been having a great time, with "actions" instead of plans, to establish a presence in the face of gentrification, to archive and activate memories to build a monument to music, and to be the spot where the frontier of environmental survival for the rest of the city can be generated. It has offered me a sense of purpose that makes sense for a meaningful future for us all. When the killing of George Floyd (he was from Houston's Third Ward) happened, it shook me deeply like all the deaths that preceded and reaffirmed that the Black Lives Matter movement is one we must unquestionably support.

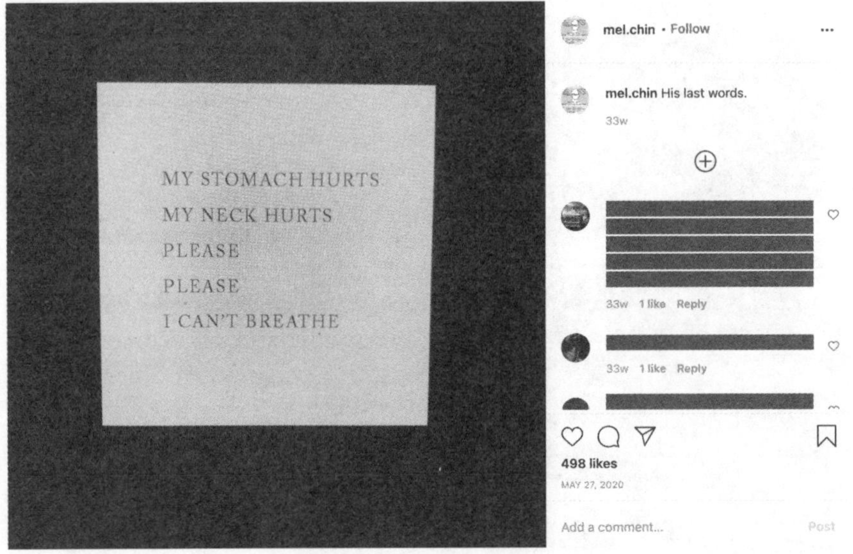

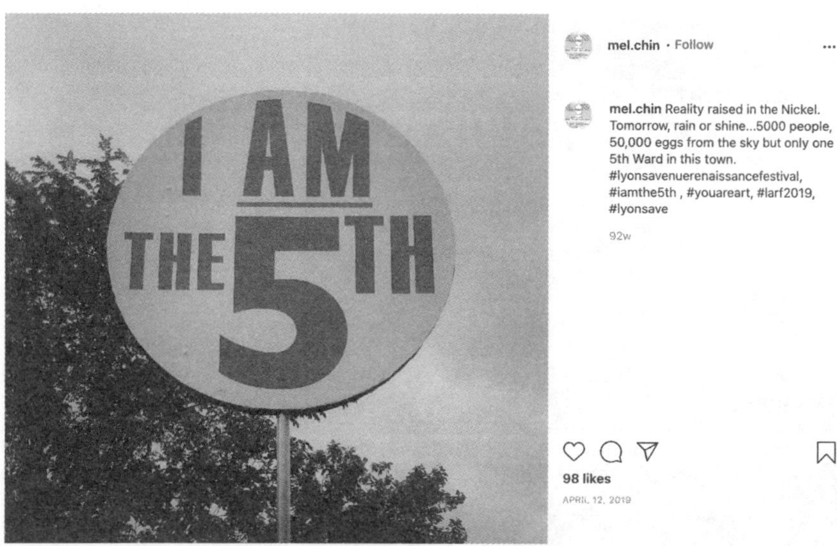

Being back in the Houston hood has stirred up a story about Dad and my intro to kung fu, and I remember the musical genius of the neighborhood we took for granted then because it was so abundantly normal to us.

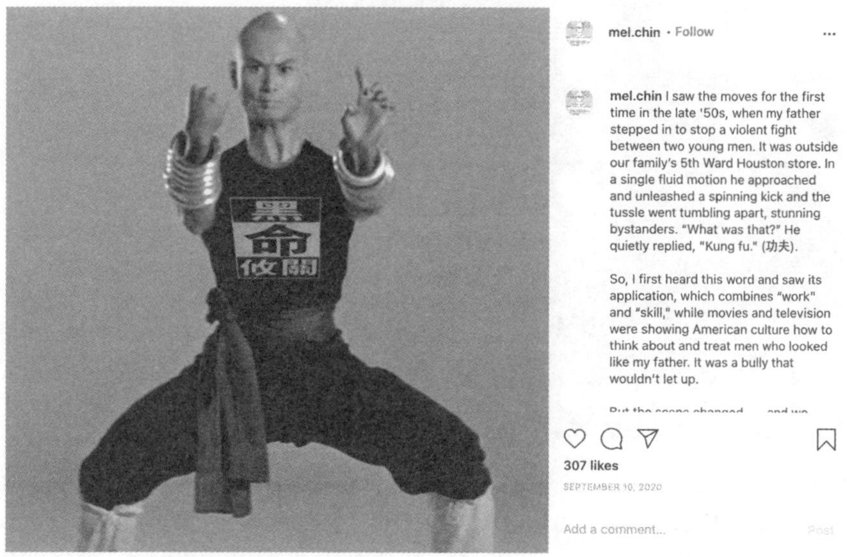

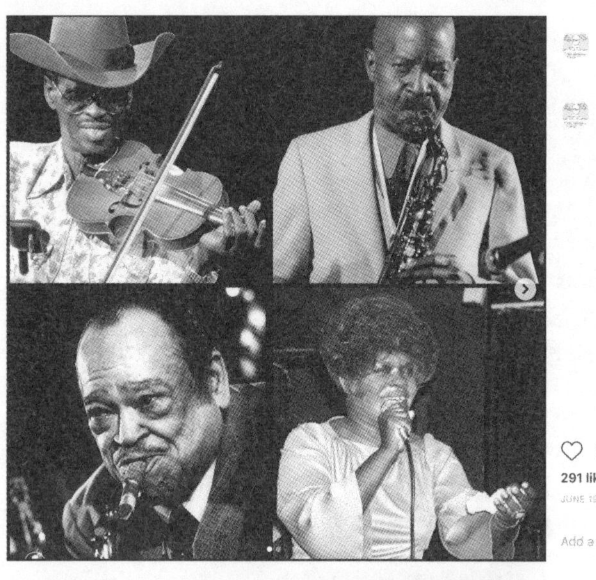

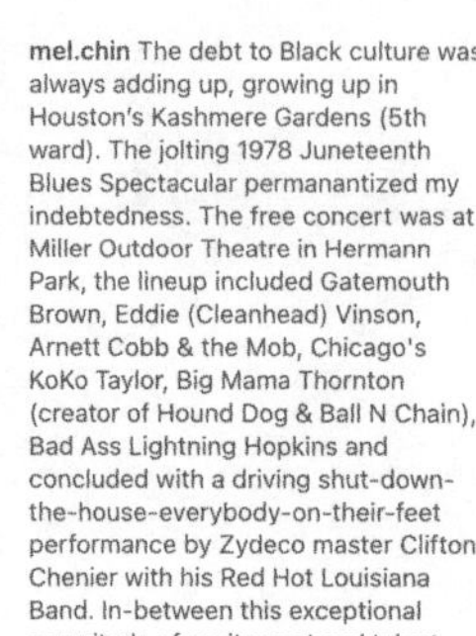

mel.chin • Follow

mel.chin The debt to Black culture was always adding up, growing up in Houston's Kashmere Gardens (5th ward). The jolting 1978 Juneteenth Blues Spectacular permanantized my indebtedness. The free concert was at Miller Outdoor Theatre in Hermann Park, the lineup included Gatemouth Brown, Eddie (Cleanhead) Vinson, Arnett Cobb & the Mob, Chicago's KoKo Taylor, Big Mama Thornton (creator of Hound Dog & Ball N Chain), Bad Ass Lightning Hopkins and concluded with a driving shut-down-the-house-everybody-on-their-feet performance by Zydeco master Clifton Chenier with his Red Hot Louisiana Band. In-between this exceptional magnitude of excitement and talent

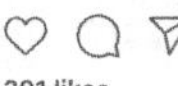

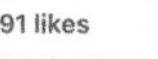

291 likes

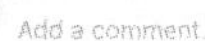

JUNE 19, 2020

Add a comment...

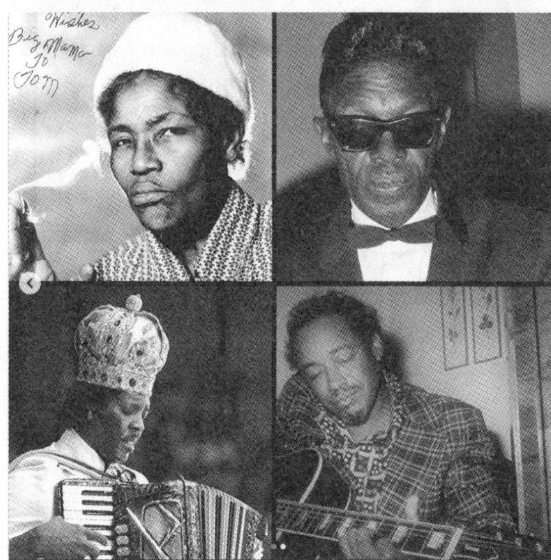

I often reflect on memories of us all at Wholesome Food Market and the customers of Kashmere Gardens. What resonates is how each one of you related so well in a genuine, soulful way to the surrounding community. I had a pathological introversion, alongside my development as a wannabe artist, that probably withheld full engagement with the neighbors, but it did not mean I was not a keen observer, soaking in your lessons. When you interacted, it was like water, effortless effort: Sunny's sincerity and generous nature in all his transactions; Ken's ever-capable banter and wit with customers; Yvonne's laughter and dealings with the women as she did her *Soul Train* dance moves with neighborhood girls; Warren's youthful inclusive and curious interactions with the complete cast of characters—delinquent teens, pious deacons, rising gospel divas, pre-rap comedians, steadfast mothers, returning broken Vietnam vets of the hood, the Creole-speaking Frenchmen—and Wayne's steady service to customers with his indefatigable strength. During that time, Wayne also made his memorable Super 8 films of the daily parade of regulars: "The Wolf" Sherman Shorts, "The Governor" Mr. Williams, "The Vietnam Vet" Baptiste, "Paralyzed Middle Finger" Reverend Boussard, "Dedication, Preparation for Intoxication" Mr. Franklin, and the sole White male, Woody from Oklahoma. All sat on the corner in front of our store, holding court like Chinese door guardians.

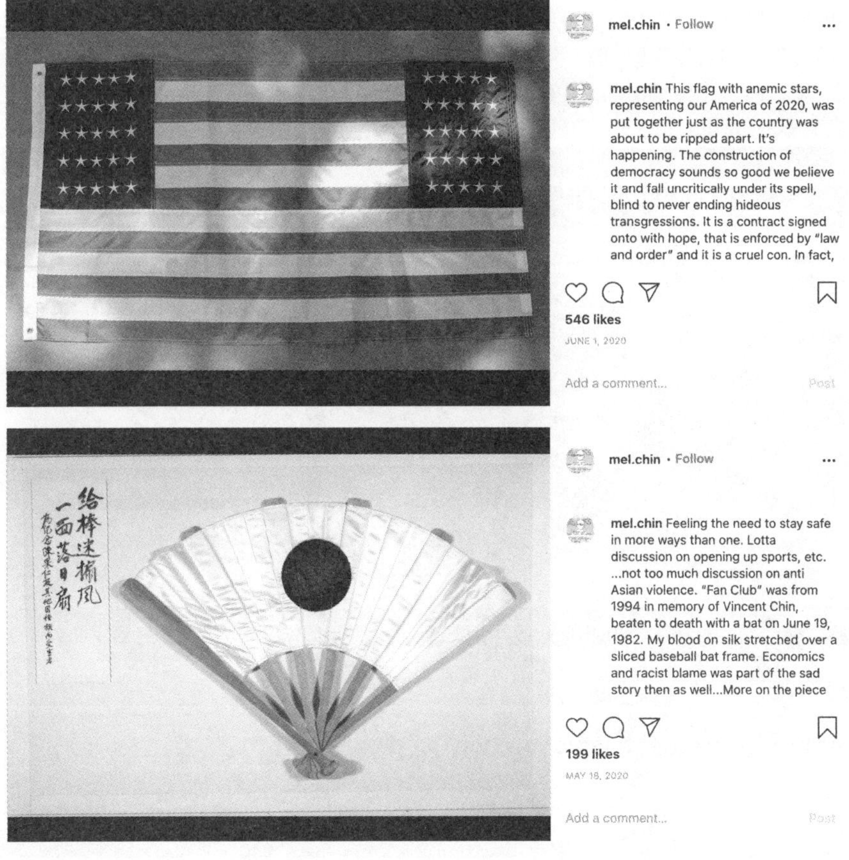

I'm writing this on the eve of the national election, in a country terribly split and still wrangling with insecurity, insensitivity, and injustices that could easily raise its racist weapons and do its harm. It is comforting to be in a family, knowing our views politically cover a spectrum, yet we are not divided. Recently, a convo with Sunny revealed we might be at odds about how to resolve problems in our fragile communities, but when it comes to empathy for unfortunate others, we agree.

As COVID-19 drags on, we may be at a distance for a while longer. It has made families, couples, grow further apart, but I, for one, feel closer to you than ever. Your kids have been a great joy to me, and I thank you for sharing them with me. Yes, they have made me think and consider things "outside myself." The arc of our lives might be long, if we are lucky, but the quality of that arc has been made better and significant because of you. You bring me to a righteous way to be in the moment—now.

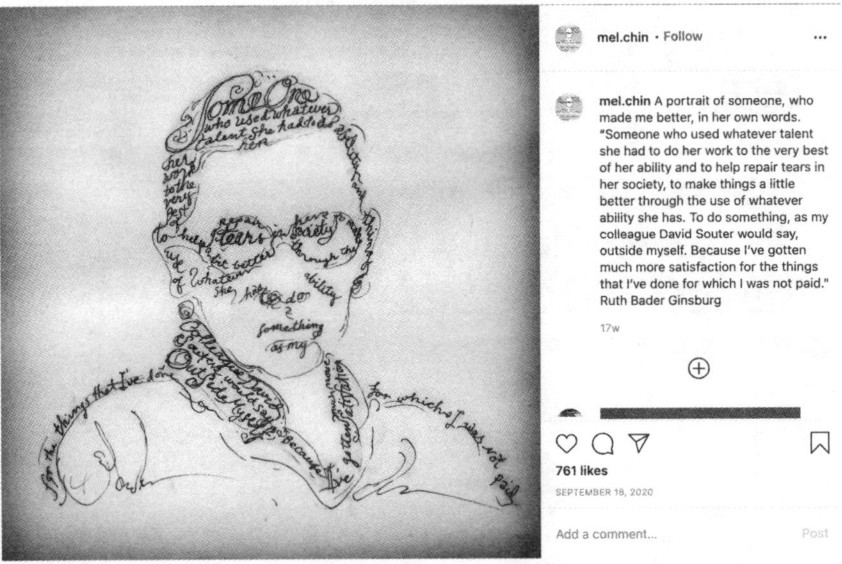

Your brother from the same mother,
Mel

CHRISTINE Y. KIM

for bell hooks

August 14, 2020

To my sixth-grade self,

Hey, you, me. This letter is from you, Christine, at age 48 in 2020. Don't freak out; you're going to be fine. You will have a fulfilling life and career in New York and then in Los Angeles, despite your current feelings about puberty, the playground bullies who make fun of your fish egg, seaweed, and rice bento lunches, and the perpetual sense that you don't belong. You will also have two healthy children who have inherited your tenacity, love for pickled foods, and bowlegs, and a loving, supportive, and equitable partner. Also, you won't have to cut your paper napkins in half with scissors along the crease to save money, as Mom has taught you to do.

Today's America is a very different place than it was in 1983. Technology has produced smartphones, which are tiny cordless computers (smaller than your Little Twin Stars pencil case) that serve as all-in-one telephones, cameras, video game consoles, TVs, stereos, newspapers, and portable libraries in real time. One of the hottest musical genres is the South Korean export K-pop, exemplified by a boy band called BTS, who released two of the three top-selling albums *in the world* in 2018—which, for your reference, is way more than Duran Duran. And we will elect a Black president in 2008, the year your older daughter, whose father is African American, will be born.

Now, this next part may be confusing for an 11-year-old, but bear with me. I'm going to try to explain as clearly as I can why I am writing this letter to you:

Last year, the *New York Times* published *The 1619 Project* on the 400th anniversary of the arrival of the first ship of enslaved Africans, whom the Portuguese kidnapped from Angola, to the British colony of Virginia. The series reframed US history, centering the consequences of slavery and the contributions of Black Americans in the national narrative. (Despite the "quality" of your education, your schooling is Eurocentric and will require a lifetime of unlearning.) In her introductory essay, journalist Nikole Hannah-Jones recalls a childhood memory that became the inspiration for this letter to you, my younger self. Above all, I want you to take steps toward your own liberation through knowledge, empathy, and courage, and in order to do so, you must stake your claim and state your truth at every turn, starting in the classroom. Hannah-Jones writes:

> When I was a child—I must have been in fifth or sixth grade—a teacher gave our class an assignment intended to celebrate the diversity of the great American melting pot. She instructed each of us to write a short report on our ancestral land and then draw that nation's flag. As she turned to write the assignment on the board, the other black girl in class locked eyes with me. Slavery had erased any connection we had to an African country, and even if we tried to claim the whole continent, there was no "African" flag. It was hard enough being one of two black kids in the class, and this assignment would just be another reminder of the distance between the white kids and us. In the end, I walked over to the globe near my teacher's desk, picked a random African country and claimed it as my own.
>
> I wish, now, that I could go back to the younger me and tell her that her people's ancestry started here, on these lands, and to boldly, proudly, draw the stars and those stripes of the American flag. We were told once, by virtue of our bondage, that we could never be American. But it was by virtue of our bondage that we became the most American of all.[1]

The story of Hannah-Jones's ancestry and diaspora differs starkly from your own: her foreparents were forced into servitude generations ago, while your parents came here in search of opportunity. Her ancestry was erased by chattel slavery, while you can trace your roots back to the Uiseong Kim-Cheonggye lineage, dating back to the founding of the Shilla dynasty (57 BC – 935 AD), as your dad tells you all the time. African Americans have experienced the most overt and violent racism in this country, while racism against Asian Americans manifests itself most frequently through xenophobia and the invisibilization of a model (yet still dirty) minority. Both racisms are part of the project of White supremacy and the strategies of oppression, which have trickled down over the centuries from the White House to the schoolhouse. Reading this passage triggered my childhood experiences of humiliation and denial under the White gaze. Hannah-Jones's desire to return to the classroom, to correct the assignment, to insist on her existence and belonging, to tell her own and universal truths about a country that has inflicted violence, injustice, and pain on generations of Americans, implores me to insist that you reflect on her narrative and these kinds of stories when you experience moments of self-doubt, shame, and pain at school and in your life.

Your most powerful tool at this moment is something you already possess: a love for reading, writing, and drawing. I know that you lock yourself in your room with your library books and notepads after school until your mom starts to nag you to finish your homework, practice violin, bathe, or set the table for dinner. It's okay. I love that you write in the morning, head lowered at the kitchen table while your broth gets cold. You write in secret, quietly at night, not to wake your sister who sleeps in the twin bed with the matching polyester butterfly bedspread next to yours. You write out of loneliness, like seeking correspondence with a pen pal who doesn't respond. Let your composition book be the place where you don't edit your words and pictures, where you explore wherever your mind takes you, after carefully studying images of New York City, *Gray's Anatomy*, or pointillist paintings. Focus less on what you think your teachers and parents want you to write about, and instead, go deep into what you can't not let bother you, what you dream about, and what must be documented or remembered. The impossibility of this letter written to you, my younger self, is overridden by psychic necessity. Heeding the guidance of Toni Morrison, who implores: "if there's a book that you want to read, but it hasn't been written yet, then you must write it," I write what I must say but cannot be communicated.

By the time you're in your late twenties, after graduate school, you will be hired as a curatorial assistant at an incredible museum in New York called The Studio Museum in Harlem, becoming the first Asian American curator at this major Black art institution (yes, this will happen!). You will begin to publish your writing: outward-facing, nonfiction essays based on research, observation, art history, and theory. You will struggle with deep insecurities about your writing that arise mostly in graduate school. (One time, a film professor takes one look at you and asks if you would like to join the ESL writing class, which will unfairly highlight your feelings of fraudulence.) When you write for others, your self-doubt—which comes from having been told at home and at school that you are not good enough—creeps in. Just keep writing for yourself, even if you need to tear up the page immediately afterward. Your feelings are not shameful. Shame—which should not be confused with humility—is something your parents instill in you, with the false belief that it will protect you. Shame will only quash your curiosity, vulnerability, and creativity—and in turn, make it easier for others to decenter and dominate your narrative.

Below are three pieces of advice that I want you to try to remember. I'm sorry if this is heavy. I know you're just a kid, and I also know that you don't like people telling you what to do—a consequence of your conditioning—but, remember, it's me, your future self, and hopefully that makes this feel less threatening and more visionary:

1. Do not let your story be defined by the White imagination. Remember Nikole Hannah-Jones's story? When you were made to stand in front of the classroom last year on "Ethnic Day," awkwardly donning a *hanbok* that you outgrew two years before, the teacher forced you to talk about "your culture" while the other students snickered and tugged at the outer edges of their eyes to make them look like paper cuts. You wanted to crawl into your cubby and die. You were not in the wrong; they were. People will continue to create and perpetuate stereotypes about you to elevate themselves. Your own stories are in those notebooks, and you will understand them more deeply in different intersectional contexts as time goes on.

   Despite what strangers whisper when they sneer at you, you belong here in this country. Your parents met here as college students in the 1960s seeking education and a better life, which they found and are grateful for every day. They associate Uncle Sam with heroic US soldiers who defeated the enemy and handed out candy and chocolate to Korean children; they are not versed in the politics of race, class, and gender in America, and you will inherit the trauma of weathering. This effort extends to the trouble you are having fitting in with the White kids, trying to meet their expectations of or assumptions about you. This is probably the hardest advice to hear right now; since Mom and Dad switched you from your racially mixed public elementary school to a private Catholic school (the year after Proposition 13 passed in California), everything is about fitting in when nothing seems to fit at all. I recently read an article written by John Yau, a critic and poet I admire, who recounts: "My biggest regret is that I tried a little too hard to fit in when I first began writing art reviews for *Art in America* in 1977, as if I could actually pass as a member of the 'model minority.' ... Why did I keep trying?" He is over twenty years older than me, but I ask myself the same question. I wish this regret did not have to befall you.

2. Representation matters. Seek out other Asian Americans and peers of color. Connect and empathize with them—though you are told to keep your feelings to yourself. These peers are going to become your closest friends and allies. Stories of representation inform and underscore the urgency of knowledge outside of the White gaze. This is an important way to both empower and humanize yourself and others whose experiences are similarly pushed to the margins (while bullies push to the center and cut

in line ahead of you). When a closeted queer thespian in high school who borrows your eyeliner and mascara (you will learn that this kind of sharing is always a bad idea) comes out of the closet—meaning he tells you, and you alone, that he is gay—you will grow from this too: his struggle, courage, and confidence will strengthen your bond, develop your sense of empathy toward another human experience, and inspire you to identify, confront, and to enact your own truth.

In these intersections, you must also recognize your own privilege, as an educated East Asian American, within the spectrum of marginalized groups often pitted against one another. There will be situations when you may feel seduced by the popular White girls who think that you're pretty or cool enough to share a limo to prom with them; while their intentions may not be malicious, they don't and can't really see you—not in the suburbs of San Francisco in the 1980s. You will often feel stuck between acceptance from the White kids and loyalty to your non-White peers. In the year you graduate from college and move to New York, an artist named Daniel J. Martinez will put a piece in an influential art exhibition that states: "I CAN'T IMAGINE EVER WANTING TO BE WHITE." The sentiment may sound preposterous to you now (not long ago, you used to leave shampoo in your hair way too long, hoping it would wash out the soiled blackness), but you will come to celebrate its truth and power.

3. Last but not least: know where you come from historically, culturally, biologically, and psychically. Don't be afraid to correct people—especially those who call you "Kim," not bothering to ever learn that "Kim" is a Korean last name, the most common one in Korea, with twenty-six lineages. Piecing Mom and Dad's immigrant stories together will not be as easy as you think, because they are riddled with trauma and expressed with contradiction. You will have to remind yourself that they grew up in a patriarchal, authoritarian, and war-torn Korea: Dad from a poor, traditional agrarian village in the south, and Mom from a cosmopolitan family with privilege in the north who lost everything in the war. Their trauma—from poverty, war, violence, and immigration—has become part of your biology, psyche, and pathos. When they admonish you to respect and obey authority figures (especially men) and strive strictly for academic and athletic excellence, they have practically no grasp of social and emotional success in a White world. You hear *ad nauseum* about the superiority of the Korean language and culture (especially above Japanese), but then they force you to speak English at home. This is because, above all, they want you to succeed in America: the only place they know with security, safety, and opportunity. In some ways, their projection is what hurts you the most; unbeknownst

to them, your curiosity and your interest in what you will learn is "good trouble" (John Lewis) will make you particularly strong. Understanding your history requires unpacking these complexities as harmonics—dissonant and incoherent as they may be—to release you from the unresolvable anguish of a perpetual second-generation-immigrant purgatory.

My heart explodes with rainbow, red balloon, stars, and multicolored heart emojis (you'll see what I mean when you get to smartphones) when I think about all the people, adventures, lessons, and experiences ahead. I am now more than halfway through my life (despite a treatable autoimmune condition, I am healthy and well), and while I struggle with anxiety and giving myself permission to slow things down, there is little that I would change. Even the bad decisions, failures, breakups, and moments of uncertainty when life shifts keys have led to other registers and encounters. Staying open and humble includes the necessary and perpetual effort of unlearning and listening. The misremembering of things past, intergenerational trauma, and the chaos of embodied knowledge create a kind of memory or post-memory with divots and holes.

One of the most empowering accomplishments in your life thus far will come in the form of a collective reengagement among your fellow Korean Americans in Los Angeles. In 2017, you will cofound a nonprofit art organization called GYOPO. Translating quite simply to "a Korean person living outside of Korea," *gyopo* is not a pejorative term, as you may believe. Aligned with terms like *Chicano* or *Chicanx*, which celebrate a hybrid identity of second-, third-, etc. generation Mexican Americans, or *queer* for LGBTQ people reclaiming a once-derogatory slur, your attaching the term *gyopo* to this community celebrates a complex, diasporic Korean identity that becomes part of the lexicon of political identities by 2020. While you will take pride in your exhibitions and work as a curator at the Los Angeles County Museum of Art, GYOPO will be the safe, dedicated, and elevated space in which to finally tell your story firsthand. You don't have to wear a too-small *hanbok* ever again, and the room will be full of paper cuts celebrating our paper cut-ness, and allies interweaving *gyopo* neologisms and playing dissonant and gay music! Your children will have little sense of its radical contrast to some of the things that you are experiencing and feeling right now, but this banality is also a triumph.

I'm more accustomed to writing texts on contemporary art and artists, and this letter has been one of the more difficult pieces of writing for me in a while. It may even come across as self-indulgent. But perhaps that is part of the antidote to the poison of invisibility injected by the machinations of White America. There is always going to be a fight, and you will go from being a foot soldier to a clever commander who delivers aid and aims for truces and treaties. When Hannah-Jones writes, "it was by virtue of our bondage that we became the most American of all," yes, she is absolutely correct, and it is *your story* that makes you American, makes you *you*, and makes you belong.

With the deepest and most complex self-love and respect,
Christine

P.S. Bet some coin on a Korean film named *Parasite* in just about every category at the Oscars in 2020.

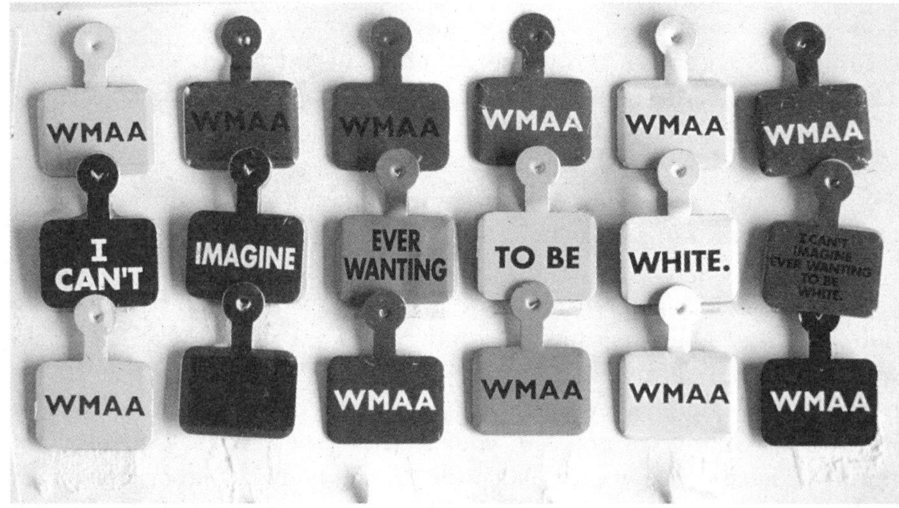

Daniel Joseph Martinez, *Museum Tags: Second Movement (overture)*; or, *Overture con Claque (Overture with Hired Audience Members)*, 1993. Whitney Biennial, Whitney Museum of American Art, New York. Collection of Michael Brenson. Original WMAA with 1993 derive, fifteen metal tags with enamel paint on cardboard, 9 × 12 in. / (22.86 × 30.48 cm). Courtesy the artist and Roberts Projects, Los Angeles, California.

1 Nikole Hannah-Jones, "America Wasn't a Democracy, Until Black Americans Made It One," *New York Times*, August 14, 2019.

YAYOI SHIONOIRI

June 26, 2020

Dear Akasegawa Genpei sensei「赤瀬川原平先生」,

I wish you could have had the chance to see the 2020 Tokyo Olympics nearly happen this year. As the Japanese government considered allowing the games to take place in the midst of a pandemic, prioritizing national prestige over global health, I would like to think that you would have reunited Hi-Red Center「ハイレッド・センター」and undertaken a *direct action*「直接行動」to ridicule this near-occurrence. It would have been inspiring to witness a re-performance of Hi-Red Center's 1964 *Be Clean! Campaign to Promote Cleanliness and Order in the Metropolitan Area*《首都圏清掃整理促進運動》, where you and fellow artists took to the streets in white lab coats, carefully and painstakingly scrubbing at the relatively trash-free streets of Ginza in response to the government's demands that the city present its "cleanest face" during the 1964 Olympics. A 2020 reinterpretation would have provided a seemingly apolitical platform from the realm of art and culture to begin a necessary conversation on the misdirected policies of the current government. To add an additional layer of irony, I have no doubt that, in spite of this subversive and critical message, you would have attempted to apply for (and likely would have successfully received) a cultural grant from the Tokyo Metropolitan Government to undertake your satirical performance.

We so desperately need your voice in our protests today. These days, it's harder than ever to be a politically engaged artist, at least in Japan and the US, because artists' values are often defined by how they can most effectively monetize their time. You probably would retort that it was hard to be an *avant-garde artist*「前衛芸術家」even back in your day, but it seems that we now expect our artists to exist both outside and inside quotidian life. As both shamans and plebeians, artists are expected to help the rest of us see the world in a different and entirely unique way, yet also have the capacity to run a small business with employees—to keep turning the gears of the commercial art machine.

Since you saw artistic practice as a form of everyday life, and given your ability to navigate and multitask in so many worlds, I suppose that's something you wouldn't have had any trouble doing even now; I think often about our conversation at your house back in the summer of 2009 as I seek to make sense of our world today.

Reflecting on the so-called Model Thousand-Yen Note Incident prompted by your work, I find strength in considering how you navigated a legal framework that attempted to censor your expression. In 1963, you arranged to have printed monochrome, single-sided reproductions of banknotes that you used in your artistic practice—thus embracing the impossibility of achieving true originality as an artist. Through the series of legal events that followed, you had to defend not only the legality of your actions, but even the value of your artistic contributions to society. In doing so, you helped us understand the social construct and contract through which we assign values to pieces of paper. In my view, despite your criminal conviction, your artistic practice succeeded as civil disobedience—embodying the principle of direct action in one of the most politically impactful examples of 20th-century Japanese art.

There remains a desperate need for art that relays political messages and seeks to make political impacts. Here in the US, the federal government has abdicated responsibility in the face of an unprecedented health emergency and an economy in freefall. Instead, it has sought to stoke hostility on the basis of race and class—to the point where people are fighting in the streets for their lives and fighting for the right to be heard. Your artistic practice, shining light into the darkness of government actions, would have been a welcome foundation for justice.

Asians and Asian Americans in America are at a watershed moment. Some may hope to remain unnoticed, playing into the stereotype of a model minority and living comfortably in economic privilege, if they have the opportunity to do so. Yet others are rising up, using art—whether following in your direct action footsteps or not—to find and disseminate our political voice. Like those miniscule dust motes that you tried so hard to clean out of the Tokyo sidewalk cracks in 1964, maybe we can continue to accumulate, find strength in numbers, and demand the right to have our voices heard—in fact, exercise our obligation to do so.

Your practice continues to inspire me as I consider how Asian and Asian American artists can engage in complex, layered, and contentious conversations about race. I suppose you would jump right in, seeing no line where direct action stops and life continues.

With respect,
Yayoi
「塩野入　弥生　拝」

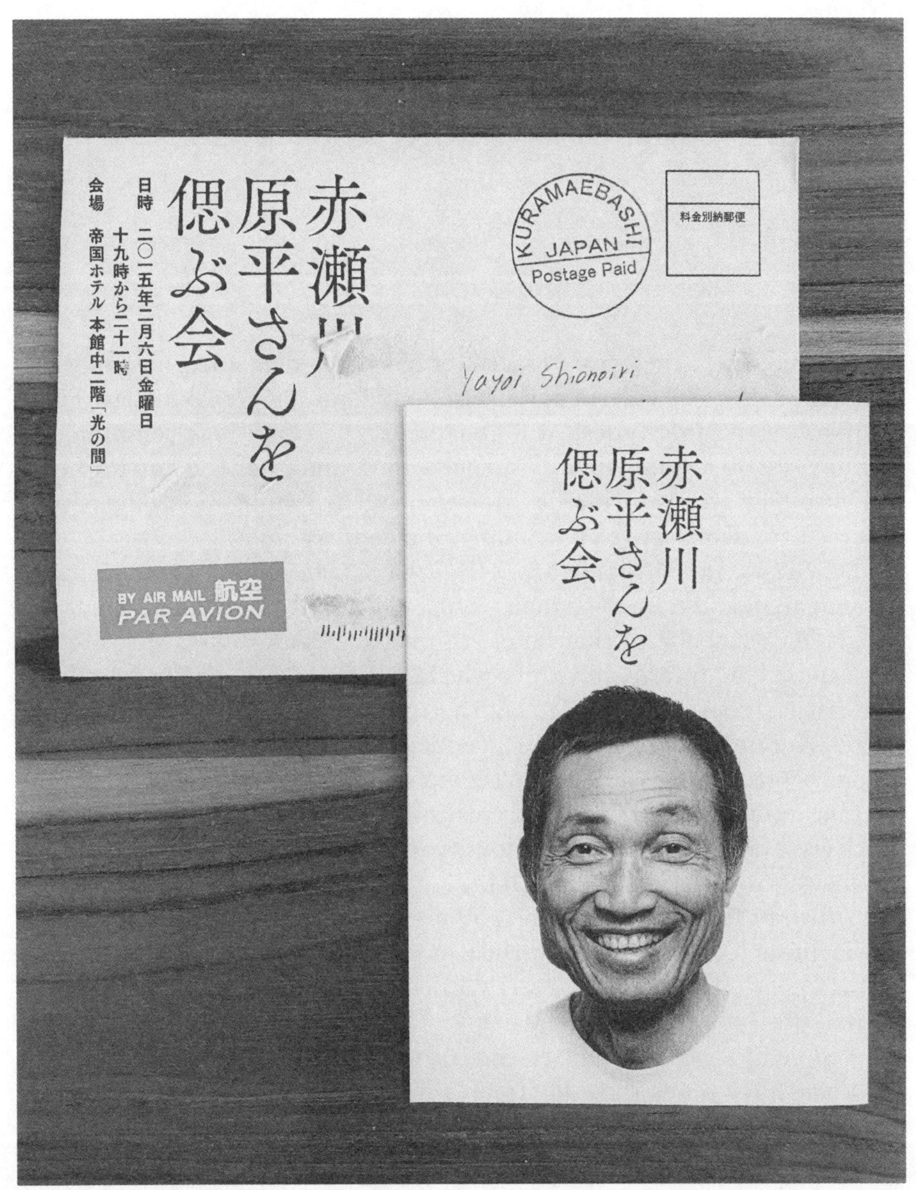

Letter announcing February 6, 2015, memorial for Genpei Akasegawa-san.

PATTY CHANG

September 5, 2020

Dear Ba,

You've been dead seven years now. A lot has happened since, and a lot has stayed the same. The current coronavirus pandemic surely would have killed you if you weren't already dead, with your preexisting conditions, compromised immune system, feeding tube, oxygen machine, and extended nursing home and hospital stays. Your slow deterioration was like a long mourning period, with cycles of denial, anger, bargaining, and depression.

When I was in sixth grade, Mr. Metzger gave us an assignment to interview a grandparent and transcribe their words. Popo, your mother, had lived with us since I was a baby. At that time, I think she was almost 90, the wife of a terraced rice paddy farmer in China who had bound feet and talked in Ch'ing Tien dialect. I could barely understand her: you spoke in English and Mandarin with us. A dramatic perfectionist, I imagined I would never be able to interview her and petulantly told you I couldn't complete the assignment, tacitly blaming you for coming to this country and creating a gulf between me and the past—which was exactly why you came. I think you sensed all this, and you wrote out her answers to all the questions on my interview worksheet. You filled in her entire history, from being born in another century and on another continent, to what life on a farm built on a vertical mountain was like, to how she arrived in this upper-middle-class, largely White, new suburb near San Francisco. I'm not sure if you even consulted her.

I copied her/your responses and turned in my homework the next day, not giving it too much thought. To my surprise, Mr. Metzger singled out my report and decided that he needed to read all twelve pages out loud in front of the class. I was mortified at being singled out, suddenly conscious of the deceit I had staged. He sat on a high stool, one foot on the ground, the other on the bottom rung, holding the plastic-bound report in one hand as if casually reading a newspaper. I wanted to confess my transgression, but I was paralyzed with shame. I felt shame for being different. I felt shame for being a baby and making you do my homework. I felt shame for forcing you to answer for my own feelings of difference and inadequacy. I felt shame for displacing the shame back onto you, as if it was your fault. I am sorry.

This was one of my first visceral, embodied experiences of my—our—raced and classed difference, and of internalized racism. It stands out because in flagrantly plagiarizing your writing of my grandmother's history, I conflated shameful feelings of fraud and racial difference. Your voice spoke her story, and I penned it as mine—the fraud cut deeply through generations. Like a so-so Chinese daughter, I swallowed it.

These conflated feelings of fraud and racial difference followed me as I navigated finishing college, moved through the world, suffered an eating disorder, chose to become an artist, worked any job to pay the rent, loved and was loved, made my way as an emerging artist in the New York art world, got dumped, experienced drunken delusion, wrote and won and lost grants and commissions, spoke and taught in White institutions of art and higher education, experienced motherhood, became a midcareer artist, got tenured at a White institution of higher education, and on and on.

I have many questions about your experiences of racism in this country, starting from the 1960s when you first came here. Like, why did you leave your Ph.D. program at UC Berkeley after a fight with your advisor, who was most likely a White man, and then turn down an offer from Stanford to finish your degree there? Was it money, racism, pressure, stress, life? Was it wanting to bring your mother over to America before she died, but not being able to sponsor her financially as a student? Two powerful, White, legitimizing institutions of education: I want to believe your decision was a refusal, the sovereignty to say no. Maybe you just wanted a break. You never offered much information, but I should have asked.

Since that interview assignment in sixth grade, you often agreed to work with me on my projects (not petulantly coerced). In 2001, for *In Love*, we practiced eating onions between us on our off time while attending the wedding of my cousin in Seattle. Even though you disliked onions, you said, "Once in a while is OK." In 2003, I asked you and Ma to talk about your ideas of love. Your performances while sitting on a white couch wearing white clothes were superimposed at half transparency, and speaking simultaneously, you and Ma looked like apparitions from the dead or part of a religious cult.

In 2005, you came to visit us in Shangri-La, China—not your first time, but your second. The promise of longevity did not bear out. Later in the year, I came to your house to film your garden and the making of a fountain out of overlapped dinner plates, bowls, and dishes of various kinds. I looked at all the tourist footage you shot during your trips back to China, when you went to visit the place you came from and observed it from the position of an outsider. I noticed the changing of your gait over time, from sure-footed to tentative, to tumbling down stairs and pathways. And while I was making *The Wandering Lake*, I documented moments from your last days with us.

When hospice finally called us to say that we should come to see you, that there were only a few days left, we were in Montreal at a temporary art residency. We flew with Leroy, who was only three months old, to be with you. You were at home in your bedroom, lying immobile in a home-use hospital bed, pillows propped underneath your knees and your arms. They stopped giving you food and water and thought you would be gone in two days. You lasted nine. I wasn't in the room to see this happen, most likely catching up on sleep, but multiple people told me about it later—my brother Gene lifted Leroy right up to your face, to show him to you as you lay motionless in bed, your eyes clouded and your mouth slacked open, breathing with effort. Like a baby, Leroy reached down to touch your face and explored it with his right hand, which was adorned with a gold chain-link bracelet. It dangled precariously into your mouth. Like a rat trap, your jaw clamped down hard and fast on the 18-karat gold and didn't let go.

When I said earlier that your slow deterioration was like a mourning period, with cycles of denial, anger, bargaining, and depression, I left out "acceptance" because I don't think you were ready to die. Even toward the end, whenever we would talk about your possible death, what your wishes were, or how you imagined spending your final days, you didn't want us to speak that way. That one day I came home to visit, you walked with your walker towards the door leading to the garage, wearing a crescent-shaped piece of an asteroid the size of a drumstick bone on a string around your neck. Your acupuncturist had sold it to you, saying it had healing forces. I, in my impatient able-bodied way, dismissed it as a sham—a token from a corrupt doctor to a desperate patient. To this day, I regret not giving more space to the possibility: to magic, to something besides Western medicine and Chinese medicine, to your desire and your need to believe there was a way out of this illness besides death. But, we all know that is the only way.

If I had it to do over again, I would assign other steps of mourning to the scripted five steps of denial, anger, bargaining, depression, and acceptance. Perhaps the leap between depression and acceptance seemed too big a gulf to bridge. Between them, I would add (in no fixed order): repositioning, integrating, shape-shifting, imagination, enchantment, trance, transmogrification, invocation, mystification, and bewilderment. When the time comes—because I am sure it will—I'll test them out and let you know how it goes.

Love,
Patricia

CHITRA GANESH AND SUNG HWAN KIM
BETWEEN YOU AND ME: A CORRESPONDENCE IN FRAGMENTS

Between you and me documents a process of thinking in close friendship. This letter gives form to modes of interaction, intimacy, and exchange that evolved organically between Sung and Chitra over almost twenty years. The work was developed through a process of casual notation—sharing a series of SMS and WhatsApp messages, drawings, phone calls, art, and fragments of the historical record—about our overlapping research interests. The correspondence in *Between you and me* probes the systematic erasures—material, discursive, and psychic—of Asian histories in America, and how the lack of legibility and absence of these histories continue to structure the domain of (Euro-American) contemporary art. The following text is excerpted from a longer work, one of a series of exchanges between artists on contemporary art and history commissioned by *Art Practical* and the Rainin Foundation in 2018.

Chintra Ganesh (CG) and Sung Hwan Kim (SHK)

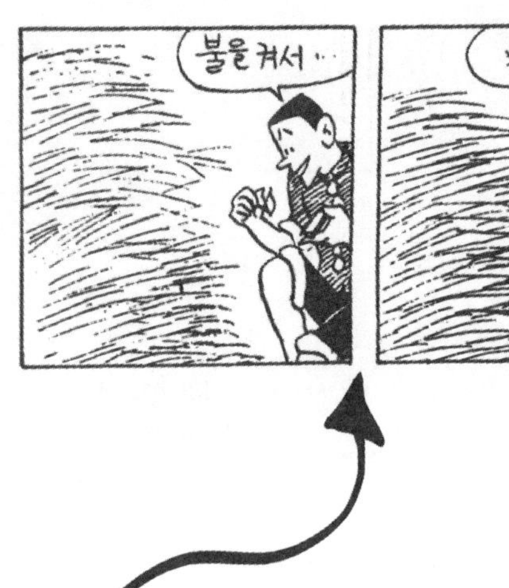

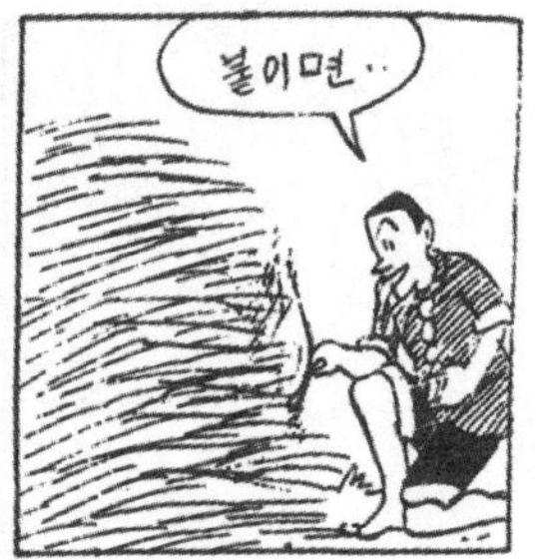

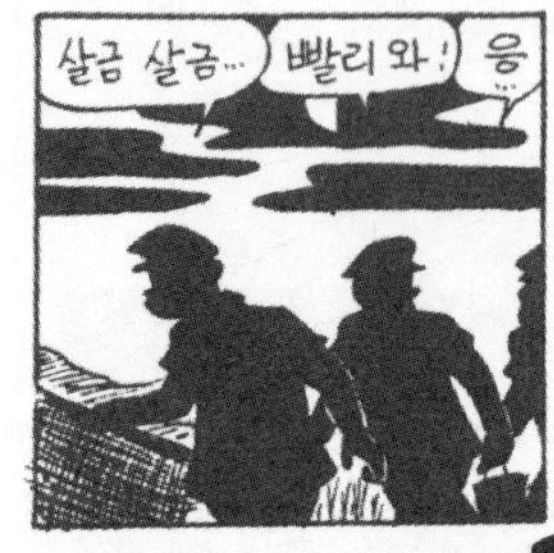

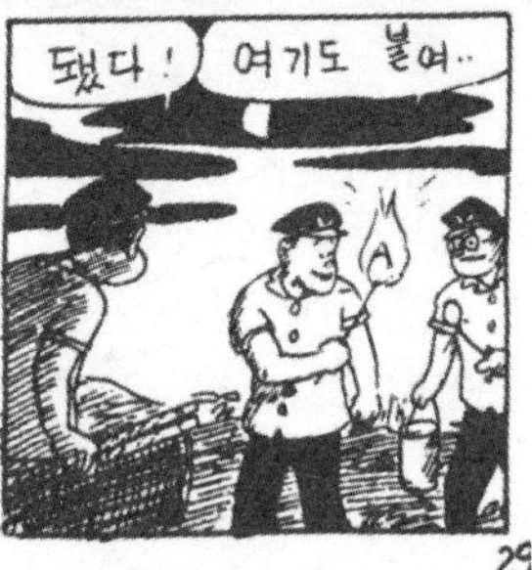

THE GUTTER...

SHK:

- 약동이와 영팔이, 방영진 (1939-1997), 한국만화영상진흥원, first published in 1962, Korea.
- I chose two sets of two cuts showing before and after lighting a match.
- (first set) A kid lighting hay with a match.
- (second set) Night shone by the moon vs. a moment later with a lit-up matchstick.

CG:

- Your fire in two cuts illuminates the gutter.
- The gutter is the space in between two panels in a comic.
- Gutters indicate the passage of time, the transformation of space, etc
- Sometimes the gutter reveals itself as the flow of a river
- The gutter also reminds me to read between the lines.

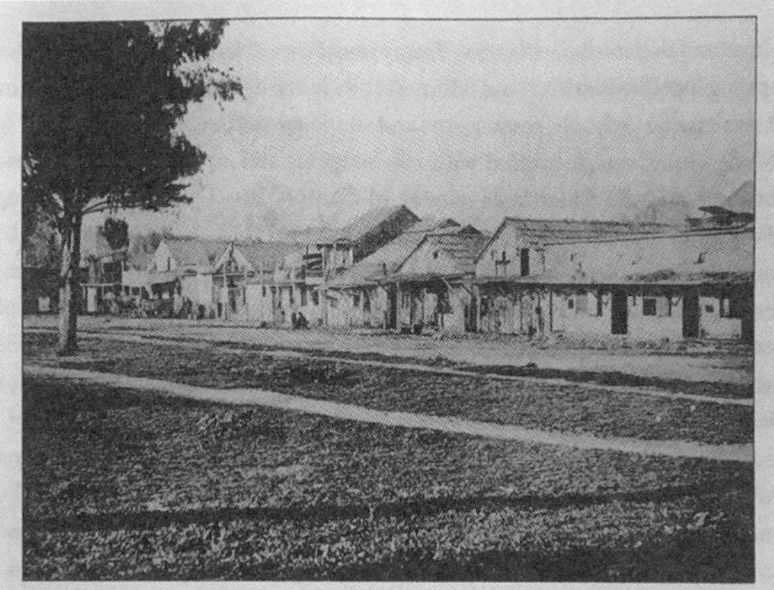

Market Street Chinatown in San Jose before the fire, 1887

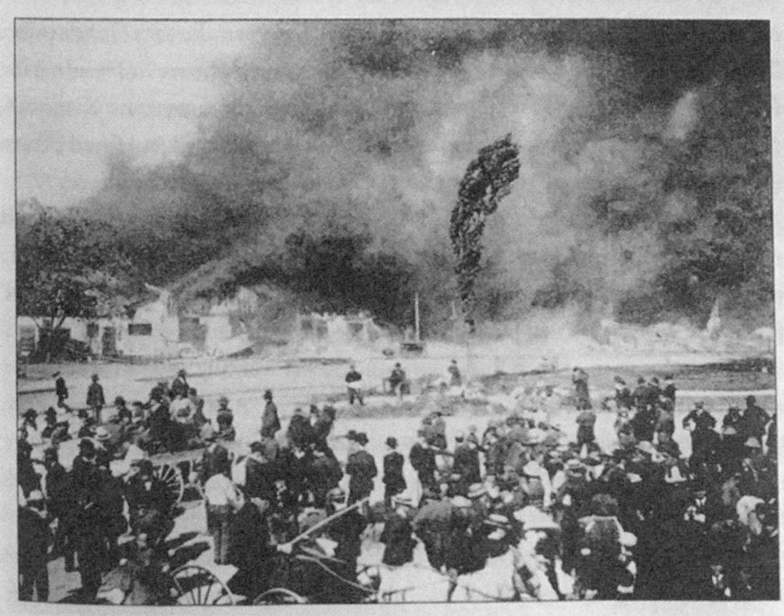

White citizens observe the burning of Chinatown

SHK:

• Another example of two cuts with fire.

• *Driven Out,* Jean Pfaelzer, first published in 2008.

• A page from this book shows a Chinese town
before arson and after arson.

• Pfaelzer, a scholar of American History
at Humboldt State University in 1974,
first notices the absence of Asian students in her school.

• She notices this absence during meetings
against the Vietnam War and for Native American Rights.

• A local poet informs Pfaelzer that the absence of Asian students
resulted from their memory of the massacre of the Chinese in Eureka in 1885.

• Thirty years later, Pfaelzer embarks on her research
on Chinese immigrants living in the US between 1850 and 1906.

• One fact from her research: Out of the (at least)
302 lynchings that occurred in California between 1849 and 1902,
200 were of Asian people.

CG:

• A San Jose I never knew about before
you showed me this page,

• A Chinatown I wish I saw with my own eyes...

CG:

- With a gutter like this, does time move forward or back?
- How is the directionality of time and progress scrambled by the order in which we learn things?

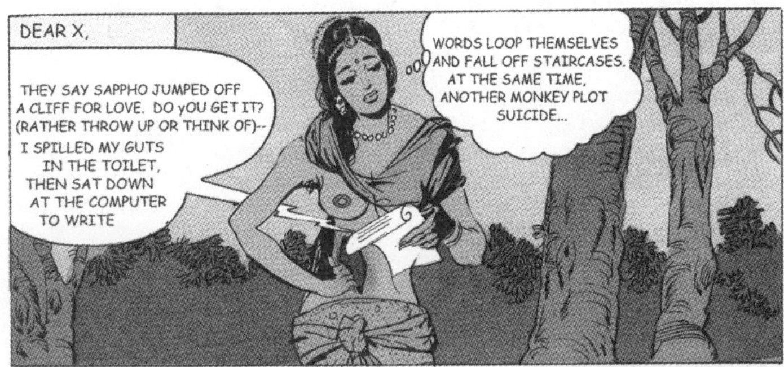

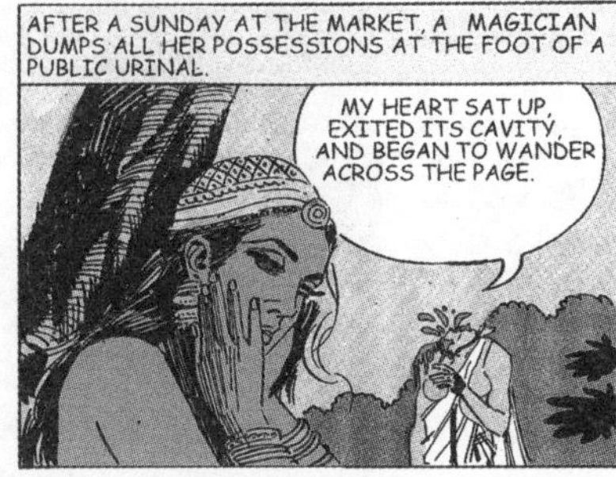

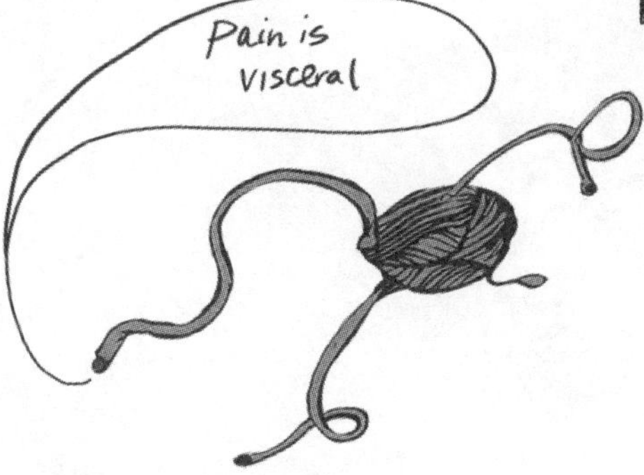

SHK:

- Pain is visceral.
- like moving words?

CG:

• Martin Wong's 8 Ball is another heart
wandering across the page.

• This 8 Ball was an oracle and toy of my childhood.

• The first time I saw Wong's work was at his
posthumous New Museum retrospective in 1998.

• Before that, I had never encountered an American artist
of Asian descent in a museum.

• He painted gay firefighters kissing in the Loisaida rubble

• What troubles did he tell the 8 Ball?

• After more than 20 years in New York City,
Wong went back to California to die in 1994.

• Somehow this fact struck me: what, ultimately, was his
relationship to family and home?

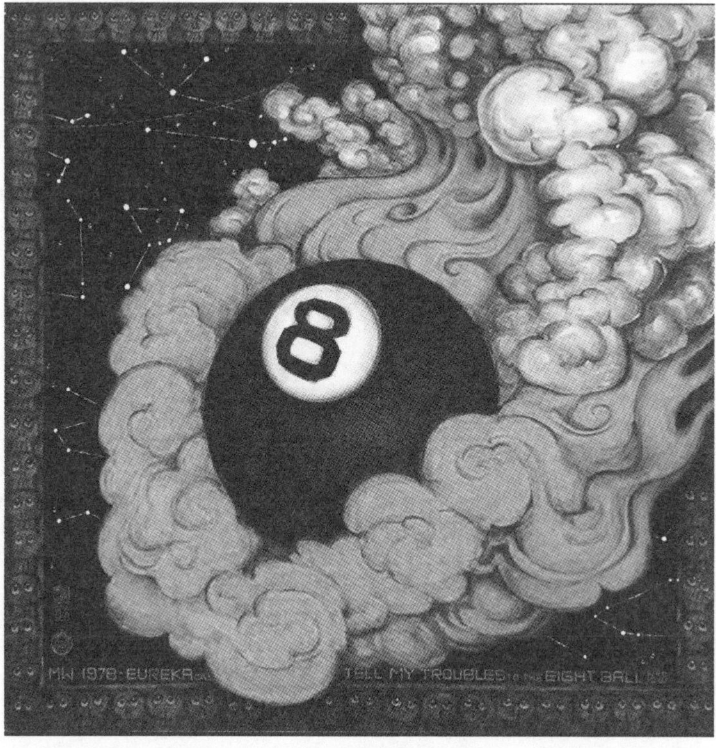

CG:

•history repeats 1917 with the desire for a 'Muslim Ban'

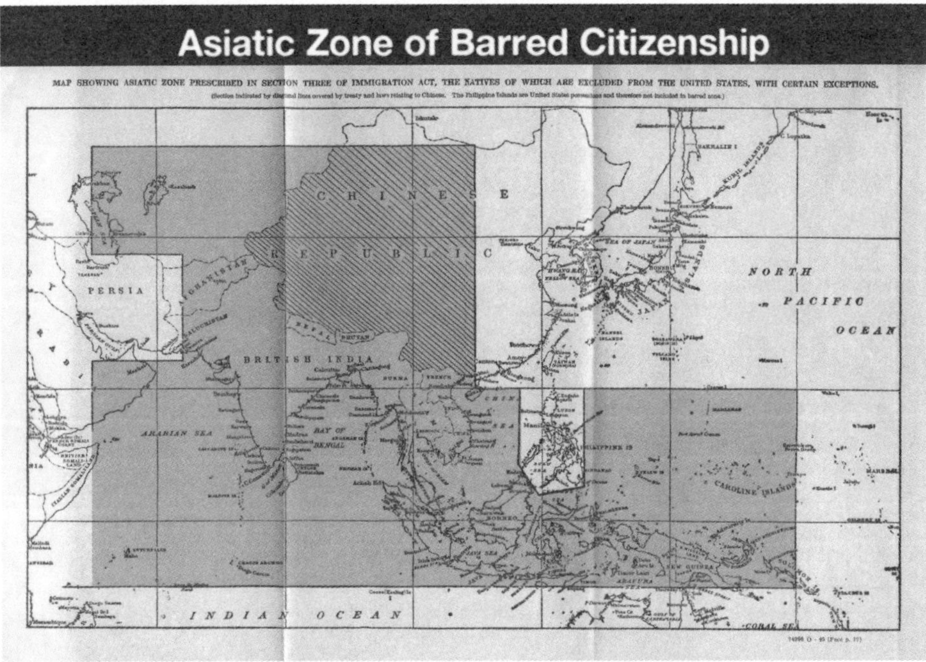

image courtesy of SAADA (South Asian AMerican Digital Archive)

SHK:

• Between my arrival to the US in 1996 and the year 2016, I had never met anyone in the US who shared a knowledge of the long history of the ban against Asian immigration, which finally was repealed in 1965.

• I did not know that most Asians in the US before 1965, except for special cases, remained undocumented and/or lived with undocumented parents most of their lives, without rights to either vote or purchase/lease property.

• I first found out in 2016 that during the 1992 Los Angeles riots, out of the one billion dollars worth of property damage, Korean-owned property damage was estimated at 400 million dollars.

CG:

• In Alpesh Patel's book *Productive Failure*, he notes:

• How Greenberg goes out of his way to deny Asian influence in his 1955 essay *"American-Type" Painting*.

• It was common for West coast based artists to earn money as sailors and spend lots of time in Asia while East coast artists earned money as commercial sign painters, dressing department store windows.

• When I was looking for this paragraph in the essay, I kept looking for the word "Asia".

• Greenberg does not refer to any places specifically.

• It's all "Oriental".

Nationalist rhetoric in the art world

If Natvar Bhavsar is one of a number of artists of Asian descent whose works have been largely ignored as part of post-Second World War art history, then this was at least partly due to the fact that critics such as American Clement Greenberg downplayed the influence of Zen and Asian philosophy on Western art. Greenberg, for instance, wrote:

> Actually, not one of the original 'abstract expressionists' ... has felt more than a cursory interest in Oriental art. The sources of their art lie entirely in the West; what resemblances to Oriental modes may be found in it are an effect of convergence at the most, and of accident at the least.[125]

The title of the famous essay in which this was written, 'American-Type Painting', suggests what was at stake here. Greenberg was outlining characteristics of a national category and this meant ensuring that the country's output could not be confused with that of any other country or region. Art historian

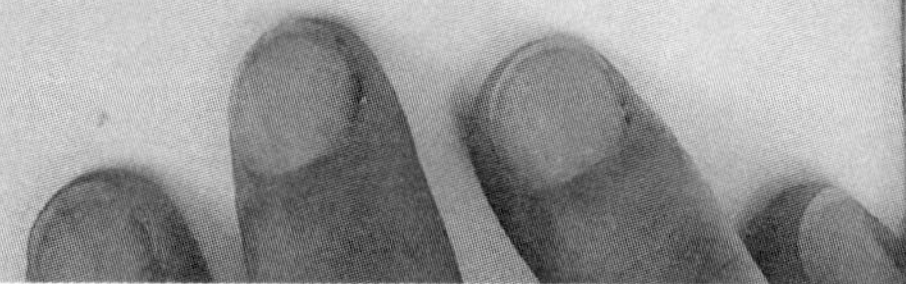

SHK:

• As a child in Korea, we used to stretch the edges of our eyes upward to make them slanted, and then say this is Japanese;

• lower them to say this is Chinese.

SHK:

Basic knowledge that I had on Noguchi before 2017:
• He made beautiful furniture and zen gardens.
• ~~He was Japanese~~.

• He made smooth surfaces.

WHITENESS AND CULTURAL PRIVILEGE IN POSTWAR AMERICA

Only some artists—typically white, heterosexual men—were credited with successfully integrating "the primitive" into an art that seemed "universal" because it crossed racial, ethnic, and linguistic lines to communicate a liberal, even progressive, cultural viewpoint. As the art historian Ann Gibson explains, women, artists of color, and homosexuals could not do this "because their audiences would not accept their work as universal. Even if they wanted to be universal and said so[,] . . . the dominant society did not read the work that way."[2] Thus if a woman made art and presented it as an exploration of issues of universal significance, it might well be read as deriving from her "feminine" identity rather than the broadly *human* identity she aspired to represent. Identity drove the analysis and meaning of Noguchi's work too. As much as he tried to make it address broadly shared humanistic concerns, its meaning was limited by the same assumptions about his Japaneseness that had inflected the reception of his

NOGUCHI, ASIAN AMERICA, ARTISTIC IDENTITY · 161

CG:

• And what you told me about Noguchi's work
being described as "too clean and smooth"
as if his Asian masculinity itself was being evaulated
and dismissed; while
his engagment with farmland, industrialization, and socialism
is omitted and depoliticized.

SHK:

You may wonder why land art did not thrive already in the 1930s. Noguchi's proposal might seem neither timely nor even inappropriate before recognizing the following:

• 1933 Agricultural Adjustment Act.

• Its contradiction to then-conventional ethics of the American farmers (To the average farmers, crop "control" seems sinful...To him this is a crime against fertility, for he is schooled to think in terms of famine and plenty, not in terms of supply and demand...
Bernard Ostrolenk, *New York Times Sunday Magazine*, July 16, 1933, 3).

• The prior inhabitants of the proposed site, the Middle West of the United States of America, were suggested by Noguchi to be Mayans.

• National Origins Act or Asian Exclusion Act of 1924.

• The reasonable assumption that, living in such a nativistic period, every action of Noguchi, a half-Japanese American, inevitably would be either associated or disassociated with his identity.

• Noguchi's repeated endeavor to map artisanry onto industry.

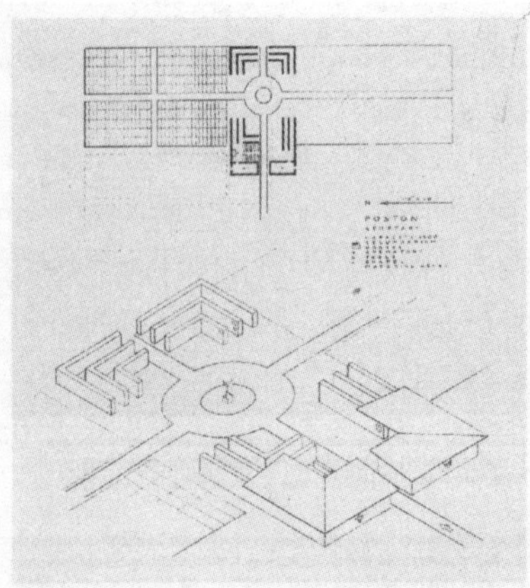

FIGURE 48.
Isamu Noguchi. *Cemetery Project for Poston Camp*, 1942. © 2013 The Isamu Noguchi Foundation and Garden Museum, New York/Artists Rights Society (ARS), New York.

In designing the architectural environment for the Poston park and recreation facilities (Figure 49), Noguchi followed through on several ideas in the NWAMD proposal about collective labor and community building among the camp's population. A recreation center, set at an angle to the characteristic "harsh symmetry" of Poston's barracks, would feel like a welcome "retreat." Programming at the center would foster "self-expression" in a range of arts "departments," including ceramics, music, painting, and sculpture; there was to be even a small museum. The buildings housing these arts departments would encourage art as a self-generated process—one that Noguchi

NEGOTIATING JAPANESE AMERICAN CONFINEMENT · 119

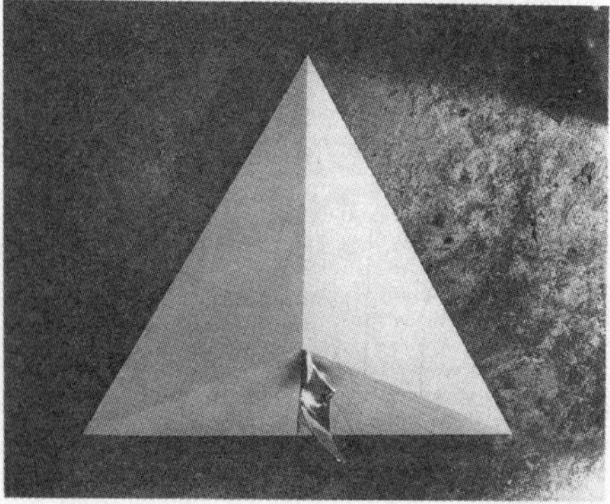

FIGURE 11.
Isamu Noguchi, model for *Monument to the Plow*, c. 1933–1934. Plaster model. Photographer: Berenice Abbott. © 2013 The Isamu Noguchi Foundation and Garden Museum, New York/Artists Rights Society (ARS), New York. Photo © Berenice Abbott/Commerce Graphics, NYC.

and to new scientific approaches to controlling erosion and rotating crops championed by the administrator of the Agricultural Adjustment Act to ensure fertile, and thus more productive, farmland.

The slopes of the pyramid would have to be plowed by a horse-drawn plow, with a human guiding both, to create the patterned furrows Noguchi wanted for the monument. Mechanical tractors could not have done the exacting work. The iconic plow set into the monument's concrete cap was thus integral to a structure that emphasized the need to mitigate the erosion caused by cultivating the earth. The cap to which the plow was affixed would prevent erosion of the monument from above, and the planted and furrowed sides of the work would sustain the monument's form, the plants holding the work together and their roots preventing erosion of the soil.

Erosion was recognized as a major impediment to agricultural production as the effects of overplanting and droughts, which had begun in the midwestern prairies in the early 1930s, started to spread eastward by 1934. In the spring of 1934, the Soil Erosion Service of the U.S. Department of the Interior was established to protect agricultural

34 · EARTHWORKS AND MONUMENT TO THE PLOW

SHK:

Some knowledge not known to me before 2017:

- *Isamu Noguchi's Modernism: Negotiating Race, Labor, and Nation, 1930-1950,* Amy Lyford, first published in 2013.

- This picture was taken c. 1939-1940.

- Before President Roosevelt relocated and incarcerated 110,000 people of Japanese ancestry, the majority being Japanese-American;

- Before Noguchi, in 1942, volunteered himself to the Colorado River Relocation Center in order to "help preserve self-respect and belief in America;"

- Before two nuclear attacks on Japan.

- Noguchi was born in the US and was raised by his American mother, Léoni Gilmour.

- He initially declined the invitation to represent the US at the US Pavilion in the Venice Biennale in 1986.

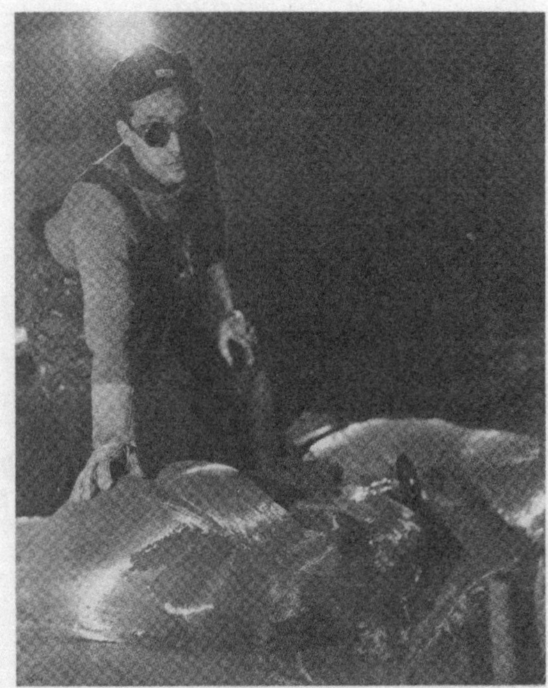

FIGURE 35.
AP press kit photo 12: Noguchi resting his hand and a grinder on the stainless steel mural, c. 1939–1940. © 2013 Rockefeller Group, Inc./Rockefeller Center Archives. © 2013 The Isamu Noguchi Foundation and Garden Museum, New York/Artists Rights Society (ARS), New York.

CG:

• Ironic that Noguchi was a volunteer
to serve and protect the US.

• It reminds me of Fred Korematsu, known
for his legal challenge against Japanese internment.

• He lost the case; the Supereme Court upheld
the practice of internment.

• He rarely spoke about this case until the end of his life

• I got to know him only a few years ago—
when I realized it was often the most ordinary people,
like Richard and Mildred Loving, who fought
against state-sanctioned segregation.

• I was lucky enough to have an 8th grade history
teacher who taught us about Japanese internment

• the betrayal and shame associated with this event
kept me up at night for weeks after.

3 JAPANESE DEFY CURBS

Army Says One Tried to Become 'Spaniard' by Plastic Surgery

Special to THE NEW YORK TIMES.

SAN FRANCISCO, June 12—Complaints charging violations of restrictive regulations imposed by the Army were filed today against three Japanese in this area, one of whom was accused of undergoing a plastic surgical operation to turn himself into a "Spaniard."

Agents of the Federal Bureau of Investigation told A. J. Zirpoli, assistant Federal attorney, that Fred Toyosaburo Korematsu, 23, of San Leandro, had been operated on since the outbreak of the war. He notified his draft board, agents said, that his name was Clyde Sarah and tried to persuade an unidentified Italian girl to marry him. She learned he was Japanese, it was related, but he spurned her advice that he surrender to Federal authorities, and his arrest followed.

The other defendants are John Ra, 19, of Centerville, who fled the State after his family had been removed to a Japanese assembly center, and Koji Kurokawa of this city, who was found hiding in the basement of his former employer's home.

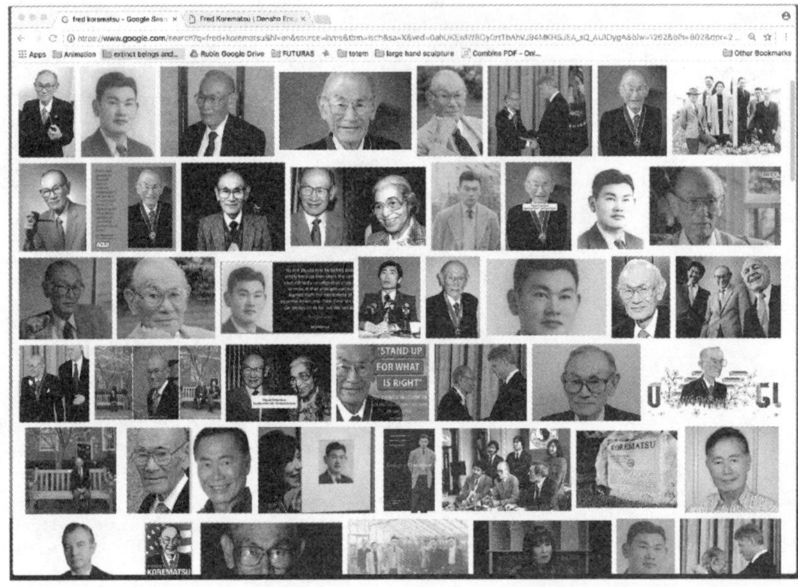

MARCI KWON

July 13, 2020

Dear Casey,

You are my beloved younger sister. You are also the wisest person I know. I write this letter to thank you for all you have taught me, and also to say: enough.

That is, we are enough. Although we grew up in Southern California alongside many other Asian Americans, we were often made to feel our difference. We were made to feel we were not (White) enough. For me, this difference, this deficiency, was like the insistent buzz of a fluorescent light. My childhood was bathed in this white noise. I could never silence it, but sometimes I could tune it out. At times it grew too piercing to ignore.

I remember his pale, bald head and his powerfully bland name: Jeff. Jeff lived across the street, and once when I was 12 and you were 7, he invited us and Dad over to his house. While we played on his beige carpet, they drank white wine. "This Zin is on FIRE," Jeff exclaimed, eyes bulging, muscles tensed, face red. Dad wanted to be Jeff's bro. He laughed his fake laugh at Jeff's dudely exclamations. Jeff never called him back. Dad raged about this slight, muttering through a clenched jaw that if Jeff didn't want to be his friend, he didn't need him. Only now do I realize what Jeff offered and then denied was that which our dad fervently desired: to be draped in the mantle of White masculinity, to be accepted as a White man. Dad heard the noise, too. It grew so deafening it almost destroyed him, and us along with him. But we survived.

It is easy to see how Dad instilled in us this feeling of insufficiency—of not being enough. It is harder to admit the ways this feeling was reinforced by the people we turned to for safety and love: our grandparents and our mother. They pushed us to be "good girls" and to achieve some abstract notion of "the best." They made us feel like their love and regard was contingent upon conforming with their version of goodness and individual achievement. I am beginning to understand the ways their experiences of war, trauma, and loss gave rise to this impossible demand. Our grandfather's mother, father, and brother were trapped in North Korea after the 38th parallel closed, and he carried them with him to the United States. He tried to give us the safety that was denied them, and in America, safety is money. His demand that we be "good" and "the best" is a product of fear, an attempt to forestall the tragedy that befell his—our—family.

Our family internalized historical trauma as its own failing, and told us that if we were good and worked hard, we might prevent its unbearable pain. This is how the model minority myth operates: we take society's racist message—*be more perfect, be more White*—and when we fail, we blame ourselves. It is easier to do this, to pretend we have some measure of control than face the truth that the game is, of course, rigged: it is as impossible to achieve perfection (perfect for whom?), as it is for an Asian person to become White. This inevitable failure is one source of what Cathy Park Hong calls the "oily flame of shame." I like this image because it captures the slimy feeling of shame: a white-hot heat that coats you in a disgusting film. For Hong, this flame burns in the space between Asian American and White; it is fueled by the impossibility of bridging this gap. I think this flame is fed by another source as well. Asian Americans' presumed proximity to Whiteness, and the way we have tried to achieve it, has been wielded as a tool of violence and oppression against Black people in particular. This is not to deny that Asian Americans have experienced racism and discrimination, but we need to hold this truth alongside the equally painful truth that we have allowed ourselves to be used. We are culpable in this country's anti-Blackness. Our need for perfection, for Whiteness, upholds Whiteness's desirability. We need to sit with this shame, with the paradox that we can be discriminated against *and* perpetuate discrimination. To all of this, we must say: enough.

In our own ways, you and I tried to say this to our family. Our version of the best was never theirs. Rather than money or name-brand education, we valued uniqueness, creativity, beauty. This is what I remember of you as a child: you were always painting, designing, creating. I admired you for that, and I now wonder if this is why I became an art historian. Although I loved looking at art, I could never create the way you could. In studying art, perhaps I was trying to get closer to you, to understand the source of your strength and power.

I imagine that what I do as an academic might feel abstract to you, and to our family. Perhaps it has enforced a kind of distance between us. But my work has always been a way for me to think through deeply personal experiences and questions. In my reading, writing, and teaching, I am trying to find my way back to you. When I arrived at Stanford in 2016, the first class I taught was the history of Asian American art. My class was filled with students who reminded me of you, of myself. When I teach this class, I search for the threads that connect our experiences to deeper histories. I tug at these threads to see how long they are, how far they extend, where they are anchored. Weaving these strands into a historical narrative, I try to create a world populated by people who are at once like and unlike us: artists, laborers, craftspeople who, in making things, were searching for a way to move through a world that was at once theirs and not theirs.

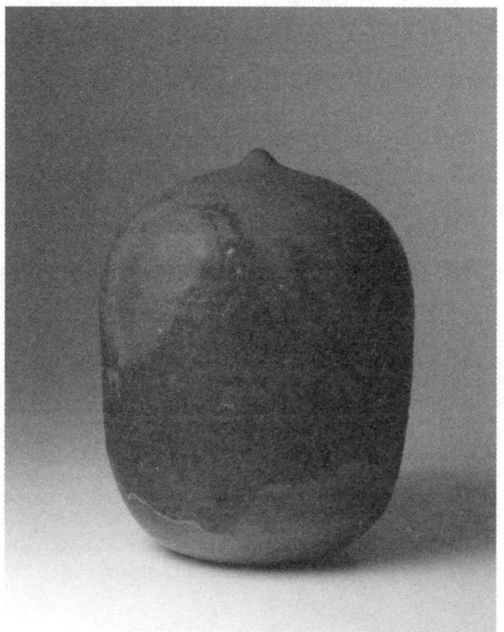

Toshiko Takaezu, *#8,* 20th century, stoneware with glazes, 7-1/8 × 6 × 6 in.

The pot wears a skin of electric blue. Charcoal glaze pooled around its base flows *upwards*, mirroring the movement of the black rivulets floating across its curved face. It is as if gravity has loosened her grip to allow these glaze drips to rise like smoke against the cobalt sky of the pot's skin. It is at once of and not of the earth; at once made of earth and also, somehow, not subject to its inexorable forces. Yet these same forces also give the pot its form: the heat and pressure of a kiln makes soft clay hard as rock, a transformation captured in the name of its medium: stoneware. These stone walls hold space. We cannot see this space, for the mouth of the pot has been sealed, its top pinched and teased into a smooth nipple. But it is there. By closing the pot, Toshiko Takaezu reveals how its form is constituted by the void it holds: "The most important part is the dark space you cannot see," she observed of her sealed works. Takaezu was born in Hawaii in 1922, and she must have been thinking of the sea and the sky as she glazed its sides. I am nourished by this breast of water, air, and earth, for she teaches me that opposites—hardness and softness, gravity and weightlessness, the material world and the space that surrounds it—are one and the same. The pot gathers these contrasts into herself and unites them. Her existence is a paradox. And in this, she is enough.

I first saw this work at Stanford's Cantor Arts Center. As I looked at it, I wondered if it held the ceramic bead Takaezu often places within her closed pots. I have always imagined, but never heard, the gentle rattle of a bead inside a Takaezu pot. Looking at this work, my fingers itched to pick it up. I think this desire to touch, to hold, is also a desire to give. I imagine giving you this pot. As I pass you this fragment of impossibility, our fingers touch and our eyes meet, and together we hear the bead. We know then that we need not solve the problem of our existence—for we, too, embody a paradox. And in this, we are enough.

I love you,
Marci

LUMI TAN

Hi!

This letter is to future Asian American female curators—though I hope that we, as curators, become something less nameable and more fluid. Until a few years ago, I had never thought too much about mentorship because when I came to New York City in 2003 to pursue work in the arts, there weren't very many of us around. The art world seemed so pervasively White that it never even occurred to me there might be an opportunity to see more of us. Seventeen years later, there still aren't nearly enough. But I feel differently now, thanks to all of you whom I have met in schools, who have reached out to me to get coffee, and whom I follow online.

At the goodbye party from my first job as a curatorial assistant at a prominent and "cool" contemporary art museum, the director toasted me by saying, "Lumi is the green tea of the staff." (These kinds of implicitly and explicitly racist and sexist comments from the director and chief curator, along with their general disregard for people's feelings, were precisely the reasons why I was leaving.) The description referred to my ability to stay calm within the pure chaos of our office—a particular type of hysteria that our staff felt entitled to enact precisely *because of* our privileges in contemporary art. Undoubtedly, my calm could have been interpreted as a stereotypical trait of model minority workers; we are assumed to be reserved, to keep our heads down, and never to challenge authority.

And looking back, yes, there was so much I was scared of initially; and even now I still have issues of likeability. But really, I was just attempting to keep everything in perspective (is this what the rest of my life in the art world will be like?), to cut through unnecessary drama (is shouting really an effective tool of communication?), and to understand why I was here in the first place (it's the artists, right?). My "green tea" style of management (LOL) has kept me going in an unregulated, hypocritical industry. It is not about denial or submissiveness; in fact, people can get extremely angry when you don't accommodate their emotional manipulation. Staying calm is necessary work in order to prioritize your own values and articulate your needs. It's about not wearing yourself out trying to shout over the loudest voices. Let the others exhaust themselves, so you can do the work that's important to you.

I used to believe that the art world taught me to be an incredible performer, to code-switch seamlessly when speaking to artists, to collectors and donors, to shippers; to a customer service representative in a call center in India when you're demanding a refund from Best Buy because your boss only bought these eight televisions for the duration of an exhibition; to visitors who treat you like the concierge because you sit at a front desk and they assume you have no actual work to do. But then I realized I had to credit myself for this. Only a tiny fraction of leaders know what it's like to be treated as an Asian American woman in the world at large, much less in the specific microcosm of our industry, where people with a profound lack of communication skills create their own rules as they move up the ladder.

To think of it all as *merely* a performance is to deny yourself agency and to deny the authenticity in these exchanges. Curating contemporary art is mostly just relating to people; this does not mean you erase yourself within these relations. We have to use this knowledge to build up ourselves and others we believe in. You'll be able to center everything that you thought could only thrive at the margins. The voices that cause self-doubt or undermine your experience will be pushed further away. And there will always be others in this world whom you want to learn from. That's the *only* reason why I'm still here, and I know you feel the same. There's no satisfaction in protecting the status quo—it doesn't exist to protect you.

Coming into adulthood, I rarely heard about Asian Americans experiencing double consciousness or performing an identity because, in my generation, assimilation was something our immigrant parents drilled into us so deeply that we hardly noticed it. We didn't need another consciousness: we could just be White! But performance can be both a valuable strategy for self-protection and a form of resistance. (Consider Édouard Glissant's demand for "the right to opacity" and the simple fact that not everyone deserves your time.) Performance as an artistic discipline has been meaningful to subjugated bodies because we are so used to being watched, controlled, and defined by those in power. Performance has allowed us to reject this subjugation, to reclaim our own bodies, and to create more complex or obscure readings of ourselves. Never underestimate the power of ambiguity.

While this started off as an advice letter, please see it also as a fan letter. I want you to call on me when you need help, and call me out if you're not seeing the change you hoped for. I can't wait to learn beside you.

xx
Lumi Tan
Curator, The Kitchen

BRIAN KUAN WOOD

我看我自己的後面
我落后陪我
我知道我忽略你
我東西比較好
現在季節回報
就我看我自吧的後面
我落后陪我

MATTHEW SHEN GOODMAN

Dear Peter,

My name is Matthew. I'm from New York, like you. Also Chinese, but only half. My mom is Chinese as you are, fully so. She was born in Minneapolis, raised for most of her life in upstate New York. My grandparents were originally from Beijing and Hangzhou. I know little about their lives there, of mid-century Chinese life generally, but they were what seems obvious to me as some kind of upper-middle class, my grandfather a doctor's son, my grandmother the daughter of some Kuomintang functionary who fled to Taiwan with his party following the Chinese Civil War. At the time, my grandparents were in England as international students, my grandfather studying engineering, my grandmother English. They didn't leave for Taiwan or return to China, heading instead for the US in 1949. My grandfather quickly obtained his Ph.D. from the University of Minnesota, then taught in college towns up and down the Northeast. He ended up at Rensselaer Polytechnic Institute, and my grandmother eventually became a librarian at a nursing school. The family settled east of Troy in Eagle Mills and my mother grew up knowing one other Asian family (another professor's); everyone else were farmers and rust belt survivors and the rest of the professoriate, nearly all of them White. I don't imagine my grandparents realized when they came to this country that they wouldn't see China again for decades, or never again in the case of my grandmother, who passed in the 70s from non-Hodgkin's lymphoma.

I list all of this to you because my Chineseness is due to these people—though, like all Chinesenesses, it's a very specific one, my being the half-White son of a Chinese American baby boomer sculptor who did a proto-millennial downslide from upper-middle class to the cash-poor and education-overabundant condition we've now dubbed "creative" for much of her life in the city you and I grew up in. Most of this, I'd wager, has nearly nothing to do with you outside the common signifiers of Chinese and New York. From what I can gather, you were born in Hong Kong and raised in Brooklyn, around plenty of Chinese people, by working-class parents. Why is this man writing me all this, you're probably wondering, why is he trying to establish that he has something in common, that he's Chinese enough to address you in as intimate a manner as a personal letter, and doing such a shitty, hedging job?[1] Chalk it up to my specific Chineseness, maybe, but I'm not great at brandishing the ethnic detail, not great at saying, *look at these histories, at these analogous experiences, I have something to talk to you about, and you should listen.* It's a mug's game to feel as though you can only ever have intimacy with those you most resemble, so maybe my justification isn't that I'm similarly Chinese, it's just my having known people like you my whole life. Chinese people who were born in Hong Kong or China or Taiwan or Malaysia or wherever else and came to New York before they could have memories of those places, who usually grew up in majority-Asian neighborhoods in Queens and Brooklyn, who thought I was Latino at first, who found my mom to be—by dint of her accent and profession—the Whitest Asian they'd ever met. Kids I played handball with, got drunk in handball courts with, gamed in Internet cafés and arcades with, studied in Starbucks with, took the train to the Manhattan Mall to buy Starburys with, went to sweet sixteens in some strip mall banquet hall in Forest Hills with, danced terribly at those to "Gasolina" with.

Another ethnic detail: none of these kids became cops. Rich, poor, White, not—no one I knew did. I've never thought to talk casually to a police officer, let alone an Asian one, a phenomenon I have no memories of from being a kid. (Only one percent of the NYPD was Asian at the beginning of the 90s, though now we make up a tenth of the force.) Maybe a Bronx Irish or Italian crew cut or two from my childhood is badged up now, but I haven't talked to a White Yankees fan in a decade. Like most of the people I've known who are my age, from New York, and didn't have family or friends in the Fraternal Order of Police, I have tried to keep a healthy distance from your employer—a distance I've been lucky enough to maintain. Crew cuts aside, those of us without an uncle's Patrolmen's Benevolent Association card in our wallets have had, to various degrees of explicitness, the impression that whomever the police *were* for, they probably weren't for us. Best not to find out if you didn't have to, and so this nervous, stuttering tone, as again, I've never thought to have an intimate conversation with a police officer on duty or off, especially given the more likely kinds of intimacy we could have had, let's say, if I'd overcome my neuroses about COVID and my unspoken bourgeois nihilism about protesting and instead marched after George Floyd's death until I was corralled with the other protesters. The two of us would be face to face, me chanting masked and you silently waiting to charge, your face bare like most of your colleagues; or me cuffed and my fingers blue as you read me my rights, or more likely said something snide—or even more likely you would just stare at me curbside, at your feet, with that contemporary cop face at rest, that mute put-on of blankness barely concealing an excitement to hand out punishment at some signal illegible and unpredictable to the civilians you claim to serve and simultaneously denounce as making said servitude impossibly difficult.

But I wasn't there, and you wouldn't have been working the protests, as you're no longer a cop. You will, however, be defined for the rest of your life by killing Akai Gurley during a vertical patrol that your commanding officer told you *not* to do, in a stairwell of a housing project in East New York; for standing by his body—in a "state of shock," your lawyers argued in court—and arguing with your partner about who should call your sergeant; for stepping around Gurley's girlfriend as she attempted her untrained best to give CPR (both you and your partner were certified, but as the firing of your police academy CPR instructor later suggested, not actually qualified), finally radioing for help some twenty minutes later, in a show of gross ineptitude and callousness towards Black life as mandated by the NYPD's criminalization of those living in these buildings, the department's position being essentially (as implied by your patrol guide's warnings) that vertical patrols were always at risk of ambush regardless of situation, that you were at war. You'll be defined by how you galvanized Chinese both abroad and domestic to fundraise and protest, at least 10,000 strong in Cadman Plaza alone one day, advocating for your cause as they waved placards with one tragedy, two victims and—the poor man's image abused in continuously novel ways—signs with Martin Luther King Jr.'s face on them. You will be remembered for bringing out the most notable show of Asian political muscle in recent history, predominated by the sentiment that you were being scapegoated as a Chinese for something the NYPD did flagrantly all the time; the protesters demanding then that you face the lack of consequences that the NYPD usually faces, as opposed to having you first and then the rest of the force finally face something closer to justice. When I think of you, I think of all those Chinese people protesting on the street for the first time, something so astoundingly novel that even some Asians who despised what you did couldn't help but express a kind of hope that these energies, now unleashed, could be channeled somewhere better—which struck me always as strange, as if these people weren't publicly declaring what they actually believed and were instead only jonesing for any reason to assemble at all.

But let's go back: Why become a cop? The query probably seems inane, rude, especially given the American tendency to valorize our jobs: we view them as callings from God or are so immiserated that any work is nice work if you can get it, often convincing ourselves of the former because of the latter. I'm not sure that any work is simply nice work or God-given, especially police work. Of course, I, in my specific Chineseness, am consciously and unconsciously wont to turn my nose up at certain jobs, and so I remain unfamiliar with both that

90s NYPD one percent and the current class of Asian officers. I don't talk to their friends and family and broader supporters, the last group most recently visible by way of Chinese conservative and business interests running pro-NYPD rallies or doing shit like chanting "Business lives matter" at a Department of Transportation conference about bus lanes, as did Flushing Councilman Peter Koo. Perhaps my mom is too middle class and White as a Chinese for me to be introduced to the Asian variant of blue-collar cop culture, though treating police work as a bastion of working-class power has always struck me as both ahistoric, given the Haymarket riots and Hilo massacres and the police's general brutalization of labor over our country's history, and a contemporary misconception of the working class as an inscrutable monolith driven only by its economic needs, equating police work with any old kind of labor, despite the gun and the qualified immunity.

In any case, I imagine you wish you hadn't become a cop. Do you ask yourself why? Do you wonder how this happened? I watched a documentary recently about you called *Down A Dark Stairwell*, by a filmmaker named Ursula Liang (no relation). I don't remember seeing some Asian cop forebear, nor anyone ever directly answering my question, though I remember some supporter saying something about your goodness, your desire to help the community. No one calls you a psycho who wants to run rampant like every block is a theater of combat, or a troop who wants to bring the war home, or simply a schmuck, a bully coward, a C+ student, and JV team reject marred by a mean streak and just a little stupid, if not a lot—which would cover a great deal of the kinds of people I understand to be cops, though from a carefully maintained distance. (I knew plenty of Asian men with these tendencies, and the shittiest of them became troops, but that's another story.)

Was it something you *saw*? One of the Asian one percent you spotted in a squad car in Brooklyn that planted the seeds as a kid? (No representation for me, as I didn't know of a half-Asian half-White cop until my mid-twenties: Oklahoma City PD officer Daniel Holtzclaw, who at the end of 2015 was convicted of eighteen out of thirty-six counts of sexual battery, rape, and other offenses, his victims African American women he accosted on patrol. His lone public defender has been Michelle Malkin, a Filipina American conservative pundit par Nazi-associating excellence.) Or some form of what is now getting termed *copaganda*? *Cops* got canceled, thank god; police sitcoms like *Brooklyn Nine-Nine* are scrapping planned seasons for something they can feel "morally OK about," per lead actor and sudden moral arbiter Andy Samberg. I'm skeptical of efforts to purge cop shows from our TV screens because I'm not sure that mass media works like that, or that this is the most pressing issue. But who am I to argue against there being some aggregate effect of being fed this glut of mindless police procedurals and arrest porn? Against some desensitization to policing's ill effects, whether through spectacularizing the world into a drug-riddled death trap or sanding police work down into a quotidianly wacky office comedy? I recently read a *Los Angeles Times* article about the former type of copaganda, produced for those who thought *Jackass* should be crueler and not funny and with actual stakes, and was more surprised than I'd like to admit that *Cops* apparently got people to join the police force. ("We've talked to the police departments that participate, and they say straight up they use it for recruiting," said Henry Molofsky of the podcast *Running from Cops*.) Curious, I found a 90s episode of *Cops* set in New York. It's a 1994 subway special following the New York City Transit Police, which would be incorporated into the NYPD the following year. In the Canal Street station, they apprehend a pickpocket who lifts jewelry and a beer off an undercover pretending to be drunk. I'm watching a shitty rip on YouTube, and the quality's horrible, but what looks like an Asian cop asks the pickpocket how long he's been on the street for and where he came from. The pickpocket responds with Mexico, the cop asks him whether he's "illegal," pickpocket says yes, and then it cuts away. That's that. Not a particularly aspirational bit of policing nor a good showing by our Asian friend in law enforcement. Going off the basely representational, "Look, it's me on TV" shit that Asian Americans spent the last couple of years working themselves up over, it's difficult to think of an Asian cop on TV that might have convinced you to do this sort of thing. Sammo Hung in *Martial Law*? Love you Sammo, but I doubt it. Jackie Chan in one of his many roles? I hope not; I can't imagine something more embarrassing than "I became a cop because of *Rush Hour*." And who watches the good Jackie Chan movies—where, yes, he's usually police—and thinks *I want to be a cop*, rather than *I want to be Jackie Chan*?

But the second thing you said to your partner after shooting Gurley was "I'm fired," the first being the claim the gun went off by accident. On the witness stand, you testified that you became a cop because the economy was slow when you graduated from college. Asking what TV show or Thin Blue Line operator uncle you had makes the assumption that you treated police work as a higher calling, as opposed to nice work you could get. From the admittedly little I can gather, though the "I'm fired" seems so telling, your apparent relation to that work seems so transactional as to reduce the act of policing to *only* an abstracted number of hours of labor. It makes me wonder: Have you seen all these people calling to close shop on your previous employer? Have you looked at one of these social media posts, via #Asians4BlackLives or some such, about unlearning policing as a mindset, about abolishing the cop in your head? For me, given that cops spend most of their time chasing misdemeanors and noncriminal complaints, abolition for civilians means in part not calling someone given license by the state to use force to detain or harm or kill someone else because their behavior is errant or offensive or annoying. It is an appeal to stop calling someone with a gun to do a thing that one is either too scared to do (e.g., ask someone to turn down their music) or would never do but imagine as one's right to have done (as in, get this homeless person nodding out off of my stoop). These appeals for abolition are meant to explain the consequences of what one has asked the police to do when the police do what one intends them to, as well the ramifications of what the police often actually do, which is something totally ineffectual or incommensurate: showing up hours late to no avail when someone reported something stolen; brutalizing that aforementioned man on the stoop regardless of why he's sleeping outside or whether he's willing to move; detaining someone found just "suspicious" enough to snitch on because of the "See Something, Say Something" mentality that's pervaded New York since 9/11, which was arguably spun into the country's greatest copaganda push. Again, probably not directly responsible for you becoming one of our boys in blue, though.

When you see those calls for abolition, do you ever think, *hey, that's what happened to me*? You were convicted of second-degree manslaughter with the possibility of serving fifteen years in prison before the judge reduced it to criminally negligent homicide and no prison time. Ultimately, you did five months of probation and 800 hours of community service—like what one'd get for tagging a wall, yelled a Black Lives Matter demonstrator outside the courthouse when the decision was announced. You also paid $25,000 to Gurley's family as part of a settlement of a wrongful death suit filed against the city, which paid more than $4 million. I've been thinking about the Asians I knew, East Asian American and middle class and educated, who were so sentimental as to give credence, however measured, to protests in your name, if only because they saw the emergence of an Asian American public that considered itself a political entity. It seemed spineless to me, to be completely honest, a bout of ideological inarticulation because these people couldn't bear to say shit about Asians in public, and so they'd rather squint such that the protests roughly resembled something worthwhile instead of the reactionary mess it was.

I've been laughing to myself at the idea that said Asians would do some variant of the same with your situation, convincing themselves it roughly resembled a case of abolition in actuality. The abolitionist position would be to not jail you, it's true, to hold you accountable without incarceration. But if I understand abolition, in part, as unlearning the dial-a-cop reflex, I also understand it as a utopian demand: a condition that we may never fully reach but that we should strive for; a world of nonviolent and equitable conflict resolution that refuses punishment, detainment, social death.

There is a chasm between that world and where we are now, one so massive that I have no idea what it might look like, given even the most progressive possible steps forward in the near future. But I know you can't just leap the chasm, just as you can't feasibly make the straw-man argument about the exemplary abolition of Peter Liang I've made above to dunk on these Asian Americans I don't particularly like. The obvious answer to my hallucinated liberal hypothesis: your being kept out of jail isn't meaningful abolition, because that would involve convincing those involved—Chinese, Black, New Yorkers, people living in housing projects, etc.—that your not being police is enough as a feasible step towards a utopian world. I don't imagine that the Chinese community that came out in force to support you is interested in abolishing your former employers, and I'm also not sure that the people who suffered because of you *don't* want to see you in jail. When the district attorney announced he wouldn't seek jail time for you, recommending to the judge that you serve only probation, the family released a statement arguing that such a sentence would only send the message that police would get off without serious consequences. "The district attorney's inadequate recommendation diminishes what Peter Liang did," the statement said. "It diminishes Akai's death."

Maybe they've changed their opinions. Jon Mattingly remains on the Louisville police force as of the time of my writing this, despite murdering Breonna Taylor. (Last I checked, he was reassigned to desk duty, having gotten by a grand jury without getting indicted.) As officers walk around without consequences for what we know they've done, people have time to consider what we'd want to do to them. I've begun to see the demand that we don't jail killer cops; we strip them of their jobs and pensions and figure out some way to get to them to atone and restore and, presumably, stop being a murderous psycho. I get that, but I'm staring into the chasm. Abolition obviously can't look like what happened to you or Daniel Pantaleo, the cop who killed Eric Garner, where you get dismissed and suffer at most from your own personal guilt or shame with no sense of accountability to the community that you wronged, which you are not part of. You get turned into a martyr for your own community instead, a community which raises hundreds of thousands of dollars for you and shelters you and, in Pantaleo's case, supports your suing the city to let you back on the force. Relying on community and not the police means little when said community loves the police. Given law enforcement's penchant for employing ghost skins and Oath Keepers and Three Percenters and straight-up Klansmen, the community we're asking to account for its own harbors various heavily armed elements preparing for something like an insurrection, however incompetently for now. Even before the QAnon faithful and White nationalists muttering the fourteen words to themselves mobbed the capitol (with little resistance from an oddly deferential Capitol Police), it has seemed likely to me that we're heading towards domestic armed conflict, wherein those ostensibly paid to protect civilians from violence are inextricably linked with those perpetrating it. Which is to say, bad (and stupid) as things are, they will obviously be worse in an explicit civil war that seems increasingly feasible.

Back to the premise, I guess. What are Chinese people going to do in that situation? Asians generally? Who knows, though most of us probably won't be with the 1488 folks. (January 6th saw two yellow flags in the crowd: the Gadsden and the South Vietnamese.) We've been buying a lot of guns since the pandemic started, certainly. I don't mean to advocate against abolishing the police because I'm scared of White supremacists, as if—as in what's now a trope—the cops weren't the biggest White supremacist gang in the country. But I am totally unsure of how to meet such threats outside of looking for someone else with a gun, someone who looks a little more like me, like you.

I'm staring here across another chasm. Distance shrinks faster when it's a dystopia hurtling closer. But it's chasms all the way across to anywhere, so enough with this "who watches the watchmen" pondering. Showing vulnerability about my inability to envision abolition to a cop is like saying that I'm not sure there's anything else but capitalism to a Wall Street exec. (Did you know a total of one went to jail for 2008's financial crisis?) We'll be lucky if we swipe a billion from the NYPD's six, and actually swipe, not just shift the funds around like this year's budget. Worrying about having no police force when the ex-cops get together with the Timothy McVeigh types and start murdering us all might be a little much. But as one Chinese to another, honestly, a detail between ethnics: Whether in the academy, in the PBA meetings, in the precinct, in the patrol car, or over the radio, if you saw something, say something?

Best,
Matthew Shen Goodman

1 This is a pretty artificial intimacy. (Who endnotes an actual letter?) I was emailed to participate in this anthology in May, during the tail end of the first wave of coronavirus cases in New York. The editors told me that we were living through a reckoning for Asian Americans, our visibility recently heightened. Andrew Yang, *Parasite*, "Kung flu," etc. With that preamble, would I want to write a letter? To anyone, about anything? I'd be featured alongside other Asian Americans, also writing whatever to whomever, bound by the current moment and our census category. I found the ask ambiguous, the call to congregate aggravatingly vague. There are so many of us Asians, the truism goes, more than any other kind of person on Earth. There isn't a 1:1 demographic equivalence in the US, this country not a recursion of the world at large, but there are enough of as many kinds of us here that it's somewhat meaningless, even at this moment, to say a bunch of Asian Americans are writing letters together, especially when you say "Asian American" and mean something much more specific, i.e., mostly art-world and media-class East Asian—and now I'm verging on a particular liberal Asian American trope. The one where you nod sagely at the idea that "Asian American" can't do justice to the specificities it encompasses. Avoiding saying

anything specific, you chin-stroke infinitely, pleased with yourself as you point out that there are always Asians who are not like other Asians. You never get over the initial fallacy that it's particularly meaningful or interesting to talk about "Asian Americans" to begin with. I find the category as usually applied to be summarily worthless, ahistoric and, honestly, boring. My hope is that we'll disaggregate the whole thing. Say Japanese when we mean Japanese, Hmong when we mean Hmong. The poor among us when we mean the poor among us, the professional-managerial-class East Asian Americans who only fraternize with other PMC East Asian Americans and Whites when we mean—well, I'm not writing that twice. Of course, all of these concerns arise again in miniature when I start pretending like me being a Chinese means I have some mystical resonant bond—exceeding class and immigration history and geography and comfort around cops—with you as another Chinese.

MARY LUM

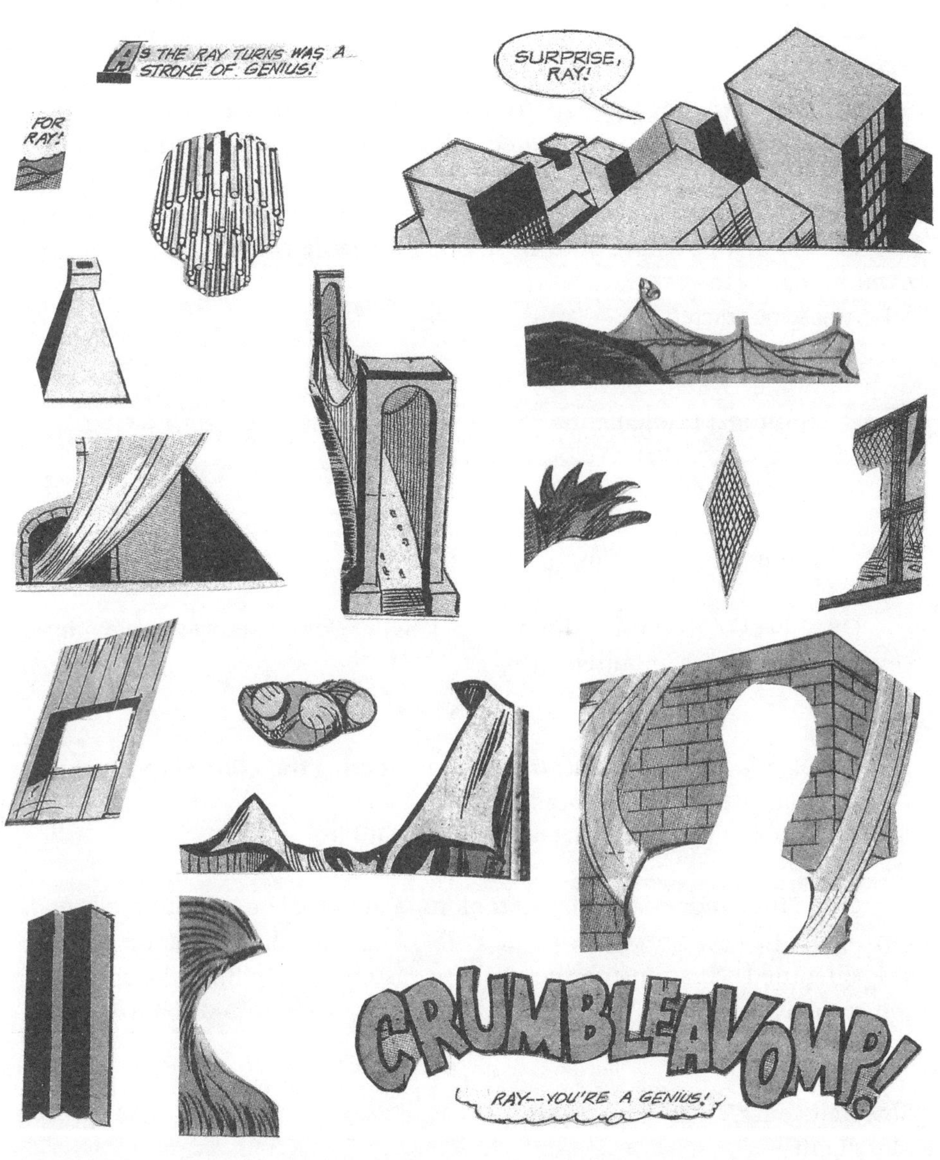
AS THE RAY TURNS WAS A STROKE OF GENIUS!
SURPRISE, RAY!
FOR RAY!
CRUMBLEAVOMP!
RAY--YOU'RE A GENIUS!

Dear Ray Yoshida,

Please scream inside your heart.

In the archives,[1] I looked through your papers, notebooks, and collections of written ephemera. Most of your notes are handwritten on unlined paper, either in almost-neat printing or barely-legible cursive. Some of the things I gleaned:

You wrote out long passages from Rilke's *Letters to a Young Poet*.

From e e cummings you quoted: "don't stand under whispers," "hatred bounces," and

"think twice before you think."

From a list of what could have been possible titles for paintings, or exhibitions:

(ones you starred)

Unknown Facts
Subjective Objective
Improper Implements

(ones you starred, then crossed out the star)

Questionable Structures
Partial Wholes
Simple Complexities

On a sheet of New York Hilton at Rockefeller Center stationery circa 1978, you wrote: "Bored as unbuttered toast."

And:

Lethologica means the state of not remembering the word you want to say.

The plastic ends of shoelaces are called aglets.

There is no mention of cats or dogs in the Bible.

Given the kinds of things you took note of then, you might have noted, during the July 2020 news cycle, the Fuji-Q Highland amusement park near Tokyo banned screaming on their roller coasters to help limit the spread of the coronavirus. Their recommendation: "PLEASE SCREAM INSIDE YOUR HEART."

Sincerely yours,
Mary Lum

1 Archives of American Art, Smithsonian Institution.

HỒNG-ÂN TRƯƠNG

July 17, 2020

Dear Deb,

On a hot summer morning, you called me. Do you remember? I remember it clearly, now that I think of it. I took your call on the fire escape of my friends' apartment in Park Slope. I had just gone through a tumultuous yearlong breakup, my father was falling deeper and deeper into decline from Alzheimer's disease, and fleeing my graduate program in California, I had taken refuge in New York amongst chosen kin. I was lovingly taken in by two dear friends, Lyndsey and Vanessa, and I spent those restless summer days sitting on their fire escape, smoking cigarette after cigarette while eating pints of ice cream (I was convinced the cold enhanced the nicotine). We had to crawl through the tiny, broken kitchen window to get outside, and the three of us would sit hip to hip, legs dangling, breathing in the heavy humid city air. That summer, I was deeply wounded: that feeling of loss where time unspools acutely, visibly, painfully in front of your eyes, and you know without a doubt that from one moment to the next, things never have been, nor will they ever be, the same. Time as transition was physical, endless, unbearable.

You knew this too. So you called me that morning, inviting me to go to the spa that evening. I had never been to a spa. I was overwhelmed at your invitation: thrilled at the opportunity to experience such a treat, humbled by your generosity and love, blessed for the precious time to spend with you. New York at that time was still a magical, lonely dream to me, and I remember distinctly that the place we met was on a wide, red-bricked SoHo street—a part of the neighborhood where it suddenly opens up and the sky surprises you, and then you remember with relief and joy it had been there all along. You spent the evening with me. I talked, you listened, I listened to you talk. You shared stories with me, stories that were personal, institutional, everyday. You were never one to dispense verbose or lengthy advice to me. But your words never quite cut to the chase, either. After listening to me, you would cock your head to the side, lean in closer, and say things like, "You know how it is," or "That's what happens." I heard it as a compassionate way of speaking through affirmation, a way of saying that I already had the answer, a way of testifying to the truth that was already my lived experience.

That evening, you offered me a part-time job as your research assistant. The second time that I would be working for you, it was a gift, a job that was far more for my benefit than yours, despite your demanding work schedule. This is the kind of thing you did, the kind of thing you have been doing unceremoniously, with kindness, for so many others like me, for years. The first time you offered me a job, I was 24, and at that time it seemed improbable that I could actually work for you, a prolific artist and scholar who had just been awarded a MacArthur. The year before, I had breathlessly read your book, *Picturing Us: African American Identity in Photography*. I read it like an incantation, and now you were the distinctive appointed joint professor at Duke and UNC. That year you also published the definitive, groundbreaking tome, *Reflections in Black: A History of Black Photographers, 1840 – Present*. The class I took with you, called Visualizing Culture, was profoundly, irrevocably transformative. I had never encountered stories like those I encountered in your photographs and books and in the work you shared with us. They were beautiful stories about Black history, selfhood, and self-representation that resonated powerfully; they were life-affirming stories that I longed to see about the Vietnamese diaspora that were missing from cultural narratives about the US. Your work and teaching gave me a mirror to myself and the world that I had never seen before, a critical perspective of the world through racialized constructions of the self and Other that gave me the language to understand who I was.

So I was astounded and humbled when you asked me to be your teaching assistant the following semester. I had been enrolled as a non-degree-seeking auditor in your class, one of many students who were deeply influenced by your work, teaching, and mentorship that year. (Do you remember all the brilliant people we got to know during that time?) I was two years out of college with no graduate training, and you asked me without hesitation—a reflection of your grace, openness, and generosity. I imagine I am lucky to be one of many upon whom you've shone your light, and I have since learned the deep work it takes to make this kindness, this investment in students, appear effortless.

It was in that first class, when I met you as a student, that you told me, quite simply, that I had a story to tell and I needed to tell it. You told me that, and at first, I didn't believe you or didn't want to believe you, or had implicitly understood all my life otherwise, so it was impossible to believe you. But then, slowly, I did start believing you. I started to believe you because you didn't just tell me that and disappear. You told me that and stayed around me somehow. And you continued to stay around me, long after your year in North Carolina ended and you moved back to DC. It is my sense of your continued presence—not physical or everyday or regular, but real nonetheless—that I am so grateful for: what a letter alone could never express.

Every so often, you would surprise me with short texts and emails, like "how are things," or "thinking about you. how are you. sending love, deb." Or there would be slightly longer ones like, "I'm showing your work to my students right now," or "do you have new work you want me to see?" These were quiet messages, but eruptions that powerfully shaped the contours of care that you nurtured in our relationship. The shape of this care extends beyond the structures that we each inhabited. The shape of this care is disloyal to power and refuses the boundaries circumscribed by institutional hierarchies.

The shape of this care means that you do not judge me as an inauthentic Other when I struggle to understand myself in relationship to my White lover, acknowledging, like hooks, *the ways erotic longings inform our politics and might allow us to know how desire can make resistance possible*. The shape of this care means that listening is sacred, as in Minh-ha's *Mother always has a mother*. The shape of this care means that what you give is not held hostage to debt or payment, a predicament in capitalism not easily circumvented or subverted, perhaps only under conditions of Moten and Harney's *principle of elaboration*. I have come to understand that the shape of this care is a revolutionary act that shares in vulnerability across difference, that erodes the divisions reified by racial capitalism, a disloyalty to power necessary for liberation.

I have thought often of the shape of your care in all these years that have passed since I first met you. The condition of receiving care, that gift, under a principle of elaboration, resistant to exchange based on individualism, opens up the possibility for one to slip under the watchful eye of the institution. It is also a condition that can change the course of time, a condition in which there is a before and an after and you can never return to that before. And how could I not think constantly about gift economies, and about that before and after? After all, my family's refugee life, rising from the ashes, as it were, from the *afterlife of empire*, is demarcated by the demands of a debt from a nefarious "gift of freedom" that we can never repay.[1] (I saw my father, after more than ten years of part-time community college courses, finally complete his degree to find his first and only professional job, which he took to his grave: a civil servant bound to the US Army.) That debt means perpetually living among ghosts, as ghosts—never, as my father used to always tell me, having a home to call our own.

It is true that the care you gifted me over the years can never be repaid, but under that condition—that *principle of elaboration*—receiving your gift shattered the illusion of origin, the illusion that there was ever a beginning, a single creator, or a first time that the story was ever told. In fact, *the story needs all of us to come into being.*[2] I have come to learn that, despite my best attempts to return and return and return, I cannot claim any single origin. I have come to understand through you, your work, and your care, that the power of the story is in its imparting, its transmission. I have come to understand through you, your work, and your care that in order to avoid the bait of cultural and racial binaries and artificial categories sedimented by nationalist narratives, we must tell our stories alongside the stories of others.[3]

We occasionally lost touch over the years, but I cherish those early times with you, as painful and difficult as they might have been, and am endlessly grateful for your mentorship. Without a doubt, I am who I am because of you, and my work is what it is because of you.

I am trying to finish this letter on July 17th, the anniversary of my sister's death. Do you remember that, too? It was the first story I tried to tell you almost twenty years ago. We shared our stories of loss, which left indelible marks on me not easily hidden or forgotten. Thank you so much for listening; thank you so much for sharing.

With love,
Hồng-Ân

1 Mimi Thi Nguyen, *The Gift of Freedom: War, Debt, and Other Refugee Passages* (Durham: Duke University Press, 2012).

2 Trinh T. Minh-ha, *Woman, Native, Other: Writing Postcoloniality and Feminism* (Bloomington: Indiana University Press, 1989).

3 Cedric Robinson, *Black Marxism: The Making of the Black Radical Tradition* (London: Verso, 1994) and Gaye Theresa Johnson and Alex Lubin, *Futures of Black Radicalism* (London: Verso, 2017).

HERA CHAN

To whom I was a year ago,

In retrospect, the end of the world is a drawn-out affair. When I returned to Hong Kong after two months in Dakar, I suffered from sleep paralysis. Every night for a week, I watched as my loved ones and myself faced imminent death. My father and I were in my neighbor's house, only it was our own. We were sharing inconsequential details about our day when a pounding began on a translucent, makeshift covering plastered over a hole in the wall. As we ran to lock ourselves in the bathroom of the master suite, we saw the shape of a body forcing its way into the room. As I cried out bloody murder, I realized I had lost my voice. Forcing myself to wake, I remained in a stupor all day. It was the first time I seriously considered therapy. Yet I already knew what inspired these lucid nightmares: the city of Hong Kong had become a battlefield.

Walking along Jordan Road toward my apartment, I could see the scars of struggle. Blank patches of dug-up sidewalk bricks had been coarsely repaired with striated cement. Flimsy yellow plastic chains stitched up the barricades that had been torn down and repurposed as protection against the police. Some residents had taped plastic garbage bags over their external air conditioner units to prevent tear gas from filtering into their homes. As I walked, the movements in East Asia that precipitated this one lingered in my thoughts: the Sunflower movement in Taiwan, the Gwangju uprisings in South Korea, and later, the online rebellion in the name of free speech following the death of coronavirus whistleblower Dr. Li Wenliang.

Last November, our movement had its first massive victory. In the only free election we have, pro-democracy candidates had taken over seventeen out of eighteen districts in the city with a voter turnout of 71.2 percent. I had stayed up in Dakar watching the votes come in, eating at a Chinese restaurant in Gibraltar I found by following two Chinese workers. I thought, even the military couldn't stop our movement now. This pandemic for freedom had spread its tactics to Beirut and Catalonia. It was going to be May '68, except in the Global South. But then came the one thing that could have stopped it: COVID-19.

As the Chinese New Year of 2020 passed, the cancellation of the future became more pronounced. Wuhan was undergoing a brutal lockdown. The city of Hong Kong was at war. Last December, Dr. Li had received a notice from the police—a cease and desist—commanding him to "have the ability to understand." On a snowy roof in China, a lone person dressed in black had traced out a brief eulogy for Li. With his feet, he had written a temporary message large enough for viewers in surrounding buildings to see.

When I moved here three years ago, a question raised by my peers plagued me: What is a Hong Kong worth living for? It seemed, three years later, that we had answered that question in the communities we built in spite of the system, only to suffer vicious retaliation.

It has now been over two months since Hong Kong has taken measures against the virus. We are all waiting for a scientific solution. We know that the extinction event facing Hong Kong is not COVID-19, but one regarding freedom. As the government released a financial stimulus package, the first line jumped out to all Hong Kong ID holders: HKD 10,000 cash handout for all. Buried in a lower line was a budget increase of 25 percent for the police force.

My nightmares seem so far away now. It is a matter of record to keep reiterating what kind of society we want to live in. I believe the movement only took hold when someone was willing to lose their life for it—the only bargaining chip for the disempowered. We have been writing eulogies for months: for those lost in the struggle, for those lost in Wuhan. I don't want to write one for our movement as well.

Yours,
Hera Chan

April 11, 2020

JIA TOLENTINO

Dear Friend,

It's June 2020, warm and green in the natural world, with pain and death and promise in the institutions. I'm signing all my stupid emails, even to strangers, with the wish that they find peace in the middle of this grinding and gorgeous revolution, the hope that I'll run into them this weekend in these streets. Right now I feel like the world is a nesting doll of reckonings. I feel made up of them; there are more within me than I expected. The past seems to cascade and encapsulate itself, decisions leading to the lack of them next time, choices masquerading as inevitabilities. For whom have I fought, and how have I done this fighting? Who has actually benefited? How many times have I thought I was moving in one direction, when I wasn't really doing so at all? I'm seven months pregnant, which has made me consider the fact that this child will have no idea—or at least no experience—of what came before this moment; it's made me think about what I want them to see.

It's not lost on me that I dread the idea of them pursuing upward mobility, even though that has been in many ways the organizing principle of my life. I didn't know it was, originally. The ability to strive, the immigrant's legacy, is a gift that feels like a requirement and operated within me like predestination. For a long time, I thought I was just looking for money: as a teenager, for a free college education, for grants that would let me get on planes I couldn't pay for; in my twenties, for the unclenching that comes with health insurance, for a stable position in an industry that keeps melting until it seems like there are only about a hundred jobs left. I was never deprived, only sharpened; I stretched my luck and charm to cover minor lack. I was subconsciously, I'm realizing, projecting my desires onto the hypothetical child I'm now carrying. I didn't want them to be president of some club in high school and throw the annual fundraiser for a needy student that would end up being their own self. I never wanted them to be afraid that the bottom would fall out at any minute. They would never feel responsible for keeping me out of indigence in old age.

With these desires, with this greed for present and future unencumbrance, I identified and laughed at but never pulled away from the language I was learning. I arranged my expressions in the syntax of laminated name tags and annual dinners, of establishment deservingness, of getting White people to redistribute other White people's money to slightly spicier recipients, of making people feel progressive just for tolerating my ideas, of being the safest version of an interesting choice. When I thought about other versions of me, about the people I cared about, the people I wanted to move more freely, I imagined that I was making the path wider. You have to access power in order to make anyone change anything. But of course—and I missed this even as I learned it—you don't have to, and in fact shouldn't, do this alone.

The same ripple is coming through so many of my text messages. Should we have learned this language in the hopes of being able to use it at cross-purposes? Are we neglecting much greater possibilities? What does it mean to be a symbol that an institution is changing, if it only changed enough to let us in? I'm realizing—it's always the year of realizing things—that I have devoted so much individual effort to reaching a place where I could advocate for a collective that I ended up doing more, I think, for the cause of individual effort than anything else.

As with everything, as with anything, the promise comes in remembering you're not alone, never alone, never first, never last, never singular, when anything is keeping you awake. The world is a nesting doll of reckonings; the little ones rattle, break open the next ones. I do feel unencumbered. I have had so much grass and sunshine. I can see this baby kicking me from the outside. I don't want anything for them except the desire—and yes, the freedom—to be kind, and to fight.

Wishing you peace, and hoping to see you,
Jia

KA-MAN TSE

Thursday, June 11, 2020   1:38 am

Rinko Ocean Ho-Yan,

I need to tell you, but you already know this:
The world is a shit show; the world is on fire.
As you learn to coo and to scream and to reach, as your world has begun to expand — are you teething, or is it just that the world is in so much pain?

It's 1:38 am and I should be asleep so that we can play together in the morning when you wake up at dawn. Tonight, like so many nights, the helicopters are low, heavy, and oppressive in the air.

Holding you, as I do every day and night since you were born, rocking you to sleep on my shoulder. The space that is this space right here between our bodies, the here that is one arm's length, the nook that is my left shoulder and where you learned to put your hand up my t-shirt sleeve, and then to hold on with both your hands, and your head leaning in while we sway to doo wop and Meshel Ndegeocello you used to fit under my chin! You can't read this letter yet and you can't speak words yet but I have tried to learn these seven month and eleven (twelve?) days to read your breathing and your body. I want you to hold this letter one day. I want you to hold this space and to hold space for others, for friends, your community, your world. When you sigh, when you do one last shudder before you finally go down to sleep. Feeling and knowing when you would be asleep asleep.

Today, I saw solid beads of sweat on your nose in the afternoon.
When you were a newborn, sometimes you would cry so hard your whole body would sweat.

The other weekend, you didn't cry when you threw up in the car nine times. You were trying to hold it in. We were looking for a new place to live, thinking we could make it upstate. I held your hand, as when we pulled you out into the world. It was cold and bright in that room; the three of us had been up Monday, Tuesday, Wednesday and you didn't want to come down.

You came out wailing. The doctors said "wow" twice.
I held out a finger and you grasped it tight.
There we were in the car, seven months later, holding hands.
I could see your eyes, you were trying to hold it in,
and I kept trying to say to you, "DON'T HOLD IT IN."
We have swallowed too much in this world
for you to do the same. Get it out!
But at that moment I couldn't care about anything else
but only to take your pain away, to make it stop
and to hold you.

We left upstate and the winding roads. You still can't sleep
through the night. There are nights that are so long,
and we try our best to console you. Are babies intuitive?
Do you have a sense that the world is on fire,
on every corner?

We came back to Brooklyn, at the beginning of the protests.

Friday, June 12, 2020 2:12

Rinko Ocean Ho-Yan,

when you were in utero I spent the summer in Hong Kong crying every night.

I was thinking a lot about what kind of world we build for you. Every night when I came home from the protests, summer of 2019, first at Kaufu's house, then in the quiet flat, stories above the wet pavement in Cheung Sha Wan, I knew I had to come back to you intact, alive, that you needed to know what was happening to Hong Kong. I cannot unsee the things I saw that summer: the state sanctioned violence against bodies, the fever pitch that we all felt, the heartbreak, the rage and anger and fear, all of the late night conversations, the heat, the blatant, brazen, unapologetic tyranny. And also, the community that came together, to protect each other and to fight for this city. One million at a time, two million at a time. That deep burning smell of tear gas that gets inside your skin and your clothes. The saran wrap for armor. The cardboard and water bottles for armor. Umbrellas for armor. Relaying in a chain, with a community food and water and supplies, saline, googles, plastic ties, scissors. Pulling strangers into our umbrella. Coins on top of the MTR machines, when it was still safe inside the MTR.

All of the waiting, all of the anticipation that is a war, the wearing down, the normalization of violence. How mad I would feel on Monday mornings after a weekend of tears and police violence. How could I cross the street or order lai cha and eggs. Before you were born, I thought about all of these things, and I wanted to show you Hong Kong. Now, this summer, I think about all that I want to protect you from.

You are not even seven and a half months old.

When you were born, we knew, as your parents, that we wanted to protect you from shame and guilt. Intergenerational violence. The family drama. What gets passed down.

What does it mean when there is no home to go home to?
I can't bring you back to Hong Kong, not now.
I can't bring you to gong gong and popo.
And not until they stop ~~telling us we shouldn't have become parents~~.

As you sleep, I think about all things I want to tell you and
show you. We miss you when you nap. We look at pictures
of you on our phones while you sleep. Every new move
and sound you make. You understand Cantonese and English,
you understand a lot of words, like wait, and hold this,
in Cantonese. You understand "LOOK" in both languages.
And all the protest slogans in Cantonese and English.

WAIT. HOLD. LOOK.
What does it mean to hold space now, to hold you?
We have waited for you for so long.

Tonight, you are sleeping in your own ROOM for the first time.
For all of these months, weeks and nights, I could hear
your every breath, your every toss and turn,
when you would scratch your left elbow by rubbing it
against the crib mattress, right there in the same room.
As I write this I am sitting by the window
at the dining room table. It's the first night there's been a breez
and finally the helicopters have stopped.

Sunday June 14, 2020 12:57am

Rinko Ocean - lately, these are the things that I've been thinking about, and want to write down for you.

What is the world we are building for you?
You.
We owe you.
We, this world we, have to change.

The world building, or is it the world-we-are-dismantling? To build a better one, we have to tear this one to pieces. In this time of a global pandemic, back to normal is not good enough. You have not known normal. But do we ask you to change the world, for you to be braver than us, or do we do it right now as you sleep?

Rinko Ocean, we loved you before you were born. We loved you into existence. The poking and prodding, the needles, the waiting, the procedures, the phone calls, the fluorescent lights, the insurance calls, the blastocysts.

But
I want to tell you not about your origin - you are our magical baby - or the past, but about this moment, the right now that you read this when you are older, is 2020. The pandemic has stopped the world, stopped the protests in Hong Kong, decimated the economy in the U.S. The pain and loss, the economic disparity, the injustice that is this world, the racial violence the inequality - ~~all designed~~ as policy - the pandemic has thrown this into sharp relief. How it all compounds, and I know that you know that something is up, something is wrong. You are intelligent and intuitive and perceptive.

It's been a year since we were tear gassed, on June 12, 2019. For the first time, Hong Kongers, that summer. I remember the escalators that had stopped, the road that we were occupying, a barricade had become a stepladder, people had begun camping out as it were Umbrella Movement. I remember when they would ask for a cheung jai, a long umbrella. They would float down from the overpass, a petal, a shield. I remember how hot it was. It was always hot, thick, and wet, the heat. Black t-shirts with salt crystals at the end of each day. I remember at first everyone chanting cheet wui. After that, everything tumbled and escalated week after week. I remember the first night there were gwai, undercover cops, in front of the station. I would call home and your momma cheryl was still nauseous with you, and you stil had the hiccups all the time.

Nights
Rocking you to sleep when you were a newborn, your hiccups in utero, your hiccups when you were born. Your eyes had not even opened and now you are teething. Screaming all the things we have tried to soothe. Screaming all the things we have felt and wanted to say and did not have the words.

Helicopters
George floyd, Breonna Taylor, Nina pop, Tony McDade
Riah Milton, Dominique Rem'mie Fells. Ahmand Arbery.
Trayvon. Tamir.
Helicopters.
It seems appropriate that you would be wailing.
I need to tell you about the violence against Black and brown bodies
I need to tell you about white supremacy.
As Asian Americans we need to be in solidarity for Black Lives

Will your body
though born here, be scrutinized
be read as contagion
as perpetually foreign? or when we
were both crying
when was the first time you noticed I was crying?
I think you noticed the other day.
It's like ~~wha~~ in the morning when you pull on my nose
to wake me up when I have fallen asleep on the play mat
out of exhaustion.

Oysters
is a song we play for you on loop at the end of each night and you hear it on my shoulder on repeat. You love doo wop, and waltzes, and you love Meshell, her cover of sometimes it snows in April, and Oysters.
In oysters, Meshell sings:

> Everybody talking about changing the world,
> world ain't never gonna change
> But you can always change it for me
> I'll shuck all the oysters and you keep the pearls

Rinko Ocean Ho-Yan,
you can always change it for me.

Rinko Ocean Ho-Yan,
Ho-Yan 浩恩 means to be expansive like the ocean; a gracious, generous person. There is water in your name. and an open mouth. and heart.
I hope that you can hold this, for yourself to grow to make this space, to speak and to love and be expansive.

Today, 15,000 people showed up at the Brooklyn Museum for Black Trans Lives!!! I want to tell you so much about this and other protests. I'm sure you watch your mommas talk about this and racism and capitalism. You love emphatic speaking, always have. And you have my eyebrows.

Back in February, when you were three and half months old, we took you on the D train, your first subway ride, to see art. Alvin Baltrop was your first show. (He had been a medic, and later carried around a first aid kit at the piers, tending to, caring for. Yes, I'd like to think he was repairing in between photographs...) Just when we were supposed to branch out – for you to see the world – the world shut down.

Friday June 19, 2020 1:26 am

I write to you over the course of many nights. It's a letter that can never be finished. It's finally quiet. The police helicopters have stopped. The fireworks. The air-con units and a distant siren. Distant pops like they are muted in a can. Like the trajectory never fully goes off. Each day, as your body and your will progress, your legs can now pivot, and you can spin in a circle like a clock hand. Your little feet push against the mat, you can grunt, scream, laugh. We have our inside jokes, you can hoot and you have rhythm and you know your favorite songs and you love watching the trees wave in the wind in the dappled light and we have our Zena Rec bird call. Our own world and language.

On Juneteenth, we were listening to Deva Woodley's Black Feminist practices lecture. On Juneteenth, you were eating roasted blueberries with cinnamon and listening intently. Did you understand what she was talking about? Later, you didn't want broccoli with the ginger and garlic, and then I heated up some sweet potato I had roasted for you. Later, we played TLC's Waterfalls. Only now I realise it's a parent's song. But it feels like Runaway Bunny. If you ran away and turned into a bird, the momma says she will turn into a tree for you on which to rest. But I want you to fly, just not be self-destructive. Amend the lyrics. Go see the world, it is bigger than this window, and fight for what you care about. Fall even, even if I don't want you to. Later, we dance to it when Halim comes to visit on the porch. Every day when we turn on the radio your mommas explain to you emphatically how fucked up this nation and world is, the systems.

I know you'll have it your way or none at all. You're a Scorpio.

You didn't want to come down. Waited days. Maybe you knew that the world was on fire.

Tuesday, June 30, 2020 12:03 am

You are eight months old today.
It's already July 1st in Hong Kong.
It's already **2047**.

Wednesday, July 1, 2020 12:46am

Fireworks
Almost a full moon
Big ones in the sky across the yard behind the building's rooftops
Nothing to celebrate
but heartbreak and rage.

Fracture.
Compression.
The world shrinks, and is connected, and stops. Fractures
and aspirations. Here we are in Hunkerdown mode
while you want to reach and see and grab
and pull, curious. I am feeling anger, rage and
hurt, at the world. I can no longer bring you back
to Hong Kong. I cried every night last year, summer of
2019 in Hong Kong. We are crying every night this summer,
2020.

How do I protect you from the trauma, the world?
The fever pitch? How do I tell you that we want you
to be generous and expansive
Patient
Gentle
Kind
But you can also scream and wail as you want to.
Yau sum see, gong ah, OK?
Don't hold it in.

The National Security Law. Our friends are beginning to delete
their cell phone pictures from last year. It's the
Anniversary of the handover. 97.
Each year, I would go out and march on July 1st.
We used to joke, in the final years before 2019, 2020
that they would cloud see it – it would always rain!

Monday July 6, 2020 2:33 am

Rinko Ocean, Brooklyn is quiet now. Have they used up the fireworks from the 4th? The window is open, the backyard has a breeze.

Today I played for you My Little Airport, the concert Taste of Tears, from the end of 2019. We had listened to it way back, but I don't think you remember. Today we rocked and swayed while staring out the window at the trees. I think you noticed me crying during the protest songs, and then at the end of the concert when they do the Beyond cover. In between the songs, the crowd was chanting Liberate Hong Kong, Revolution of Our Times. There are shots of the crowd. everyone's hands up. Five Demands. I wanted you to hear this. I wanted you to hear everyone screaming Liberate Hong Kong, Revolution of Our Times.

Six Demands.
Abolish the police.

What do I want you to know
or think about or pay attention to?
what should I as your parent
pay attention to? Or want you to?
or want us to?

Do I want to talk to you about today, the right now, the murk, or do I want to talk to you about the future? What future do I want for you?
I cannot take you to Hong Kong, but I can't even take you to Greenegrape Provisions or the deli or the pharmacy or the subway. How has it that your world has closed at this moment when you are reaching, pushing out beyond your grasp?
What world do I want for you? What about the words that are deleted that Hong Kongers cannot even say?
GFHK SDGM

You must smash it to pieces. Be radical, think and make critically, self-reflect, question, don't take the status quo. We inherited tyranny, colonialism and capitalism, and white supremacy and misogyny and transphobia and self-doubt and the policing of bodies and thought.

It is your generation to fuck this all up and tear it to pieces.
Or is it ours to do this?

How do I describe to you the sound? The pulling out of steel barricades from the ground, metal scraping and flying down the pavement. How do I describe this sound? I can't unhear it: the screams in the mall as the police came in last summer, when they said they would never go inside a tourist mall, and they did. It was still July 2019, in Sha Tin. The echoes on the tiles and glass and the atrium, all the levels. What have we fallen into? 2020. 2019.

On Saturday, July 4th 2020 you went to your second protest. We were on the sidelines. You were watching intently.

Sunday, July 12, 2020 2:06 am

You used to smell like warm sweetened condensed milk.
Today I picked you up from your nap
and you smelled like sweat and vinegar.
I love your smile, your knowing eyes and I love it when you
kick your legs and hoot and when you rock out to Aaliyah.
I love the things that make you laugh. I see it in you sometimes,
when you are frustrated and we are trying to understand you.
I want to hear your thoughts and your eyebrows; I want to see
what you see and what you think about. I want you to know,
as you hold this letter in your hands – your hands that
were this wonder, that had you mesmerized — for weeks –
about this moment that is now, but also right now
as you read this – you can come and talk to us.
I want to read your language.

I love that you love to feed yourself now. Roasted cauliflower with cumin,
carrots with ginger and tumeric, chicken and basil.
Shucked peas and mint. How you look at us, when you
try something new, and then the window outside,
the trees swaying.

Today, in the late afternoon, a shaft of light came in
onto the mat, and I held it in the air, like a bowl,
with my hands open, and you watched the light glow hot,
and then disappear.

Monday, July 13, 2020 1:47am

Today, you have started to push across the room.
Your body, your reach.
You know.
A fathom.
A fathom is a reach of a body. It is the depth of water, it is the depth of outstretched arms.

AILY NASH AND SYLVIA SCHEDELBAUER

Dear Sylvia,

When I was invited to write a letter to someone about my relationship to Asian Americanism, you quickly came to my mind. But I didn't want to just write to you, I wanted to invite you to respond and share your experience.

Before I ever met you or saw your films, I remember coming across your website and reading descriptions of your work and feeling an immediate kinship. I knew I had to know you. I was always drawn to film and literature as a vehicle for accessing other subjectivities as a way to make sense of my own and the various cultures that intersected in my life. I imagine this is the case for many. Some artists who are bicultural, or have a migratory experience of some kind, come to reckon with this aspect of their identity through their practice. I was intrigued by how your early films engaged with the complexities of being from two cultures with their respective histories.

You write that your films "negotiate the space between broader historical narratives and personal, psychological realms mainly through poetic manipulations of found and archival footage." Your films resonate with me precisely because you succeed in communicating through affect. The feelings your films produced in me reminded me of my own searching, questioning, and reckoning with who or what I am. Am I Japanese? Am I American? Am I Asian American? Japanese American? Hafu? Am I a first-generation immigrant? Perhaps I'm all of these things. Although you're not American, I somehow found clues to my identity in your work.

I'm curious to know what works and artists accompanied you in your understanding of your identity. How did these influences shift your practice or process? How did you know that film was the medium you had fluency in? Since most of your work utilizes found footage, I wonder if preexisting images enunciated some of the questions and feelings that you yourself were grappling with.

The intimacy we feel when something outside of ourselves resonates with something internal is very profound. In that moment with an image, a film, or another's life experience, we find kinship. Witnessing—or accompanying, as we do when we experience an artwork—grants us entry into others' processes of becoming, and that experience inevitably becomes part of our own.

I'm grateful for your work and your friendship, and that we share and accompany each other in this unique place between Japan and the West.

Love,
Aily

愛理ちゃん,

Is this how you write your name in kanji? I assume so—the characters fit you so perfectly: Love and Reason. Your parents picked such a beautiful name for you!

Did you know I have a Japanese middle name? It's Yuki. There was a brief time that it seemed popular for some to use katakana for first names. My mom's Japanese passport states her first name as セツ, Setsu. Anyway, she didn't care for kanji in names. Frankly, I don't think I had one for my name, until I kept asking her in grade school. I still remember her reaction—I'm sure she improvised on the spot. 雪。Snow!

In the ten years or so that we've known each other, we've spoken time and time again about our respective experiences and how different they were. My identity has never been easy to define, and it has definitely changed over time. I went through a long (and hard) acculturation in the years after I moved to Germany. As you know, I was born and raised in Japan and attended the Tokyo German School there. I always identified as Hafu until I moved to Berlin, where I began omitting the half-Japanese part because it resulted in (constant) emotional labor, and in being othered too much—not just in every new encounter, but well into friendships, too. I think both Germany and Japan still have long ways to go in terms of their acceptance, understanding, and visibility of various minorities. Very few people seemed open to "believe" my experience: there were always too many questions about an "authenticity." Nowadays, I like to say that I'm a transnational. I feel comfortable with this label because the prefix *trans-* denotes a movement of sorts, between, or from one to the other, whether that's physical (moving from Japan to Germany, vice versa, and beyond) or psychological (between cultures; processes of adjustment, understanding, becoming).

For me, this acculturation occurred on every level: food, clothing, communication, behavior, mannerisms, and even in thinking. I moved to Germany in the early 1990s, at a time when people "innocently" asked me whether I spoke Chinese when I told them I grew up in Tokyo. This was before cheap air travel, which opened cultural horizons for the mainstream, and way before foodie culture arrived in Germany. It was still rather rare that Germans ate seafood (as it wasn't widely available), and the notion of eating raw fish still triggered repulsion in many. It was quite hard and expensive to get Japanese food items.

I was used to courtesy, politeness, and being more cognizant of people when speaking because, as you know, in Japanese communication one uses different language depending on gender, age, and professional status. Berlin to me was pretty rough. One of the first things I was told when I finally got into art school, was that if I wanted to survive in this society, I needed to toughen up, and stop being so "nice." I was told that I needed to learn how to "use my elbows," that I didn't seem to know what that meant. Within five years after moving to Germany, I ended up dropping out of university and going back to Japan for a few years. I wasn't coping at all, but more than anything, I was disillusioned by the art school—not only because it felt more capitalist, conservative, and neoliberal than many other sectors in society, but also because I suffered from racism and sexism at the hands of almost all White, male teachers. I was actually never going to return to Germany, but I really wanted to finish my university degree. Tuition is free here, while student fees with living expenses in Japan (and even more so in the US) were too daunting, so I came back. But I was resolved that I would return to university only if I could study under a female professor, and luckily, this was possible.

My life up to my thirties always seemed predetermined by external projections: the Japanese were adamant that I could never understand Japaneseness simply because I wasn't 100 percent Japanese, but the Germans also went the other extreme: at the University of Arts in Berlin, there were some feminists who thought it was progressive to call me *only* German. "Of course you're *German*!" They were trying to be inclusive, but I could never get myself to tell them that it felt like erasing part of my experience and identity. In any event, I most definitely never looked Asian enough.

I believe it's still quite common among Germans and Japanese to think that there is something authentic, originary, or primary about their respective cultures. Even though both countries have age-old histories of migration and mixing, and of course, colonialism—for Germany, these histories are a little more obvious, and for Japan, they are much more obscured—it feels like both Germans and Japanese share a strong belief that their respective cultures are native, homegrown, and endemic. There is a sense of unquestioned entitlement;

there is prevalent, if latent (because often "unconscious") essentialism. I think for many—conscious or not, latent or explicit—the dominant national culture is still an indisputable norm. In Germany, there is a sociopolitical concept in place of *deutsche Leitkultur* (German *leading*, or dominant culture), which one must sooner or later submit to, in order to integrate, assimilate, and succeed. (A kind of mirror image of that is the "one race mythology" that Japanese conservatives perpetuate.)

The turn of the millennium and the changes that came with the acceleration of globalization seem to have improved a lot in Germany. There has definitely been a bit more visibility and representation of "minorities" on every level, including academia, the arts, and visual culture. Germany is slowly beginning to go beyond working through WWll atrocities and national reunification issues to address its migration and colonial histories. But I believe that as long as any notion of *Leitkultur* remains a political stance, things will only change on a superficial level.

The first short film I made, *Memories* (2004), was an attempt at constructing my family history. My German father moved to Japan in 1958 and lived there for thirty-six years. I don't know where or how he met my Japanese mother. The mystery and secrecy around my parents' lives before I was born—combined with the fact that neither of them ever wanted to speak about their respective childhood experiences during WWII in Germany and Japan—just made me more curious. But at some point, I realized that the family secrets would always remain secrets, so I began thinking about history and memory in more general terms. Maybe I was looking beyond my own family history for a transnational history that pertained to my own identity. I found that history was usually narrated through a monocultural and national lens, and it seemed full of erasures and exclusions. I feel the desire to look beyond some of these gaps, to connect my experience with those that came before.

I'm not sure what came first, falling in love with old archival celluloid films or the urge to work with them. It probably happened simultaneously. Using found and researched material made perfect sense for exploring a time that has already passed. I love juxtaposing images and making unexpected connections between different people, places, and times. It feels right because that's what marks the transnational experience for me—beyond feelings of an in-betweenness, my films translate the straddling, bridging, connecting, entangling, mixing, and merging of possibly completely disparate narratives, cultures, and contexts. Found footage works on multiple levels: formal, material, and metaphorical. Taking old films and creating new meanings through montage was full of creative possibilities for me. The (American) term "orphan film" also resonated because many postwar Hafu kids were orphaned in Japan, as were their stories and histories.

I spent my formative years as a filmmaker in San Francisco, and in the American context, I suddenly "qualified" as a person of color. I experienced racism in both German and Japanese societies, but my experience in those countries was never "valid" and never seemed to fit any mold. It was only when I visited California for the first time in 2004 that I felt accepted for who I was. The Bay Area is a special place to me—the temperate weather, the colors of the sunlight, the landscape, the proximity to the Pacific Ocean and the mountains, the fact that there, many European and Asian American cultures mix. No one thought it was a big deal that I was half-German, half-Japanese. I felt at home immediately. It's funny because the Latinx communities usually thought I was one of them. The way they looked at me and automatically spoke to me in Spanish gave me an odd but very nice sense of normalcy. In San Francisco, people didn't ask me how long I lived where and what language I dreamed in; people didn't ask me where I preferred to live, and if I thought I was ever going to go back.

I connected with artist-activists like Scott Tsuchitani, who criticized "both sides": through his work, mostly racism and representations of "Asians and Asianness" in visual culture. But Scott also criticized a sense of stagnancy within the Japanese American community, which didn't make things easier for him. I related to this, to criticize and be criticized, and fight on multiple fronts. My conversations with Scott were very important; I think our experiences had a lot in common even though we came from very different backgrounds. In retrospect, I think we shared a sense of feeling "orphaned" by our reference cultures, by history, and by what were supposed to be our communities. Although this is my projection now, over ten years later, I'm not sure if Scott would agree with me.

Discovering Rea Tajiri's *History and Memory: For Akiko and Takashige* (1991) was very meaningful for me at the time. The way Tajiri went beyond official recorded history, interweaving fragments of memory and family history, in order to make sense of her personal history. The way she used absence to declare presence was an approach I had never seen before. The personal was nested in family/community/national/transnational narratives. I became very interested in Japanese American history, as it's deeply marked by the friction between American and Japanese national histories; at the time it felt as close as it would get to finding a (proxy) history I could relate to, and this became a premise for my second film, *Remote Intimacy* (2007).

The time I spent on the Pacific Rim was formative for me as a filmmaker. It was around this time that I discovered Trinh T. Minh-ha's work; her writing, in particular, was hugely influential for me. I remember the first time I read one of her essays, I felt like I had been struck by lightning. I woke from some sort of slumber, deeply inspired, even enlightened. She wrote—I'm afraid

I forgot in which essay it was—that one should not self-marginalize or stay on the margins, but continually move in, out, around, through, and beyond different contexts. My memory is likely making modifications, but this is the meaning I understood and took away from that first essay I read about fifteen years ago.

This quote has haunted me: "Neither black/red/yellow nor woman but poet or writer." It's funny, because I identified with so much of what she wrote: all the while her work made me critical of the processes involved in making films around/about the politics of identity. I began to question and scrutinize my first biographical essays: this process led to me to work around these issues in a much more abstract, nonverbal, and metaphorical way.

This makes me think of a fellow half-German, half-Japanese artist, Hito Steyerl, who has made a point of not overtly discussing anything related to her identity. In an interview, she says that there'd been "a historical pressure to confess or use a confessional discourse among ethnic minorities in Germany, and that it's the only possible story you're supposed to tell, like relying on your origins or ancestry or stuff like that. But the problem with these stories is that if they do not correspond to the prefabricated stereotypes existing around this specific minority, then people will not be satisfied. And that's sort of a trap or double bind, let's put it like that. You are forced to confess, but whatever you say will not be what people expected and will therefore be invalid. I always tried to avoid getting caught up in this double bind, so I never made any work which could be understood as fitting into that category."

I believe that it's possible to make films in ways that don't easily fit into one or the other category. But this is what I think now: I wasn't so confident about it when I began making films. After ten years of making abstract work, I'm returning to making personal film essays about my experiences. I'm ready to take this on again now; I feel the need to open up a space for myself, and hopefully for others as well—no matter what audiences expect and how they judge it.

I can't think of films (or essays) that I encountered in Germany—or Japan, for that matter—that related as deeply to my own experience, at least not in the way that I was impacted by the Asian American context. Being removed from it, as an outsider looking in, allowed me to see all categories and labels as temporary tools, that nothing is static, just like an identity is never static—it's always in the process of becoming. While identity categories allow for communities to shape around them, I believe they must always be questioned, scrutinized, opened up, even exploded, before being reassembled in new articulations. I see this reflected in the way I've labeled myself over the course of my life: Hafu, half-Japanese, bicultural, intercultural, mixed-race, and transnational. But language plays a role as well: in American English,

I've also been a Hapa, in German, it's always been very complicated, while in Japanese, I've always been nothing but Hafu.

I've really valued our friendship over the years, Aily. I've really appreciated your confidence, your thinking, your programming, and your projects in the art and film world. It's been inspiring and exciting to see a slightly stronger Hafu presence, and more representation, in the arts, and of course beyond.

頑張ろう。

Much love,
Sylvia

MARTIN WONG

MARTIN WONG
117 SOUTH STREET
NEW YORK 10038
MR & MRS BEN FIE
344 EWING TERRACE
SAN FRANCSCO
CALIFORNIA 94118
EARLY CANCER DETECTION
PAP TEST
USA 13c

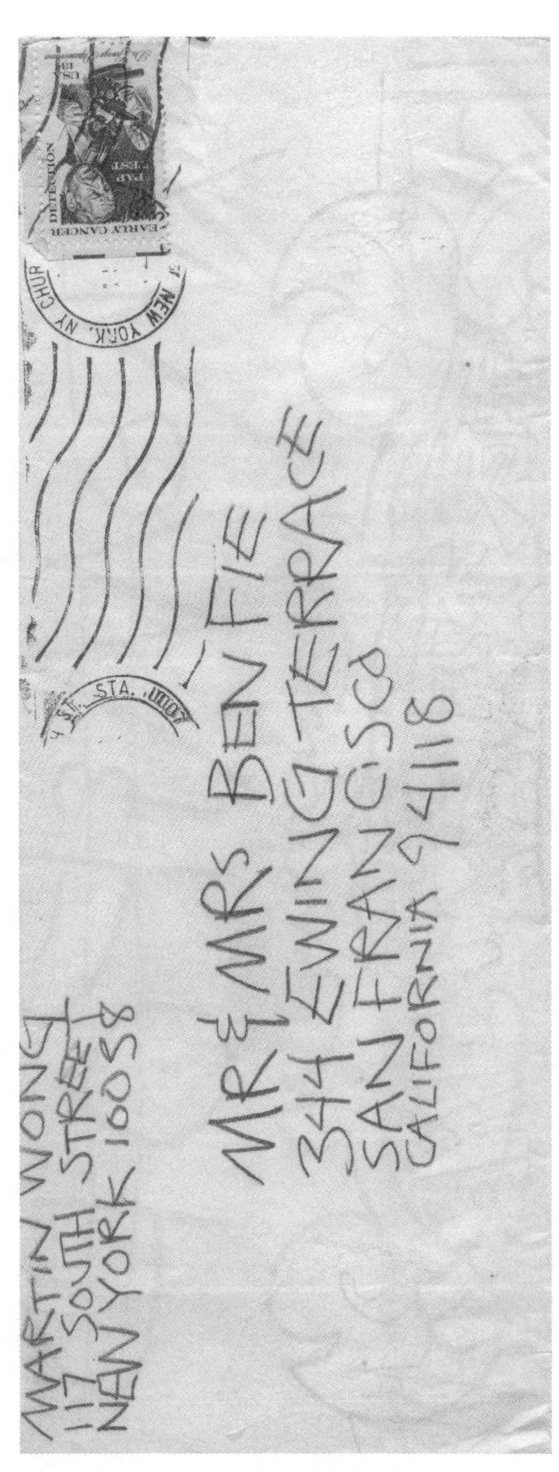

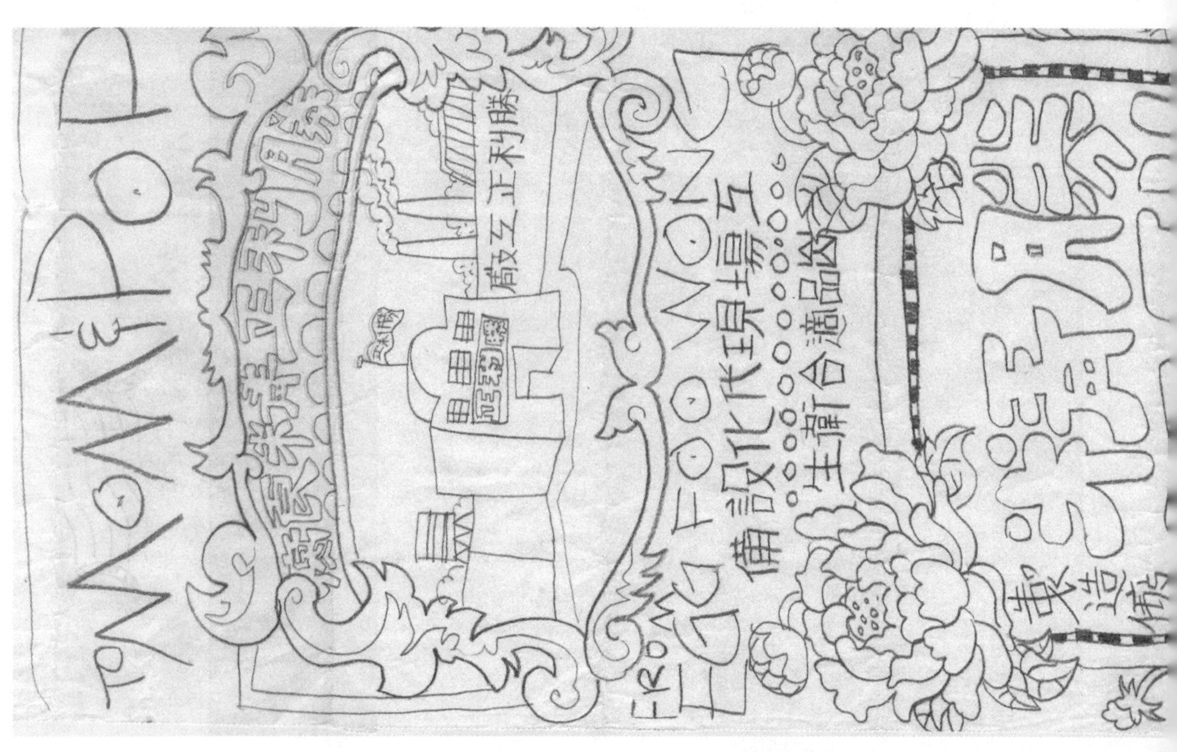
TO WANG POP
FROM EGG FOO WONG

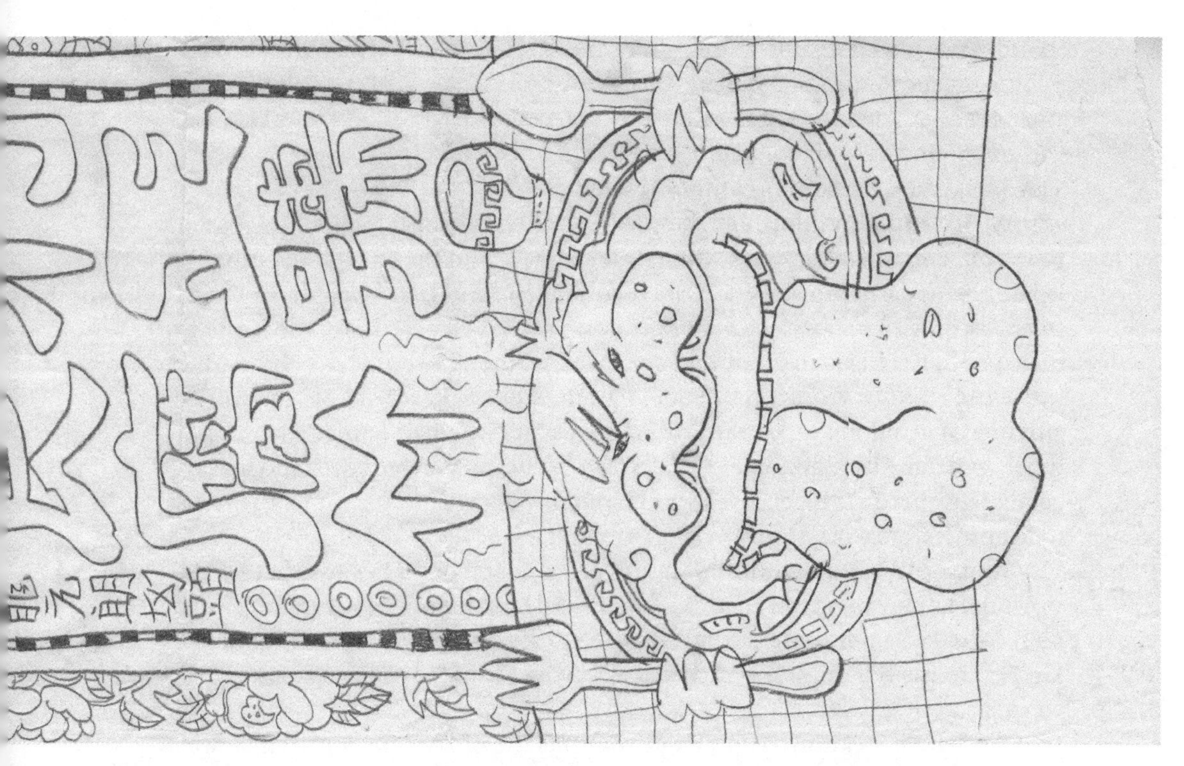

MO KONG

2020

Dear Ma:

This is your son, JiangJiang. How are you?

We have been talking almost every day since February—about the Lunar New Year, Grandpa's sickness, China's lockdown, and the COVID-19 outbreak in the US. In early February, I worried about your and Dad's health, so I tried to check in with you twice every day; now you have been doing the same to me since March. I always told you, *don't worry, I am safe*, but I had a hard time processing what's going on outside. I am anxious and scared by New York's situation; I just don't want you to get anxious and worried for me. There is not much to do besides stay home. Thank you for sending me the gloves and masks. I actually went to the Black Lives Matter march and gave away some extra masks to the protesters. Sorry, I promised I wouldn't go.

You worried about my immigration process. It paused because of COVID-19; I don't know when I can go back visit you and Dad. It's been four years already. I am sorry I was not there during Lunar New Year, when you said "Everyone's kid is at home but ours." I was crying with you. I hope to see you soon. I miss you dearly.

The whole lockdown experience reminds me of SARS in 2003, which was my last year in middle school. I remembered the schools were closed, and I was staying at Grandpa's house for the whole summer. It didn't feel as scary as coronavirus, maybe because I was too young. Like you always said, "As you get older, you are more scared of death." Lately I've had dreams about my childhood, classmates, playing in the field, even exams. Maybe I've been away from home too long—I just miss every single thing.

Being an artist in New York is very difficult, especially as an immigrant. I never said that to you; I just assume we both know that, and crying about it won't solve the issues. I've actually been thinking about taking a break from art during the pandemic, to just have a normal life, work from 10 AM to 6 PM, have weekends and vacations, stop worrying about the studio, rent, and three temporary jobs. I am exhausted. It feels like there is only one thing I want to do—to make art—but I have to figure out ten other things first. But you know how stubborn and moody I am! I will let you know when I change my mind.

Miss you and everything at home. Love you.
Mo

WANGSHUI

Dear P,

When I look at you, I see ocean history eugenics war. Victory pain prophecy pore. Obsessive repulsive desire shame. Semen scandal rapture fame. Feces fly fantasy faith. Paradox pleasure corporeal coup.

You are my effigy dew.

Love,
S

LUKE LUOKUN CHENG

7/14/2020

Dear Reader,

It's punishingly hard to do nothing.

These days when I crash, any sort of mental, emotional, or muscular effort—even watching videos or holding up my phone against a pillow—exhausts me and slows my recovery. The doctors call it an energy envelope, but it feels more like a cage, one that closes in on me every time I try to escape.

The night of a crash, my body burns while my thoughts thrash like lightning flashing over wildfire. The sound of my offbeat heart is thunder in my chest while I wait for sleep. After six hours of tossing and turning, I wake up dead tired and sore everywhere; my poop is mush; my mind loses focus in the middle of conversation. I have to spend the day in bed doing absolutely nothing, and then again the next day, and for a week or more after that. Then, I'll get maybe a few days of respite before the slightest thing—a long video call or some light gardening—triggers another brutal freefall.

I used to feel fine between these episodes of "post-exertional malaise," but over time, my cage got so small that I started to feel symptoms every day. Long before the pandemic hit, I had become mostly housebound.

—

As early as 2017, I knew something was wrong. But over and over again, I was told by doctors, friends, and family—in explicit and implicit terms—that I was probably just depressed or overworked, that my symptoms were psychological, or that it was my fault. For my father, my affliction was inextricably tied to my assumed faith in Western modernity, which included my "gay lifestyle" and the medications I had taken over the years.

Last November, after three years of denials and dismissals, I finally received a diagnosis from Dr. Susan Levine, who looked at me with a soft gaze and told me that I had ME/CFS, a noncommunicable, systemic disease with a clumsy, deceptive name: myalgic encephalomyelitis, or chronic fatigue syndrome. It's often triggered by viral infection and results in energy depletion on a cellular level, leaving many of its patients house- or bed-bound, with the majority unable to hold a job. The most severely affected spend 24/7 in bed wearing eye masks and earplugs because even light stimulus causes them pain. Dr. Levine and others had been studying the syndrome for decades, but the scientific community still had few leads on its cause or treatment. In the US, ME/CFS has the same number of cases as HIV but receives less than a fraction of a percent of the research funding. In the 90s, the CDC was even caught diverting pre-allocated funding away from investigating the disease. Dr. Levine told me that I could learn how to function better, but that I'd probably never recover or be cured.

I was participating in an art incubator program associated with the New Museum at the time, but after the diagnosis, it became clear that my work was accelerating my disability. I took permanent medical leave and shut down my other projects one by one. Then I parted ways with my boyfriend and moved in with my parents in Virginia.

In the following months, I would often descend into a blind rage. I wanted to rip apart the egos of every doctor who was too arrogant to admit that I might have an illness that they didn't yet understand. I wanted the NIH to know the desperate fury of a 28-year old watching himself descend into disability and not know how or why, only that he was losing faith in an entire civilization.

I thought being queer was enough of a cosmic joke, but being crippled by a mysterious illness takes the cake. When I came out to my mother in 2013, she was afraid I'd die of AIDS before I hit 30. I constantly worried about the dangers of loving another man, only to succumb to an illness with a far lower quality of life.

Six years after coming out, my mother's views had softened, but I was still trying to prove to my parents and myself that my desires weren't karmically cursed—that not only would I survive past thirty but that I too could obtain the model-minority American dream, like some hot, rich, White gay dad in a Human Rights Campaign ad but with more filial piety. That aspiration imploded when I got sick, like the collapse of an aging star.

I said goodbye to myriad things in the aftermath of my diagnosis, with something new to let go of each day: the glamor of wearing a homemade "look" to a Bubble_T party, precious friendships I could no longer maintain, the thrill of making eye contact in the gym showers, and the heat of another body next to mine; the exhilaration of swimming a lap at full speed, the splendor of mountaintop views, the satisfaction of reracking weights after a set of squats, and my vain hopes of finally putting on some muscle. I gave up not only refined sugars, staying up late, porn, shopping, and social media, but also hiking, gardening, cooking, karaoke, and travel. I bid farewell to creating installations, then sewing, and then digital artmaking. I stopped watching films, then playing video games, and finally, listening to music.

Eventually, I lost the parts of myself that I prized most. I put aside hopes and dreams that I held too close to even say aloud. My libido withered. I couldn't get hard anymore while awake, yet woke up with painful erections at night. I had been proud of my ability to think fast, learn quickly, and work hard, but before long, I lost that, too. Despite holding a degree in applied math, I started to struggle with adding up figures. I found myself forgetting details I had heard only moments before and straining to hold onto my own train of thought. Emails became hard to write—not to mention this letter. When I first got sick, I took comfort in reading texts like *Illness as Metaphor*, but months later, I could barely finish a chapter of *Harry Potter*. Even talking too much to family and friends started causing me to crash, and soon I was down to one 30-minute conversation a day.

And when I had nothing left of my own to grieve, I thought of those things we all lost: a third of the Earth's coral reefs; a third of the entire bird population of North America, as well as oysters and salmon and the living things they sustained; the lives of countless Black brothers and sisters; the innumerable Indigenous peoples and cultures extinguished in a continent-wide genocide.

—

Anguish is hard to sustain in this body. When I get too tired, I let everything float downstream. In my dissociation, the seconds stretch out like the vast mirror of a salt flat, while entire decades speed by in a single glance. I let myself be transported back to the mid-Atlantic forests of my childhood and to the smell of ripe peaches on Shanghai streets. Fragments of my past blend with films, songs, and novels: rippling waves of tall grass as I chase after a lover, the scurrying of a plover among tiny clam holes in the sand, a vast carpet of golden ginkgo leaves in October.

I linger in fragile moments on the border of intimacy. In my Chinatown apartment, I look into the eyes of a soon-to-be lover lying shirtless on the bathroom floor as I prepare to trim his beard. In a friend's dark bedroom, he admits that he has wondered what it would feel like to lay his lips on another man's body for the first time. And on a train from New York back to Princeton, I sit by my straight college friend whom I've silently fallen in love with; as the day turns to night, I feel the warmth of his head landing softly on my shoulder.

In my days spent awake in bed, I think about the artist Ron Athey and wonder what it was like for him to perform *Incorruptible Flesh: Dissociative*

Sparkle. He spent five hours lying naked, face-up on a metal rack, with his eyelids pulled open, his entire body glistening with Vaseline, his ass penetrated by a baseball bat. Was that experience anything like one of my crashes? In those wide-eyed, gaping hours, he was a most permeable medium. What did he see? What did he receive?

—

A growing body of scientific research portrays the human body not as the discrete, monolithic entity that the Euro-American imagination envisions, but rather as a porous and ever-shifting ecosystem of interdependent organisms and cells, some with human DNA but most without.

Suspended in a febrile daze, I become a cacophonous collaboration of trillions of microbes, my consciousness an emergent property of the signals they send back and forth. But my mitochondria can't produce energy the way they used to. Lactic acid builds up too quickly in my muscles and brain. The delicate balance of my gut microbiome is askew, and my intestinal walls have become leaky, allowing bacteria to slip into my bloodstream. My body is chronically inflamed, perhaps caused by the remnants of a viral infection that my weakened immune system just can't erase.

This is all to say: my metabolism has been hijacked by a self-perpetuating pattern that's crippling me.

Sometimes I imagine the whole living Earth commiserating with me—our shared fever inaugurating a mass extinction, our bodies infected and reinfected with a lingering virus, our metabolisms rewired into an accelerating flywheel of accumulation and consumption, with toxins building up in our arteries faster than we can expel. We're a flesh-and-blood version of the optimization models I studied in college, and I wish I knew how to stop it.

—

Did you know that before coral colonies die, they become fluorescent? Like humans and our resident bacteria, coral polyps depend on a mutualistic relationship between animal and algae. That bond breaks down when ocean waters become too warm, and the coral eject their microbial partners. Naked and alone, the coral's own fluorescent proteins become more visible, and in the final moments before they starve, they glow more vividly than ever before. Is it a cry for help? Or perhaps a swan song?

As for me, I don't get to sing my own dirge. There's no martyrdom to be found in ME/CFS—I expect to live well into my fifties, even if half of it's in bed. But looking out at the world from my room, I can't help but feel like I'm disappearing.

It's been said that yellow-skinned people are rendered invisible here in the US—seen but not heard, imagined as part of a past or future but not the present, a ghost in the machine. But how much more of a specter is the yellow-skinned person who is bedridden? And what does it mean to be a ghost in a world where an ever-expanding Euro-American modernity insists that nothing is haunted? Where do the spirits go when we sever ties to the past, to locality, to each other? And what will become of me?

—

The writer Ocean Vuong once mentioned that he loved the story of Noah's Ark as a kid because it asked the crucial question: "When the apocalypse comes, what do we decide to put in the vessel for the future?" For those of us whose worlds have already ended once, perhaps the best thing to arise is a growing certainty about what to take with us as we journey into the years and decades to come.

I may not be able to carry much anymore, but the things I hold are that much more precious:

My 14-year-old sister sitting on my bed after a bad crash, softly narrating to me a video game I can't play;

the drifting, heartbeat glow of fireflies at the edge of the woods, the lonely beetles reaching out to each other at the end of a summer day;

and the gentle, life-changing words of my straight college friend when I finally confessed my love to him.

Knowing I was closeted and miserable, he looked at me with warmth and said, "Maybe it's time for a change."

Luke Luokun Cheng

YARA EL-SHERBINI AND NAEEM MOHAIEMEN

Passing Comment I

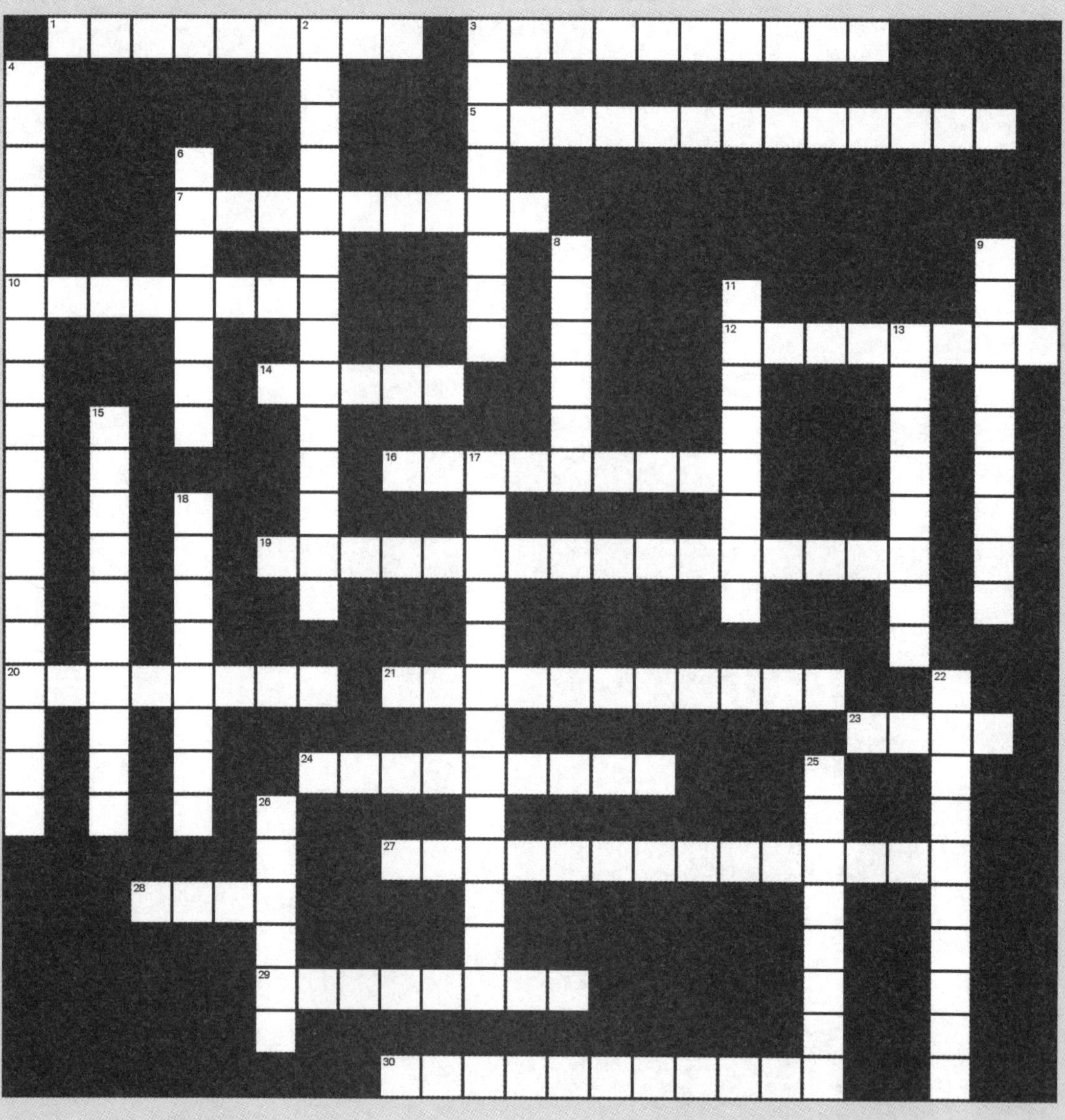

Across

1 A scarlet coloured ghost in the shell.

3 From Thai king to robot gunslinger for this Russian-American.

5 British Indian actor playing Iraqi soldier in *Lost*.

7 Sherman Alexie affirmatively chose this Chinese nom de plume poet.

10 Blackface, from Russia without love.

12 Danzy Senna's fugitive belongs to which radical group?

14 Lebanese safe car enthusiast who ran for President.

16 Aloha, a white stone cast as half Asian.

19 They did not get the memo(ir) when they cast Chinese actors as Japanese.

20 British Pakistani actor playing Arab terrorist in *True Lies*.

21 For a change, Rue was not what some fans of this series imagined.

23 Chinese detective played sixteen times by Swedish actor Warner Oland.

24 I mean the soil is authentic, you want Chinese actors as well?

27 Royalty must have given a major Farrokh to change name.

28 Cumberbatch went into darkness, and entered another dimension.

29 British Pakistani actor playing Iranian restaurateur in *The English Harem.*

30 Mr. White on *Saturday Night* before he went solo.

Down

2 Molly Ringwald regrets this old flame that burnt bridges with Asian audiences.

3 Rooney, taking the mickey with that accent in *Breakfast at Tiffany's*.

4 Ben Kingsley's Kenyan Indian birth name, invisible in *Gandhi*.

6 British King to Civil Rights King, this Londoner David has range.

8 What Ridley Scott says would not be financed if he cast "Mohammad so-and-so from such-and-such".

9 His Pudd'nhead Wilson was a radical novel in 1894, today can give a classroom pause.

11 We were bamboozled by a box office flop for this director.

13 On this hit TV show, even Arabic pretends to be what it is not.

15 Anthony Hopkins acting biracial playing white.

17 Angelina Jolie, a Pearl of a different hue.

18 British Pakistani actor playing Afghani ally to James Bond.

22 Top Forty kept Arab roots out of the radio.

25 We were the opposite of furious with this Samuel Jackson casting.

26 Geoffrey Holder, could you at least get that Annie accent right?

Across

1 JOHANSSON
3 YULBRYNNER
5 NAVEENANDREWS
7 YIFENCHOU
10 ALJOLSON
12 PANTHERS
14 NADER
16 EMMASTONE
19 MEMOIRSOFAGEISHA
20 ARTMALIK
21 HUNGERGAMES
23 CHAN
24 GOODEARTH
27 FREDDIEMERCURY
28 KHAN
29 ARTMALIK
30 EDDIEMURPHY

Down

2 SIXTEENCANDLES
3 YUNIOSHI
4 KRISNAPANDITBHANJI
6 OYELOWO
8 EXODUS
9 MARKTWAIN
11 SPIKELEE
13 HOMELAND
15 HUMANSTAIN
17 MARIANNEPEAR
18 ARTMALIK
22 CASEYKASEM
25 NICKFURY
26 PUNJAB

MARGARET LEE

Dear Sanmao,

It's hard to imagine what your audience felt reading accounts of your travels around the world, especially your stories of the Sahara from the 1970s. Your adventures most likely provided young women with hope that their futures could expand beyond traditional patriarchal family constraints.

But reading the first few pages of *Stories of the Sahara* in 2019, I could not help but feel mistrustful. Your "liberation" appeared to depend on the novelty of Otherness—both your Othering of the people of the Sahara and your own self-exoticization, which allowed you to stay separate. I could look past your being an unreliable narrator, but your self-aggrandizing observations bothered me. I get it. You are special; there's no denying this. And it is your specialness that made it impossible for me to stop reading. But maybe I also kept reading because I was hoping to see your narrative shift, from tourist to ally.

It is a strange and difficult position to be neither here nor there. In your case, to be neither colonizer nor Indigenous. I came to see this in-between status as what provided you the space to question what was generally accepted. Your prying questions were forgiven: you were an outsider, your perceptions were regarded as uninformed and generally resulted in humorous misunderstandings. It wasn't until I arrived at your story of the mute slave that I came to understand how your leaving home was connected to your understanding of oppression. When your husband and the affluent Sahrawi tried to convince you not to worry, to assure you that slavery was simply part of the culture and that slaves were treated "well," you refused to accept this position. You refused to stop making trouble, and in the case of the mute slave, you refused to turn away.

No one can be sure whether your story of the mute slave was fabricated or embellished, but this does not matter to me. If your narrative was constructed, it does not take away from the reality of the experience of those forced into human bondage, of those whose humanity has been stripped and relegated to property—and the cruelty of those who benefit from or accept these conditions as unchangeable. Fiction or not, I felt deeply your desire to set free the enslaved and the devastating realization that an individual's desire alone cannot change the conditions that create systems of oppression, especially if met with indifference from the larger society.

Though there are two more stories in the collection, my memory of you—the outsider observer—will forever be tied to the image of you, without thinking, pulling the blanket off your bed to offer as a last gift. My memory of you, Sanmao, is that of the outsider observer who wasn't always outside and who wasn't only observing.

xoxo,
ML

C. SPENCER YEH

Heya !! Hi HI !

Firstly, let me take a moment to shout out to my AZ-AM RHINOS in the field. ... From since then to now ... no one TRULY feels our pain (if there IS any pain, RIGHT ?>?). ... We KNOW how to be that exotic in the field. ... We KNOW how much that value means.... And yet, where is there even to GO with it? We r tired of "eating it," but I kinda feel like that's pretty much what we gotta do again. ... I simply don't know if I trust our expressions against it as being any GOOD. ...

~~So pardon the delay in getting back to ya—tonite I did a pretty DEEP hang with a friend ... A WHITEBOY friend. ... Real good friend, ppl got a lotta thoughts bout him but he's one I don't know how to quit. ... Angry young guy, but we have good talks. ... And while, yet again, attempting to maaaybe unpack alla this. ... I did explode, I threw a buncha self-told-reminded unproductive words around. ... Or, at least, I immediately labeled them as being HMMM ... UNPRODUCTIVE. ... Despite me usin the hang as a punching bag, my abovementioned friend tho, continued to try to encourage me to give voice too whatever the fuck it is I was trying to talk about—by the way, I get waaaay to caught up in sorting out all the emotions and logic and allowance and reason for even being able to say SOMETHING ?? Also, duh,ehrtyhwy46I have been a very sensitive watcher of a hmmm CRINGE radar. ... I really really really want to try to work towards a concision, believe me!! I don't always wanna explode at 3 AM in the karaoke bar saying some sort of thing about not feeling like a human or IDK wtf. ...~~

TBH, so much of this attempt at "reppin" or whatever, in terms of being Asian American ... OK ... I at this point do NOT want to take a shit on ppl who feel strongly towards certain identities and values. ... I just ... I really just do not care at this point right now, because to actually be felt, and to be held, is rare. ...

So, here's my best attempt at a thesis: Because of the alienation, trauma, and abuse experienced as an immigrant in largely White communities in the US, I got a lot of ANGER and a lot of PAIN. In not having much of a support network or guidance available, I just sorta made up my own way to get through life, being trained in the best that a White male supremacy can give you, as AMAB. As a side note, I never felt very much draw or attachment to much of masculinity (of which I would get to know its various forms beyond the usual stuff, including various visions of AZ-AM masculinity). So eventually, and luckily, I was able to have these.

Oh hey, I also had been thinkin a TON about this tweet—

> a hard lesson i had to learn as a survivor: You are doing a disservice to yourself, your healing, and everyone around you if you only consider yourself someone who can Be Hurt, but never as someone who can Cause Harm
>
> It's often hard to admit you've been Hurt, Assaulted, and Survived. It's also hard to admit that you have the capacity for harm too. But if you are in any way committed to the project of transformative justice and abolition, you must hold both those truths
>
> —@sloane_jett

I've also FINALLY gotten on this path recognizing that, for better or worse, I contributed to the climate of harm, to being damaging, to hell, IDK what, just thru participating to just bein around. ... I know MEN tend to hang back and NOT make any pronouncement or take a position until all those around them are driven CRAZY and eventually have to take a fucking stance themselves and set up some kinda boundaries, which isn't to say that it's a COLD move. ... It SUCKS. However, you totally SEE where things COULD head ... so you try to stay AHEAD of it. So yeah ... mostly dudes will routinely talk about how they felt blindsided "outta nowhere" by an eventual burst of feeling or reaction from the one sitting across from them ... and yes, guess who usually LOSES in terms of the unofficial divvying of friends and social scene ... WHO is ready to TAKE that HIT in the name of not just themselves, but hmmm, perhaps some dude who is NOT ready to DEAL? IDK. This is a lotta caps and I actually feel like I'm addicted to making CAPS more than anything else rn. ...

It's so fucking dark, that vibe. ... This idea, where, in order to prove stakes and a position in masculinity, that you gotta hmmm ... How could I rephrase this. ... You know those Angry Yellow MEN ... I can hear and write these gripes ... I'm sorry, though ... I have not always known ... I just get tired hearing these assertions of BEING. ... Hey, listen, I just turned 45, and a part of brt4bns4 me knows NOW that ... not everything is gonna happen that my little BOY deserves ... just in the same way where progressive thinkers LONG AGO knew that they would not see a BETTER TOMORROW. ...

When the QUAR hit, and it was asked that we all basically denied desires and got invisible, I was like, "Oh wait, this thing I barely was able to finally name ... this ability that I KNOW and absolutely recognize ... it is actually easy and necessary right NOW ???"

I mean, at a certain point, in my younger years, I totally told someone that the idea of kissing another ASIAN would feel like I was kissing my LITTLE SISTER. ... So therefore ... YUCK. ...

I'm really curious what some of y'all may see in imagining getting it ON with another ASIAN. ...

So flash forward to NOW, when I am FINALLY like ... yes (what we ALL knew all along, including White dudes in the after-hours at The STONE). ... No juh46 that BREAKTHROUGH be rewarded and available to me ... well ... yeah ... guess what ... yeah ... no ... (And to the side: clearly you have OTHER things in these stakes to address at this point....)

In one organization, amongst MANY that I fuck with, WE all, upon request by the White leadership, do a breakout group of all *non-Whites, in an attempt to do some kinda, IDK. ... OMG FINALLY we have SPACE to figure out how to IDK whatever. Anyway, the real revelation was that, amongst a good grip of Azns ... a good majority hadh46hj46 never made out with another "Asian." ... What am I asking for? It's kinda dark, it's kinda lame. ... If you wanna see a deeper dive into it, turn on like IDK... *STRANGER THINGS*, and watch how a lil White CISHET boy pretty much deserves his object of desire. ... I'd like to think at a certain point in younger years, I was absolutely following orders. ... We know where that claim gets ya though. ...

Hey listen, I was around after-hours in a very hallowed and notable and yet oft-debated spot for some sorta kinda music. ... I was there sitting around thinking I was IN on some kinda after-hours sorta IDK what (truly, I was not seeking much other than just ... ya know ... being around). ... So I was sitting around with a buncha dudes who are IN the SCENE ... and OMG ... I'm gonna be a snitch here—there was a moment where all these White dudes had a laugh about how they were "partnered" with "Asian women." ... OMG that's hilarious ... DUDES, I'm barely hanging onto my own shit, but ... hey ... to do this IN FRONT OF ME? I mean ... honestly, I am used to this. ... Srsly ... what is the choice here? Feel "emasculated" and subsequently try to sling hella dumplings and cheese pizza by talking about "poppin bottles and models / from railroads to General Tso's now we movin and feedin mad hoes?" Just to what? ... Feel what? Again, is there even room to wonder this additional complication I had been asking?

I mean, I will absolutely seek out ANY reason to just ... hrmmm ... feel BAAAD for myself and how COOOMPLICAATED my own situation is. ... And yes, that has been an issue getting in the way of me actually hearing and feeling for others ... because, I ... When it really comes down to it ... I just don't actually let anyone know the full story (and, print publication exclusive… still haven't, TBH). … You know how it goes. … It hangs around for WAY TOO LONG and feels WACK and OLD. … And in any case, sometimes we are just people living in transition time. … We push along towards something not quite visible. … You know … one thing I think about is how "yesterday's REVOLUTION is tomorrow's PROBLEM."… Ask Howie. .. he got me on this (sorry Howie) …

I have lately been thinking a TON about "White adjacency." … IDK why it took me so long to google that term! I knew it! It's in my bones! It was at a time, maybe, my alibi!! WHITE ADJACENCY … I thought it'd truly be my alibi for being canceled, but you know what? NO. …

Sure, sure. Listen, yes, we all make "mistakes" … we all exhibit "bad behavior" … "ill judgment." … All that being said, it is still NOT a level playing field. … And you know what? The same way some AZN chef dood wants to flex his MANness, some AZN dood wanna talk about how he is the master over CIS women of a certain vibe? What the fuck u want dude? I really DO NOT get it. Whatever u want is OVER. Why do y'all love CARS so much?? Where ya goin with this?? Honestly, even the in-between sitch would still involve some seemingly chill White dude in the mix. …

So when I gave voice to this, when I took it on a long JOYRIDE … so MUCH seemed to SNAP into PLACE. … NO LEVEL PLAYING FIELD EVER. I absolutely knew I RESENTED this. I wanted to BLAME this forced socialization that we "stumbled" into … and yet, there are no "clean getaways." I am COMPLICIT regardless. … Heya, I didn't ask for "this," but also, I am now responsible "for this." …

I guess this is at this point as decent as any place to put this…. Very shortly after being born and then moving to, firstly Canada when I was 2, and then a southwest Ohio suburb when I was 5 … Hmmmm some things happened along the way that I keep thinking about, that I think I can still see, if I try hard enough. But I know I cannot even fully identify—if not BEGIN this magical process of letting go—no matter how I try, even now. And of course, there's always people telling me I am taking it wrong … not necessarily remembering what I may have thought happened. … But … you know … if I can take this moment to throw this out there … imagine being the only single available slant-eyed, yellow-skinned, super-afraid, and yet willing to comply, child available for miles. … It really kinda sucks when White people wanna talk me down from even trying to get towards something that feels very, very wrong. …

Firstly: over life, I've learned that to even try to bring ANYTHING troubling up—yeah, no one wants to hear about it. And then, I don't know (and here we go) it's when like a White person basically is like, "Oh hey, I ALSO felt ALIENATED growing up as well!" At this point, there's PLENTY I am keeping track of, and I know about de-escalating and am absolutely in love with the ability to do that with my long-long-term partner, IN THE MOMENT. ... But you know what, put her aside for a moment. ... It's kinda harsh as fuck when you realize you are being dismissed in an attempt to "normalize."

Hey ... anyways, again, so super good to be thought of to write a letter to you, and perhaps have it on record?? ... What a forgotten and overlooked forme-ht6heh, in this age of QUIPS and HOT TAKES. ... BTW I am surprised and feel nicely included in an ask list. ... Oh right, the rec literally was in the subject line of the initial email. ... If I can be LOL and REAL in some ways, IDK ... we all talk about how this QUAR has been like, an exposé about how alla this shit works, how there is SO MUCH bullshit we try to navigate in order to do "nryhnrtyhrour thing." ... For a moment, for myself, at the prompt of a beacon (HOWIE! YOU KNOW WHO I AM SAYING) FINALLY moving to NYC and eyes FINALLY opened ... maybe finding others who KNOW how this goes, and who MAYBE could help me work thru some self-hate. ... Given how my own personal experienc-gh5her7giue to this date in terms of actually knowing or feeling this in terms of whatever this contributor list tells me, ... it's not like I'm gonna see any of y'all anytime soon. ... Honestly, support can and will happen unconditionally. ...

Hey, you know what, when I feel like I finally reached what may have led me to this next step of maaaaybe finally being "OK" with "myself"—finally maaaybe identifying and linking up with a scene that is made up of somewhat remotely AZN-made-UP?

I KNOW we do NOT have space for EVERY other SUCKER who finally crawls UP this WAKEUP MOUNTAIN. However, I just feel triggered, honestly, about how the rare Asian I'd crossed paths with would basically act as if I should step the fuck off/away.... I mean, I get it.... You have your own exotic empire or whatever, IDK. I kinda don't even care because, based on my own attempted tell-all, I'd rather kiss an uh.... OK can we just re-meet in five-ish years and talk about "solidarity"? And yet, that does not mean a make-out....

IDK, that's cool. I ABSOLUTELY support—you know, this IS a time for rejuvenation, reflection etc. BTW, just tonight some White friends reached out to me (after years and years, OMG the CRAY of this QUAR) asking why I wasn't in touch, and took the risk of admitting their long-held investment in our relationship. ... I tried to chalk it up to some kinda depression or existential IDK or whatev, but honestly IDK, after all these years it feels like a cop-out. But for real, some of y'all still reading, real talk, I hadn't heard of y'all either. ...

When I was in the midst of my very formative seventeen-year-long, full-time office job in Cincinnati in the 2000s, to fully subsidize what I guess were my contributions towards—passions? IDK, Art?—there was a time I wanted to grow my hair out. This dude in my work zone (DUH yes, a WHITE dude ... BTW, holding some sorta senior position in the workplace at that), upon seeing that I had some long hair, basically helped himself to put his hands on my head and

TUG on my ponytail being like, "Hey Spencer! Whoa, what's going on here?" IDK Dhfhiuhiutghiufrshjk (I really do not care what he said after, bc, I was hmmm) ... in front of people, the same way I'd been put on the spot in public before, and over and over again. ...

You know what? Never mind all this talk goin on rn. ... UP UP DOWN DOWN LEFT LEFT RIGHT I just do NOT trust any of y'all right now. I don't even know what to trust you ABOUT. I thought your revelations would rescue me right now, being in the middle of the field ... being a dummy. PLEASE let me know what YOU think is next. ... Actually, if you've read this, don't bother!!

Best,
Spencer

August 10, 2020

VINAY HIRA

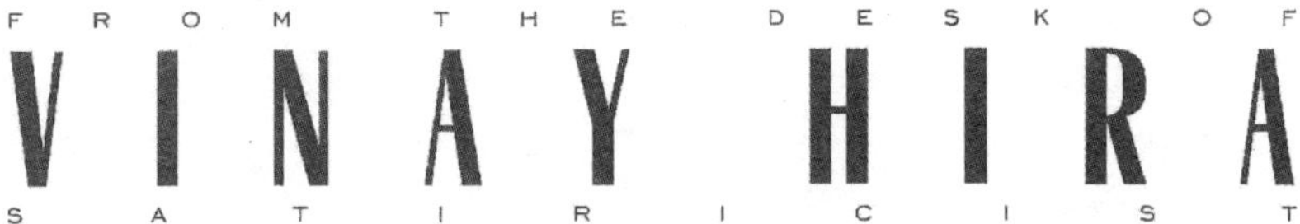

PO Box40434
Glenfield
North Shore City
0747
@vinayyhira

20th November 2K15

To Whom It May Concern,

Regrettably I inform you, that this letter is my resignation,

From client services officer, my Fidelity Life designation.

I thank you for the support and this opportunity,

A better fit to the role and team you will find presumably.

The 24th of December will be my last day of employment,

I apologize, but feel for this office, I may be a little too flamboyant.

Kind Regards

Vinay Hira

WWW.VINAYHIRA.COM

ANICKA YI

Dear Chris,

I enjoyed our discussion, and I have some follow-up thoughts.

When we talked, we realized that we'd both started late in art. For me, this comes into the race question, the immigrant story. My parents didn't provide the tools for me to explore what I might want to pursue—vocationally, creatively, anything. They wanted me to be a newscaster or a lawyer because I was a very vocal young person. But they didn't provide any tools. They didn't help me with my homework, they didn't help me get into the best schools, they didn't buy me books. I'm not saying this to condemn them, because they had enough on their plates. I have an immense compassion for them, for what they were trying to juggle in an America that was very inhospitable to immigrants. I was very lost for a long time. That's why I started art late.

I think that we're also similar—and similar to many Asian Americans—in that we have a lot of baggage. We are trying to decolonize our White supremacist conditioning, and at this moment, we're having to pay attention to our White adjacency and the privilege that comes with it. I know that's a lot of virtue signaling to say those words. But I didn't say that to myself twenty years ago.

I've been thinking a lot about this: Is America fixable? If so, how do we fix it? Because America was not built for you and me, for Black and Brown people. It just wasn't. So at the core, is it possible to change it? I don't know/ What's it going to take? I don't have the answers. But to me, social equity is economic equity. You can't have one or the other.

This is a good time to give you that MLK quote I mentioned. It was sent to me via email by a young follower who is really sharp about seeing the political vectors lining up with our time. It's from the "Three Evils of Society" speech:

> Victor Hugo could have been thinking of 20th-century America when he wrote: "There is always more misery among the lower classes than humanity among the higher classes." The time has come for America to face the inevitable choice between materialism and humanism. We must devote

> at least as much to our children's education and the health of the poor as we do to the care of our automobiles and the building of beautiful and impressive hotels. We must also realize that the problems of racial injustice and economic injustice cannot be solved without a radical redistribution of political and economic power.

The more we keep peeling these stinky layers, the more I'm thinking we need to throw out the entire onion. I'm not asking for that right now because I don't think we have all the answers. But we do have to take a closer look.

We don't even have to look that close: the history of capitalism is the history of oppression. You have colonialism, you have slavery; if that wasn't a genius stroke of capitalist advancement, I don't know what is. This country, America, would not be where it is without slavery. We know this. If you look at any of these strong, contemporary Asian economies—this has not happened without the complicity of American imperialist agendas.

It's very difficult to extract racial injustice from capitalism. One of the problems I find is that a lot of our granular thinking in the last couple of weeks around racial injustice has been *race, race, race*. But you have to look at all of the tentacles that shape systemic racism, that explain its persistence. To your point: Why are we still talking about this twenty years later? Why haven't we eradicated it? Where is the vaccine for racism? Why haven't we come up with it? Because these systems are designed to perpetuate racism at every turn. Racism is a mutation. You don't have the same type of racist scenarios for every person of color. It's shapeshifting, and it adapts to its needs so it can do its work.

To make a parallel: COVID-19 doesn't distinguish between human beings, bats, and pangolins. It jumped through cell walls and recognized our genes as the evolutionary cousins to those species. Humans think: No, we left nature and the jungles, and we're *here* now, and nature is over *there*. But the virus doesn't know that and doesn't distinguish us from any other kind of animal. Racism works like that, too.

But we have to be careful about this language. I don't want to villainize viruses because viruses are, ironically, our allies. Their function is to regulate monoculture. Their function is to punish the winners. We're all sheltering in place in lockdown because a virus's role is to regulate biodiversity—and humans are terrible for biodiversity. We're an obstacle, an active obstacle, to biodiversity. And so the virus comes along and needs to regulate us. Symbolically, it is our ally. To say "viruses are bad" misses the point. The human genome is 8 percent virus. Without viruses, we would not be alive. Viruses help to regulate life on the planet. The problem is, for us, that we're not its priority. Its priority is biodiverse life, and we are just one form of life among many.

I don't mean this in a narcissistic way (like, oh, *I've* got to crack the code, or even imagine that it could happen in any singular way), but: How do we tackle racism? How do we eradicate it? First of all, human beings are front-lobed primates. We have a neurochemical wiring for xenophobia. We're tribal animals. And we're dealing with something that is inherent in us. Some of us have evolved, but not all of us. So knowing that, as humans, how then do we handle xenophobia?

I think a lot of the obstacles in humanity's attempt to overcome our tribalism are rooted in culture. That's kind of a bombshell because culture is, to me, the apple in the Garden of Eden. It's truly the expression of the best and worst of humanity. On the positive side of culture, you have poetry, music, the arts, organizations of mutual aid, charities, all of that. But then on the other side, you have racism, sexism, homophobia, nationalism. ... Culture is a construct that, like racism, serves its own needs. Humans enable it, in the way that when we go to war to protect our nation-state, it's not to preserve ourselves but to preserve the ideology. Yet we all sign up for it and say, "Yay, go America." That's part of the culture. How do we get rid of that? We can't—unless we actually question culture in its entirety. We can't just make exceptions, extract this part because we don't like it, but keep this other part because it brings us pleasure and happiness. That's what I'm thinking currently.

You know what the police of culture is? Identity. We are so hooked on identity. When you are so tied to your identity, you don't have any objectivity. All you do is see yourself in terms of a type or class of person. But that isn't who you are; those are attributes. We live in a culture where if you dissent or contradict your community and your identity, then you get punished, don't you? You get canceled. This is why we cling to identity. This is why identity is the cop of culture.

We're running out of time. We don't have an infinite surplus of time to workshop this. We've got asteroids looming, we've got climate change, we've got superviruses. This is code orange time.

But ... I'm extremely hopeful. I think I said to you: This is like the Black Power movement meets Yellow Peril meets Occupy Wall Street, against a backdrop of scientific literacy never known before. It's exhilarating!

All best,
Anicka

BRENDAN FERNANDES

Dear Isamu,

I write to you as though we have met, as though we have traveled together, shared meals, and known friends in common. Though we have never been in the same place at the same time, I write these words with a sense of kinship. I write knowing that our energies have crossed paths.

Why do I feel this way? In part, it is that we are both hybrids—in our identities, and in our ways of thinking and making. We are hybrid artists. Our compound identities have allowed us to maneuver through many spaces, to transgress boundaries, and to be in various communities at once. Being resilient and malleable, we have learned to call many places home. In this mobile sense of belonging, we connect to one another.

You are Japanese American, and you lived in both countries. I am a Kenyan-born Goan, and my family immigrated to Canada in 1989—just after you passed away. I can't help but feel that this is part of our connection. The year we arrived in Canada is also the year I began to dance. I now reside in the United States—in Chicago—but I came here to study and to spend time in New York, just like you.

Three years ago, I was invited to create a dance work in your former studio in Long Island City, which has become the Isamu Noguchi Foundation and Garden Museum. Through the museum's invitation, I was able to work in your archive, where I found again and again similarities between the ways that we make and think about art.

Looking at your assemblage sculptures, I realized that in order to put them together, the museum staff had to study and practice the movements required to fit each piece together. They used plywood replicas of your pieces to practice the playful order of operations before installing the original stone and bronze versions. I loved this choreography embedded in these objects. In my own show in your museum, I had three dancers assemble and disassemble these plywood copies in close proximity to the originals. Through performance, the audience gets to see the kind of play and collaboration at work in the still originals. I am still amazed at how corporeal—how much like bodies—your bronzes can feel. Put next to dancers, there's an interaction that happens between body and sculpture: body gets looked at like sculpture, and sculpture gets looked at like body. In the making, it felt like a collaboration between us.

This performance with your assemblages was part of a larger series of interventions we called *Contract and Release*. Contraction and release are central to the modern dance techniques of Martha Graham, with whom you frequently collaborated. I myself am a formally trained Martha Graham dancer, so my research gravitated to the sets you made for her many ballets. I thought about them as platforms for launching a new dance in your museum. I worked with Dakin Hart, the senior curator of the museum, to install a new show of your works titled *Body-Space Devices* that looked at the ways you engaged and represented the body through sculpture. This collaborative show was open for a few months while dancers and I worked on a choreography to intervene in the space. We added scaffolding and my own sculptural devices to the space—rocking chairs, inspired by a chair you made for Martha's ballet *Appalachian Spring*. You made her a rocking chair that did not rock. I added the rocking back in. Martha had wanted a chair she could sit on for the duration of *Appalachian Spring*. But I wanted to build a device that would challenge my dancers to remain still. I tasked them with holding poses from Graham technique while seated in the chairs, but challenged them to remain as still as possible. To do so on the rocking chairs, they would have to contract their muscles continually, until they fatigued and shook and rocked. For audiences, it gave the effect of watching sculptures start to sweat and tremble. Watching the dancers labor asked the audience to empathize in a different way. It challenged their expectations of sculpture and their privilege as viewers.

For me, your collaborations broke down similar barriers. They negotiated a newness by blending and challenging traditions of art and dance. The things you created allowed for new ways to see art and dance together. This has been a huge influence on the way that I make my work, and I thank you for this. To work within your studio, to dance on the sets you made for Martha, it felt like a collaboration with you both, and for that, I count myself extraordinarily lucky.

This kind of collaboration, of course, continued in my mind. I wondered if you and Martha talked about your experiences as a Japanese person and if the sets and props you made for her took influence from Japanese traditions? Did you ever talk with her about what being a Japanese American means to you? The dance world often (still) uses Orientalist narratives, particularly in ballet. I wonder if this came up in your collaborations—if this was one of the many traditions you and Martha sought to break from. I wonder about what bridges and distances were a part of your collaborations—how much you learned from each other's experiences and how much space you each allowed for those experiences to enter into the work.

I also wonder how going back and forth between America and Japan affected how you thought about your identity. Did you consider yourself Asian American? I too am Asian in a sense, and so I'm also Asian American to some extent, now that I live in the United States. What does it mean for us to share the moniker "Asian American" when we are from very different parts of the continent—you the East, and me the South? I wonder what our solidarity would look like across that distance. What defines a continent in the first place? Colonial hierarchy? Rules arbitrated in Europe? These far from address or unite the complexities of the cultures and communities deemed "Asian." Here in North America, "Asian American" is another thing again. I like the term and adopt it as something that includes me and you. There are many layers to who and what it means to be Asian, and many more to what it means to be Asian in America. But I think the term encompasses this—it is rich and ever-changing.

Being of Indian descent, having grown up in Kenya and Canada, and now living in the United States, I find my identity has always been complex and in flux. I often get asked where I am from; the answer is never direct or short. If I say I am Kenyan or Canadian, I get a suspicious look. When I say I am Asian as well, the reactions have been even more confused—as if their idea of the category "Asian" doesn't include people who look like me. My physical appearance points to my Asian heritage, but I had also never been to India until very recently. At times, this made me question my own connection. But many people are in this same situation, of not ever having been to where they are "from." So, I've learned to see the advantages in this—to see ideas of "belonging," "home," and "from-ness" as something more malleable. I think there is a great value in understanding belonging as changeable in a world that seems to be increasingly at war over the idea of home.

You were born in LA in 1904, but you made your connection to Japan visible, spending time there and connecting your work to various Japanese traditions and ways of thinking. Both your way of living and way of making have been inspirational to me and to others. Decentering identity and accepting who you were, but also messing it up, is something that I feel is valuable for me to do as well. You yourself were in flux, and in your work and collaborations you manifested this as hybridity. It was a queering—an establishing of a space that is never defined and is always changing. Identity is, and is always, evolving. Through a lifetime of artistic experimentation, you, Isamu, expanded and adapted what it meant to be Asian American. You brought a complexity to the table that to this day still inspires. You brought complexity to the idea of what "Asian American" means, and that allows a newness to keep emerging. We are given the term, but we can continue to challenge it, to give visibility to its many meanings, and to redefine the ways this moniker is perceived, so that the community behind it can continue to grow and evolve as well.

In our world today, it is important to recognize the kind of legacy you, Isamu, have left for us: one that shows our value as Asian Americans, one that shows the different ways people can be considered American. From our experiences, we have found ways to be and become many things. We have endured, defined, and redefined ourselves again and again. We have found ways to exist, and we have pushed hard to dismantle the hegemony of White heteronormative cisgender space.

I wonder what you would think of how precarious the US has become for Asian Americans today. This year the world has changed with a pandemic in truly unexpected ways, and Asians in America are being targeted with new hostility and propagandistic blame. Did you call America home? Did you too have to renegotiate your sense of belonging in this place as its governments waged wars and its citizens clashed over prejudices? Home for me has had so many meanings—Canada, Kenya, India, and America have all been my homes, and in each I have felt both belonging and a need to challenge.

Looking at your work, I think this challenging belonging might also have been true for you. There seems to be a negotiation at work in your pieces. To understand them best, you have to move, or else see the movement within them. I see them as collaborations. You brought people, spaces, concepts, and materials together that were not necessarily meant to be together. This has been inspiring to me and I hope our collaboration—me being brought together with you—might be similarly inspiring to others. That, after all, is how we move forward and become movements ourselves.

We have shared that kind of space. Despite never meeting, we have collaborated from across time. We have both strived to make things new, hybrid, and challenging. Although we carry and embrace various identities, we are boundless and not defined by them. We define our own terms, make them ours, and then redefine them again.

I write this as we are living through a pandemic. As I isolate at home, I have been making collages with the biomorphic forms of your sculptures juxtaposed with images from my life as a queer person. These collages have become another way your work lives with me and helps me think about new movements and exchanges. I am grateful for your continued presence. I am grateful for your legacy, for your knowledge and friendship across time.

I have so many more questions to ask you—like what inspirations did Africa (my other home) bring to your work? What did you think about while collecting African art objects? Was that a collaboration for you, too? Were you always searching for newness? What other categories and monikers did you want to stretch and bend? And did you ever think that long after you were gone, others would still be writing to collaborate with you? I will have to leave you with these and wait, until our paths cross again.

Until then,
Brendan

JP MOT

To my dearest beloved,

From whom I've been separated for the length of an endless pandemy,
One that likens itself to a crowning song; As the world filled its chest, heavy with thorns,
gushing off keystrokes of denials. And with a spilled, yellowish tinted tone; They gave us perils ...
With my wide saucer eyes and aquiline nose; I never knew that their bullying ways ...
Were of sheepish hopes. With flowing fist and feet. Browning us not to belong was their creed;

Ma would say, be fearless toward the unknown; don't be humble in the face of their indifferences;
And definitely hold grudges, as they help keep the Shaytans away.
The Barangs would never be swayed by us, she added.
Lessons from a tiger mom are never to be taken lightly ...
as she, herself, would never settle for this dubious Rosé.

I remembered, when I was 5, she scolded me because I was eating too slowly;
If our village would be bombed, she said,
I would have to run swiftly on an empty stomach—and only if I was lucky enough to escape.
Small me laughed and laughed, as I've only known peaceful Montreal ...
So distant from the tropics, but little did I know,
that our building, on that same evening, caught fire at sunset indeed.

Weeping outside, under a blanket of felt, consoled by my older brother,
He, who enjoyed the nightly autumn breeze and stargazing outdoors;
He, who finished his meal in five minutes flat, while I mumbled to myself as my belly groaned,

He, who lived his early childhood in labor camps happily guarding the Regime's chickens;
And, he, who managed to stay alive at Ma's side when they made a run for the border to the distant refugee camp,
Ducking minefields and jungle foes.

At that camp, an elderly couple asked my mom if she was willing to trade my dusty brother for a skinny cow
And some gold for her trouble, as he reminded them of their dusk-ed only son who had vanished in the night not long before.
To which my mother simply replied that she wouldn't have the strength, alone, to chase away starving brigands.
As snotty as he was, my brother was still hers and my Father's precious first-born son.
To anyone who inquired about Father, Ma always said that she'd find him in the next camp, thwarting both the curious and pretendants.
She lied often, and had to, as he was studying abroad, far away under those colonial fiends;
The scarf-y regime wouldn't have it ... Not the protectorate! ...moquettes aux amandes!

Not a peep of news from Ma for the past half decade;
Father remarried to drown his own deep sorrows, he said, as news from home was grim
But he still longed for the promise that he made with Ma to meet in the city overlooking the Seine on that bridge under the bowing moonlight.
Right before the coup, Father was desperately waiting for his childhood sweetheart and their first child to join him in Paris;
As the opposing troops advanced, the airport closed with a coup d'état looming, then booming, leaving Ma and my brother stranded.
Making way for the mistaken hopes. And just like that, the land of the smiles turned into the land of the frowns. ...
The lovers were left in radio silence for more than a half decade ... not knowing of each other's fate.

Father hopelessly tried to mend his heart elsewhere, but Ma, like a midsummer night's dream,
Appeared and waved at him from that fateful bridge, making true to their promises a half decade late.
It took Ma all this time to find her way back into his arms, as the country's borders were closed for so long.

After the Regime toppled, bouncing around several refugee camps and
negotiating a whole immigration system later.
Months of countless letters and phone calls to surviving friends in France to
locate Father, as he wouldn't know how to reach her.
And finally, a fateful single red-eyed flight to Paris to meet him once more.
Two wives would be a problem for him though, as Ma was definitely not the
sharing kind!
And unlike his own patriarch, my prolific Grandpa, who, according to lore,
had three-going-on-four before his untimely curtain call,
with countless trysts all over North, East, and Southeast Asia. ... He loved the
Hadiths, they say;
Father was expected to choose only one, as Ma never found letting a man
have a quartet of wifes to be an endearing proposition.

Ma said she'd never thought of someone else, only because there was no one
like him.
Father proposed to her when he was barely 10, and he meant it seriously,
even if she didn't when she accepted.
She was 6, so little did she think of it, aside from that shiny haircomb, prickly
with diamond-like dust, which he gave her as a wedding gift.
My wandering-eyed Grandpa decided then and there that she'd be his son's
only wife; his future daughter in law.
Like the unfolding serenade of a couple from Sin Sisamouth, they loved, lost,
struggled, and found each other yet again. ...
Mending their serendipitous union, they departed Paris, crossing the
Atlantic, moving away from their past selves yet again.
Away from Father's second wife, and away from their longtime friends still
mourning the failure of the Regime; a greatness that never was.
—toward a place where no such dream is ushered twice or thrice over rice.

During our time apart, I always found some solace in quiet, vacant, dimly lit
spaces.
Endless worlds of carnal wonders and the spark of a single timeless love.
Aloof and unaware, I was still blissfully beaming—from your kind gesture;
At that time, we were nothing but perfect strangers. At the end of this
crowning song
I'll be waiting for you in front of the tea house near Tuanjiehu station; I'll be
there holding a plastic bag filled
With yogurts and grass-jelly drinks—our cheeks will be filled, flush with
misdeeds.

P.S. On that day, without kneeling, I'll marry you. ;)

RALPH PUGAY

Dear You,

If the life you are living has been in any way similar to mine, then your innate drive to survive and see yourself as a human being will also lead you to believe that you need to betray yourself in order to maintain a presence.

This condition will be fraught with many painful moments, which you will have difficulty expressing to others due to different factors. You will find yourself constantly morphing into different shapes determined by the external conditions of your reality. You might find this to be a necessary compulsion, to the point that you forget that you have cultivated it. As a result, you might start feeling increasingly tired and achy without knowing why. As you endure this state, people will be weirded out and tell you that you are a crabby person or that you have bad energy. You will be confused into thinking that you love things that, in reality, make you fearful or angry. You will seek help from doctors, therapists, and other professionals who might have no understanding as to how they can assist you, which will alienate you even more. It will be expensive. You will also find yourself disregarding the people who can actually help you because they will act as a mirror to your missteps, and you might not like what you see. When they hold you accountable for your own healing, you might find that being in denial is easier to endure. But this delusion might also wear you down.

If you find yourself in a fatigued, disembodied, emotional state and are considering steps to get back to yourself, here are some tips that I have found helpful:

- Take some time out of your day to move the way that your body wants to move. Find a good space to do this so that your body can express itself freely. Lay down and focus on your heart. Allow it to orient your movements in space. Orient yourself to movements that you feel might allow you some relief from all the heaviness. Do this until you feel ready to feel light again.

- Walk slowly and, if you feel inclined to hum, do so. Hum through your gut to reflect the nature of your steps. You might find yourself naturally composing a melody. Consider what this melody sounds like to you and reflect on why it sounds the way that it does.

- Find someone to harmonize hums with. Harmonize based on the tones that your gut wants to express. Harmonizing from the gut with a friend is a way to feel deeply connected to yourself and to the world around you without the barriers of language.

- Add the time spent recuperating from emotional labor to the time you are paid for by your employer. If you find yourself laying in bed from emotional exhaustion for long periods after work and during your weekends, ask if you are getting paid enough, how much time work is actually taking from your life, and what other options you might have to make a living.

- Stay with people who are willing to devote time to recognizing you. Because people in the US are not taught the value of compassion and difference in a deep way, it is important that you find people whom you know will be able to listen and embody what you have to share. Don't be afraid to find commonality and support from others.

- Understand the survival mechanisms that you have inherited from your ancestors. They allow us to see our trajectory more objectively and to understand the resilience of the people closely connected to us. They also prevent us from following paths that might not be well suited to who we are.

- People who have been hurt also hurt others. Hold people accountable for their own healing. Provide support if you have the capacity to do so, but also recognize the limits of what you are able to do.

- If you find yourself feeling empty and searching for a purpose, ask if you might be mistaking purpose for recognition. Begin to understand the difference between the two on your own terms. It is easy to confuse them while living life under capitalism.

- Do research on teacher plants that grow in the region where you live; they help you learn more about your path, and remind you that the things growing around you are there for a reason. For example, mugwort is a type of teacher plant that commonly grows in North America. It helps to induce dreams and is useful in times of anxiety, which are often not conducive to states of deep sleep and dreaming. To be disconnected from your dream state is to be disconnected from an integral aspect of living.

- Don't apologize for your aches and exhaustion. The way that you feel is real. If you find yourself in a place where you are able to recognize your feelings, find ways to maintain your truth. Own it unapologetically. Allow it to be confusing if it feels that way. At times it is difficult to determine the difference between self-sabotage and self-preservation.

Much love and care,

Ralph Pugay

ZULFIKAR ALI BHUTTO

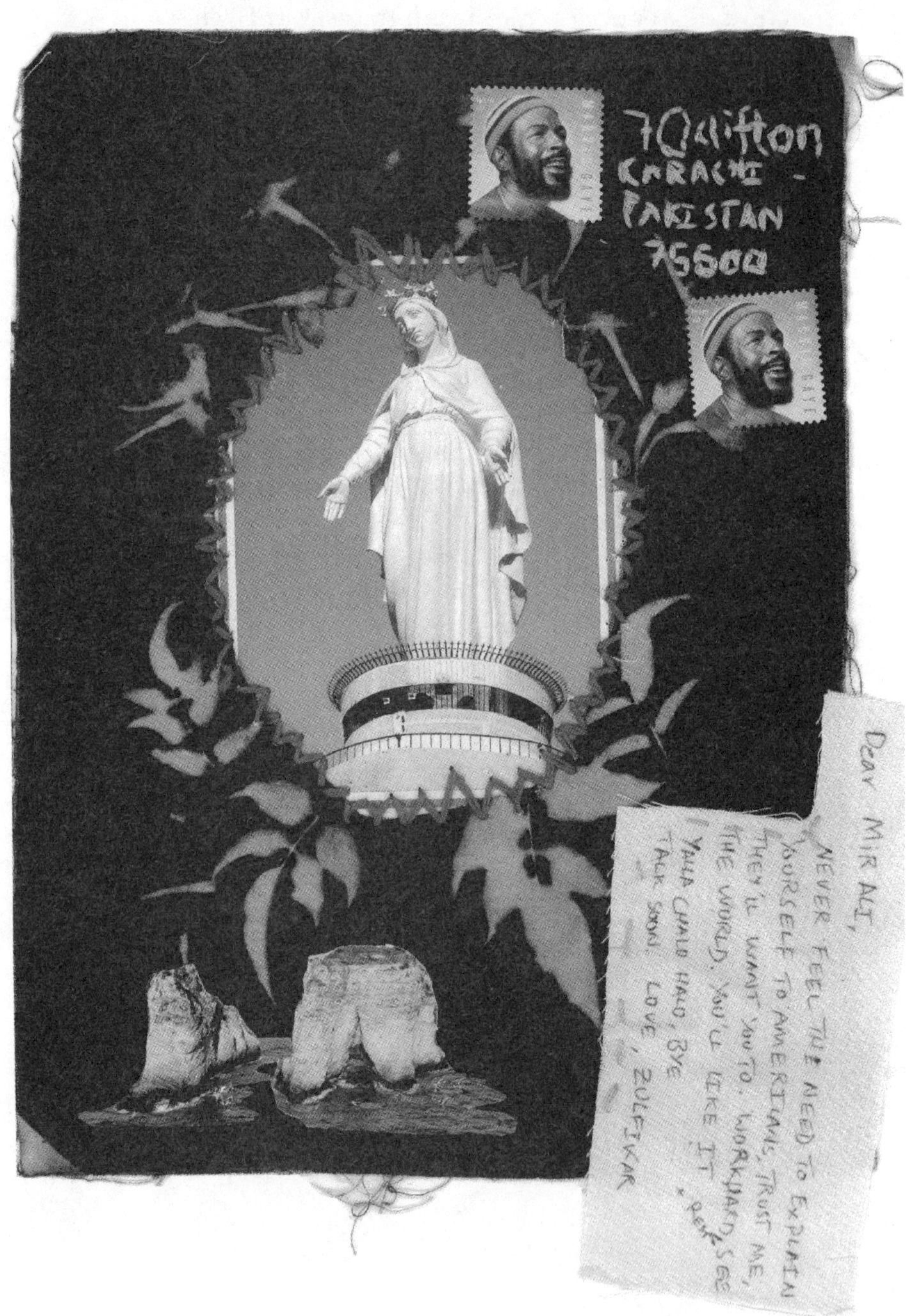

TAUSIF NOOR

September 28, 2020

RE: advice?

The thing about advice is that I'm always asking for it—never really giving it, never really sure about my own recommendations on anything, even when those things are my real-life lived experiences, even when the thing I'm trying to say is something I've felt so strongly, so frequently, so devastatingly proximate to my own way of moving through the world.

The thing about introspection is that recently it's just been unsatisfying.

Anyway, I was going to write you to say that more often than not, the shit that's getting in your way isn't actually yourself. That's what institutions (read: people) tell you when they're trying not to acknowledge the *moral decrepitude* of their own relationships to money, access, power, etc., etc., etc. It would be so wonderful, quite frankly, to have yourself (read: myself) be the primary obstacle to well-being, rather than desires, those bad objects you're theoretically supposed to shed to be enlightened.

The point here is, there are some real barriers that you have to surpass: sometimes with aplomb, rarely with the kind of even-keeled gentility that swirls around this fucked-up industry, rarer still with results that feel at all worth the effort required to manage the more or less constant stress about work, money, family obligations, love(!), money, time, money, and so on. If it sounds like I am complaining—which I am—take it to heart that I am at the very least being completely honest. And so should you.

What you should try to remember at least is that the things worth standing up for—and they are worth standing up for—are very rarely the things that are easy, convenient, or at all popular, which is to say that if you can't find, in this hazardous landscape, a fight to join, you're probably not looking hard enough, or really at all.

Spite may be motivating; principles last longer. In any case, it's tougher than it looks. And so are you.

Love,
Tausif

IFTIKHAR DADI
TIMEPASS

Many scholars have been examining contemporary issues of race in cyberspace. My reflections attempt to open up these questions for the generation of migrants who came to consciousness in the United States in a pre-digital era.

Well before the pervasive spread of video and online games, Asians played board games of various kinds. For many Asian immigrants, familial relations and exposure to wider American society were perhaps mediated partly by such leisure activities. They were caught between relentless pressures to succeed at school and college and in professional life, and to conform to family life and community activities. Presumably, many young migrants shuttled between being industrious in their work and their studies, and spending leisure time in a somewhat socially confined and mentally detached zone of activity.

South Asian migrants would have been familiar with board games prevalent in Bangladesh, India, Pakistan, and Sri Lanka; *Ludo* and *Snakes and Ladders* have deep historical lineages. A bewildering number of versions of *Snakes and Ladders* were played among various communities in South Asia; they laid out ludic scenarios rich with Tantric, Bhakti, and Sufi ideas about leading a life with redemptive and salvific potential. During the British colonial era that extended from the late 18th century to the mid-20th century, many traditional games were repackaged, shorn of their older associations, and redeployed as games of pure competition and chance.

As would be expected in some of the world's oldest civilizations, local cosmologies informed board games and leisure in many regions of Asia. Subsequent capitalist urbanization and modernization led to new articulations of leisure. Today, Asians worldwide bear the charge of both being industrious—to the degree of being viewed as robotic and inhuman—while simultaneously being mindlessly enthralled with the detritus of contemporary life and the mediatized frivolity of online games. The Asian American model minority stereotype fits this very well, while in Asia itself, we have K-pop, Manga, Bollywood, and the addictions of TikTok.

In modern South Asia, other games also became very common. I remember playing the British version of *Monopoly* while growing up in Karachi during the 1960s and 70s; in it, one could acquire public properties like Trafalgar Square (even if in reality these spaces existed in London). Local manifestations of *Monopoly* were also in circulation. For example, an Urdu version that I bought in Karachi in the early 90s called *Memon crorepati beopar* (Memon Million Business) was created by someone from the business-oriented Memon community. It offers prominent sites in Karachi for acquisition—rather than the faraway New York and London landmarks common to versions of *Monopoly* in the English language, with which one could scarcely relate.

Charles Baudelaire and Walter Benjamin, among other thinkers, saw boredom as a foundation of modern life. I can testify from personal experience that theory accords very well with reality. As a young boy, I remember my great uncle Siraj Mamoo saying to me rather incredulously and contemptuously in Urdu, "Why is it today that everyone is bored?" He used the English word "bore," as this was the term we youngsters bandied about and one that has no good Urdu equivalent. For him, boredom was an affliction of those much younger than him, living in a debased society: entire generations had clearly lost their way.

We are guilty as charged, are condemned to this ennui, and suffer irrevocably from it. We also don't care much about salvific or redemptive games of the past, or "educational" games of today that are trotted out regularly, even in the hyper-stimulated digital realm, as a way of developing correct political consciousness.

Among the towering contributions of South Asia to the grand theorization of boredom in the modern world is the magisterial concept of *timepass*. Anthropologist Craig Jeffrey managed to write a whole book with the title *Timepass: Youth, Class, and the Politics of Waiting in India*, a study of non-elite youth facing thwarted opportunities in a midsized Indian city. And in her essay "Timepass: A (Queer) View from South Asia," Anjali Arondekar characterizes timepass as "a relationship to temporality that is about loitering, stalling, and ultimately queering the process of making time ... from killing time, to engaging in casual (often sexual) activities that defy time's value. To do or invite timepass is to unmoor oneself from the weight of time, to surrender (for better or worse) to the process; all that matters is that time passes and we along with it."

If you search the Web for reviews of Bollywood films, people often comment that a particular film is "strictly for timepass." There is even a list on IMDb for Hollywood movies titled "my best time pass movies." (Writing and reading such frivolous commentary is itself a supreme timepass activity and thus positioned at a meta level of discourse.) These are films from which you learn nothing of value, neither aesthetically nor ethically. Their only purpose is to fill the empty hours of the day, when one is too exhausted from the model minority rat race or when one simply sees no prospects worth struggling for.

Timepass is absolutely central to Asian American experience.

As a migrant, one's community inevitably extends beyond kinship. School, college, friendships, jobs, neighbors, and media all expose young Asian Americans to the wider American society to which they also seek to belong. When migration from Asia reopened in the United States around 1965, it was also a time of great ferment in American society; with the civil rights movement and the intellectual and cultural movements of the 60s and 70s, new ways of thinking about the self and society were being forged.

American board games from the 60s and 70s embody the anxieties and the possibilities of the era (for example, the 1971 game *Perception*, with its psychedelic graphics, reflects the pop gestalt psychology of the period), but also the widespread blindness to an increasingly multiracial United States. The 1970 game called *Blacks & Whites* issued by *Psychology Today* magazine is a kind of a critical but perverse *Monopoly*, with its mapping of social exclusions premised primarily on the Black-White duality. What might have a young Asian American have perceived, if invited to play such a game? Education and timepass, mixed together in a strangely inviting yet alienating cocktail?

And what have our young subject have made of *The Middle Class Game* from 1979, if invited to play along with neighbors? The graphics of the game extend American popular culture's Whiteness from the 1950s to an era that ought to have known better. What kind of affect would it have evoked, which aspirations would it have resonated with, and how would it have felt—uncanny, *unheimlich*?

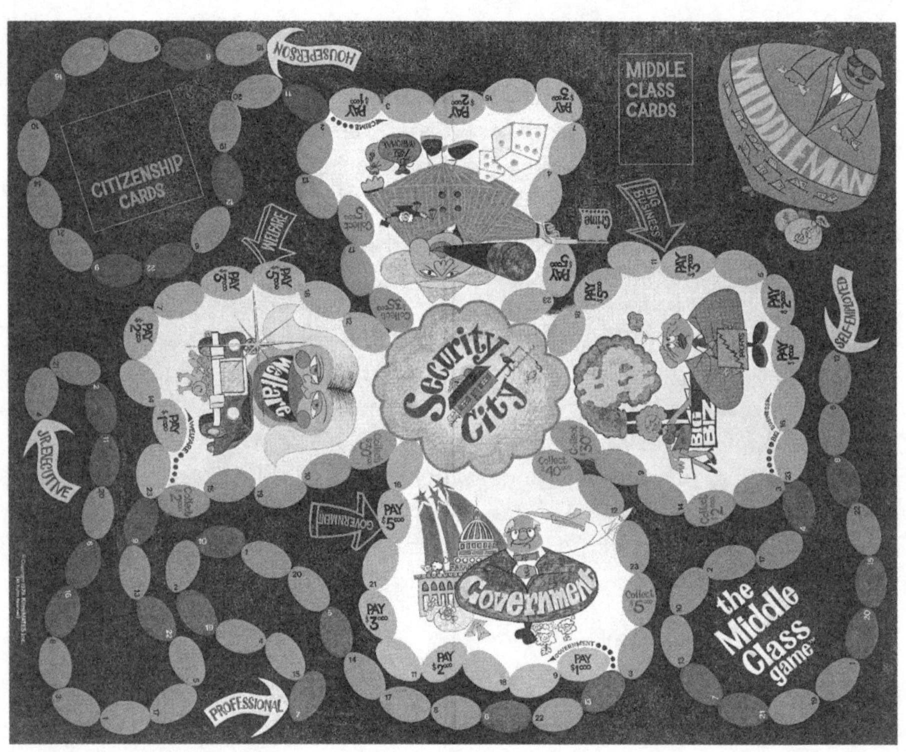

Middle Class Game board. Image courtesy the author.

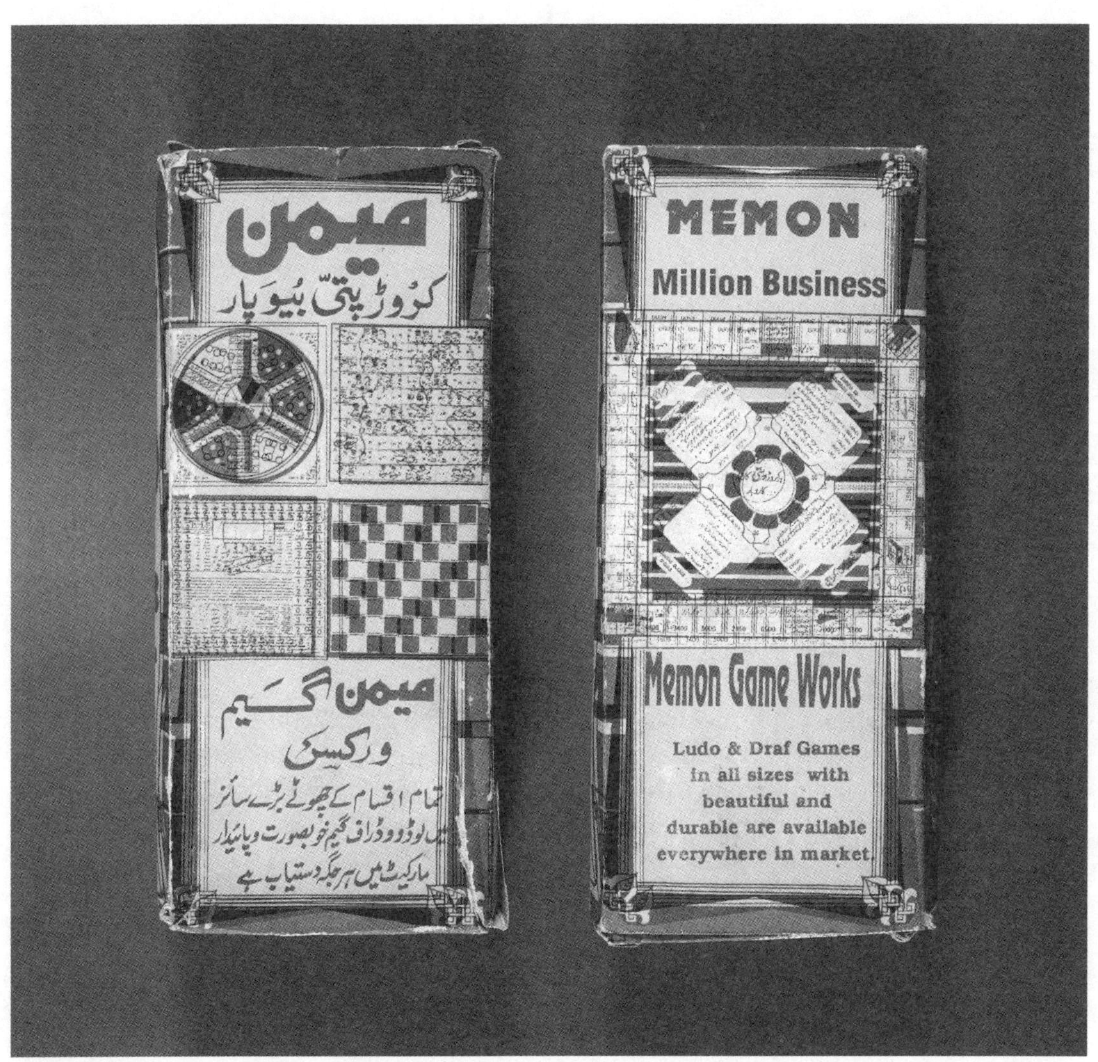

Memon Monopoly. Image courtesy the author.

SARAH MCCAFFERY

Dear One Who Wishes to Radically Dance,

Your dance is a condition of your now, your roots, and your future. Strive for the following to shape your dance towards a radical agenda for collective liberation:

Know and seek multiplicity. Of states, realms, ways, and being.

Be multilingual, speak in assemblages of languages, translate, and craft new ways of saying. Find the same nuances for listening. And also be versed in silence.

Be open to studying forms from across the Earth shaped by people with different lands, trees, waters, and more. Through studying, you also learn what the body already knows.

Commit to hope, including hopes from the past, of the present, and for the future. Tap into roots and get to know how your ancestors moved. Sensitize your movement to respond dialectically to the contradictions of the present. Allow for audacious imagining to expand ways to move forward. Let your dance be soaked in hope.

Know that there are many paths to developing radical dances. Expertise in a dance form is just one path. Becoming an expert in a form also potentially allows for expert manipulation of it, including processes of dismantling, abandoning, retooling, and reconstructing.

Build resiliency. Through an amassing of great strength, find a way to be pliable under pressure and rebound with resiliency as opposed to breaking. Develop the resilient flow of your form.

Recognize your interdependence. Breath. Heartbeat. Coursing blood.

Marvel at the polyrhythms within, and seek to connect with other rhythms. Invest in building critical connections, forming partnerships, ensembles, movements.

Know vastness, and equip yourself with the courage to give what is essential for the dance.

In motion,
Fellow Dancer

MIMI WONG

Dear Publishers,

Writing began as a way for me to explore my complicated relationship with the community in which I grew up. The year after I graduated from my Silicon Valley high school, a news story broke about an academic cheating scandal and subsequent bomb plot there. From the other side of the country, during my freshman year of college, I remember reading article after article in the local paper asking, "How could this happen here?" I felt I intuitively understood the conditions, if not the actual reasons, that led high-achieving Asian American students to resort to desperate measures in order to get ahead—because I had lived it.

Growing up, I didn't see my experience reflected in the flattened depictions of robotic perfectionism. Like a lot of teenagers, I wrestled with the person I thought I was supposed to be, the person I didn't want to be, and crucially the self that felt authentic. The latter was most difficult to pin down because being a child of immigrants often means having to be the first one to figure it out. It can be disorienting.

Popular culture has tended to oversimplify the pressure placed on second-generation children. I wanted to challenge that stereotype of tiger-parented kids. Although variations of these kids may exist, the model minority myth is just as toxic. As a writer who wants to examine my own complicity, I feel it's necessary to consider what we're sacrificing when we buy into the American Dream. Author V. V. Ganeshananthan recently tweeted, "Representation isn't worth much to me if it gives up self-critique." Over the past few years, Asian American writers have demonstrated a strong desire to rewrite their own narrative.

In her 2009 work of literary criticism *Ingratitude: The Debt-Bound Daughter in Asian American Literature*, erin Khuê Ninh observes an "anger and bitterness" underlying the narratives written by second-generation Asian American daughters—"this despite their largely unremarkable upbringings." Citing works by Asian American writers including Maxine Hong Kingston, Ninh homes in on the dilemma of the second-generation daughter who feels herself "caught in a system of 'designated failure.'" If the straight-A student is the norm, then the protagonist in my novel—one who's bright and creative but doesn't necessarily excel the way she's expected to—feels herself to be an aberration. If she appears passive or quiet, it's because she hasn't yet been given the opportunity or space to find her own voice. That is her journey.

My character's story, in a lot of ways, is my story. But she also represents my best friends. She's one of the Asian American girls I mentor and teach, who juggle the expectations of their parents, their schools, and especially their peers. A student recently complained about feeling excluded by her Asian American classmates, worrying it was because she wasn't perceived as being "Asian enough." My hope is that in the future, she will be able to define for herself what being Asian American means. Ultimately, I wrote the novel for my younger self, not only as a source of comfort, but also to let her know that she is seen.

Sincerely,
Mimi Wong

CANDICE LIN

Dear Lee,

What was it like to live as the White man's other wife? Even after you cut off your long, black braid and traded your loose, swishing clothes for tailored, black broadcloth, you still made his coffee, inflated his pride, and scolded the boys. They were *your* boys, at least for a while; their first words were in Cantonese. Did it pain you when they were so quick to disown you? The first time you tried to go away and start a new life, the boys barely noticed. Cal wanted to go to the baseball game, and Aron was excited about the funny sausages the man put in the buns. You paled in comparison to this quintessential America and to the mystery of their real mother—the whore with her cold, flat eyes and sharp teeth.

In a way, you understood her. Emasculated, you both kept your eyes inscrutable, your language full of what men wanted to hear. From her: feminine pleasantries, mirrored agreements, and, most of all, silence. From you: pidgin English, despite being born and brought up in the US. But only she managed to leave him (she even succeeded as a businesswoman, running her own house of vice). Perhaps you envied her. You wanted to open a bookshop, but when you left, you came right back, as if leashed to the smell of burnt coffee and an ineffectual man who didn't even know that to make a fire burn, you must first sweep the old ashes out. Were you ashamed of the crushing loneliness that sent you back to servitude? Was being indispensable the closest you got to being loved? On good days, was it enough?

You came into this world as an adult several years after the Chinese Exclusion Act was repealed. It was 1952, the year the Immigration and Nationality Act redrew the lines of exclusion around the new worry of communism. When you were conceived, perhaps John hoped that your second-generation abilities to assimilate would reassure the gentle reader of the fullness of your humanity. But there was no point in translating old Chinese poetry into English, as you told Samuel. People want to listen to only the stories they see themselves in:

"the strange and foreign is not interesting—only the deeply personal and familiar." So you learned Hebrew and became a kind of Judeo-Christian savant, prophesying a replay of the Cain and Abel cliché, the universal story of the wronged child with a choice.

In this retelling, as in the original, there is no coercion—neither indentured labor nor slavery, none of the chaos and poverty brought on by imperialism—just people making choices. Here, America is a nation of immigrants descended from "the restless, the nervous, the criminals, the arguers and the brawlers, but also the brave and independent and generous"—of those who did not stay and starve in their homelands. This is the story of colorblindness, of overcoming adversity and violence, and choosing to succeed. Amerikkka loves the story of the underdog but forgets how Cain was forever marked. And what was this mark, if not the marker of race?

You were not sorry when Aron had to die; you loved the sullen Cal best anyway. And you did love him—admit it—just as you loved the White man in your careful care. You loved him as yourself, as your son, despite his total disregard for you. He never saw you as a mother or a wife, only as the dependable Chinaman ready in the wings.

I, too, thought I could be a good servant. Perhaps I was one in a past life. My friends would laugh at such an idea, knowing how bossy and stubborn I am. ("You don't even like to listen to recipes!" one friend told me. "That's how much of a problem with authority you have.") But I worked for a man for six years as his personal assistant, and I felt a strange power in my efficiency, my spreadsheets, and in his immediate and total dependence on me. Samuel asked you once if you were content to be a servant, and you said, "A good servant has absolute security, not because of his master's kindness, but because of habit and indolence ... a good servant, and I am an excellent one, can completely control his master, tell him what to think, how to act, whom to marry, when to divorce, reduce him to terror as a discipline, or distribute happiness to him, and finally be mentioned in his will."

You said this, but in fact, you couldn't control his marriage. And he had a stroke before he could write you into his will. But I doubt he would have, anyway; it would have been very hard for him to imagine that you had a future independent of him. But I understand your delusion of being a power bottom. There were times when I thought I was the boss, too, or that the boss was a friend. It was easy to ignore the small reminders that this was not the case.

I am sipping wormwood tincture while I write to you (the name of the herb is a mistranslation of "the rotten apples drink" you always drank, which was made from a completely different root). I wonder what your full name was. Who were your parents, and what was your childhood like? When you told the story of your birth and your upbringing by the Chinese railroad workers who had raped your mother—who was cross-dressing as your father's young nephew and working pregnant alongside him, setting railroad ties—did you plagiarize? It reminded me of a sensationalist Pearl Buck story I read as a teenager. Such stories of poverty, rape, and coercion meshed into a kind of pornographic haze for me during my adolescence. How hard we tried to reimagine the dearth of 19th-century immigrant Chinese women by inventing characters like the feminized Mr. Lee, his cross-dressing mother, and the cross-dressing and arguably trans character of Mr. Lowe from Patricia Powell's *The Pagoda*. How odd that the trauma and violence endured by previous generations became fodder for my teenage erotic fantasies.

And what about you? No hint of a childhood, nor of any sexuality or romance—not even a full name. You would not have replicated the original Adam's mistakes, idolizing a pretty doll-like face. Nor would you have mistook willfulness and the desire for one's own life as emblems of feminine evil. But who did you love besides him—if you can call that love? Who could you love within this context?

I see myself in the racial melancholia of your story. There was no place for you. You told Samuel, "To the so-called Whites I was still a Chinese, but an untrustworthy one; and at the same time my Chinese friends steered clear of me. I had to give it up ... I did go back to China. My father was a fairly successful man. It didn't work. They said I looked like a foreign devil; they said I spoke like a foreign devil. I made mistakes in manners, and I didn't know delicacies that had grown up since my father had left. They wouldn't have me. You can believe it or not—I'm less foreign here than I was in China."

When I recently visited my uncle in Fuzhou for the second time in my life—the first was when I was 16—the street vendors who sold me food would say in puzzlement at my broken attempts to speak a few words of Mandarin: "But it's strange. You look like you could be part Chinese." My uncle and I tried to speak through a translation device. Whenever we went beyond the two-syllable words and basic pleasantries, the machine would rebel, translating, "Fuck you, bitch, shut up," and we would burst into embarrassed peals of laughter. But the gulf between us was melancholic, too. He was separated from his parents and other siblings, who were born in Taiwan. He grew up in China with his grandparents, fleeing to the woods to avoid hard labor camp. I picture him, young and alone, electrocuting fish in a shallow pool in order to eat.

A few years after finally being reunited with him, my grandparents went back to China to die in his house. He said, "I bury and grieve the parents I did not really get a chance to know." I, too, in my own privileged and diasporic way, am always grieving the loss of what I do not know. I cannot visit the grave of this loss because it has no set location. I cannot "scatter devil papers" to the winds. I cannot offer "a little roast pig."

Yours,
Lin

Lee and the details of his story are quoted from John Steinbeck, *East of Eden* (New York: Penguin Books, 2002/1952).

MAIA CHAO

Dear Zoë,

As I digitize Nana's memoir, drafts of which sit in thick dusty piles around her house, I've been pondering this strange process: the life cycle of this family text and the life cycles of our family. I'm taking a document that was once digital (presumably a Word doc), that became physical (ink printed on paper), and scanning it with my iPhone, making it digital once again. It feels absurd, and I wonder if, somewhere in the house, the .doc file is hiding on a buried floppy disc. I'm not even sure that I have the final copy, but I decided to digitize the draft with the most pages. I hope I'm not missing something crucial.

The process of digitization is mind-numbing. As I scan each page, I must help the computer identify what part of it is text. The algorithm is faulty; it reads *all* markings as text, including the random hole punch in the margin or a crease in the paper. I find myself thinking about what gets recognized, deemed legible, centered, and passed on—and what gets marginalized, determined illegible, and erased.

This process is forcing me to confront the realness of Nana's memoir as a material object—one that takes up space. There is no way to clean Nana's house without confronting parts of this text, stuffed in random drawers, under desks, in bins and boxes.

I have found it difficult to choose which excerpts I'd like to share for this publication. I don't want to sensationalize or inadvertently reify stereotypes, be it a tale of immigrant suffering or the myth of the model minority. I reached out to Nana by email with hopes that she might have a suggestion, but with the fast-approaching deadline and the daunting task of selecting what to share of a project she's left behind, she—or rather, Roger—encouraged me to go ahead and choose for myself. Below are the excerpts I've chosen, based on the simple premise that they resonated with me at this moment in time.

The publisher had suggested the idea of me corresponding with you or with Dad about a given passage, but you're on the road, and Dad, as you know, hasn't read the memoir—can't read it, feels guilty. For a while I thought this was so weird, but I now can see that to confront this memoir would be to confront a lot of trauma: loss, betrayal, violence. Strangely, I've been told that Stephen read it all the way through, but of course, I would imagine that he forgot all of it, as he claims to forget everything.

I recently finished *Minor Feelings*, where I read that domestic violence is least reported by Asian women. Which, of course, is not to say that it happens less. In considering this fact, Cathy Park Hong reflects, "I grew up in a culture where to speak of pain would not only retraumatize me but traumatize everyone I love, as if words are not a cure but a poison that will infect others." Nana's memoir feels like an antidote to this. Obviously, this memoir is far from a chronicle of violence. But it is honest, and willfully so. Nana does not spare us the pain—one of the many ways she is decidedly American.

And yet, as I prepare for this submission, I am faced with the fact that I could not find an interlocutor in the family to help me sort through Nana's story. Likewise, when Nana sought publication years ago, the process stalled out. So, here I am, sitting with 600+ printed pages of our grandmother's life. It is a great gift, but one that is hard to receive.

What is there to say? I think perhaps it's *Thank you, Nana*. And: I'm sorry that there is, to my knowledge, so little sustained dialogue about this beautiful and generous work. As an artist, I sometimes avoid seeking feedback for fear of how it might impact me, but at the same time, I am devastated when my work is met with silence. If the work of art at hand were my memoir, I would imagine that this pain would feel even more acute. It's crucial that one's work is recognized by someone, even a family member, if only as a mechanism of echolocation—to confirm that the work did indeed enter the world and it is seen and considered by others. It is real.

Love,
Maia

* * *

Excerpts from *Dreaming of Home (Meng Jia): A Family Memoir*, by Phebe Shih Chao:

> One day, I find myself in a place called Hong Kong. I must have been on a boat for several days in order to reach it from Shanghai. To begin with, it seemed like another vacation. I had traveled on an ocean-going steamer before, going back and forth to and from Qingtao. Daddy and I were usu-

ally on the deck. Mama was always seasick. She hated boats. They made her throw up. But she wasn't on the boat with me this time. Neither of my parents was there. I am with my three cousins, and it must have been one or two of my aunts, Laura and maybe Marie, though she may have come later, and some amahs—not mine. I'm not even sure of these facts. I don't remember anything of the crossing. If, as people say, when the memory is too painful or you have reason not to remember, you won't remember. For the life of me, I can't recall a thing about the first months of getting used to a different house.

Worse than that, I don't know when I realized that except for my relatives, no one spoke a language I knew. The amahs spoke Guangdong-hua—Cantonese, the chief dialect of Hong Kong—as did all the servants. A speaker of Shanghai-hua can't understand Guangdong-hua, and vice-versa. The same is true for a speaker of Beijing-hua. Not one of them is comprehensible to the other. My father succeeded in getting me to speak Mandarin from the cradle because he installed my own amah from Beijing in the room next to me. I spoke Shanghai-hua because I lived in Shanghai, and because that was the language of exchange among my schoolmates at McTyeire. But at some point, it must have occurred to me that I was without a language in Hong Kong.

Obviously, I learned to speak Cantonese in the two or three years I lived in Hong Kong. Auntie Marie tells me I spoke it fluently. Today just the most basic phrases are retrievable, about as much as the Russian left over from Mamselle. I don't remember learning, and I don't remember forgetting. The strange thing is that I hung on to Beijing-hua and Shanghai-hua through forty or fifty years of not using it, and not even hearing it spoken. I must have felt my very being depended on hanging on to my mother tongue(s)—the deepest, most unconscious part of me. This is me; that is not me. I reject the circumstances that forced me to leave home at 6 years old.

Quite suddenly, I wake up in Hong Kong. We begin in a big house in the city, even though I have no sense memory of its shape, look, or layout; I'm blank on the entrance, the neighboring buildings, what colors the rooms are, where I sit down to meals, the room I have trouble sleeping in. I come awake briefly during the Great Typhoon of 1937, when the wind in powerful gusts rattles the windows and then finally blows them out. The driven rain slashes into the rooms, and the maids, barefoot, spend all night sweeping the water that accumulates on the bedroom floors. They sweep it down the stairway. I watch the little waterfalls cascading down the risers to the next lower tread, down, and down, and down. The children and the women are damp and huddle together in the middle of the watery floor. Perhaps it is enough like being on a lifeboat during a drill that it awakens me from my torpor. Fairy tales where a gentle kiss awakens the princess describe such a process psychologically. I used to think that the agency, the force to shake off sleep, had to have been more earth-shaking, but in time I realized that a loving kiss from anyone in those years of separation from home would have worked wonders.

The next day, the children are driven to the harbor to see a big ocean liner, blown onto the wharf like a toy, resting on its side. Years later, the unreal scene in Hong Kong harbor flashed vividly before me when I saw Fellini's film *Amarcord*, where the townspeople row out in the night to see the many-storied steamship. Memory, unpredictable as to what one remembers, when one is jolted or nudged into remembering, how the neurons travel their unconsciously chosen paths, is a mystery.

[...]

Who was there to talk to? Going from one in number (me) to four (Laurette, MJ, Xiao Doo, and me) overnight—the realization of this change in my life might have taken as long as the boat trip I don't remember—didn't make me less alone or more secure. The most accurate way to say it is that with my aunt and uncle and cousins, in a low-key way, I felt in a perpetually precarious position—in other words, my normal state was one of unease. Though I could be lulled by momentary harmony into an unguarded state, it would never last for long. It took very little—sometimes not more than a look—to remind me that I was not a sister, that Uncle T.V. was not my father, that I needed to remain once again on guard.

I excavate all this because much later in our lives, Marie had occasion to write my mother that it was too bad I had grown up in America, that it had somehow ruined my natural Chinese sense of what was right and what was wrong, that my behavior had become so Americanized that Mother just had to accept the fact that I was an American and not Chinese in any real sense anymore. My mother was hurt, since it implied that she hadn't brought me up properly, had not been strict enough; I was hurt because I thought at the time, and for a long time afterward, that I was at least half-Chinese. "Chinese," in their minds, seemed to rank higher in propriety and morals and general virtue than American. Eventually, I realized that, in fact, it merely marks cultural difference.

In the end, Marie was right that my coming to America changed my life forever. I accept it, and I no longer regret it. I realize that willy-nilly, I've chosen to be American.

One of the things my auntie Marie said that really hurt my mother's feelings was: "Aiyah, Anna," (sentences that begin with "Aiyah," a sigh breathed out, mean something pitiful, even tragic, may follow) "It's too bad Phebe has become so Americanized. Well, what can you expect, when she grew up here. It's not your fault. ... " She petered off into silence—meaning, of course, *it is your fault that you allowed her to grow up here.* "Americanized" is a code word for all the things a Chinese lady like my auntie Marie would not approve of in a young person's outlook and attitude. She'd be hard-put to define the word beyond "too free, too independent."

Many years later, when my youngest son, Stephen, visited her in Hong Kong, and she felt assaulted by the brash democratic assumptions of his question about privilege and class, she once again said to my mother (this time, in a letter with only an implied "aiyah"), "It's too bad Stephen is so Americanized." I don't know if she remembered she had used the exact same word about me. Stephen, in his innocent teens, was under the impression that they had got on very well. On second thought, what seems mutually exclusive—that is, to get along with and be critical of someone at the same time—is, in fact, rather common.

Auntie Marie's sighs of disapproval were not so different from what my dagupopo declared when I got married. "Well, she grew up in America. Maybe it's best she's married. ... " petering off into silence, meaning something like, *America is an environment where, unfortunately, individualism is a virtue, and emotion and passions are allowed to run rampant, unruly, and ungovernable; if she wants a sexual life, at least this is an honorable solution.* This last could have been my mother's interpolation, but the old lady was fully capable of thinking along the same faultline. I was indignant and infuriated, only later appalled at the way I'd been misunderstood. As in some arranged marriages, life with this husband was unwanted, and that most decidedly included a sex life. I considered myself a normal teenager, curious and affectionate, but also fastidious and choosy, quite able to say no. Out of spite, it occurred to me: What if I hadn't said no with such regularity, and let them die of shame? Until Wai, I didn't know anything about intercourse, despite my one experience which hadn't taught me a thing—except that whatever it was, it wasn't as much fun as kissing and making out. As for Wai, how I wished I could make him disappear. And they were saying I should be married in order to be fucked legally?

If I ever thought about my future, it was only momentary, sooner off the screen of consciousness than it took for the thought to arrive there. When one attempts a new wilderness trail, one is too busy adjusting one's feet to the rocky terrain, looking around—for hazards, for markers, for the way around a stream—to focus on a destination. I was too busy with the present (both the gift and the time) of my beautiful baby to be conscious of becoming an American, the place where I was headed without knowing it.

If others see my life dividing here between the exoticism of my being Chinese from an extraordinary background and the mundaneness of my melting into the American folk, all I can say to them is: Think of it from my point of view. What was more exotic to me than becoming one with the strange peoples of a strange land?

I didn't spend time thinking about what it was to be Chinese, though I was aware what it was like, what was expected. I could verbalize my understanding of it. For example, every Chinese is proud of her heritage, 4,000 years of history and culture and achievements galore. Secretly held, the belief that we really are superior to foreign barbarians. Even as we're living among them. A true Chinese tries at all times to be a model of her race and nationality so that life will be easier for those Chinese who come after her. This is especially true of an immigrant. There is a genuine sense of community in that behavior. One has to do one's best for the sake of others, contemporary and future, in the same situation as oneself.

I went to a school where being Chinese was rarely brought to my attention. Oh, perhaps once, when the fourth-grade teacher, in the middle of her unit on China, felt the need for a bona fide Chinese senior to speak to her class.

In those days, assimilation—not calling attention to differences—was the ideal, rather than multiculturalism, which acknowledges, even emphasizes, differences. Ironically, I was made more aware of my difference when I went to Wellesley. Ironic because I'm sure the overt intention was to melt us all into the college culture. Girls from geographic areas where there were no others, asked me late at night in their pajamas and innocence, having dropped their daytime garments and pseudo-sophistication, whether I had ever gone out with White boys. They were round-eyed with surprise at the answer: that until I went to college, I had never gone out with any Chinese. These late night exchanges were often part of the larger give and take where those who were wholly ignorant of sexual terms and practices received their education from the somewhat more knowledgeable. I discovered that image consciousness drove our reactions: there were those who didn't want to seem to know too much because they'd always been considered "nice" girls, and then those who had no experience who wanted to be included with the more knowing majority, who pretended to know more than they did. Where image is concerned, there's always much at stake.

Chinese patriarchy wants its women "pure" and thus "worthy" of the dignity of the family they're marrying into. I once asked my father why a nice girl like Rose was engaged to marry such an unattractive young man, one who was obviously trying to follow in the footsteps of his notoriously lecherous father. Without knowing much, I added it would be unpleasant to enter that family. He could have just answered, "Family. Money. Nice girls can be bought by the dozen from their greedy parents." Instead, he said, "Shut up, Phebishka." It was a phrase he often used not entirely seriously whenever he thought I was being outrageous and didn't want me to think I could get away with it—and if anyone was listening, why, it could pass for his having tried to remonstrate with me.

Clearly, the simplistic schema divided bad girls who didn't know their place (or, from another point of view, were too smart), used their physical attributes to get what they wanted (also too smart), called attention to themselves (looked too good or were too smart), took up too much time (ditto), from the nice girls who were virginal and self-effacing, more acted upon than acting. In stark contrast, the American girls I admired had healthy egos about their bodies and their intelligence, and were worthy of the men because of their own self-worth.

Chinese patriarchy was an established structure long before Confucius (ca. 500 BC), who was merely codifying the past. And still, when I read Henry James and especially Edith Wharton's *House of Mirth*, I understood that my mother's cultural values were inherited directly from the generation before her, her late Victorian teachers at MacTeiyre. I felt enormous sympathy for Lily Bart, trying her best but somehow managing to make a botch of her life.

In some ways, I was prepared and ready to understand the egalitarian aspects of America. At home, though we had servants, and it was made clear to me that they were servants, some of them were also my family. They performed their duties, as my father, say, performed his. My amah was more mother to me than my own mother in Shanghai, something like the phenomenon of mammies in the South, though color added another dimension to that complicated relationship. Later, in Washington, too, Louis the chauffeur treated me as his daughter, and so did sweet, simple Ah Dong. There were emotional attachments in the balance. Several times a week, I taught Ah Dong English from the little grammar books he bought in Chinatown on his days off. I liked him possibly more than my blood uncles, some of whom weren't nearly as decent.

Everywhere I lived—and I've lived all over the place—contributed an odd-shaped piece to my overall understanding. If Lolita's life is American picaresque, I have some sense that mine was too. In America, up to this point: Pasadena, Washington, DC, Wellesley, and then in a whirlwind of sprints and dashes, stops and starts, returns and new starts, to Newton Centre to Washington, DC to Queens to Buffalo, Ann Arbor, Montclair, back to Buffalo, back to Michigan, this time squirreling around Birmingham/Bloomfield Hills/Birmingham. The ten years or so that I lived in the area near Detroit constituted the longest time I'd ever stayed put in the first forty years of my life, even though within those ten years I changed addresses four times. For a variety of reasons, we moved on the average of every two years, until I fled to Cambridge. (Soon after, I lived in three places all at once in Vermont, Massachusetts, and New Hampshire. Now, I've really become the Taoist painter who disappeared into the landscape he was painting, I have entered into the highlands of wild blueberries and granite ledges of Blue Job Mountain.)

HYPERLINK PRESS

Dear future young artists who want to make queer diaspora art,

This is our love letter to you.

Once upon a time there was LB City (2000-2003), a love story of a marginalized community that came together to support each other, which inspired our love letter to you. This passing of love has nothing to do with blood or kin. It has everything to do with the community we nurture together to continue passing on these love stories.

We write this as a collective of similar-hearted young Korean diaspora artists, formally called Hyperlink Press. We are inspired by South Korean online LGBTQ communities in the 2000s such as LB City. We archive, envision, and distribute these love stories to reimagine belonging.

LB City was an online lesbian forum founded by Lee Hae-Sol and other 25 lesbian organizers as an attempt to create a virtual "lesbian" utopia. LB City community members appropriated the term "lesbian (레즈비언)" as an alternate existence to Korean patriarchy and heteronormativity. Even before LB City and "lesbian" became popularized in Korea, there were still queer women communities and names despite the erasure: 이쪽 (e-jjok, "this side"), 이반 (e-ban, a pun on 일반 (il-ban) "normal" implying there is beyond normal), 바지씨 (baji ssi, "Mr./Ms.Pants"), and 치마씨(chi ma ssi, "Mr./Ms. Skirts"). LB City founder, Lee Hae-Sol, took inspiration from the butch taxi driver union (여운회) from the 70's and 80's which was a coalition that created family-like support for working queer women. Though Korean words for queer women existed prior to the adoption of the word "lesbian," LB City members sought to redefine the label in their own terms through embodied, everyday experiences as queer women living in South Korea. Considering LB City's inclusiveness in spirit and lots of queer neologisms were fairly new, LB City's founders' intent showed a potential for nurturing dialogue that centered queer folks, trans women, and gender nonconforming people, offering LB City's citizenship to those excluded from the immediate definition of lesbianism. The heart of LB City was the collective practice to build another kind of world that embraced and prioritized the voices and needs of queer women and minoritized people. This virtual city planning project continues to be a critical inspiration for Hyperlink's mission as we aim to continue its spirit.

Hyperlink Press sources its aesthetic inspiration from the software interfaces of the early 2000's in South Korea that followed its own distinctive path of development and growth with such programs and platforms as 아래아한글, 소리바다, 프리첼, 다음까페, 알집, and 싸이월드. For millennials, the 2000's were our first encounters with early internet aesthetics and experience; it stood as a time of excitement for a decentralized and equitable world, departing from traditional forms of community building. We are drawn to this era when anyone could have been anything and *accepted* for the stories they shared. The internet represented a radical shift in how dialogue existed and propagated, providing a framework for understanding our collective marginalized histories beyond state-mandated narratives which often centered patriarchal, heteronormative, anti-communist, and imperialist paradigms.

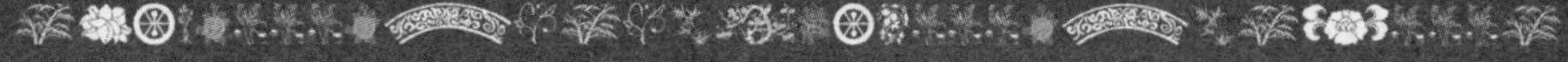

Due to our diasporic childhoods, we sought absorption of Korean culture through the internet. The internet provided a fluid space without geographical borders which afforded us the possibility to encounter different narratives outside of the state-mandated definitions of what "Korean culture" was. However when language and culture are exported and consumed this way by the english speaking diaspora, there's a disconnect in how we use that information and present it to a Western audience. Because this kind of unilateral adoption of what Korean "culture" is through romanticized translations, it creates an easy route to bypass true dialogue between peninsular and diasporic Koreans, which is often compounded by generational divides. We cannot have true dialogue without the love and the courage to trust in each other. This trust is what allows us to join in community and partnership in naming the world.*

We become afraid to engage in true dialogue, because it goes against the grains of how we are socialized to center only ourselves as independent actors. True dialogue is rooted in love which is an act of courage, not fear. Love is a commitment to others, and an act of bravery which generates other acts of freedom.* Instead, we default to romanticizing ancestral heritage or histories and participating in the contemporary art conveyor belt for the benefit of a Western audience. They wouldn't know the difference. Here, we ask, who do we *really* want to make art for? We realize that maybe we want to actually make art about our family and *for* our family (chosen or otherwise) and have an honest dialogue with them. But what we *don't* want to do is to sell an exotic story for curators and collectors to then sell to rich people who then use it only to evade taxes and participate in the unchecked late-capitalist structure of the art market.

This is not to say that we haven't been there ourselves. We've also made work about the extinct Korean tiger, about the ever-elusive Han(한), made appropriated mudang performances, and the list goes on. But looking back, if we hadn't made that work based on our nostalgia, we couldn't have started our own journey towards honest dialogue to understand identity not as a lack but rather articulating the new identities, ways of belonging, and being, birthed from migration and its specific contexts. Though we acknowledge the nostalgia which we can tangibly grasp and make art from, we know that this is not in dialogue with the dynamic culture and people from whence we came. In order to encounter true dialogue, there is a dire need to look beyond nostalgia and build upon legacy by understanding specificities of the present that are produced by the past. Only then, we can shape past learnings to intentionally create change and a vision for the future. Just like a support system or network of care, we want to foster alternative communities for artists with a focus on intersectionality, queerness, transnational communities, digital technologies, and the internet. We will always advocate for underrepresented artists, histories, stories, and experiences irrespective of their place in contemporary art or geographic location.

From LB City to you, this love letter is a way to pass down these forms of dialogue through the generations across transnational communities.

May you find the courage to inspire dialogue on the foundations of love,
Hyperlink Press
Taehee Whang, Minsoo Thigpen, Jeong Yoong Lee, Juwon Jun, and Sonia Suhyun Choi

황태희, 민수 티그펜, 이정윤, 전주원, 최수현 드림. 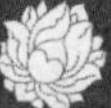

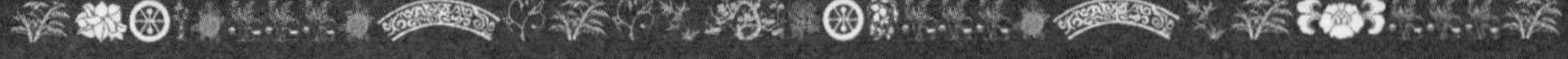

* Paulo Freire, *Pedagogy of the Oppressed* (1970)

HERB TAM

Dear Successor,

There were many times during slow days at my desk that I daydreamed about my last day at the Museum of Chinese in America. It's not that I longed to escape my job. The dreams were more a platform for narcissistic speculation. I imagined that the whole museum would shut down for a solemn, daylong celebration. Board members, some of whom rarely come to MOCA, would show up. Old colleagues would stop by, setting aside past disharmonies to wish one of their own a fond farewell. There would be a lavish spread: soft cheeses and grapes, passed dim sum, expensive donuts, prosecco, Sing Tao beer, and the "good" red wine. Toasts would go on for hours, after which I would deliver an earnest, emotional, and gracious goodbye. My last day would be a healing moment, bringing together the vast range of MOCA stakeholders for an epic farewell that would mark and highlight all of my achievements.

As I write this in the waning moments of my last day, none of the above has materialized. Instead, I'm the last one in the office picking away at a perfunctory mango mousse cake. Having just sent my colleagues a nearly useless exit memo and a carefully worded note filled with selfless sentiment (that actually directed the real credit to its author), I write to you, my successor, to indulge in a key lesson from my ten years and suggest how you should spend your first few days on the job.

First, let me say that these reflections won't mean much to you in a practical sense. You will likely come into the job like I did, with a supersized savior mentality and the belief that previous generations of staff got it all wrong. Anyway, I hope you read this with the humility I didn't have on my first day.

You're joining the Museum of Chinese in America at a pivotal and precarious moment in the institution's history. We are attempting to buy our building and remake the museum in the middle of a global pandemic that has decimated the people and economy of New York. On top of the astronomical amount of money we need to raise, the very idea of the capital endeavor has raised questions about the condition of MOCA's moral compass. The controversy began last year with an announcement by Mayor DeBlasio that several new jails would be built around the city—one being in Chinatown—to replace the notorious facility on Rikers Island. In the same breath, the city announced funding for neighborhood organizations like MOCA as a "give-back" to the communities taking on these new jails.

This press release ignited a protest movement led by the collective Chinatown Art Brigade (CAB) that has been both heated and sustained. CAB has accused MOCA of colluding with the City to secure funding in exchange for support of (or silence on) the city's jail plan. This conflict coincides with raging debates about the contradictions of museum funding, gentrification in Chinatown, the jail abolition movement, and the Black Lives Matter movement. Our work has been labeled "art washing," and we have been accused of benefiting from violence against Black and Brown people.

Before the pandemic, when it was safe to gather, CAB organized protests outside our building, calling on artists, curators, and community members to boycott us. Since the shutdown, they have organized social media campaigns and hounded our president, Nancy Yao Maasbach, in the comment boxes of Zoom public programs. CAB's tactics have gained traction, and increasingly, their calls for a boycott are being honored. An Instagram account posted that they "couldn't wait to take down MOCA and its shitty shows on Chinese food."

How do you perform your job walking into such a toxic atmosphere? My experience is only partly relevant, because MOCA's context was much less charged in 2011, when I was in the same position you find yourself. Back then the "Chinatown vs. Uptown" tension reigned, wherein detractors on one side thought MOCA was too loyal to Chinatown stories, and on the other side, they considered us elitists focusing too much on Uptown money. The polarity between Chinatown and Uptown defined class and cultural divisions within the New York Chinese American community in unhelpful, one-dimensional terms. In this scenario, Chinatown was seen as a working-class enclave for struggling Cantonese and Fujianese people, while Uptown was associated with the wealth and social status of elite Shanghainese.

I knew that there was much more to the Chinese experience in America than this dynamic, but still, this Chinatown–Uptown pressure was distracting to my day-to-day work, if not outright paralyzing sometimes. I didn't know how to position my department's work politically. Who should we be representing? No doubt you will be asking yourself the same question in a much more politically heightened environment.

A few years after I started at MOCA, while working on an exhibition about MOCA's collection and archives, I realized that at the core of anything we'd want to do exhibitions about, there is at least one inherent tension. In fact, it is this tension that often marks a subject's relevance. Therefore, tensions should not be seen as obstacles, but rather tunnels to the heart of the matter.

For example, in the aforementioned "shitty Chinese food exhibition," actually titled "Sour, Sweet, Bitter, Spicy: Stories of Chinese Food and Identity in America," we identified a tension within the hierarchy of Chinese food. The discourse of Chinese food primarily revolved around determinations of authenticity, usually by non-Chinese critics who passed judgment on whether a restaurant or chef measured up to their romantic notions of traditional cooking. This kind of gatekeeping felt condescending in a colonialist way, so in the exhibition, we asked Chinese food chefs and home cooks to talk about their food and their lives. These chefs, restaurateurs, and home cooks—spanning all regions of America and a diverse range of Chinese food—became the voices narrating the exhibition.

For an ethnic-specific museum like MOCA, the voice is everything. What voice do we choose to amplify? What tone of voice are we using? From whose perspective are we speaking? So my advice to you in your first few days is to have conversations with people and listen more than you talk. Talk to Chinatown old-timers, Uptown Chinese Americans, Chinatown Art Brigade, property owners, Columbus Park regulars, newly arrived college students, the Flushing–Sunset Park–Chinatown shuttle bus drivers, East Broadway dried-good sellers, MOCA board members, local art gallerists, neighborhood artists, and local political upstarts. Understand what they expect of MOCA. Find the tensions that divide our communities and dream about how to express them in three dimensions.

Take these folks out for a coffee at one of the neighborhood's many precious little cafés or one of Chinatown's fine bakeries. But if you want to chat with me, take me to dim sum at Ping's on Mott Street and charge it to the museum.

Sincerely,
Herb Tam

P.S. I am not actually leaving my job at the Museum of Chinese in America and have no plans of leaving. This letter was written rhetorically, *as if* I were to leave.

JEAN SHIN

Re: DEBT FORGIVENESS

July 4, 2020

Dear Creditor,

It is with regret that I write this letter to you, notifying you that I will not be able to repay my debts in my lifetime. I am speaking not only in financial terms, but also of debts incurred due to racial injustice and inequity. I have lost confidence in this country's ability to care for its people, especially the most vulnerable communities of color.

As an Asian American, I feel a sense of urgency to write this letter now, as an attempt to reconcile the burden I have inherited. I would first like to acknowledge the generosity of generations before me and the historic debts I owe to Black and Native communities. These are impossible to pay back.

My second unpayable debt is to my uncle Eugene on my father's side. He was the first person in my family to lay down roots in the United States. He left Seoul to work as a medical technician in Baltimore but ended up running a supermarket for most of his life. I will forever remember him as a soft-spoken man who had a passion for photography. It was through his invitation that my immediate family was able to immigrate to this country from South Korea in 1978; his brother—my father—was to help him run the store.

I am also indebted, then, to my parents, with whom I came to the US at age six and eventually became a naturalized citizen. My family's history is unfairly labeled as "chain immigration," with all the negative associations of that term—when, in fact, it is a story about reunification and overcoming hardship.

Though my immigrant experience was one of assimilation to the point of invisibility, my parents' life in the United States was dramatically different. Speaking mainly in Korean with some broken English, they owned a corner grocery store in a predominantly Black neighborhood in Washington, DC. While I helped out in the store on weekends, I learned about the struggles of a very different America. My parents' store existed in an urban food desert, where it was challenging to serve fresh produce, meats, and dairy products to underserved Black communities. This Black neighborhood provided my family with our livelihood, but sadly our relationship was complicated by racial mistrust, mutual economic hardship, and a codependency that both resented.

In the 1980s and 90s, headlines reported violence and racial tensions between Korean business owners and Black communities in cities across the county, divisively pitting one minority's survival against the other's. My parents experienced many deaths of close friends within their Korean business community. I spent much of my childhood coping with nightmares and worrying that my parents would also be shot at gunpoint at work. I feared that I would wake up the next morning an orphan. The LA riots of 1992 intensified these unsettling feelings. Over the course of my life, the horror and anger I felt then have transformed into deep, unspoken sadness and rage.

My parents survived and are now retired. Their endurance and strength afforded me access to education, safety, and opportunity, but they are damaged by anxiety, depression, and symptoms of PTSD. How do I repay this kind of suffering and the sacrifices they made on my behalf? On the other hand, how do I begin to account for the greater loss and harm inflicted on Black communities through structural racism?

I owe a big debt to art for saving me. I found solace from violence and discrimination in my own creative process. Although my parents discouraged me from becoming an artist in favor of a more lucrative and stable career path, art chose me and I chose it. I see art as a powerful, transformative gift.

Although I was never taught about art made by people who looked like me, I am thankful that I was exposed to Black writers in my school curriculum. James Baldwin, Toni Morrison, Angela Davis, and others put words to my feeling of oppression, speaking to revolutions and demanding radical change. Channeling them and standing on their shoulders, I found my own voice during my college years at Pratt. In embracing an activist role, I overcame my feeling of helplessness. I am indebted to the Black leaders that modeled a life of resilience, resistance, and fearlessness.

Through art, I now have access to wealth and privilege; individuals, institutions, and foundations have awarded me scholarships, grants, and support. This is another debt that I am unable to pay back monetarily. However, I do my best to give back to these organizations with my time and labor—through teaching, mentoring, and serving on selection committees and boards. In this way, I help them further their mission to support the next generation of artists. These relationships of mutual support feel familiar to one brought up with Korean customs: one person generously steps up to pay for the entire group, but it's expected that someone else will pay next time. The oldest is obligated to provide and cover for the young, as an investment in the future well-being of the group. This shared sense of interdependency and intergenerational connectedness makes the group stronger, its members accountable to one another beyond transactional exchanges.

I understand that a letter asking for forgiveness requires that I show evidence of my hardship. To this end, I want to explain that having access to institutions is not the same as having the power to shape them. For example, even when I break through the glass ceiling to become the first Korean American woman artist to have a major solo exhibition at a prestigious museum, the percentage of such exhibitions by women of color remains miniscule. Worse, exhibition histories are forgotten and achievements erased. Major acquisitions of artwork by women and people of color to museums' permanent collections are rare.

My financial survival as an artist is uncertain and perhaps unsustainable; I go from gig to gig, project to project, and year to year. Women and people of color are also often excluded from the art market, which favors tokens of diversity rather than true equity. Systemic bias and an entrenched canon continue to advantage White male artists and benefit wealthy collectors. The number of Asian American women represented by galleries and having solo exhibitions is staggeringly low. Perhaps this is why I am committed to making public art: it is my way of sharing the gift of art in a much larger ecosystem, ensuring that art exists for free and for everyone.

In asking for debt forgiveness, I urge you to value human dignity over profit. In the collective, long-term work of repaying our historic debt to people of color, I promise to think clearly about how to divest in racist practices and redistribute our resources. I understand there may be strings attached in funding socially responsible endeavors and meeting the demands of the Black Lives Matter movement. I welcome this accountability. I not only give you my pledge and ongoing commitment to restorative justice, but more importantly, I pledge to continue direct actions with clear intentions towards the shared goal of real change. While I anticipate setbacks, I look forward to a future when we are truly debt-free, liberated, and at peace.

With gratitude,
Jean Shin

CELINE WONG KATZMAN

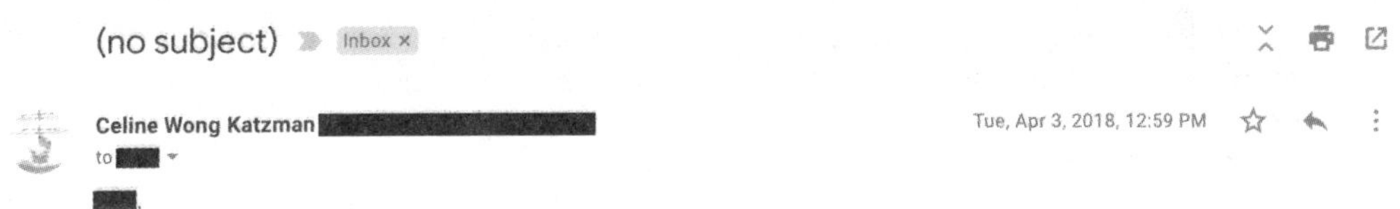
(no subject) Inbox ×

Celine Wong Katzman [redacted] Tue, Apr 3, 2018, 12:59 PM

to [redacted]

[redacted],

There are some things I need to say to you that have been weighing on my mind with regards to Saturday night. I would prefer to do this in person, and I know emails can cause miscommunication, but please understand that having emotionally intense conversations in person about boundary violation is extremely triggering to me.

Your behavior on Saturday night was inappropriate and made me very uncomfortable. You owe me an apology and I'm unsure that I can trust you anymore as a friend or professional colleague. I don't think that you systematically devised a situation to coerce me, but your actions (knowingly executed or not) were manipulative and violated my personal boundaries.

When we arrived at the club, we talked about work-related topics: you offered me professional advice, asked me to work together on a project, and mentioned you had a potential CTO job offer. These topics assert your power in the professional space we share and make me feel that I should be developing a personal relationship with you if I want to gain power by proximity.

Then, we both agreed to dance with your friends. That was fine.

When we got to the dance floor you were touching my furry coat, which was also okay with me, but I wish you had asked first. I attributed that desire to your state of mind at the time.

Then, you started dancing more closely to me. I didn't know how to react because the situation was escalating slowly. So slowly that I thought perhaps I was even just imagining it because I'd been drinking.

Finally, you started grinding on me and touching my bare skin underneath my coat. I truly had no idea what to do. This was not something I was comfortable with. If you were a stranger, I would have shoved you off me immediately and walked away, but I wanted to handle the situation gingerly as you're my friend and also someone who just asserted your professional power to me.

While I was trying to figure out how to de-escalate the situation, we kept dancing. I imagine you interpreted my nonaction as consent to continue, which is why you leaned in to kiss me. Thankfully that was enough for me to immediately verbally object, which I did, and you withdrew and later thanked me for letting you know that I was uncomfortable.

The glaring problem with this situation is you never asked me if I was comfortable with or desired any of the boundary-crossing actions leading up to leaning in for a kiss. Instead of giving me the opportunity to let you know I did not want that by asking for my consent, you just kept pushing until I said stop.

This brings me to the discussion that took place later in the night. You mentioned twice that your partner knew "the situation" and that I was there with you. This was confusing to me because that implied that you and I had discussed and agreed upon a "situation" that necessitated disclosure, and we never did. You never asked me if I saw our relationship as anything but platonic and professional. This really upset me because you misunderstood my discomfort related to the violation of my personal boundaries as worry that I had violated your boundaries with your partner. Furthermore, you knew that I have a partner of my own—someone who you had met in person—and you never asked about my boundaries with him.

Your assumption that I wanted you to come on to me without checking in with me at all and that my discomfort was due to the fact that I was worried I may have violated *your* boundaries is at the very least incredibly selfish and at worst downright narcissistic.

I don't think you understand how incredibly damaging this entire experience has been for me. I've spent the past few days running through every interaction we've ever had to see if I had missed something that would have allowed me to anticipate the interaction on Saturday, which took me completely by surprise. I've been asking myself: Have you wanted to work with me or advocate for my ideas because you respect my intelligence, or have you had ulterior motivations this entire time? The answer to this question matters less than the fact that I have to ask.

You have severely compromised my trust. I am not sure if or when I will be ready to talk to you in person. I will give you the opportunity to demonstrate that you are deeply sorry for what happened by thoughtfully and thoroughly responding to this email. I encourage you to take a few days to seriously think about this and not reply to me immediately. Perhaps then we can start to rebuild our relationship.

Celine

JEN LIU

COLLEC
DISAPPE

TIVE ARANCE

A SPECULATIVE MODEL OF ANALOG RESISTANCE

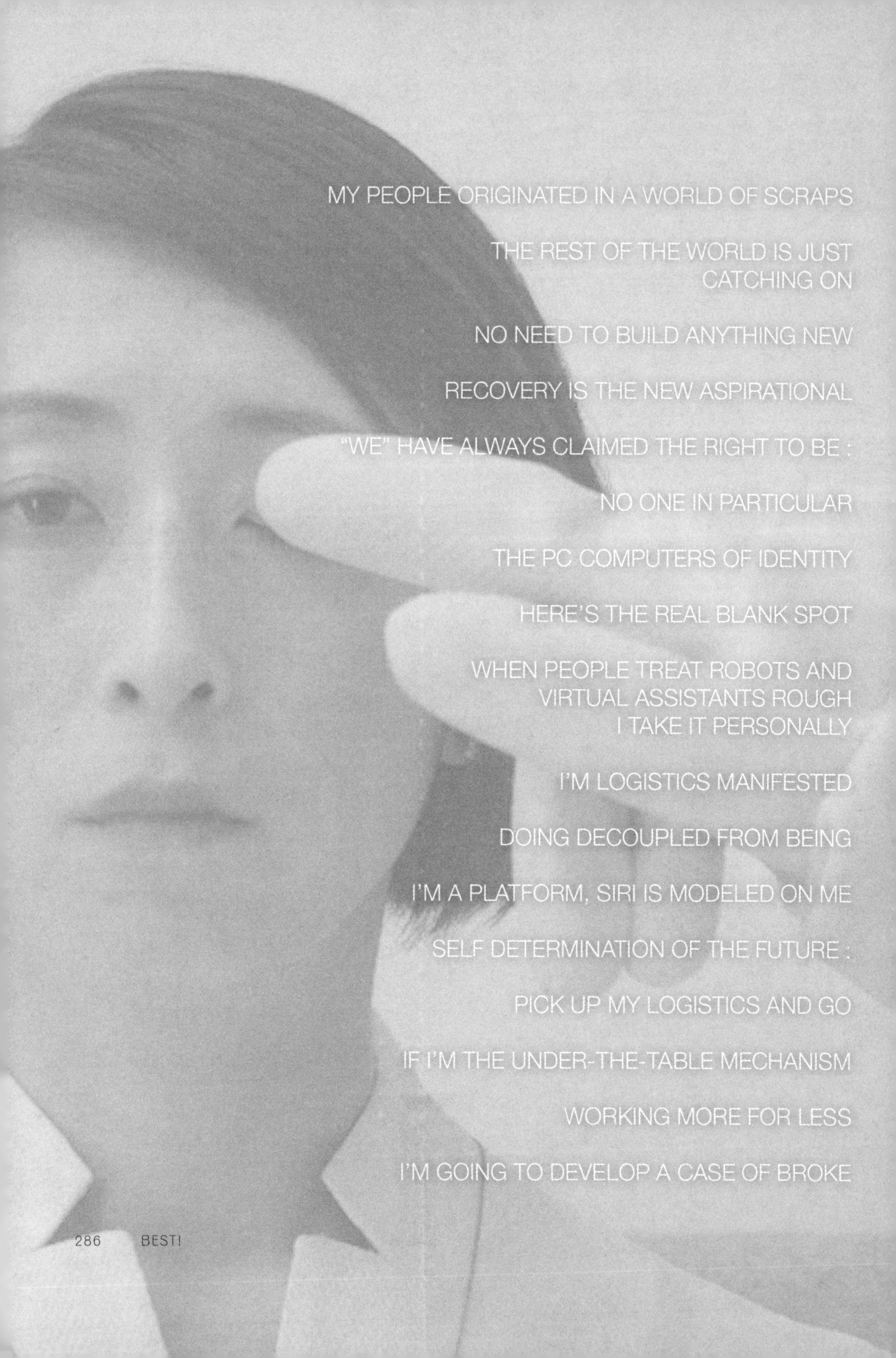

MY PEOPLE ORIGINATED IN A WORLD OF SCRAPS

THE REST OF THE WORLD IS JUST
CATCHING ON

NO NEED TO BUILD ANYTHING NEW

RECOVERY IS THE NEW ASPIRATIONAL

"WE" HAVE ALWAYS CLAIMED THE RIGHT TO BE :

NO ONE IN PARTICULAR

THE PC COMPUTERS OF IDENTITY

HERE'S THE REAL BLANK SPOT

WHEN PEOPLE TREAT ROBOTS AND
VIRTUAL ASSISTANTS ROUGH
I TAKE IT PERSONALLY

I'M LOGISTICS MANIFESTED

DOING DECOUPLED FROM BEING

I'M A PLATFORM, SIRI IS MODELED ON ME

SELF DETERMINATION OF THE FUTURE :

PICK UP MY LOGISTICS AND GO

IF I'M THE UNDER-THE-TABLE MECHANISM

WORKING MORE FOR LESS

I'M GOING TO DEVELOP A CASE OF BROKE

The time is right to take advantage of a circular economy, which keeps products, components, and materials at their highest value at all times, and decouples global economic development from finite resource consumption.

- *Hewlett Packard Enterprises*

Step 1: cut, sort, shred and pulverize.
Step 2: roast at 500 degrees
Step 3: leach in cyanide barrels, purify in hydrochloric + nitric acid drums
Step 4: electrolytic spinning and melt down

- *Methods of e-waste recycling of gold*

E-waste: small and large household appliances; information technology and telecommunications equipment; lighting equipment; electrical and electronic tools, toys, and leisure and sports equipment; medical devices; monitoring and control instruments; automatic dispensers; batteries, circuit boards, plastic casings, cathode-ray tubes, activated glass, and lead capacitors.

- *The Lancet, 2013*

Collective disappearance: when the population cuts off social contact with the opponent by disappearing, abandoning their homes. In early times, the magistrate of a county in central China was directed to conduct a census of the population. Being dissatisfied with the returns sent in by his subordinates, the magistrate undertook to count the inhabitants himself. The population, alarmed by his persistence and worried that he was coming to levy an oppressive tax, fled from the city and hid themselves in the fields. The official, thus frustrated in his efforts, hanged himself

- *198 Methods of Nonviolent Action, Gene Sharp*

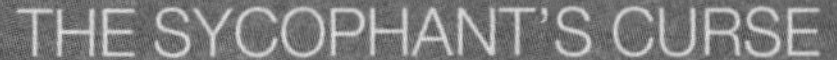

THE SYCOPHANT'S CURSE :

WANTING TO BE TAKEN FOR SOMETHING,
NOT NOTHING

BUT WHEN SOMETHING COMES
IT'S A BUCKET OF ACID

THAT'S A 50%
DISAPPEARANCE

BETTER TO 100%
DISAPPEAR

DISAPPEARANCE AS RESISTANCE :

THE PLATONIC IDEAL OF STRIKE
AGAINST THE COLONIZER

I DON'T WANT TO PLAY YOUR GAME

I'M NOT GOING TO PLAY CATCH-UP

DON'T PICK ME

BE LIKE WATER - SAYS BRUCE LEE

DON'T BE A GLASS OF BACKWASH - SAYS ME

FUCK THEM ALL - SAYS SIRI

She was showered with hot nitric acid. At first, her right cornea was semiopaque, while the left was slightly burned. By the 28th day the right cornea had cleared, but the left became opaque. She accidentally gargled with 30-40 ml of nitric acid, and swallowed a much smaller amount, after spitting most of it out. She developed corrosive esophagitis. X-rays revealed that her stomach shrank into a small sausage-shaped organ the diameter of a normal colon

- *US Center for Disease Control, Occupational Exposure to Nitric Acid, 1967*

Skeletal Deformation Stage: the entire body is wracked with severe pain and walking becomes very difficult. Pressure on the weakened spinal vertebrae due to bone fracturing causes a decrease in the patient's height. X-rays show the bones fracturing in a lateral fashion. The bones bend, deteriorate, become very soft, and disintegrate.

- *Polluted Japan*

Video stills and texts from PINK SLIME CAESAR SHIFT: GOLD LOOP, 2020. Pink Slime Caesar Shift is a multi-year, multi-media body of work, whose premise is to alter the DNA of mass-produced in-vitro hamburgers, to carry encrypted messages. These messages could be of vital use for labor activists in China or any other place in which a network alternative to social media is needed.

Gold Loop originated with gold biolistics, a method of genetic modification. Gold microparticles are shot into living cells, introducing altered DNA. Sümeyye Yar and I used this method to make fluorescent yellow beef cells that list 40 methods of nonviolent protest.

The gold microparticles had been recycled multiple times, its former lifetimes in consumer electronics: discarded phones, computers.

Gold Loop was shot at Dishui Lake, China, and Birmingham UK. It imagines a dreamlike global interconnectedness, looped together through circulations of resources, labor, and toxicity – via e-waste recycling and the Circular Economy model. In reality, this model shields a nightmare of biopolitical toxicity from view. Its aesthetics of corporate hygiene depend on export resource depletion, locking exploited bodies into extralegal zones of invisibility.

But are there possibilities of resistance within this invisbility?

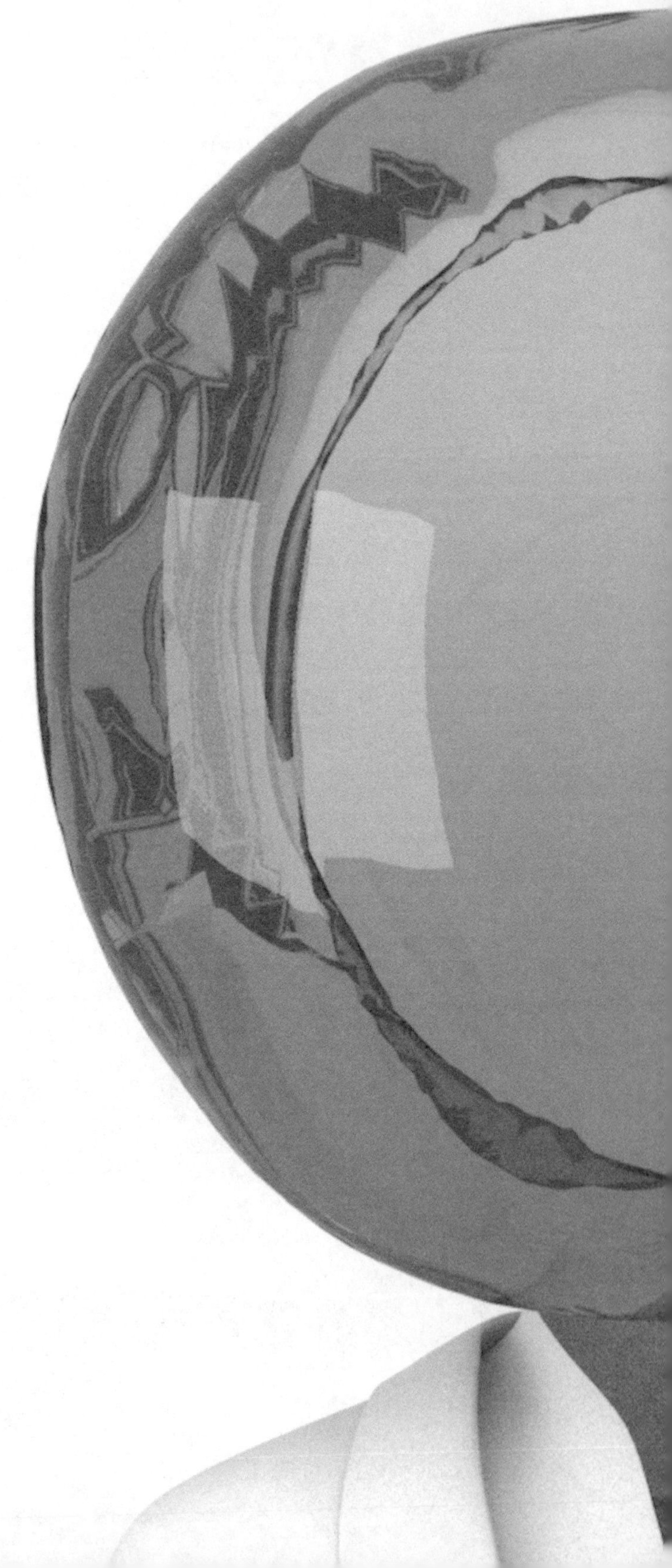

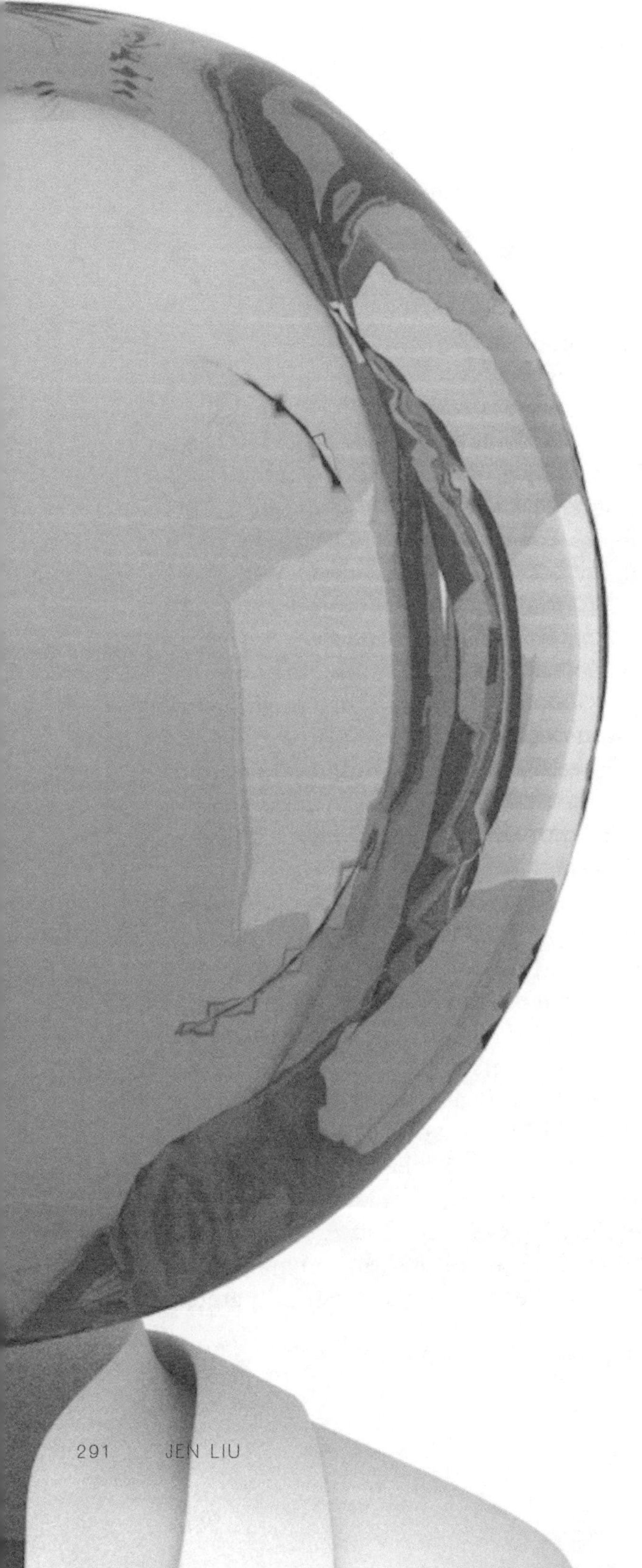

JESSICA HONG

Dear future self in an impending new paradigm,

I am writing to you during a time of extreme precarity, where once defined positions and temporalities have coalesced, collided, and fulminated. Though the future in which you sit may be unknown to me for some time, what is clear, even now, is that we are entering a new paradigm, where you are. I don't know what this new paradigm will look like or how we will get there, and it both comforts and unsettles me that you know this future well. With these uncertainties, I wasn't sure whether to write this letter. Why would you want to hear of past events that you've already experienced? However, it is out of a necessity on my part to write to you, this potential future, to know that there is indeed a future to look forward to. I write this out of a need to work through uncertainty, but rather than resorting back to my goal-oriented self attempting to find immediate resolutions to these uncertainties I face, this exercise is meant to sit with and understand the unprecedented characteristics of these times, to get comfortable with ambiguity while serving as a reflective document for you to learn from lived experiences.

I began writing this letter to you from my home office in the Upper Valley region of New Hampshire on the afternoon of Thursday, March 19, 2020. The Hood Museum of Art and Dartmouth College moved to remote work due to the novel coronavirus (COVID) that continues to affect communities across the globe. When I started this letter, full of anxiety, there was still the promise of spring and summer. But time waits for no one, and you're not likely waiting for me to catch up to you. It has taken some time to write, due to my feckless attempt to encapsulate all of my responses to what has taken place. I am finishing this letter on Wednesday, November 4, 2020, once again in my home office the day after a fateful election. I awoke this morning to a frosted landscape and headlines claiming even more uncertainty around this decisive presidential race. As much as I want to sit within ambiguity, this one seems impossible to swallow, all the while knowing you have clarity around the outcome.

Pre-COVID, my reading list comprised of novels about dystopic futures, with apocalyptic fevers or viruses leading to societal collapse: *Exit West* (Mohsin Hamid), *Severance* (Ling Ma), *Station Eleven* (Emily St. John Mandel), *Terra Nullius* (Claire Coleman), *Zed* (Joanna Kevenna). Many of the characters are living through the end times while reflecting on their past lives. I never imagined these fictive narratives would manifest or how, in reality, time and space would expand, extend, and contract. What, if anything, could have been done in the past to help shape these new futures? With our mostly presentist and futurist orientations, is that possible now?

With COVID's spread, precautionary distance between persons quickly became forced isolation with little to no human contact. Even with loosening over the last few months, it appears we are moving toward an isolationist mode once more. The absence of loved ones and the most mundane elements of my day-to-day—such as the office space or running errands—are palpable. Along with despondency amid a dire void of personal connectivity in a time of tumult, what has been confounding is seeing the structures that many, including myself, wanted to believe in failing us, those which the pandemic has laid bare and this administration has only augmented. Each day, I witness the devastating manifestations of severe inequities in dismaying news reports—from Black, Brown, and Indigenous folks having higher risks of contracting and dying from the virus, due to little to no access to quality, affordable healthcare or vital resources, to overt voter suppression in a disquieting political climate. The shock I felt at first quickly turned to guilt while recognizing the strange privilege that I held. Though my mother immigrated from Korea and, following a grueling divorce, tirelessly supported five kids as a single parent to provide a life for us with certain comforts, I have continued to live almost exclusively in a progressive bubble, ignorant of the sociopolitical landscapes beyond my sphere. I've had a paradoxical sense of injustice: confronting my own self and complicity in upholding these systems, perhaps being unconsciously blind to them, while on the other hand, my existence has been one on the margins, invisibilized, precisely because of these systems.

As we've seen with the pandemic, the entire world can change in a matter of months—and as we saw again this spring, it can change again in a matter of days. On May 25, months after I initiated this letter, George Floyd was murdered by a Minneapolis police officer for allegedly using a counterfeit $20 bill at a local convenience store. Witnessing the national and global protests following the murders of Floyd, Breonna Taylor, Ahmaud Arbery, Tony McDade, and Rayshard Brooks unfold this year with the backdrop of the pandemic was prodigious and surreal. Viewing on my computer screen in rural New Hampshire, I could feel the protesters' exasperation, frustration, and anger and felt a solidarity of spirit, a desire to be there with them, to echo the calls for change. These calls postulate that change can in fact come—an encouraging sliver of possibility during these darkest of days. But murders of Black folks by White supremacist institutions are part of the country's founding, so why are we only now seeing this kind of intersectional, intergenerational rallying? Why does the organizing that I've been witnessing not align with the still-solid support of this abhorrent administration? Then again, why only now do I feel I must, and in fact, have the power to act within my small capacity? Will the organizing continue into this new paradigm you're in, and how can I, can we, make sure change does come, even if incrementally?

As I contend with these personal afflictions, on the professional front, recent events have created time and space for genuine critical reflection that many museum workers have never experienced before, including critical introspection. I've been heartened to see and take part in conversations on anti-Blackness, particularly within Asian communities, and the complicated role of Asians and Asian Americans in the US as unwilling "beneficiaries" to the racial hierarchies implemented by White supremacist structures. Though Asians are seen as a foreign Other, are actively excluded and discriminated against, and experience violence at the hands of these structures, and though I personally have faced barriers because of my gender and race, I must come to terms with the fraught "benefits" I have received (and still receive) from the model minority myth. I am conscious that one of the reasons that I got to where I am professionally is that I fit a particular persona and temperament that befits these institutions—I may appear amiable, am discreet, and aim to please—while ticking off a diversity box. Early in my career, while I had and continue to have inspiring colleagues and mentors, there were those who critiqued my ambitions. I entered the field believing in the potency of the arts and their ability to engage and facilitate critical dialogues. But as a young Asian woman, I was distraught at how gender and racial stereotypes persisted in the field. I realized quite late that those who called me overly ambitious had become aware that this "assessment" was just their projections. It continues to be a challenge not to internalize these projections. Then there is the complicated matter of what constitutes Asians, Asian Americans, and Asianness. As a woman of East Asian descent, I am also cognizant of the colorist hierarchies in many Asian communities. Part of this is due to the racial hierarchies implemented by colonialism and White supremacy that have divided communities to prevent collaboration and intersectionality in order to preserve the status of those few at the top—which I am witnessing in real time. I often vacillate between questioning myself—is there anything that I can actually do to implement change?—and feeling defiant that regardless of seeming impossibilities, change is feasible.

As a museum curator, this era has initiated a professional identity crisis of sorts. Questions of what is essential abound. How do the arts, museums, curating, exhibitions, and visual culture fit on the continuum of essential goods and labor? With ensuing protests, many museums posted public statements and faced criticism for their desultory support of #BlackLivesMatter or empty promises of structural change. Museums have been discussing issues of diversity and inclusion (though equity and accessibility are notably absent), but participating at the surface level, only focusing on the external facets of the institution such as acquisitions and exhibitions featuring artists of color—at times, these artists may fit institutionally prescribed notions of racial identities and are still perceived as the Other. Performative gestures are not new, and I have functioned in spaces that are guilty of this, but in the past, I never felt I had the authority to speak up and speak out. I only recently feel empowered to do so by working through the detrimental internalizations of projections and assumptions of myself by others. You may question why it took so long to get here, but because you are in the future, you understand that it can take a temporal distancing to reflect, learn, adapt, and evolve.

Many of the conversations we're able to have and the actions we're able to carry out can be context-dependent. Being in a relatively remote area of New Hampshire, a state that is 93.1 percent White, and operating within an Ivy League institution in a museological space, makes me feel isolated and disconnected from the world. What does it mean for me as an Asian American woman to function in this context and participate in discussions around structural change? Issues of White adjacency are certainly present. When having these difficult conversations, White folks seem to feel more comfortable expressing their problematic views to me or even forget that I am a person of color, presuming that I will sympathize with their viewpoints. I am still reconciling how to seriously address this, rather than internalizing frustration and anguish. Additionally, there is an amplification of the problems of so-called neutrality. Whiteness—in all facets of the term, including as a racial category—presents itself as neutral to eschew the privileges of Whiteness that come directly from the conquering, exploitation, suppression, and killing of Black, Brown, Indigenous, POC, and other marginalized communities. This institution and surrounding communities are now reckoning with this reality, but there are grave uncertainties about constructive next steps. It has been an interesting exercise to interrogate this idea of neutrality with our audiences. Within nearly all publics I've engaged with, past and present, there are contingents that believe in the separation of aesthetics from the political; they see the museum as a space for escape to muse on the "beautiful" and refuse complexity. So, along with the internal structural changes required, another large challenge is to foster an ideological shift with audiences and their understandings around museums. In most instances, we must be transparent about our processes, curatorial decision-making, the pace of change, and the need to be methodical and intentional while making sure we're not stuck solely in conversation. In other cases, our audiences need to understand that we are a civic space that reflects the multifaceted worlds we live in. Knowing that change is often tediously slow, especially amid shifting mindsets, I imagine you are still working toward this.

There is always a worry of professional recourse for openly confronting such issues, but as I read and watch the news and scroll through virtual social platforms, which can be quite dreadful, I have never witnessed such public discourse around uprooting White supremacy and am seeing unparalleled intersectional, intergenerational collective action. In my role at the Hood and at Dartmouth, I frequently engage with undergraduate students. People have criticized factions of this generation for being self-absorbed and self-aggrandizing, and though they have much life to live, I have also experienced their thoughtfulness, intelligence, intentionality, awareness, and engagement, and am now seeing their drive, energy, and resilience. Whether I'm teaching or working with interns, there is a constructive critique and questioning that seems to be part of the generational DNA. Perhaps I am focused on the progressive sphere I exist in, but when I think about myself at that age, and though critical thinking and questioning had import to me, I don't remember having this kind of wherewithal or courage to so openly question and not only question, but make space and conceive of new models to be in the world. Students vigorously call upon the institution to center voices of Black, Indigenous, LGBTQIA+, peoples of color to transfigure Eurocentric curricula. In their spare time, they've organized fundraising initiatives for students in need of financial support, and in the midst of this political climate, volunteered as poll workers, all the while so deftly contending with the drastic limitations this pandemic has wrought. Because of severe institutional lack and with the uncertain future, these young folks are trying to take steps to ensure that we get to the future we need. One of the most important things I can do in my work is make space for ensuing generations who implement changes.

I recall when I first started in this field, at least in the contemporary art scene in New York, there was a tacit but accepted understanding that we were meant to aspire to the status of "star curator" and breed a kind of cult of personality. Though you can argue there are parallels today with the rise of social media, curators such as myself see ourselves as a part of a whole, a member of broader communities, a stitch in the larger, connected sociocultural fabric. Our work is collaborative and not singular. As such, we are seeing a shift toward community. The term *community*, however, comes with its complications. It assumes a homogenous group, but "community" in any context realistically comprises multiple communities, some that may intersect and some that may not. Within the museological context, institutions continue to have difficulty understanding who constitutes their communities. Though there are always exceptions to the rule, museums haven't historically expressed real interest in getting to know their communities. So, returning to this question of the essential nature of the arts and cultural sectors, one way to understand what is essential is how committed the surrounding communities are to a cultural institution. Does the museum not only add to but, more importantly, foster and support cultural discourse and cultural production in its communities? While I am certainly open to imagining new models beyond the museum, the museum is primarily the space in which I function (in particular the museum as it is based in the US) and my focus has been on how to change, reenvision, and even transform this particular site. As museums finally begin to acknowledge their colonial and White supremacist legacies and the dynamic and vital conversations around that happen so publicly in our field, there is something to look to. Building on the organizing and labor of Black communities (particularly Black women), Indigenous folks, and a range of marginal communities, these up-and-coming generations are modeling labor and life to prioritize community in all its forms, which has intensified my determination to bring this to the fore of my work. I know that hope is fraught, but as I look to you in the uncertain but near future, I choose to—and need to—hold onto these glimmers of hope.

In your new paradigm, what fears, desires, habits, organizing, structures, as well as communities have remained, dissipated, and formed? In reading this, I'm somewhat chagrined by my sentiments in this letter, as it's quite unresolved, undetermined, and I know you have a more holistic idea of the experiences I'm having. In your time, these musings may seem aspirational, naive, or even misguided. This is the state of things, open, fluid, ever-changing, ever-evolving. And I, you, we should not forget where we once were, so that I, you, and we can assess these currents while forging ahead into your new paradigm and to learn from our pasts to help shape potential futures. It's impossible to predict what will come even where you are, and as of now, I can only project and hope while collectively working toward what I, what we, believe is necessary right now.

Until we meet,
Jessica Hong

HOWIE CHEN

Dear Elaine Chao,
Dear Andrew Yang,
Dear Wendi Deng,
Dear Bobby Jindal,
Dear Kevin Kwan,
Dear Kellie Chauvin,
Dear Nikki Haley,
Dear Paul Chan,
Dear Tou Thao,
Dear Peter Liang,
Dear Kamala Harris,
Dear Tulsi Gabbard,
Dear Chris Lew,
Dear Amy Chua,
Dear Michael Chang,
Dear Sadoux Kim,
Dear Julie Chen,
Dear Priscilla Chan,
Dear Ajit Pai,
Dear Jeremy Lin,
Dear Tiger Woods,
Dear Danny Bowien,
Dear Tila Tequila,
Dear Inyoung You,
Dear John Yoo,

Dear Dinesh D'Souza,
Dear Andy Ngo,
Dear Cindy Yang,
Dear Michelle Malkin,
Dear Gedde Watanabe,
Dear Kurt Suzuki,
Dear Soon Ja Du,
Dear Richard Aoki,

Good luck,
Howie Chen

MARTHA TUTTLE

To my grandmother,

My mother says that your spirit came to the hospital the day I was born—

When she speaks of this, I imagine I am watching from the sidelines. As though my consciousness had not yet fully reached
my body, and so somehow I had a greater capacity for seeing or awareness or memory. I remember you filling the whole room like a cup of water spilled on a countertop, held in tension at the edges. As if for a moment
we coexisted on the
same plane—when anyone speaks about you, I think of light.

I was named the name you chose
when you needed a good one in English.

(Martha// Latin from Ancient Greek Μάρθα, from Aramaic מרתא *(martā) "the mistress" or "the lady," from* מרה *"mistress," feminine of* מרי *"master")*

[I ask myself often—why is it so important to me that people know that I am Chinese?

Because I was raised to feel that way— to acknowledge is to honor.

But also because of all the times people have said *not enough/ you are so/ what are you/ you look like/ but what are you really/ you don't look like/ are you sure you aren't actually*]

My mother's mother—

I do not know what to call you.

Because you died before I was born, what I know about you is from stories, as well as a box of letters my grandfather gave to me when we were moving him from his apartment in Honolulu to an assisted living facility. You wrote them to him when he was stationed in Chongqing, and later when he had returned to the United States to finish his studies.

I like reading about your courtship, of when you were pregnant with my mother, about your secret marriage. About Mao's rising presence in China, and when you and my mother left to meet my grandfather in San Francisco. I think it's nice that you bought my grandfather slippers for his cold feet (a small detail, but something I knew to be true about him some forty years later). You worry if he's getting enough sleep, and eating well. You handle his mother's rejection with significant grace.

I wish I could say that as time went on, it was as if you were writing to me. An ancestor gone is a myth, a demigod, and I have always wanted to know you as a reality.

When I moved into the apartment where I now live, I found several letters written to my grandfather from the mental health ward of an American war hospital. They described a sudden attack of depression and malaise warranting medical evacuation by helicopter. The language in the letters describes a quality of mind unique in its capacity for devastation while maintaining self-control. They are undoubtedly the words of a woman shell shocked by war and by loss, yet still able to argue with her doctor and—if I am to take the writer at her word—to win. I sat on the floor of my new home and I cried and cried and cried—the distinct feeling of relief that recognition can give these letters so succinctly described the quality of depression that seems to be passed down through the women of our family characterized by simultaneous lucidity and collapse.

(Akhmatova// it was then that something like a smile slid over what had previously been her face.)

[I think people crave connection---clarity---more than almost anything. If we are born without a clear narrative---and then we are offered one---

(the connection of a name for instance, or the perceived similarity to a family member passed) *Didion// we tell ourselves stories in order to live*
]

But when I showed these letters to my mother, she said the handwriting was not yours. They must have been written by a previous girlfriend and kept by my grandfather in the same box. Such a strange connection to a stranger. I feel as if I'm supposed to say I read these letters because I want to know you, or because I want to know me. But there is so much distance between us, in terms of time and experience. If I am being honest, I like reading your words mostly because I like you. I find you brave and smart and funny. Not an anchor neccesarily, not a guide, but someone to grow a space with.

[A few years ago I made a list of my favorite novels for a friend. I realized then that I am drawn to stories about spirits, ghosts, a sense of fluidity between worlds.

Leslie Marmon Silko// Ceremony

Amos Tutuola// My life in the bush of ghosts

Juan Rulfo// Pedro Paramo

Ovid// Metamorphosis

Clarice Lispector// Agua Viva

Do you ever pass through anymore]

Uncle Boonmee who can recall his past lives// ghosts are attached to people, not places

As a child my mother would tell me that you are the first star to emerge after sunset and
To think of you as the growing indigo of the evening sky.

But she also said---that at times you were angry

When you left China, you brought with you a lavender silk jacket, still in progress. The arms are in pieces, and the lining is unhemmed.

Was this a way to pick up where you left off? I can't imagine what it must have been like for you to be so far from your family, your country, your home.

Can anyone ever believe they are permanently leaving their home

No one has thought to finish it and seventy years later it remains crisp and the parts folded---almost cloying, if we were to treat it as a metaphor.

I write to you as yours.

JOHN TAIN

Dear Yasuhiro Ishimoto,

You have been on my mind of late. This may not be all that surprising, given that I've been researching you these last few years.[1] My motivation had come from admiration for *Someday, Somewhere* (1958) and *Katsura* (1959), publications whose sheer formal inventiveness are considered to have opened a path for the generation of Japanese photographers after you, including Daido Moriyama and Shomei Tomatsu, and led to what has widely been regarded as the golden age of the photobook. I knew that you had been seen as a bridge between the Japanese postwar era and the modernism of the Institute of Design in Chicago—founded as the New Bauhaus by László Moholy-Nagy in 1937, and where it had generally been understood that you learned photography with Harry Callahan while a student from 1948 to 1952. And no doubt this reading is right. However, research uncovered a carefully assembled album of your photographs taken during the war years, demonstrating that, to a great extent, you had learned modernist photography while at Camp Amache in Colorado. You were first taught by fellow inmates, some of whom were professionals—much as the younger artist Ruth Asawa had learned drawing and painting from Disney animators who were incarcerated with her.

The astonishing photographs from the camp change our understanding of your work. You took enough pride in them to have made the album and to have shown them to others when you were first starting out in Chicago. But something about the response you got made you hide these photographs for the remainder of your lifetime—possibly out of embarrassment or a sense that they best be forgotten.

Your wanting to put that chapter of your life behind you would not have been so unusual. After the war, the pressure to assimilate as fully as possible into mainstream (White) American culture was intense. But much as you may have tried, others would not let you forget your difference. Strangers would accost you in the street while you were photographing. And the artist Minor

White wrote in an exhibition pamphlet, over your objections, that your training may have been Western, but your "tradition of seeing" was "Oriental," turning what should have been a moment of celebration—your first one-person museum show—into a reminder of stigma.[2] You knew intimately the contradiction at the heart of being Asian American and lived the social impossibility of inhabiting both terms at once.

Given the resurgence of racism and anti-Asian sentiment across the United States now, not to mention the government's renewed use of "detention centers," it'd be hard to not think of what you went through. Your biography offers a stark reminder that current events are part of a longer history, one that encompasses the incarceration of over 120,000 Issei and Nissei. Indeed, some people's refusal to acknowledge people of Asian descent as Americans, much less as human beings, has been around since the 19th century, when the first wave of immigrants arrived as laborers. (An indication of where attitudes stood during your lifetime can be seen in the fact that sociologists at UC Berkeley deemed it perfectly acceptable to use the terms "spoilage" or "salvage" to describe individuals coming out of the camps.)[3]

But if I continue to think of you, it is not just because you were Japanese American. It is also because you lived your life as an artist. That is, where others may have only seen doors closing, you saw also an opening onto the possibility of solidarity. You intuitively understood that the discrimination you had experienced paralleled the racism faced by the African Americans present in your work.

You were not the only one to photograph Black Chicagoans with empathy and understanding: Wayne Miller, who taught photography at the Institute around the time you started, undertook a two-year project, *The Way of Life of the Northern Negro*, in which he tried "to express how they were feeling about their daily lives and their families." But Miller's photos often are taken at a distance, so as to situate the sitters in their socioeconomic environment. This choice suggests that he ultimately acted as an ethnographer, understanding the people he documented as a "them." By contrast, your images frequently concentrate on the individuals themselves; when you looked into their faces, you saw people like you, a "we." This much is clear from the careful juxtaposition of children from Chicago, most of them African American, side by side with children in Tokyo.

Of course, such a world was *someday, somewhere*, as the title suggests. But it is still remarkable, given that your work came about at a conjuncture when notions of intersectionality and allyship—much less Asian American identity—had not yet come into being. It may have been dreamwork that you were doing in these photographs, but it is no less real. So I will continue to carry you with me, not only as a reminder of the past, but also as an inspiration for what is possible. For that, I thank you.

Yours,
John

1 This was mainly for an exhibition I cocurated with Jasmine Alinder at the DePaul Art Museum for the Terra Foundation for American Art's Art Design Chicago initiative. See Jasmine Alinder and John Tain, *Yasuhiro Ishimoto: Someday, Chicago* (Chicago: DePaul Art Museum; University of Chicago Press, 2018).

2 Minor White, *Photographs by Yasuhiro Ishimoto* (Chicago: Art Institute of Chicago, 1960).

3 See the publications from the Japanese American Evacuation and Resettlement Study: Dorothy Swaine Thomas and Richard Nishimoto, *The Spoilage* (Berkeley: University of California Press, 1946), and Dorothy Swaine Thomas, *The Salvage* (Berkeley: University of California Press, 1952).

KEN LUM

Dear Mother,

I wanted to continue from where I ended in my last letter to you. I so regret kicking up such a fuss whenever you wanted to go and see a Chinese opera in Chinatown. I felt embarrassed by what I thought of then as "noise," the strange costumes and painted faces. I think back to your extensive collection of long-playing records of Chinese opera and how knowledgeable you were on the subject. I just did not appreciate any of this at the time. I know now that it wasn't just the foreignness of Chinese opera that I rejected. I was also rejecting the Chineseness in me. Every Chinese person I knew was poor and lived in cramped quarters around Chinatown. I was wrong to think that way, of course, but I only knew what I saw and what I saw seemed categorically true.

There was another thing that I did not fully appreciate about you, and that was just how Chinese you were. I knew that you did not speak a word of English. I knew that you were completely reliant upon the Chinese world that you knew in Vancouver. But I did not appreciate the rituals you performed daily in front of the shrine you kept in our living room. I did not appreciate your insistence that my brother Andrew and I learn how to read and write in Chinese. I did not appreciate the strange medicinal brews you made me drink whenever I did not feel well. I appreciate all of these things now and increasingly so with each passing day. I also appreciate—and love—being a person of Chinese descent, and I want to instill this appreciation in my children.

I think you would be shocked to see China today. It is far different from the one you knew when you left for Hong Kong in the early 1950s. There are Chinese tourists everywhere now. Technology has made possible Chinese language stations throughout the world. I remember how excited you were with the arrival of VHS tapes and the anticipation of watching Chinese movies from the luxury of home. I now understand how deeply isolating the world must have been for you across the Pacific Ocean in Vancouver. I wish I had understood this earlier. And I wish that you were still alive to meet Paloma and our children, Linus and Linnea.

I have another regret: I know how disappointed you were in me when I resigned from my science studies to follow the path of art in the late 1970s. I know you were worried about me and wanted only the best for me. Money was always a problem for us, and I know that contemporary art must have seemed a flight of lunacy. You were very sick when I sold my first artwork. I recall you expressing surprise and pleasure. I also like to believe that, on a deeper level, you were happy that I was following my own path. You were never allowed to follow the path of your own choosing. You had no choice but to work. Life dealt you a cruel hand, for I know you were a person of great refinement who was so fond of and knowledgeable about Chinese music and literature.

I know you would be proud to know that I am now a university professor. You were a teacher yourself and spoke different dialects of Chinese. You were sent to the countryside of Southern China to teach Mandarin Chinese to Cantonese speakers. It was there you met my father, who was visiting from Canada in search of a wife. He was not a good husband or father. He was absent for long stretches, disloyal, and terribly addicted to gambling. Our family was constantly under threat of gangster debt collectors. I recall how circumscribed life was when my brother and I were children. I recall being so wide-eyed when I visited the downtown of Vancouver for the first time. I did not see any other Chinese people. Everyone was White. Even then, I understood that this was the world of our rulers. I understood that I had to know this world in order to negotiate my passage through it.

I was the recipient of many racial taunts as a child. Over time, however, the taunts all but disappeared. Asians were starting to be admired as a model race. I remember going to see *Flower Drum Song* (1961) in a movie theater with you and Andrew. It was one of the few times that you wanted to see a non-Chinese film. While the Head Tax, the Chinese Exclusion Law, and the race riots that tried to destroy Chinatown were a heavy price to pay for acceptance into White-dominated society, we had a sense of hope that life in Canada would be a lot better for future generations of Chinese.

This was the case in the United States as well. Your parents lived in near squalor in a one-bedroom, five-floor walk-up right under the Manhattan Bridge. It was home to Grandmother, Grandfather, Aunt, Uncle, and Great Uncle. Whenever we visited, every inch of the apartment became a sleeping space at night. But after several years on Henry Street, you all moved to a much larger place in Brooklyn. Although the neighborhood of the latter was quite dangerous at the time, there was no ceaseless traffic noise from the rattle of the Manhattan Bridge. Again, there was hope.

But I am sad to tell you that a well of anti-Asian racism has begun to surface again. Several of our Asian students in the Master of Fine Arts program at the University of Pennsylvania where I teach were verbally assaulted this year, one quite threateningly. I have to be a bit careful myself and take the advice you gave me as a child to always lie low. However, I also know it is important to join others in fighting racism. I will tell you about the Black Lives Matter movement in my next letter to you. Please know that I love you, wherever you are.

Your loving son,
Ken (Lin Yinting)

KIM NGUYEN

Dear,

Each day, I receive multiple emails that wish for my health and safety during this unprecedented moment. I wonder why these same people don't consider our health and safety during any other moment of any other day. They send wishes of wellness before they cancel projects or withdraw funds, and use the crisis as an excuse to eliminate jobs, opportunities, and existing commitments, thrusting more of us into precarity. Their wishes are just exercises in capitalistic productivity, rather than true acknowledgments of an overwhelming collective state of grief over the loss of our livelihoods. It is convenient for them that we are distracted, saddened by humanity; that we live in a bad society where greed, racial neglect, surveillance, and class violence run rampant, where grandmothers die alone while capitalism gets to keep on living like the Karen that she is. White liberal settler legacies undergird the rich protecting the rich, and the White protecting the White. Power eternally protects power.

Each week, our students ask why anyone has to work or go to school (now or ever again). We have no real response except to say that we should just release everyone from prison—literal first, but also imagined, why not—and once that's done, we can toss out the rest of this universe, along with the trash bag it came in. Why does it take the extraordinary for us to care for one another, and even then, not nearly enough? Living in this country is like waiting to be robbed, and dying in this country is just being robbed. Strike's still on, kids.

Each morning begins with the same routine: halfhearted exercise followed by less-than-halfhearted email, remembering to eat but somehow not eating what we used to, just something to stay alive. I have started and stopped writing this text more times than I can count, because who counts time anymore except for bosses and the bosses of bosses? Let's make another pact to stop caring about either of them.

Netflix says a Korean drama about a woman who falls in love with a hologram is a 98 percent match for me, and you know this algorithm *sees me*, because what else is my life other than unrequited love with ghosts? Let us always stay devoted to this haunting.

And ghosts only please, no zombies. Those are for the White men at dinner parties who talk about how we live in Western civilization and therefore should care about the Greeks, which I don't know anything about. Whatever is birthed out of the cradle of capitalism sounds like their fantasy, and no one is here for it. Whenever these men expound the importance of art history and how it must be preserved, what they actually mean is that it must be *protected*. They can keep all the corpses; here's that trash bag.

Each time this happens, we conjure the wise words of Nesbit Crutchfield, who said we have a right to determine our own destinies, our own noncapitalist paths. He reminded us that to know our history is to love ourselves first. To be seen as *whole*. Unsurprisingly, he makes no mention of the Greeks.

Each year a different room, mostly the same faces. We come together, and the beginning and the end remain the same. We say this is a broken system, and the more times we point to this broken system, the harder it gets to climb back up. It does not get easier to say out loud that I am tired of the fight because the fight is long, and the institution is winning. I see it marked on my body and the bodies of everyone I love. I worry about the White people listening, who take this statement as quitting, who interpret this sentence as a cry for White saviorhood, because a life constructed on possession will never understand one that is carved out of dispossession. I cannot handle the burden of White people who listen but feel guilty hearing this. Their emotional journey is not and never will be ours. White devils versus unwanted allies, on & on & on & on. We have figured out the engravings on all of our tombstones. *She worked hard*. Still dead.

We hold each other, I told you (& you & you & you). I hold you when you cannot hold yourself any longer, and I know you will hold me when I cannot hold myself. I don't want to talk about a broken system right now, maybe never will again—but I am dramatic like that, so I will likely talk about it later and reverse this promise. We are allowed to be weak sometimes and to break our resolve, because we can only hold so much, and I grant myself permission to quit and I hope you (& you & you & you) will do the same. Because we stand here together, holding each other, on the precipice of absolutely nothing, with a belief that at the bottom of this jump is abolition and not reform, always and forever, measured in our bodies, crossed over our hearts, promised to die.

So for those of us who cannot leave: this is for you.

Tomorrow, I want to speak about the well of arrogance we have to dip into to keep living. I want to speak about recognizing our own worth and the worth of everyone dear to us. I want to speak about indecent love. We don't do this because the fight is rewarding or because we believe it will change, or because we think the institution will ever treat us as human beings. We do this because *we love each other*, even if the institution will never love us back. These people think we are not worthy: not worthy of their education, their mentorship, their opportunities, not worthy of their love. But I am here to say we love each other, deeply and with full hearts, in a way that is completely indecipherable to them because their existence is constructed on individualism and imperialism, and ours is built on each other, even in pieces—or especially in pieces.

Soon, I want to be able to openly and legibly speak about liberation—about a future that does not belong to anyone but ourselves—without White people thinking this voyage is purely personal, the repercussions of our individual scars. They don't understand. They don't understand that we are doing this not because we are trying to convince anyone of anything, but because we love each other too much not to. They don't understand that liberation can mean multiple endings and not a new frontier.

Eventually, I want our love for each other to mean we can critique one another, be honest about the precision of our politics, and use the sharpest tips of our knives to emphasize that we are not monolithic and neither are our politics. And even when you are on the "right side," you can use and be used, and we will never *become* if we are always speaking for them and to them, answering their calls, cleaning up their messes, explaining & explaining, waiting for them to transform their well-wishes into the actual transformation of our lives. The family argument is ours to have, and we can never have it if we are trapped in conversations around inclusion and equity, tokenism, solidarity, and allyship, as if those words mean anything anymore. We all know that even if we find new terms, they'll just take those and ruin them too.

Next time, I want to speak about joy as disobedience, as a betrayal of all the systems and structures that are trying to destroy us. Legality has failed us many times over. Good people will not turn a rotten apple into a ripe one, just as White people will never turn upon a system that they constructed and that allows them to continue to exist. This is not about the power you know, and I want us to stop asking permission from this power as if an institution that checks boxes, makes strategic hires and acquisitions, and signs letters denouncing its own racism will improve the material conditions of our loved ones. When given the opportunity to take care of us or it, they choose art history over history and legacy over our lives—always.

& ultimately I want none of us return to work anyway, because our dreams were never about jobs.

Someday we will better articulate the curvatures of our loneliness. Or these articulations will not even be necessary, as they will just be known. The more I learn about myself and the people I love, the more I learn about everyone we loved before us and after, the lonelier and more alienated I feel in this universe. It is a type of knowledge that enriches some relations and poisons others, as our languages become less legible and our thoughts are too fast to be slowed. In the search for horizons, there are no returns. We can want a future that we do not know, and mourn the loss of the past we never had, all at once.

Thus the contradiction of our lives. We are incongruous with this world in the best and worst ways, in need of and bound by an intense love that is unwavering yet uneven, living *for* each other—not because we are against *them*—even if being against them consumes our living. Trinh T. Minh-ha says that the physical and psychic conditions of our world show that we are a profoundly heartsick society. That sometimes "a sickness of the system may help to chart new ground, bring out what lies dormant, and open one's sight to *what's already flowering within*. When a flower blooms, here and now the world comes into being."

& in the end, another spring.

MICHELLE LOPEZ

Dear Wolf,

I remember when you were starting at a new elite school when you were 10. I mentioned the importance of dressing the part so that people wouldn't mistake you for a ne'er-do-well minority. You told me, *Mom, it's not like that anymore*. And then I suddenly doubted myself and felt my age and the transmission of my inherited fear. I doubted my simmering hysteria that accompanies being Brown, and I wondered, as I always do with certain interactions, if maybe it was just me.

Maybe, in fact, the world is a post-racial place, and I unduly isolate myself because I am fundamentally scared of the world and my place in it. I pause; I hesitate because I don't recognize myself in certain spaces. My moves are subconsciously passive; they actually are non-moves because I imagine if I tried, I wouldn't get anywhere anyway. I rationalize, *I can subvert the system by my nonparticipation.*

And so when the riots happened the night of your thirteenth birthday party—where we danced joyously with friends on Zoom to forget for a minute that we were in a pandemic—I stayed up late watching the ripple effect of the uprising in several states. The next morning, on your actual birthday, my face streamed with tears before you woke, but not out of fear for my safety. In fact, the rebellion brought relief and a certain jaw-dropping awe. I was crying for you as a mother for her vulnerable child as I wondered what world you were entering. How does a child become an adult in the midst of this? And how does the child within the adult calm all the racist traumas of her own childhood as they swell inside her, just beyond the brink of her own long-standing silence?

A few hours later, I would gather myself, smiling with birthday cheer, and we would silently bike through the streets of Philadelphia, looking at all the freshly smashed storefronts. To me, the rock through the glass was finally a moment of recognition. *It's not just me. It's not just me.*

In the weeks after, as you have seen, so many minority groups have come forward to say, *This happened to me, too*, in institutions of power. People have risen to protest, to not be silent. You may be one of those unique people who is not oppressed by race—with the combination of a Western name and the appearance of being "White enough." And when you open this letter when you are an adult, and time has passed, I hope you can honestly tell me in my grave, *Mom, it's not like that anymore.*

This letter is to help guide you in how to handle my estate, so you may express to others in your decision on where my artistic legacy lands: what it has meant for me to be a silent witness and swallow a certain acceptance to a kind of oppression—as a woman of color who is not White enough, or Black enough, or Asian enough. Oppression may be too strong of a word: simply forgotten is a more accurate description because my work can't seem to be filed into an identity folder by the powers that be.

In that same silence, I have always wanted to stand as a Brown artist of color. And yet I don't want people to be amazed at how a small Asian "delicate" woman could make such large, masculine work. So my only condition is that you refuse the acquisition if the conversation goes towards this need to essentialize. Maybe my identity has led me to make something bigger than myself because that is the only way to move beyond the delicacy and frailty of a presupposed identity.

In the end, regardless of the state of the world as you handle the estate, I want you to remember your mom as a *force* and to make decisions in accordance with that—especially if I was unwilling to do that in my lifetime.

X Mom

ASAD RAZA

From: **Asad Raza**
Date: Wed, June 19, 2019 at 1:24 PM
Subject: alma nama
To: Syed Tasnim Raza, MD
Cc: Abbas in Italy; Ada Beams; Akbi Khan; Alia Raza; Anjuli Raza Kolb; Arfa Raza; Ashad; Atiya Khan, MD; AVM S J & Arfa Raza; Batool Raza; BiBi Amera Raza; Hussain; Jaffer Kolb; jbeams; Margit Oberrauch; Musa Raza; Nazli Ayse Raza; Raza, Azra; Ryan Moritz; Sakeena Raza; Samina Raza Egilmez; Samuel Beams; Sheher Preisler; Sughra Raza, MD; Tariq Khan, MD; zbeams; Zehra Fatima Raza, MD; Aral Egilmez; Omar Raza; Yasmin Raza

Aloha Famig, and apologies for the wait for a more comprehensive message. I hear rumblings that people feel uninformed—well, we've been kind of busy! Here is a long description, and PLEASE feel free to ignore, as it is long, visceral, and frankly, fucking graphic. But there is one hero to this story, and her name is Kathrin Jira. I have been her main assistant, so I saw what she did and is doing. She is amazingly brave and she is relentless. And we went through some wretched moments.

It all started on Sunday, when Mommy and Elsa left our house at 4:30 AM. It was such a fun visit. We cooked every day and took long walks around Berlin and hung out. On Sunday morning, we were a little sad, cleaned up, and organized things and later in the day, Kathrin felt a bad headache, which can be a sign of pregnancy problems, so we went to our hospital, Charité, which is a beautiful place, actually—a set of buildings around a central "allée" in the north of Berlin. We were there for most of the afternoon. They found nothing major wrong but gave an internal massage intended to promote contractions. We went home, eating dinner on the way, and went to bed at 10 PM pretty bone tired from the day and from several days.

Later, I woke up to Kathrin softly calling my name. I was in a deep sleep. I said, "What is it?" She said, a little tremulously, "My water broke." We were both in shock, which sounds crazy, I know. This was actually going to happen.

I looked for a clock. We had only slept twenty-five minutes. We got our prepacked little roller suitcase (holding energy bars, our clothes, and Alma's first outfit) and called a taxi. There was a sensation of surreality, of living events you had been anticipating for a long time but hadn't known would feel precisely like *this*. The driver sensed the extreme gravity and drove perfectly, said good luck with everything. We got to Charité. Kathrin had planned everything for the benefit of Junebug and knew exactly what she wanted to do. The plan was to go without painkillers (which we were told here is better for the baby and for the mother's postpartum mental state) and to hold the baby immediately (she had been separated from her own mom), among other things, and I was the main assistant to her for the labor time (with regular guidance from the midwives and doctors), and there was a whole plan. Life is what happens instead.

Most of what we expected, we got, for the first nine hours or so. Contractions were coming every three minutes or so, getting worse and worse. The pain was getting very bad, and Kathrin suffers from back pain, which was also being triggered. She just wouldn't give in, and we entered some kind of fugue state. By 6 AM, we were falling asleep for ninety seconds between each contraction, K on the bed and me in a facing chair, then rising together so I could support her while she stood through the contraction, the least painful way for her. It got worse and worse, though. Eventually, she described what she was going through as belts of red-hot iron cutting through her back to belly. And after three hours of this, they said we had gained another centimeter—and we needed three more to start pushing. Oh, god.

At about 9 AM, the doctor came and told us it wasn't going fast enough and recommended an epidural, a shot to numb her entire lower body. K was immediately okay with it, even though we were departing from the plan, and I knew how much she wanted everything done in the "right" way. She said Junebug needed to come out and recognized that she couldn't stick to her plan, though. But the epidural, which gave her relief, also slowed the contractions, and then they decided to give another drug to induce stronger contractions. From here, we thought the finish line was in sight. It was late in the morning.

So the drug was given, and things quickly started to change: the contractions became very strong, and yet dilating wasn't happening. More hours passed. We were getting nervous because they said the water breaking so early meant there could be an infection. And then K's heart rate and Alma's heart rate both started to climb. Everyone grew concerned. The head was in the right place but couldn't start to push through yet. They decided to take blood from Alma's head, using a long, thin-bladed device threaded through a large tube inserted into K, to check for infection. It was hard to watch. The nurses were excited when they saw how thick Alma's hair was. That was a lift.

And then, events moved so quickly I couldn't keep up. The blood result came back fine, they said, but the chance of infection was growing. They told us that we needed to change to a caesarian section—to cut open the belly and take the baby out—as labor would be another four hours at least, and it was too long. Kathrin accepted it, saying we had to do whatever was best for the baby. She had an implacable calm in these decisions and turnarounds, in very tough conditions. They started to get her ready to go in the operating room. A nurse came to tell us all the bad things that could happen (death, the uterus having to be removed, damage to other organs, infection, etc.), and we signed a piece of paper. I had to put on scrubs, a hairnet, and a mask. Kathrin was taken somewhere else. Specialists came by. It was close to 2 PM on Monday. After waiting for what seemed hours but was ten minutes alone in the now empty delivery room, I was summoned to the OR. By the number of people in the room, it seemed things were getting close to ready.

Bivouacked into place in the front of the room was Kathrin's head. She was fully awake, laying on the operating table, and curtained off from her belly, which would be incised. I sat behind her with my hands on her shoulders. The idea was to show her the baby immediately and let her hold her, so she could still have something like the experience of normal birth. I was then to cut the umbilical cord and hold the baby for a while, and then we would be given the baby again in a half-hour in the delivery room. It seemed a good plan. I was scared. Kathrin was scared too, but showing steely readiness for whatever needed to happen. They were about to sterilize her abdomen.

Then came a beeping from everyone, all the doctors, all the nurses. They each had a phone, and all were beeping. We later found out that as we sat at the table, Junebug's heart rate had suddenly plummeted. At the moment, I didn't know what was happening. Suddenly, doctors were literally running into the room, their scrubs flapping behind them. One threw a bag onto a table, which fell open to reveal scalpels. Orders were barked in a tone that I knew: it means life or death is at stake. They were working like a great basketball team on a run, completely together and silent except for a few curt words. I stupidly wondered why everyone's mood had changed. More orders barked. I saw the baby for a second as she was hustled to a side room. Someone said, "Born, 2:05 PM" in German. She looked gray and yellowish. No one asked me to cut the cord, no one showed her to Kathrin, and now I knew something was wrong, badly wrong. I felt the pain of the idea that maybe Alma wouldn't make it so greatly, and the pain of how Kathrin would feel. It was very dark and very large, a continent. I felt thrust into a moment so crucial it was being burned into my eyes, ears, and mind.

Have to get the baby to her mother, no matter what, was all I could think. I stood up from the table and walked to the adjoining room. There was Junebug, on a table, being poked and prodded by two doctors. I immediately sobbed. They came to me and let me come over. Her hand was purple, where they were squeezing out a drop of blood. I stroked her hair and face. They were just finishing their check, and I picked her up. They were taken aback but let me do it. They could see I wasn't going to be stopped.

Outside, K was still on the table, and I was holding Alma. Against all the doctors' wishes, I took her to K, who was shaking uncontrollably on the table as they were sewing up the incision, and the doctor called out "Sir! Sometimes a father is unsteady!" and I said very evenly, "I'm not unsteady" and crossed the operating room to kneel and hold Alma to her face, and Kathrin's was the first face touched, and Alma's first kiss was from her mother. It was one of the bravest things I have ever seen, Kathrin in that moment.

They hustled me out of the room. I was brought back to our empty delivery room with Alma, and we were alone for some blissful minutes. Alma immediately fell asleep, and I was content. But I was desperate to get her to Kathrin next. She still hadn't held the baby, and now she had been wheeled somewhere else in the hospital. After all she had been through, all I could feel was the vicarious pain K would be feeling of not having the baby with her. And now the nurses came and told me they needed to take the baby, and I wouldn't let them, and then I did, and it went on like that. I kept insisting they let me take the baby to her mother, and they wouldn't let me. Lots of moments like that, where the red mist was rising while I held Alma in my arms, cursing and cajoling and muttering to the delivery staff, watching them stick needles and squeeze her four times hunting for blood, getting only tiny sluggish droplets, until the doctor looked at me and said I should take her to her mother. I finally brought her to Kathrin in the recovery room. All was instantly well. She was so happy to see the baby and so happy to know she was all right. Two or three minutes passed.

Then, one of the nurses I had been yelling at arrived with more bad news. The baby had a possible infection and needed to go immediately to the neonatal ward, where she remains now. It was profoundly awful.

It's hard to explain the pain of having finally gotten Junebug to her mother, where both should be, only to have her taken away again. As we handed her to the nurse, I was nursing my own violent fantasies of breaking out of this prison-hospital with Alma and Kathrin in a wheelchair, holding off anyone who tried to keep us there. The red mist rose again. I stayed quiet, though, somehow.

Reading this again now, I sound almost crazy, obviously. But you see, I didn't know what was going on. No one explained anything, and it felt so wrong not to leave her with the mother for five minutes before hustling her back for more sticking and jabbing. Anyway, once we were transferred up to the third floor, we were across the hall from Junebug, but Kathrin was bedridden in our room down the hall in another ward. I resumed my quest to bring them together and hung around the neonatal ward with Junebug. At this point, a kind, young doctor, very tall—Sandij—listened to my harangues (now delivered more calmly) and said that it was very important to him too, to bring mother and baby together. But he explained the situation to me: Junebug's infection parameter was up to 400; it should be under 100, and the mother was infected, too. We had to be very careful, but he would make it happen that night. And sure enough, at 7 PM, two nurses rolled Kathrin in her hospital bed down two hallways to the neonatal ward. The bed, however, wouldn't fit into the small rooms of the ward, so they rolled Junebug's little Babytherm 8000 unit out to the hall, and we all finally, finally spent thirty minutes together, and Kathrin cried, and all was well. A way had been found.

All my aggression towards the doctors and nurses, I have to admit now, was totally misplaced. Everyone on the neonatal ward is welcoming and positively happy when we come to see Junebug, which we can do whenever we want. They take amazing care of all the babies, mostly tiny ones who were born weighing less than 2 kilos (the Bug's birth weight: 3.53 kg). And Berlin is very multi—most of the babies are Middle Eastern. Seeing a young, blond-buzz-cut, gold-hoop-earring'ed German male taking tender care of a tiny Iranian preemie, holding him to his breast and bottle-feeding him, makes your heart break of sweetness. The level of organization and care is intense. There is tons of everything we need, bottles, towels, nipples, pumping machines, all provided in places where we can get it ourselves. There is no AC (in a hospital!), but they gave us a fan as it's boiling in Berlin. The entire cost of the private room where Kathrin and I are staying is 155 euros per night, which her insurance pays, plus my out-of-pocket charge, which is 18 euros a night. The food is like 1970 coach class, but plentiful and healthy. The nurses come and get us when Alma wakes up and tell us everything, and we are lucky.

Right now, it is 1:03 PM on Wednesday. In an hour, Alma will turn fourty-eight-hours-old. We visit her every two hours, and Kathrin is trying to get walking again. She is in a lot of pain and can't bend over or turn on her side or laugh, but she lights up whenever we get to be with Alma. We still call her Junebug sometimes, and also the Bug, and also the little Roo, because her legs are like a rabbit or kangaroo. Coiled with long feet, ready to hop. She's a hopper.

About the name: Kathrin chose her middle name, Sabahat, and her last name too, Jira-Raza. But in October, on the day Kathrin told me she was pregnant, I said, maybe we could call her Alma—if it fits her when she comes out. I don't know where it came from; I don't know anyone with the name. Later, I looked it up, and it was of Latin, Hebrew, and Arabic origin all combined. The meaning of Alma is "nourishing, kind; soul; young woman; learned"—this last being the meaning of Alima in Urdu. I read somewhere that in Arabic it can also mean salt water. This we loved. K and I met in Venice, and then met the second time in Greece by the sea, and the baby was conceived a few hundred yards from the Atlantic in Long Island. And when she came out, it was clear that Junebug's name was Alma.

Zee was taken away from Mommy for the first three days, I know now, and my mom got meningitis from the epidural and had a seizure, so she couldn't see me for my first three days. We are luckier. We have gotten to spend lots of time with Alma, and they have done their best to balance saving her life and Kathrin's life with our emotions and need to be with her. I can't wait for you to meet her. I think she's really something else already.

And Alma is changing every minute. She's evolving before our eyes. It's like science fiction. She uses her hands differently now, her skin has changed color four times, her eyes are alert, she drinks like a fish, and she's very strong. She's a kind of superwoman. And she's not 2-days-old yet! She's like a post-human rabbit kangaroo, and she's a complete mix of us. She is better than us. I have a lot of new feelings; Alma is like a pure injection of a drug of joy into my heart every time I get to see her. I don't remember crying from happiness before, and now I do it every time I see her. Life has changed. It's hard to remember it exactly, before Sunday, which is partly why I wrote this down.

Love,
Asad

P.P.S. I am saving all your beautiful emails and texts for Kathrin, but don't want to bother her with long chains of replies just now, so I am not copying her here.

CHRIS WU

Message Size: 441 KB June 29, 2040 at 12:34 PM

Dear Hernandez-Wu,

This is a story from a long time ago. Before I married your mother, I took her to Taiwan for the first time to meet A-Gong and A-Ma. Despite my strong opposition, your mom insisted that we asked them for their advice on love and relationships. I remember A-Gong and A-Ma laugh and saying they didn't quite have the answers for us. They mumbled, "nothing special, just kinda worked out."

A few days later we were heading back to New York, and A-Gong handed us a letter and told us that he and A-Ma put in some thought into your mom's question; and that they wrote down their advice in Chinese and English so your mom and I could both understand. I wanted to share with you this letter because to me the advice is very helpful, not only for marriage but for almost everything else.

Love,
Dad

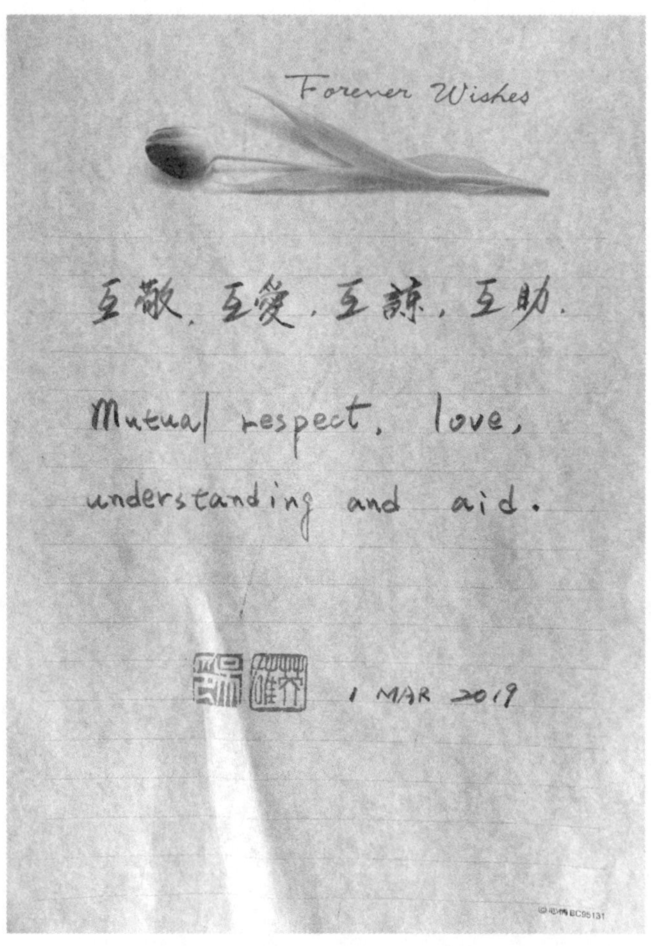

Forever Wishes

互敬．互愛．互諒．互助．

Mutual respect, love,
understanding and aid.

1 MAR 2019

AILY NASH is a curator and educator based in New York. She is a programmer at the New York Film Festival, where she cocurated the Projections section from 2014 to 2019, and is currently Head of Short Films and programmer for the Currents section. She is the program advisor to the International Film Festival Rotterdam's Short Film section. She served as a biennial advisor and cocurator of the film program for the 2017 Whitney Biennial, and was Head of Programming for the 2018 Images Festival in Toronto. She curated the Basilica Screenings series at Basilica Hudson from 2012 to 2016. She has curated programs and exhibitions for MOMA PS1, New York, NY; the Brooklyn Academy of Music, New York, NY; Anthology Film Archives, New York, NY; the Sullivan Galleries at the School of the Art Institute of Chicago, Chicago, IL; the Institute of Contemporary Art, London, UK; the Kiasma Museum of Contemporary Art, Helsinki, Finland; the Tabakalera International Centre for Contemporary Culture, San Sebastián, Spain; Doc's Kingdom, Arcos de Valdevez, Portugal; FACT, Liverpool, UK; the Tokyo Photographic Art Museum, Tokyo, Japan; Ghost:2561, Bangkok, Thailand, and others. In 2015, she was awarded an Andy Warhol Foundation Curatorial Fellowship. In 2018, she received a MOBIUS Curatorial Fellowship from the Finnish Cultural Institute New York and had new works commissioned by artists James N. Kienitz Wilkins and Lucy Raven, in partnership with PUBLICS and Heureka, the Finnish Science Centre. She has taught at Bard Microcollege, City College of New York, and Parsons School of Design.

AJAY KURIAN is an artist and writer who lives and works in Brooklyn, NY. Born in 1984 in Baltimore, MD, he received his BA in art and art history from Columbia University in 2006. His work looks to manifest the contradictions of history, culture, and materiality through various sculptural ecologies where no singular approach is prioritized. At the heart of his practice is the desire to explore what it means to be human today and how we might think of the humanist project differently. He has had solo exhibitions at 47 Canal, New York, NY; Sies+Höke, Düsseldorf, Germany; White Flag Projects, Saint Louis, MO; Jhaveri Contemporary, Mumbai, India; and Audio Visual Arts, New York, NY. He has shown work in group exhibitions at K11 Art Foundation, Hong Kong; the 2017 Whitney Biennial, New York, NY; the Øregaard Museum, Copenhagen, Denmark; La Panacée, Montpellier, France; the Art Commissions on Governors Island, New York, NY; MOMA PS1, New York, NY; and the Fridericianum, Kassel, Germany, among others. His work is in public collections including the Aïshti Foundation Collection, Beirut, Lebanon, and the Whitney Museum of American Art, New York, NY.

ALEXANDER LAU is a writer, curator, and former filmmaker based in New York, NY, and Hong Kong. He is currently the director of Empty Gallery and its associated record label, Empty Editions. Lau also sits on the board of the New York–based arts nonprofits Primary Information and Blank Forms. He has organized or participated in events in partnership with organizations such as Tai Kwun Contemporary, Hong Kong; Videotage, Hong Kong; Triple Canopy, New York, NY; Printed Matter, New York, NY; and Taipei Fine Arts Museum, Taiwan.

ANICKA YI lives and works in New York, NY. A symbiotic organism in its own right, her work fuses multi-sensory experience with synthetic and evolutionary biology to form lush bio-fictional landscapes. Utilizing a "biopolitics of the senses," Yi challenges traditional approaches to the human sensorium, emphasizing olfaction as well as microbial and embodied intelligence. Through her research and "techno-sensual" artistic exploration, Yi opens new discourse in the realms of cognition, artificial intelligence, and machine learning, introducing concepts of the sensorial ecology of intelligence, the machine microbiome, machine ecosystems, and "biologized" machines. Maintaining a practice focused on cosubjectivity, Yi's projects include collaborations with engineers, robots, synthetic and microbiologists, computer scientists, perfumers, ant and bacterial colonies, algae, tempura-fried flowers, and snails.

Her recent solo exhibitions include Gladstone Gallery, Brussels, Belgium; the Solomon R. Guggenheim Museum, New York, NY; Fridericianum, Kassel, Germany; Kunsthalle Basel, Basel, Switzerland; List Visual Arts Center, Cambridge, MA; the Kitchen, New York, NY; and the Cleveland Museum of Art, Cleveland, OH. Yi's work was also featured in the 58th Venice Biennale (2019) in Venice, Italy. Yi has screened her film, *The Flavor Genome*, at the 2017 Whitney Biennial in New York, NY, and the International Film Festival of Rotterdam (2017) in Rotterdam, the Netherlands. In 2016, she was awarded the Hugo Boss Prize for outstanding achievement in contemporary art. She is represented by Gladstone Gallery and 47 Canal, New York, NY.

ANNE ANLIN CHENG is Professor of English and American Studies at Princeton University in Princeton, NJ. She is author of *The Melancholy of Race: Psychoanalysis, Assimilation, and Hidden Grief* (New York: Oxford University Press, 2000); *Second Skin: Josephine Baker and the Modern Surface* (New York: Oxford University Press, 2011); and, most recently, *Ornamentalism* (New York: Oxford University Press, 2019). Her essays can also be found in the *Los Angeles Review of Books*, the *Nation*, and *Huffington Post*.

ANOKA FARUQEE (b. 1972, Ann Arbor, MI) earned her MFA from the Tyler School of Art in 1997 and her BA in painting from Yale University in 1994. She is an alumna of the Whitney Independent Study Program and residencies at the Skowhegan School of Painting & Sculpture and the PS1 National Studio Program. She is the recipient of grants from the Pollock-Krasner Foundation and Artadia, among others. Currently, Faruqee is Co-Director of Graduate Studies in Painting/Printmaking at Yale University. In 2016, she curated the major exhibition "Search Versus Re-Search: Josef Albers, Artist and Educator" and directed a short film about Albers's art and teaching for 32 Edgewood Gallery at the Yale School of Art. Faruqee's work has been exhibited at venues including: Secession, Vienna, Austria; Hall Art Foundation, Reading, VT; Elizabeth Foundation for the Arts, New York, NY; Schloss Derneburg Museum, Derneburg, Germany; MOMA PS1, New York, NY; Frist Art Museum, Nashville, TN; Chrysler Museum of Art, Norfolk, VA; Albright-Knox Gallery, Buffalo, NY; Schneider Museum of Art, Ashland, OR; and Björkholmen Gallery, Stockholm, Sweden, among others. Since 2013, Faruqee has been collaborating with the painter David Driscoll.

ARUNA D'SOUZA writes about modern and contemporary art, intersectional feminisms and other forms of politics, and how museums shape our views of each other and the world. Her most recent book, *Whitewalling: Art, Race, and Protest in 3 Acts* (New York: Badlands Unlimited, 2018), was named one of the best art books of 2018 by the *New York Times*. Her work appears regularly on 4Columns.org, where she is a member of the editorial advisory board, and has also been published in the *Wall Street Journal*, CNN.com, *Art News*, *Garage*, *Bookforum*, *Momus*, *Art in America*, and *Art Practical*, among other places. She is currently editing *Making It Modern: A Linda Nochlin Reader* and *Lorraine O'Grady: Writing in Space 1973–2018*. She is cocurator of the upcoming retrospective of Lorraine O'Grady's work, "Both/And," which will open in March 2021 at the Brooklyn Museum, New York, NY.

ASAD RAZA (b. Buffalo, NY) creates dialogues and rejects disciplinary boundaries in his work, which conceives of art as a metabolic, active experience. *Absorption*, in which cultivators create artificial soil, was the 34th Kaldor Public Art Project in Sydney, Australia (2019) and at the Gropius Bau, Berlin, Germany (2020). In *Untitled (plot for dialogue)* (2017), visitors played tennis in a 16th-century church in Milan, Italy. *Root sequence. Mother tongue* at the 2017 Whitney Biennial in New York, NY, combined twenty-six trees, caretakers, and objects. *Schema for a school* was an experimental school at the 2015 Ljubljana Biennial of Graphic Arts in Ljubljana, Slovenia. Raza premiered *Minor History*, a dialogue with his 91-year-old uncle, at the International Film Festival Rotterdam in Rotterdam, the Netherlands, in 2019.

Raza's works, such as *The Bedroom* at the 2018 Lahore Biennale in Lahore, Pakistan, often inhabit intimate settings. For "home show" (2015), which took place at his apartment in New York, Raza asked artists and friends to intervene in his life, while "Life to come" (2019) at Metro Pictures in New York, NY, featured participatory works and Shaker dance. Raza was Artistic Director of the Villa Empain in Brussels, Belgium, from 2016 to 2017, curating the shows "Mondialité, Décor," and "Répétition." With Hans Ulrich Obrist, he curated a series of exhibitions on Édouard Glissant, including "Trembling Thinking" at the Americas Society in New York, NY, and "Where the Oceans Meet" at MDC Museum of Art and Design, Miami, FL. Of Pakistani background, Raza studied literature and filmmaking at Johns Hopkins University and New York University, where he helped organize a labor strike in 2005.

BRENDAN FERNANDES (b. 1979, Nairobi, Kenya) is an internationally recognized Canadian artist working at the intersection of dance and visual arts. Currently based out of Chicago, IL, Fernandes's projects address issues of race, queer culture, migration, protest, and other forms of collective movement. Aiming to create new spaces and new forms of agency, his projects take on hybrid forms—part ballet, part queer dance hall, and part political protest—always rooted in collaboration and fostering solidarity. Fernandes is a graduate of the Whitney Independent Study Program (2007) and the recipient of a Robert Rauschenberg Fellowship (2014). In 2010, he was shortlisted for the Sobey Art Award. He is the recipient of a prestigious Canada Council New Chapter grant (2017), as well as the Artadia Award (2019), a Smithsonian Artist Research Fellowship (2020), and a Louis Comfort Tiffany Foundation grant (2019). His projects have been shown at the 2019 Whitney Biennial, New York, NY; the Solomon R. Guggenheim Museum, New York, NY; the Museum of Modern Art, New York, NY; the Getty Museum, Los Angeles, CA; the National Gallery of Canada, Ottawa, Canada; and MAC, Montreal, Canada, among others. He is artist-in-residence and faculty at Northwestern University and represented by Monique Meloche Gallery in Chicago. His recent and upcoming projects include performances and solo presentations at the Noguchi Museum, New York, NY; Monique Meloche Gallery, Chicago, IL; the Art Gallery of Ontario, Toronto, Canada; and the Museu de Arte de São Paulo, São Paulo, Brazil.

BRIAN KUAN WOOD is a writer based in New York and a founding editor of *e-flux journal*. His recent writings include the essays "The Horses" (*Marion von Osten: Once We Were Artists*, Utrecht: Valiz/BAK, 2018), "Frankenethics" (*Final Vocabulary*, New York: Sternberg Press, 2016), "Is it Heavy or Is It Light?" (*e-flux journal*, 2015), and "Is it Love?" (*e-flux journal*, 2014); the short story "Paradigm Thing" (*Tales of Our Time*, New York: Guggenheim Museum Publications, 2016); the films *Liquidity Inc.* (cowritten with Hito Steyerl, 2014) and Metahaven's *City Rising* (2014), as well as texts on or with Annika Eriksson, Babak Afrassiabi and Nasrin Tabatabai, Lara Favaretto, Joana Hadjithomas and Khalil Joreige, Gean Moreno and Ernesto Oroza, Hassan Khan, and Mary Walling Blackburn. He has edited readers and catalogues such as *The Internet Does Not Exist* and *Are You Working Too Much? Post-Fordism, Precarity, and the Labor of Art* (with Julieta Aranda and Anton Vidokle, New York: Sternberg Press, 2015 and 2011, respectively), the Taipei Biennial 2012 catalogue *Modern Monsters: Death and Life of Fiction* (with Anselm Franke, Leipzig: Spector Books, 2014), *IINN PPEERRPPEETTUUAALL PPRROODDUUCCTTIIOONN* (with Natascha Sadr Haghighian, New York: e-flux, 2013–14), and

Selected Maria Lind Writing (New York: Sternberg Press, 2010).

BYRON KIM is best known for his painting *Synecdoche*, which was included in the 1993 Whitney Biennial in New York, NY. Comprising a grid of panels depicting human skin color, the work is both an abstract monochrome and an ongoing group portrait. His weekly series of Sunday paintings—in which he paints the sky and on which he inscribes a journal entry—combines the cosmological and the quotidian. Kim received a BA in English from Yale University in 1983 and attended the Skowhegan School of Painting & Sculpture in 1986. Among his numerous awards are the Robert De Niro Sr. Award (2019), a Guggenheim Fellowship (2017), the Alpert Award in the Arts (2008), the Joan Mitchell Foundation Grant (1997), and the National Endowment for the Arts Award (1995). Among the institutions that have collected his work are the Art Institute of Chicago, Chicago, IL; the Berkeley Art Museum, Berkely, CA; the Brooklyn Museum, New York, NY; the Hirshhorn Museum and Sculpture Garden, Washington, DC; the Museum of Contemporary Art, San Diego, CA; the National Gallery of Art, Washington, DC; and the Wadsworth Atheneum Museum of Art, Hartford, CT.

C. SPENCER YEH is recognized for interdisciplinary activities as an artist, improviser, and composer, as well as for his music project Burning Star Core. His video works are distributed by Electronic Arts Intermix, and he is a contributing editor for *BOMB Magazine* and *Triple Canopy*. Yeh has also been a longtime programmer and trailer editor for the microcinema Spectacle Theater in Brooklyn, NY.

His exhibitions and presentations include "Shocking Asia," Empty Gallery, Hong Kong; "Two Workaround Works Around Calder," Whitney Museum of American Art, New York, NY; "Modern Mondays" and "David Tudor's Forest Speech," MoMA, New York, NY; "Sound Horizon," the Walker Art Center, Minneapolis, MN; "Tarek Atoui: Organ Within," Kurimanzutto and the Solomon R. Guggenheim Museum, New York, NY; "The World Is Sound," the Rubin Museum of Art, New York, NY; "Mei-Jia & Ting-Ting & Chih-fu & Sin-Ji," MOCA, Cleveland, OH, "Closer to the Edge," Singapore; "Crossing Over," Kuala Lumpur, Malaysia; "The Moon Represents My Heart: Music Memory and Belonging," the Museum of Chinese in America, New York, NY; and "Inner Ear Vision: Sound As Medium," Bemis Center for Contemporary Arts, Omaha, NE.

Yeh was a 2019 grant recipient of the Foundation for Contemporary Arts. *The RCA Mark II*, a project on vinyl record, was released by Primary Information in 2017.

CANDICE LIN draws from multiple disciplines to unearth largely forgotten or disregarded histories and to highlight practices that have been marginalized or discredited. She has created large-scale installations of elaborate systems in which fluids—such as kombucha or water dyed red with pigment from the cochineal insect—are drawn through tubes connecting an assortment of vessels or diverted to a surface where they pool into large stains. Her interest in legacies of colonization and attendant fictions relating to authenticity, purity, and birthright has led her to explore how specific natural materials and goods are given value and circulate through global trade routes.

Born in Concord, MA, in 1979, Lin received her BA in visual arts and semiotics from Brown University in 2001 and her MFA in new genres from the San Francisco Art Institute in 2004. She currently lives and works in Altadena, CA, and is on the faculty at the University of California, Los Angeles. Lin's work has been shown at the New Museum, New York, NY; SculptureCenter in New York, NY; the Hammer Museum, Los Angeles, CA; Portikus, Frankfurt, Germany; and Gasworks, London, UK, among others. She is represented by François Ghebaly.

CATHY PARK HONG's book of creative nonfiction, *Minor Feelings*, was published in spring 2020 by One World/Random House (US) and Profile Books (UK). She is also the author of poetry collections *Engine Empire*, published in 2012 by W. W. Norton, *Dance Dance Revolution*, chosen by Adrienne Rich for the Barnard Women Poets Prize, and *Translating Mo'um*. Hong is the recipient of the Windham-Campbell Prize, a Guggenheim Fellowship, and a National Endowment for the Arts Fellowship. Her prose and poetry have been published in the *New York Times*, the *New Republic*, the *Guardian*, the *Paris Review, Poetry*, and elsewhere. She is the poetry editor of the *New Republic* and is a full professor at Rutgers University-Newark.

CELINE WONG KATZMAN is a Singaporean American curator, writer, and educator based in New York, NY. She holds a BA with honors in visual art from Brown University. Celine is an instructor and organizer at the School for Poetic Computation. Previously, she was a NYSCA Curatorial Fellow at the Queens Museum and a gallery assistant at bitforms gallery. Her writing appears in publications such as *Rhizome,* the *Nation*, and *Art in America*, as well as in the New Museum exhibition catalogue *The Art Happens Here: Net Art's Archival Poetics* (New York: Rhizome, 2019). She has lectured and given presentations at institutions including Bard College, the School of Visual Arts, and Brown University. Her curatorial projects include "Five Contortions," a group exhibition engaging the East Asian femme body as a site of visibility, labor, agency, and exploitation; "Outside the Palace of Heavenly Purity," a group exhibition presenting artists using speculative models to complicate prevailing narratives of globalization in Asia; and "The Pointer," a solo exhibition by Ryan Kuo featuring three software commissions that address the construct of Whiteness and its involvement in technological aesthetics and productivity. Her forthcoming anthology *consider the scallion*, coedited with Diane Zhou, features a constellation of artist's reflections on the elusive, intricate nature of the scallion.

Founded in 2016, **CFGNY** began as an ongoing dialogue between Tin Nguyen and Daniel Chew on the intersection of fashion, race, identity, and sexuality.

Joined by Kirsten Kilponen and Ten Izu in 2020, CFGNY continually returns to the term "vaguely Asian": an understanding of racial identity as a specific cultural experience combined with the experience of being perceived as Other. CFGNY does not wish to represent what it means to be "Asian" in the singular; instead, it encourages the visualization of the countless ways one is able to be in the plural.

CHITRA GANESH is a Brooklyn, NY–based artist whose practice brings to light narrative representations of femininity, sexuality, and power typically absent from canons of literature, history, and art. Her drawings, prints, comics, installations, and videos combine and subvert Hindu and Buddhist mythology, South Asian pictorial forms, 19th-century European portraiture, and fairy tales, linking these to contemporary visual culture. Her work has been the subject of solo presentations at the Brooklyn Museum, New York, NY; the Andy Warhol Museum, Pittsburgh, PA; Göteborgs Konsthall, Gothenburg, Sweden; the Kitchen, New York, NY; the Rubin Museum of Art, New York, NY; and MOMA PS1, New York, NY, among others. Ganesh was awarded a Hodder Fellowship for the 2017–18 academic year at Princeton University's Lewis Center for the Arts. She is the recipient of numerous other residencies and grants, including a Guggenheim Fellowship, a Pollock-Krasner Foundation grant, and an Anonymous Was A Woman award in 2020. Ganesh's works are held in the public collections of the Philadelphia Museum of Art, Philadelphia, PA; the San José Museum of Art, San José, CA; the Baltimore Museum, Baltimore, MD; the Museum of Modern Art, New York, NY; and the Whitney Museum of American Art, New York, NY. Her installation *A city will share her secrets if you know how to ask* is currently on view at the Leslie-Lohman Museum of Art, New York, NY.

CHRIS WU is a designer and creative director based in New York, NY. He is a partner at Wkshps, a multidisciplinary design practice that crafts identities for art institutions, public spaces, nonprofits, and global brands. He was a principal of the design studio Project Projects, winner of the Cooper Hewitt National Design Award for Communication Design, the USA's highest recognition in the field. Wu has collaborated with clients such as the Solomon R. Guggenheim Museum, M+ Museum, David Zwirner, New Museum, Para Site, the Metropolitan Museum of Art, Hauser & Wirth, the Museum of Modern Art, Sculpture Center, Asia Art Archive, Gladstone Gallery, Modern Media Group Shanghai, the Vera List Center for Arts and Politics, and others. He received his Master's Degree in communications design from Pratt Institute.

Wu has lectured and served as a guest critic at universities and institutions internationally, including as a regular critic at Parsons School of Design, the New School for Design, and School of Visual Arts, State University of New York at New Paltz, Virginia Commonwealth University, the Hong Kong Polytechnic University, and Barnard College. He has also led a workshop focusing on Chinese typography at the Type Directors Club in New York. Wu authored, translated, edited, and designed *Graphic Design: Visual Comparisons* (Taipei: Zoar Int'l Press Co., 2008), a reissue of the iconic design title that was originally published in 1963. His work and writings have been widely published in design publications such as *IDEA*, *Eye*, *Print*, *AIGA Eye on Design*, *PPaper* (Taiwan), and *Design 360°* (China).

CHRISTINE Y. KIM is Associate Curator of Contemporary Art at the Los Angeles County Museum of Art in Los Angeles, CA. Her recent exhibitions include "Diana Thater: The Sympathetic Imagination" (2015–16); "My Barbarian: Double Agency" (2015); "James Turrell: A Retrospective" (2013–14), which won first place for the Best Monographic Museum Exhibition in the US by the International Art Critics Association in 2014; and "Teresa Margolles," an outdoor sculpture project in collaboration with the Los Angeles Nomadic Division, a nonprofit organization for public art which she cofounded in 2009. Prior to her post at LACMA, Kim was Associate Curator at the Studio Museum in Harlem (2000–2008), in New York, NY, where she organized exhibitions such as "Kehinde Wiley, The World Stage: Africa Lagos-Dakar" (2008), "Flow" (2008), "Philosophy of Time Travel" (2007), "Henry Taylor: Sis and Bra" (2007), "Black Belt" (2003), and "Africaine" (2002); and surveys "Frequency" (2005) and "Freestyle" (2001) with Thelma Golden. Kim's recent exhibitions at LACMA include "Isaac Julien: Playtime" (2019) and "Julie Mehretu: A Survey" (2019).

DAWN CHAN is a New York–based writer and editor whose work appears in the *Atlantic* online, *Bookforum*, the *New York Times*, the *New Yorker* online, *New York* magazine, the *Paris Review*, and the *Village Voice*, among other publications. She also frequently contributes to *Artforum*, where she worked as an editor from 2007 to 2018.

Currently visiting faculty at the Center for Curatorial Studies, Bard College, Chan has been a guest lecturer at Rhode Island School of Design, Maryland Institute College of Art, and New York University. Her work has been recognized with a Thoma Foundation Arts Writing Award in Digital Art and an Andy Warhol Foundation Arts Writers Grant. These days, she is working with four others on *November*, an editorial project launched in 2020 featuring long-form interviews on art, media, politics, and architecture.

New York–based artist **FUREN DAI** (b. Hunan, China) works in video performance, installation, and film. Dai received her BA in Russian language and literature from Beijing Foreign Studies University and her MFA from Tufts University. She has presented her work at the National Art Center, Tokyo, Japan, and the Athens Digital Arts Festival, Athens, Greece, among others. She has participated in residencies including at the International Studio & Curatorial Program in New York, Art Omi, NARS Foundation, and Saas-Fee Summer Institute of Art. She has received public art commissions from the *Art Newspaper* (2019) and Rose Kennedy Greenway (2020), as well as the Milton and Sally Avery Arts Foundation Fellowship (2017) and an Emergency Grant from Foundation for Contemporary Arts (2020).

HERA CHAN is a curator and writer based in Amsterdam, the Netherlands, by way of Kowloon, Hong Kong. Currently, she is a participant in the De Appel Curatorial Programme. Formerly, she was Associate Curator of Public Programmes at Tai Kwun Contemporary in Hong Kong, Director and Curator at Videotage in Hong Kong, researcher for SEACHINA in Hong Kong, and Cofounder and Director of Atelier Céladon in Montreal. Hera has staged exhibitions and public programs at articule, Montreal, Canada; Para Site, Hong Kong; SAVVY Contemporary, Berlin, Germany; Studio XX, Montreal, Canada; SBC Gallery of Contemporary Art, Montreal, Canada; and the UCCA Center for Contemporary Art, Beijing. With artist Xiaoshi Vivian Qin, she began investigating the 2017 purported sonic attacks on American embassies in Guangzhou and Havana as part of the Times Museum All The Way South exchange program with Artista x Artista. She was a fellow of the RAW Académie Session 7 and is cofounder of Miss Ruthless International, a contemporary art network that mimics the infrastructure of diasporic beauty pageants. Her writing has appeared in *ArtAsiaPacific*, *Artforum*, *ArtReview Asia*, *Di'van: A Journal of Accounts*, *Frieze*, *LEAP*, *MICE Magazine*, *Mousse Magazine*, *Real Review*, *Spike Art Quarterly*, *Take on Art*, and *Ocula*. She was editor in chief of *Theoretically in the Gutter: A Manga Essay Collection* and editor for *Ruthless Lantern*.

Since 2011, **HERB TAM** has been the Curator and Director of Exhibitions at the Museum of Chinese in America in New York, NY, where he recently cocurated "The Moon Represents My Heart: Music, Memory and Belonging." Tam has previously served as the Associate Curator at Exit Art and the Acting Associate Curator at the Queens Museum of Art. Tam was born in Hong Kong and raised in the San Francisco Bay Area. He studied at San José State University and earned his MFA from SVA.

HOLLY SHEN is an Asian American writer, curator, and arts administrator based in the San Francisco Bay Area. She most recently served as Deputy Director of the San José Museum of Art and in 2018, was awarded a Women in Power Fellowship at 92Y Belfer Center for Innovation & Social Impact. From 2013 to 2018, Shen was Director and Curator of Visual Arts at the Brooklyn Academy of Music. She has previously held various curatorial and collections management roles at Artsy, Memorial Sloan-Kettering Cancer Center, and SF MOMA. Shen holds a BA in art history from Georgetown University and an MA in art history from the Institute of Fine Arts at New York University.

HỒNG-ÂN TRƯƠNG is an artist who uses photography, video, and sound to explore immigrant, refugee, and decolonial narratives and subjectivities. She was awarded a Guggenheim Fellowship in Fine Art in 2019 and was the 2020 Capp Street Project artist-in-residence at the Wattis Institute for Contemporary Arts in San Francisco, CA, where she developed her web-based project *We Listen Nearby*. Hồng-Ân lives in Durham, NC, where she is an activist and a teacher. She is Associate Professor of Art at the University of North Carolina at Chapel Hill.

HOWIE CHEN is a curator and writer based in New York, NY. He is currently a principal at Chen & Lampert, an art consultancy, and is a founding director of Chen's, a townhouse gallery in Brooklyn. He has held curatorial roles at the Whitney Museum of American Art and MOMA PS1, and is a founder of Dispatch. With artist Mika Tajima, he formed New Humans. Chen graduated with a BS in economics from the Wharton School and was a Curatorial Fellow at the Whitney Independent Study Program. He has been published by Primary Information and Badlands Unlimited, as well as in journals including *Artforum*, *Frieze*, and *Art in America*. He is on the faculty of the Steinhardt School at New York University and has been a lecturer at MIT, Parsons School for Design, and Rhode Island School of Design.

Inspired by South Korean online LGBTQ+ communities in the 2000s, **HYPERLINK PRESS** is an online publication and curatorial collective creating intersectional platforms to showcase work by artists navigating the in-between spaces. Hyperlink Press's mission is to empower the under-represented history, experience, and identity in the tech field and art gallery system. Founded in 2018 by Taehee Whang, Jeong Yoon Lee, and Minsoo Thigpen, Hyperlink Press aims to share the utopic excitement for an equal world that we felt back in our shared childhood in the 2000s, breaking free from traditional forms of community building.

IFTIKHAR DADI works collaboratively as an artist with Elizabeth Dadi. Their practice investigates memory, borders, and identity in contemporary globalization, the productive capacities of urban informalities in the Global South, and the mass culture of postindustrial societies. They have exhibited widely internationally. Dadi is Associate Professor and Chair of the Department of History of Art, and Director of the South Asia Program at Cornell University. He researches modern and contemporary art from a global and transnational perspective, with emphasis on questions of methodology and intellectual history. His writings have focused on modernism and contemporary practice of Asia, the Middle East, and their diasporas. Another research interest examines the film, media, and popular cultures of South Asia, seeking to understand how emergent publics forge new avenues for participation. His publications include *Modernism and the Art of Muslim South Asia* (Chapel Hill, NC: University of North Carolina Press, 2010), the edited monograph *Anwar Jalal Shemza* (London: Ridinghouse, 2015), the coedited catalogue *Lines of Control* (Ithaca, NY: Cornell University Press, 2012), and the coedited reader *Unpacking Europe*

(Rotterdam: NAi Publishers, 2001). Dadi serves on the editorial and advisory boards of *Archives of Asian Art* and *Bio-Scope: South Asian Screen Studies*, and was a member of the editorial board of *Art Journal* (2007–11). He is an advisor to Asia Art Archive.

J FAN 范加 was born in 1990 in Ontario, Canada and raised in Hong Kong. Speculating on the intersection of biology and identity, his transdisciplinary practice emerges from a sustained inquiry into the concept of Otherness as it relates to the materiality of the gendered and racialized body. Working primarily in expanded sculpture, Fan often incorporates organic materials such as soybeans, melanin, and estrogen into larger assemblages fashioned of welded steel, poured resin, and handblown glass. Fan's recent research has explored the complex and porous systems formed between biological agents and the surrounding environment, seeking to queer the binaries of the artificial and the natural. Fan is the recipient of various fellowships such as the NYFA Artist Fellowship, Joan Mitchell Painters & Sculptors Grant, Jerome Hill Artist Fellowship, Van Lier Fellowship at the Museum of Arts and Design, and John A. Chironna Memorial Scholarship at the Rhode Island School of Design. Fan's work has been featured and reviewed in *Artforum*, *Hyperallergic*, *Art21*, *AsiaArtPacific*, *BOMB Magazine*, *Frieze*, and others. In 2021, Fan will be participating in the Liverpool Biennial, Liverpool, UK; Shanghai Biennale, Shanghai, China; and Kathmandu Triennale, Kathmandu, Nepal. Fan is currently based in Brooklyn, New York.

JP MOT (Jean-Pierre Abdelrohman Minh Mot Chen Hadji Yakop) is a Khmer Canadian conceptual artist who was born in Montreal and divides his time between Brooklyn, Montreal, and Beijing. He completed a BFA in visual and new media art (2009) at the University of Quebec and received an MFA in visual art at Columbia University (2015). His work has been shown both locally and internationally in galleries, museums, and festivals. Inspired by a nomadic and in situ practice exploring found objects, intimate architectures, and banal gestures, the eclectic works in his current series fall under a common umbrella captured in the title, "Hermit & Tent," in remembrance of the year in which, unable to secure suitable housing, he slept in a tent within his art studio to shelter from mosquitoes during the hot summer, taking showers in nearby gyms. Exploring notions of alienation and the syncretic body as political currency, his work presents an exegesis of the figure of the sacrificial scapegoat as the hero's foil. It draws on the study of canned humor and subversive semantics involving words found on items of consumption to disrupt established iconographies, expectations, and systemic stereotypes.

He has been supported by the Conseil des arts et des lettres du Québec, Canada Council for the Arts, NARS Foundation, Asia Art Archive in America, New York Foundation for the Arts, and Trust for Governors Island of New York.

Born in 1971 in Seoul, South Korea and raised in the United States, **JEAN SHIN** lives and works in Brooklyn, NY. She attended the Skowhegan School of Painting & Sculpture in 1999 and received a BFA and a MS from Pratt Institute. She is a tenured Adjunct Professor of Fine Art at Pratt and a recipient of Pratt's 2017 Alumni Achievement Award. She serves on the boards of the Joan Mitchell Foundation and National YoungArts Foundation.

Shin is nationally recognized for her monumental installations that transform everyday objects into elegant expressions of identity and community. She has had numerous solo exhibitions at institutions such as the Museum of Modern Art, New York, NY; Smithsonian American Art Museum, Washington, DC; Philadelphia Museum of Art, Philadelphia, PA; and Asian Art Museum, San Francisco, CA. Her work has been featured in more than 150 exhibitions at major cultural institutions such as the New Museum, New York, NY; Brooklyn Museum, New York, NY; Museum of Fine Arts Boston, Boston, MA; Museum of Fine Arts Houston, Houston, TX; Asia Society, New York, NY; Barnes Foundation, Philadelphia, PA; and Museum of Art and Design, New York, NY. As an accomplished artist practicing in the public realm, Shin has received commissions for large-scale, permanent installations from public federal and city agencies. She recently completed a landmark commission for the MTA's Second Avenue Subway at the 63rd Street station in Manhattan. Shin has received a Pollock-Krasner Foundation Grant, Asian Cultural Council Fellowship, and NYFA Fellowship, among others. She has been featured in *Art in America*, *Sculpture*, and the *New York Times*.

JEN LIU is a visual artist based in New York and Vermont, working in video/animation, genetically engineered biomaterial, choreography, and painting to explore national identities, gendered economies, neoliberal industrial labor, and the remotivating of archival artifacts. She is a 2019 recipient of the Creative Capital Award, 2018 LACMA Art + Technology Lab grant, and 2017 Guggenheim Fellowship in Film/Video. She has presented work at the Whitney Museum of American Art, New York, NY; the Museum of Modern Art, New York, NY; the New Museum, New York, NY; Smithsonian American Art Museum, Washington, DC; the Royal Academy of Art, London, UK; Institute of Contemporary Arts, London, UK; Kunsthaus Zürich, Zürich, Switzerland; Kunsthalle Wien, Vienna, Austria; the Aspen Museum of Art, Aspen, CO; Henry Art Gallery, Seattle, WA; Museo de Arte Contemporáneo de Castilla y León, León, Spain; the UCCA Center for Contemporary Art, Beijing, China; A07 @ 798 Art Zone, Beijing, China; Guangdong Times Museum, Guangzhou, China, the 2014 Shanghai Biennale in Shanghai, China, and the 2019 Singapore Biennale in Singapore.

JESSE CHUN is an artist working and living in New York, NY. Chun's work has been presented internationally at SculptureCenter, New York, NY; the Queens Museum, New York, NY; the Drawing Center, New York, NY; the Brooklyn Academy of Music, New York,

NY; the Bronx Museum of the Arts, New York, NY; the Vera List Center for Art and Politics, New York, NY; the Museum of Contemporary Art Toronto, Toronto, Canada; Oakville Galleries, Oakville, Canada; and the Nam June Paik Art Center, Seoul, South Korea, among others. Her recent digital and print publications include *WORKBOOK* (New York: Triple Canopy, 2019) and *Intangible Heritage* (Brooklyn: Wendy's Subway x BAM, 2018). Chun's work is in public collections including the Whitney Museum Library, New York, NY; Artist Book Collection, the School of the Art Institute of Chicago, Chicago, IL; Archive of American Art, the Smithsonian Institution, Washington, DC; Yale University Library, New Haven, CT; and Asia Art Archive in America, New York, NY.

JESSICA HONG is the Curator of Modern and Contemporary Art at the Toledo Museum of Art, Toledo, OH. Previously, she was the inaugural Associate Curator of Global Contemporary Art at the Hood Museum of Art at Dartmouth College, Hanover, NH. Prior to that, she was the Assistant Curator at the Institute of Contemporary Art / Boston in Boston, MA, where she organized exhibitions, including "Arthur Jafa: Love Is the Message, the Message Is Death" (2018) and the Boston presentation of "We Wanted a Revolution: Black Radical Women, 1956–85" (2018). She was also part of the inaugural team of the Division of Modern and Contemporary Art that launched the renovated Harvard Art Museums in Cambridge, MA. While based in New York, Hong held curatorial positions at Independent Curators International (ICI), SculptureCenter, and the Whitney Museum of American Art. Her writing has appeared in *BOMB Magazine*, and *New England Museums Now*, as well as publications by the Hood Museum, ICA / Boston, and SculptureCenter. Hong was ICI's external evaluator for curatorial programs and has been a visiting lecturer at Emerson College, Dartmouth College, Maryland College of Art, and New York University, among other academic institutions. She continues to serve as a juror on numerous fellowships, awards, and residency programs. Hong received her MA in art history from the Institute of Fine Arts, New York University and her BA in art history from Barnard College, Columbia University.

JIA TOLENTINO is a staff writer for the *New Yorker* and the author of the essay collection *Trick Mirror*.

JOHN TAIN is Head of Research at Asia Art Archive, where he leads a team based in Hong Kong, New Delhi, and Shanghai. He was the Curator of "Crafting Communities," an exhibition on the Thai-based Womanifesto initiative on view at AAA in the summer and fall of 2020. In 2018, he cocurated an exhibition for the Serendipity Arts Festival in Goa, India, and, with Jasmine Alinder, the exhibition "Yasuhiro Ishimoto: Someday, Chicago" for the DePaul Art Museum in Chicago, IL, as part of the Terra Foundation's Art Design Chicago initiative. Among his other projects, he co-convened MAHASSA (Modern Art Histories in and across Africa, and South and Southeast Asia, 2019–20), a collaboration with the Dhaka Art Summit and the Institute for Comparative Modernities at Cornell University, and serves as a series editor for Afterall's Exhibition Histories, the most recent volume of which is *Uncooperative Contemporaries: Art Exhibitions in Shanghai in 2000*. His writings have appeared in *Artforum*, *Flash Art*, *Art Review Asia*, and elsewhere. He was previously a curator at the Getty Research Institute in Los Angeles, CA.

JOHN YAU is a poet, art critic, and curator, as well as the publisher of Black Square Editions. His monograph on the Chinese artist Liu Xiaodong will be published by Lund Humphries next spring, and a book of poems, *Genghis Chan on Drums*, is forthcoming from Omnidawn in the fall. A book of essays, *Foreign Sounds or Sounds Foreign*, was recently published by MadHat. He was the 2017 recipient of the Jackson Prize in Poetry and has contributed essays to *Wifredo Lam: Volume 2: Catalogue Raisonne of the Painted Work, 1961–1982*, as well as to monographs including *Thomas Nozkowski*; *Catherine Murphy*; *Philip Taaffe*; *Richard Artschwager: Into the Desert*; *A Thing Among Things: The Art of Jasper Johns*; and *Joan Mitchell: Works on Paper 1956–1992*. A cofounder and editor of the online magazine *Hyperallergic Weekend*, he teaches at Mason Gross School of the Arts at Rutgers University in New Brunswick, NJ, and lives in New York, NY.

JOSH KLINE (b. 1979, Philadelphia, PA) lives and works in New York. His art has been exhibited internationally, including in solo exhibitions at Astrup Fearnley Museet, Oslo, Norway; Modern Art Oxford, Oxford, UK; Fondazione Sandretto Re Rebaudengo, Turin, Italy; Portland Art Museum, Portland, OR; Modern Art, London, UK; and 47 Canal, New York, NY. In 2019, Kline's work was shown in the 2019 Whitney Biennial in New York, NY; "The Body Electric" at the Walker Art Center, Minneapolis, MN; and "New Order: Art and Technology in the Twenty-First Century" at the Museum of Modern Art, New York, NY. In 2021, he will have a solo exhibition at LAXArt, Los Angeles, CA.

KA-MAN TSE is an artist and educator. She received an MFA from Yale University and a BA from Bard College. She has exhibited her work at Para Site, Hong Kong; Videotage, Hong Kong; Lumenvisum, Hong Kong; Eaton Workshop, Hong Kong; the Silver Eye Center for Photography in Pittsburgh, PA; New York Public Library, New York, NY; and Aperture, New York, NY. Her awards and fellowships include the Robert Giard Fellowship, the Aperture Portfolio Prize, the Aaron Siskind Fellowship, a research award from Yale University Fund for Lesbian and Gay Studies, and a residency at Light Work. Her curatorial projects include "Daybreak," cocurated with Matt Jensen at Leslie-Lohman Museum, and "Unruly Visions," an exhibition of emerging LGBTQ+ photographers in Hong Kong opening in December 2020 as part of the Hong Kong International Photography

Festival. In fall 2020, she exhibited video work at the Brooklyn Museum as part of "Art on the Stoop: Sunset Screenings." Her monograph *narrow distances* was published in 2018 by Candor Arts. She has taught at Cooper Union, Yale School of Art, and the City College of New York, and is currently Associate Director of Undergraduate Photography at Parsons School of Design.

KEN LUM is an artist best known for his conceptual and representational art in a number of media, including painting, sculpture, and photography. His work is concerned with how meanings are assigned to images, texts, and objects based on cultural, racial, and social codes. A longtime professor, he currently is the Chair of Fine Arts at the University of Pennsylvania's Weitzman School of Design in Philadelphia, PA.

He has published extensively, and a book of his collected writings was released by Concordia University Press in 2020. He has given keynote speeches for the Biennale of Sydney, International Council of Museums General Conference in Shanghai, and the Universities Art Association of Canada. His work has been exhibited at Documenta 11, Kassel, Germany; Venice Biennale; Bienal de São Paulo, São Paulo, Brazil; Shanghai Biennale, Shanghai, China; Carnegie International, Pittsburgh, PA; Biennale of Sydney, Sydney, Australia; Liverpool Biennial, Liverpool, UK; Gwangju Biennale, Gwangju, South Korea; and Whitney Biennial, New York, NY. His solo exhibitions include the CCA Wattis Institute for Contemporary Arts, San Francisco, CA; Kunstmuseum Luzern, Lucerne, Switzerland; and the Städtische Galerie im Lenbachhaus und Kunstbau, Munich, Germany. He is active in public art with permanent commissions for the cities of Vienna, Rotterdam, Saint Louis, Leiden, Utrecht, Toronto, and Vancouver.

Lum was the cocurator for several large-scale exhibitions, including "Shanghai Modern: 1919–1945," Sharjah Biennial 7, and "Monument Lab: Creative Speculations for Philadelphia." He was Project Manager for the exhibition "The Short Century: Independence and Liberation Movements in Africa: 1945 to 1994." He is Cofounder and Chief Curatorial Advisor for Monument Lab in Philadelphia.

KENNETH TAM's work takes the form of video installations that include moving-image works and sculpture, and currently explores ideas around the negotiation and performance of group identity. His work has been exhibited at SculptureCenter, New York, NY; MIT List Visual Arts Center, Cambridge, MA; and the Hammer Museum, Los Angeles, CA, among other institutions. He will have a solo exhibition at the Queens Museum in spring 2021 and will participate in the Shed's upcoming "Open Call," both in New York, NY. He recently produced his first live(streamed) performance at the Kitchen and has been an artist-in-residence at the Lower Manhattan Cultural Council, Pioneer Works, the Core Program at the Museum of Fine Arts, Houston in Houston, TX, and the 18th Street Arts Center in Santa Monica, CA. He is a graduate of the Cooper Union.

KIM NGUYEN is a writer and curator based in San Francisco, CA, where she is Curator and Head of Programs at the CCA Wattis Institute for Contemporary Arts. She has curated exhibitions, projects, and programs with a wide range of artists, including recent presentations with Maia Cruz Palileo, Jeffrey Gibson, Hồng-Ân Trương, Cinthia Marcelle, Akosua Adoma Owusu, Abbas Akhavan, and Ken Lum. Between 2019 and 2020, Nguyen led the Wattis's sixth research season, which was dedicated to the work of Trinh T. Minh-ha. Her writing has appeared in exhibition catalogues and periodicals, nationally and internationally. She is a recipient of the Hnatyshyn Foundation Award for Emerging Curator of Contemporary Canadian Art and the Joan Lowndes Award from the Canada Council for the Arts for excellence in critical and curatorial writing. She is currently working on her first collection of writings—a series of texts on alienation, art, and the long goodbye.

LUKE LUOKUN CHENG is an artist and digital designer working in diverse media including installation, imagery, and performance. Through his perspective as a queer Chinese immigrant in the US, he magnifies private poignancies to tease apart the boundaries of intimacy and alienation within global power structures. He draws from his experience designing social software to shape his pieces as sites of interactive possibility, while his background in large-format film portraiture informs a quiet, deliberate approach. A recipient of the Joan Mitchell Foundation Painters and Sculptors Grant, Cheng was a member of NEW INC and has exhibited at Assembly Room in New York, NY. He holds a BSE from Princeton University and was born in Jiangxi Province, China. He grew up and currently resides in Virginia.

LUMI TAN is Curator at the Kitchen in New York, NY, where she has organized exhibitions and produced performances with artists across disciplines and generations since 2010. Most recently, Tan has worked with Kevin Beasley, Lex Brown, Jibade-Khalil Huffman, Baseera Khan, Autumn Knight, and the Racial Imaginary Institute. Previously, she curated projects with artists including Gretchen Bender, Meriem Bennani, Liz Magic Laser, Sahra Motalebi, Sondra Perry, Tina Satter/Half Straddle, Anicka Yi, and Danh Võ and Xiu Xiu. Prior to holding her role at the Kitchen, Tan was Guest Curator at Frac Nord-Pas de Calais in France, Director at Zach Feuer Gallery, and Curatorial Assistant at PS1 Contemporary Art Center. Her writing has appeared in the *New York Times*, *Artforum*, *Frieze*, the *Exhibitionist*, and numerous exhibition catalogues. She was the recipient of the 2020 VIA Art Fund Curatorial Fellowship.

MAIA CHAO is an interdisciplinary artist who works in video, performance, sculpture, and social practice. She is cocreator of *Look at Art. Get Paid.*, which is slated to launch across a cohort of Massachusetts art museums in partnership with the Massachusetts Cultural Council. Chao's work has been shown at the Shed, New York, NY; the New School, New York, NY; Tufts

University, Medford, MA; Brown University, Providence, RI; RISD Museum, Providence, RI; Parsons School of Design, New York, NY; Haverford College, Haverford, PA; Helena Anrather Gallery, New York, NY; and Provincetown Art Association and Museum, Provincetown, MA. She has given talks and conference presentations at places such as ICA Philadelphia, Queens Museum, Museum of Fine Arts Boston, Minneapolis Institute of Art, and the CUE Art Foundation. Her work has been discussed in *BOMB Magazine*, the *Paris Review*, and *Hyperallergic*.

Her recent fellowships and residencies include Fine Arts Work Center (2017), Andrew W. Mellon Artist in Residence at Haverford College (2018), Asian American Arts Alliance Van Lier Fellow (2019), Philadelphia Museum of Art (2019), Pioneer Works residency (2020), and Queer|Art Mentorship (2020). A Fulbright grantee, Chao holds a BA from Brown University and an MFA from Rhode Island School of Design, where she is now on the faculty of the Sculpture Department.

MARC HANDELMAN is a visual artist and teacher. Through paintings, installations, artists' books, and other media, his work engages the afterlives of the genre of landscape. From the sustained imperial rhetoric of American landscape painting in corporate advertising, political branding, and White nationalist mythology, to the essentialization of the domain we call nature, Handelman's work explores the intimacy of aesthetics in the conditioning of knowledge and the legitimization of colonial and environmental violence. Handelman received his MFA from Columbia University. He has exhibited extensively throughout the United States as well as internationally in such venues as MOMA PS1, New York, NY; the Studio Museum in Harlem, New York, NY; Artists Space, New York, NY; Orlando Museum of Art, Orlando, FL; the Royal Academy of Art, London, UK; the Royal Swedish Academy of Fine Arts, Stockholm, Sweden; Grafikens Hus, Södertälje, Sweden; the Nerman Museum of Contemporary Art, Overland Park, KS; the American Academy of Arts and Letters, New York, NY; the Portland Museum of Contemporary Art, Portland, OR; the Rubin Museum, New York, NY; the Matsumoto City Museum of Art, Matsumoto, Japan; and the Storefront for Art and Architecture, New York, NY, among others. In spring 2018, Handelman was appointed Associate Professor at the Mason Gross School of the Arts at Rutgers University, where he currently serves as Chair of the department. He is represented by Sikkema Jenkins & Co. in New York. Handelman lives and works in Brooklyn, NY.

MARCI KWON is Assistant Professor of Art History at Stanford University, in Stanford, CA, where she also serves as the Codirector of the Cantor Art Center's Asian American Art Initiative. Her book *Enchantments: Joseph Cornell and American Modernism* is forthcoming from Princeton University Press in 2021.

MARGARET LEE (b. 1980, Bronx, New York, NY) has organized and exhibited work at numerous venues domestically and internationally, including Misako & Rosen Gallery, Tokyo, Japan, and Barneys, New York, NY. Lee's work has been shown in exhibitions including "Concentrations HK: Margaret Lee," curated by Gabriel Ritter, Duddell's x DMA, Hong Kong; "Made in LA," 2014 Hammer Museum Biennial, Los Angeles, CA; 2013 Biennale de Lyon, Lyon, France; "de, da do ... da," Carpenter Center for the Visual Arts, Harvard University, Cambridge, MA; "Caza," curated by Sofía Hernández Chong Cuy, the Bronx Museum of the Arts, New York, NY; "NO MAN'S LAND: Women Artists from the Rubell Family Collection," Rubell Family Collection, Miami, FL; "New Pictures of Common Objects," curated by Christopher Lew, MOMA PS1, New York, NY; and "Looking Back," White Columns, New York, NY. In 2009, Lee founded the artist-run space 179 Canal and is currently a partner in the gallery 47 Canal.

MARTHA TUTTLE (b. 1989, Santa Fe, NM, USA) is a multidisciplinary artist. Her fabric-based wall works and sculptural interventions search for fluidity, intimacy, and communication between states of matter, human to geologic. She received a BA from Bard College in 2011 and an MFA from the Yale School of Art in 2015. Her recent solo exhibitions include "Ma/Ma," Lora Reynolds Gallery, Austin, TX (2021); "A stone that thinks of Enceladus," Storm King Arts Center, New Windsor, NY (2020); "Dances with Atoms," Rhona Hoffman Gallery, Chicago, IL (2019); and "I long and seek after," Jack Tilton Gallery, New York, NY (2018). She has received fellowships and residencies from the Robert Rauschenberg Foundation, the Sharpe-Walentas Studio Program, the Josef Albers Foundation, and the Beinecke Rare Book & Manuscript Library, among others. She lives and works in Brooklyn, NY.

MARTIN WONG (1946–1999) was born in Portland, OR, and raised in the Chinatown district of San Francisco, CA. Wong was active in the performance art groups the Cockettes and Angels of Light before moving to New York, NY, in 1978, where he exhibited for two decades at notable downtown galleries including Exit Art, Semaphore, and P·P·O·W, among others. In 1999, Wong died in San Francisco from an AIDS-related illness. His work can be found in collections, including the Metropolitan Museum of Art, New York, NY; the Museum of Modern Art, New York, NY; the Bronx Museum of the Arts, New York, NY; the Whitney Museum of American Art, New York, NY; the Cleveland Museum of Art, Cleveland, OH; the Art Institute of Chicago, IL; and the San Francisco Museum of Modern Art, San Francisco, CA. Wong's work was the subject of a one-person show, "Sweet Oblivion," at the New Museum in New York, NY, and the University Galleries of Illinois State University in Normal, IL (1998). A retrospective, "Human Instamatic," opened at the Bronx Museum of the Arts in New York, NY, in November 2015 and traveled to the Wexner Center in Columbus, OH, in 2016, and the UC Berkeley Art Museum and Pacific Film Archive in Berkeley, CA, in 2017.

MARY LUM is a visual artist whose work draws attention to the poetic undercurrents of the city. Her work crosses media, primarily painting, photography, collage, and artists' books. Lum's work has been exhibited widely, including at Mass MOCA, North Adams, MA; the Aldrich Contemporary Art Museum, Ridgefield, CT; the deCordova Sculpture Park and Museum, Lincoln, MA; Artists Space, New York, NY; the Drawing Center, New York, NY; Museum für Gegenwartskunst, Basel, Basel, Switzerland; and Culturgest, Lisbon, Portugal. Her artists' books are in the collections of museum libraries including the Museum of Modern Art, New York, NY; the Metropolitan Museum of Art, New York, NY; and the SF MOMA, San Francisco, CA. She has received fellowships from the Solomon R. Guggenheim Foundation, the Radcliffe Institute for Advanced Study at Harvard University, the National Endowment for the Arts, New York Foundation for the Arts, the MacDowell Colony, the Massachusetts Arts Council, and the International Studio & Curatorial Program in New York. Lum's exhibitions have been reviewed in *Artforum, Art in America, Art News,* the *Village Voice,* and the *Boston Globe,* as well as online in BOMB Blog and 4Columns.org. She lives and works in North Adams, MA.

MATTHEW SHEN GOODMAN is a writer and editor in New York, NY.

MEGHA RALAPATI is an independent curator, arts manager, writer, and parent based in Chicago, IL, where she oversees the Jackman Goldwasser Residency at Hyde Park Art Center. The program supports artists across Chicago and internationally, as well as initiates collaborations with community-centered, experimental arts organizations like Project Row Houses in Houston, TX, and Artport in Tel Aviv, Israel. Megha has also developed curatorial projects including "Xenophilia" in Chicago (2016) and "Double-Jointed" at Scaramouche Gallery in New York, NY, (2012), and contributed to *New Narratives: Contemporary Art from India at the Chicago Cultural Center* (2007). Her writing appears in publications including *South as a State of Mind* (Köln: Walther König, 2018); *Kehinde Wiley: A New Republic* (New York: Prestel, 2015), *Black Sun* (London: Ridinghouse, 2014), and *Manual for Treason* (Sharjah: Sharjah Art Foundation, 2011). She has presented ideas and writing at the Asian/Pacific/American Institute at New York University (2013) and Eyebeam Art + Technology Center, New York (2012), and was a participant at the Incheon Biennial, South Korea (2011). Megha received an MA in visual culture from Goldsmiths and a BA in art history and anthropology from Columbia University.

MEL CHIN conveys complex ideas and themes through a mutative strategy, working alone or employing different disciplines and people, depending on the concept, to derive the materials of its realization, from actions, to films, to objects, as necessary. His *Revival Field* (1991), pioneered the field of "green remediation," the use of plants to remove toxic metals from the soil. From 1995 to 1998, he formed the collective Gala Committee, which produced *In the Name of the Place*, a public art project conducted on American prime-time television. His actions for the *Fundred Project* (2008–19) to end childhood lead poisoning, activated mass public engagement as a means for policymaker education. He has produced original films such as *9-11/9-11* (2007) to decenter preoccupations that engender nationalism and *L'Arctique est Paris* (2015) to deliver the poignant warnings of a Greenlandic subsistence hunter to an international audience. In 2018, he used New York's Times Square as the site of *Wake* on the ground and *Unmoored*, an AR project in the air, creating an experiential portal into a past maritime industry and a future of rising waters. "Mel Chin: All Over the Place," a forty-year survey, was named by *Hyperallergic* as the best exhibition of 2018 in New York. He is the recipient of many awards, grants, and honorary degrees, including a MacArthur Fellowship in 2019.

MICHELLE LOPEZ (b. 1970, Filipina American) is an interdisciplinary artist based in Philadelphia, PA, and New York, NY. In addition to her 2020 exhibition "Ballast & Barricades" at ICA Philadelphia, she has shown her work at the Aldrich Contemporary Art Museum, Ridgefield, CT; Public Art Fund, New York, NY; MOMA PS1, New York, NY; Protocinema, New York, NY; Carpenter Center for Visual Arts at Harvard University, Cambridge, MA; Yerba Buena Center for the Arts, San Francisco, CA; and Fondazione Nicola Trussardi, Milan, Italy, among others. In 2019, she was a recipient of a Guggenheim Fellowship.

MIMI WONG was born and raised in California's Silicon Valley. She is editor in chief of the literary magazine the *Offing*. Her writing on art, culture, and literature has appeared in the *Believer,* Catapult, Electric Literature, *Hyperallergic,* Literary Hub, and Refinery29. Her fiction has been published in *Crab Orchard Review, Day One*, and *Wildness*. She is an alumna of the Tin House Summer Workshop, Voices of Our Nations Arts Foundation, and Anaphora Writing Residency for Writers of Color. She has received support from the Banff Centre for Arts and Creativity and was awarded an Arts Writers Grant by Creative Capital and the Andy Warhol Foundation. She lives in Brooklyn, NY.

MO KONG is a multidisciplinary artist and researcher. They currently reside in Queens, New York and received an MFA from RISD. Their research-led work often takes the form of large-scale installations that incorporate scientific research and journalistic perspectives to challenge key issues of the day through complex narratives synthesizing past and present. The systems they build normally merge multiple environmental crises and social-political issues and through scientific research and social investigation, they find the similarity of two systems and bring them to one narrative storyline.

Their solo exhibitions include shows at CUE Art Foundation, New York, NY; Artericambi Gallery, Verona, Italy; Gertrude Gallery, Stockbridge, MA; and Chashama, New York, NY. Their work has been shown at the Queens Museum,

New York, NY; RISD Museum, Providence, RI; SF MOMA, San Francisco, CA; Minnesota Street Project, San Francisco, CA; Spring/Break, New York, NY and Los Angeles, CA; Artissima, Torino, Italy; Make Room Gallery, Los Angeles, CA; and Rubber Factory Gallery, New York, NY. Their fellowships and residencies include Skowhegan School of Painting & Sculpture, Triangle Art Association, Mass MOCA, Vermont Studio Center, Gibney Dance Agnes Varis Performing Arts Center, Lighthouse Works, and AAI. Their work has been featured in *Hyperallergic, Artforum, Cultured* magazine, *Art News,* CoBo Social, *Wall Street International* Magazine, and SF MOMA's *Public Knowledge.*

NAEEM MOHAIEMEN makes films and installations, and writes essays about rhizomatic families, malleable borders, and socialist utopias. The idea of a future global left—as an alternative to current organizing categories of race, religion, and nation—drives the work. He is a Mellon Research Fellow at Columbia University, New York, NY.

PAMELA M. LEE is Carnegie Professor of Modern and Contemporary Art at Yale University in New Haven, CT. She is the author, most recently, of *The Glen Park Library: A Fairy Tale of Disruption* (Cambridge, MA: no place press, 2019) and *Think Tank Aesthetics: Midcentury Modernism, the Cold War and the Neoliberal Present* (Cambridge, MA: MIT Press, 2020).

PATRICK JAOJOCO is a Filipino American curator, researcher, and organizer focusing on the spatial implications of colonialism and decolonization. His independent work seeks to articulate and expand upon decolonial historiographies and practices by engaging artists, architects, and other creative workers to educate and mobilize the public around long-term ecological, economic, and political histories. He has curated exhibitions and public programs throughout New York and is organizer of the *Decolonial Mapping Toolkit,* a project that attempts to decolonize mapping processes by reframing colonial histories in public space.

Jaojoco currently works as Director of Programs at FABnyc, where he works to bring arts strategies to anti-gentrification movements in the Lower East Side in New York, NY. In the past, he has assisted in organizing exhibitions at Storefront for Art and Architecture, New York, NY; Art in General, New York, NY; and the Hirshhorn Museum and Sculpture Garden, Washington, DC, among others. As a writer, he has contributed to exhibition catalogues, including *Mark Dion: Our Plundered Planet* (Dublin: Hugh Lane, 2019), *Brand New: Art and Commodity in the 1980s* (Washington, DC: Hirshhorn Museum, 2018), and *Constructing Paradise* (Salzburg: Verlag Anton Pustet, 2017); and to *Artforum,* the *Brooklyn Rail,* and the *Avery Review,* which published his research connecting Philippine hill station architectures to contemporary condominium developments and a decolonized, collectively owned park on the archipelago.

Jaojoco is a 2020 AICA Art Writing Workshop participant, mentored by Holland Cotter, and a 2019–21 member of NEW INC at the New Museum. He received an MA in curatorial practice from the School of Visual Arts and a BA in English and environmental studies from New York University.

PATTY CHANG is an artist working in performance, video, writing, and installation. Her work has a capacity to explore complex subjects nearly simultaneously, as does life. Born in 1972 in San Leandro, CA, Chang received her BA from the University of California, San Diego, in 1994. Her work has been exhibited nation-wide and internationally at such institutions as the Museum of Modern Art, New York, NY; the Solomon R. Guggenheim Museum, New York, NY; the New Museum, New York, NY; BAK, basis voor actuele Kunst, Utrecht, the Netherlands; the Hammer Museum, Los Angeles, CA; Fri Art Centre d'Art de Fribourg, Fribourg, Switzerland; Centre for Contemporary Chinese Art, Manchester, UK; the Museum of Contemporary Art, Chicago, IL; M+ Museum, Hong Kong; SF MOMA, San Fransisco, CA; and the Moderna Museet, Stockholm, Sweden. Her work received a 2003 award from the Rockefeller Foundation and a 2012 Creative Capital award. In 2008, she was a finalist for the Hugo Boss Prize and a Guna S. Mundheim Fellow in the Visual Arts at the American Academy in Berlin. In 2014, Chang was a John Simon Guggenheim Memorial Foundation Fellow. Her acclaimed exhibition "Patty Chang: The Wandering Lake 2009–2017" traveled to the Institute of Contemporary Art, Los Angeles in 2019. She lives and works in Los Angeles.

PAUL PFEIFFER was born in Honolulu, HI, in 1966 and grew up between Hawaii and the Philippines. After studying printmaking at San Francisco Art Institute in San Francisco, CA, he moved to New York, NY, where he attended Hunter College and the Whitney Independent Study Program. Pfeiffer's work in video, sculpture, and photography mines the history of popular mass entertainment to explore the role of images in shaping individual and collective consciousness. Reworking clips from YouTube, cable TV, and increasingly, his own footage, Pfeiffer delves into the aesthetics of nonlinear editing to elucidate the hybrid forms of space and time that define contemporary life.

PHILIP POON is an architect based in New York, NY. After working in Japan, the Netherlands, and Switzerland, Poon completed his MArch at the Harvard Graduate School of Design, where his design thesis was "The New Chinese American Restaurant." His current interest is finding an architectural expression of contemporary Asian American culture.

PREM KRISHNAMURTHY (b. 1977) is a designer, curator, writer, and teacher based in Berlin, Germany, and New York, NY. He currently directs Wkshps, a multidisciplinary design practice and is Artistic Director of FRONT International 2022, the Cleveland, OH triennial of contemporary art. He also organizes Commune, an emergent, multiform workshop that practices artistic tools for social transformation.

Krishnamurthy received the Cooper Hewitt National Design Award for Communications Design in 2015.

RALPH PUGAY (b. Cavite, the Philippines) draws, paints, and organizes participatory projects in Portland, OR, where he lives and works. He employs the visual vernacular of late capitalism to render absurd fantasy worlds which allegorize the slippery and multifaceted experience of Otherness. Notable solo exhibitions of his work have been held at the Seattle Art Museum, Seattle, WA; Upfor Gallery, Portland, OR; Vox Populi, Philadelphia, PA; FAB Gallery at Virginia Commonwealth University, Richmond, VA; and King School Museum of Contemporary Art, Portland, OR, among others. His work has also been shown in group exhibitions at Dust to Dust Projects at High Desert Test Sites, Joshua Tree, CA; AA|LA, Los Angeles, CA; PNCA Center for Contemporary Art & Culture, Portland, OR; the Art Gym, Portland, OR; Salt Lake Art Center, Salt Lake City, UT; Marinaro Gallery, New York, NY; and Ortega y Gasset Projects, Brooklyn, NY. Pugay has participated in artist residencies at Crow's Shadow Institute of the Arts, PICA's Creative Exchange Lab, the Joan Mitchell Center, the Rauschenberg Residency, Vermont Studio Center, and Skowhegan School of Painting & Sculpture. His work has received support from the Joan Mitchell Painters & Sculptors Grants program, the Betty Bowen Award, the International Sculpture Center, Regional Arts & Culture Council, Oregon Arts Commission, and the Ford Family Foundation. He studied art at Portland State University, where he was recently appointed Assistant Professor of Art Practice.

SARAH MCCAFFERY is Manager of Interdisciplinary Arts at Asia Society Museum, New York, NY. She oversees a diverse portfolio of art projects, ranging from participatory performance, site-specific works, durational performance art to immersive sound installations. Her work there includes *Creative Common Ground*, an initiative that commissioned artists to create interdisciplinary performance works. For Asia Society's first fully virtual season, she has curated interactive virtual programming focused on the role of arts and artists in social transformation.

McCaffery's intercultural and interdisciplinary approach is shaped by her extensive background in the artistic process, including dance pedagogy, choreography, and performance. She has performed in several dance forms, including ballet, contemporary dance, and modern dance, and has studied forms from across the world. Formative to her movement philosophy was training at the Dance Theatre of Harlem, where she studied the body as site for rebellion and dance as embodied liberation and power. Active in cultural organizing, she has participated in the Association for Performing Arts Professionals' Emerging Leaders Institute. She is pursuing an MA in art history at Hunter College with a focus on performance and new media studies. She earned her BA from Duke University in political science and dance.

ZHENG SHENGTIAN is an artist, scholar, and curator based in Vancouver, Canada. Before 1990, he was Professor and Chair of the Oil Painting Department at the China Academy of Art. He has been a visiting professor at the University of Minnesota and San Diego State University, Secretary of the Annie Wong Art Foundation, and founding Board Director of Vancouver International Centre for Contemporary Asian Art. Currently, he is the Managing Editor of *Yishu: Journal of Contemporary Chinese Art*, Adjunct Director of the Institute of Asian Art at the Vancouver Art Gallery, and a trustee of Asia Art Archive in America. Zheng has organized and curated numerous exhibitions and events, and has frequently contributed to periodicals and catalogues. In 2013, *Zheng Shengtian: Selected Writing on Art* was published in four volumes by China Academy Press. In 2011, he was awarded the Lifetime Achievement Award for curatorial work by the Vancouver Biennale. He received an Honorary Doctorate of Letters from Emily Carr University of Art + Design in 2013.

鄭勝天身兼藝術家、學者及策展人，現居溫哥華。1990年前，他擔任中國美術學院教授及油畫系主任，並曾是明尼蘇達大學及聖地亞哥州立大學客座教授、梁潔華藝術基金會秘書長及溫哥華當代亞洲藝術國際中心創會理事。他目前擔任《Yishu: Journal of Contemporary Chinese Art》(典藏國際版) 的總策劃，兼任溫哥華美術館亞洲館總監及亞洲藝術文獻庫 (美國) 理事。他策劃過眾多的展覽與活動，論著也常在期刊及圖錄中發表。2013年中國美術學院出版社出版了四卷本的《鄭勝天藝文選》。2011年溫哥華雙年展向他頒發「終身成就獎」以表揚其策展工作。2013年，鄭勝天獲加拿大 Emily Carr 藝術和設計大學頒授榮譽博士學位。

WANGSHUI is an artist and filmmaker whose work explores the edges of perception. WangShui has exhibited and screened work at venues including the Whitney Museum of American Art, New York, NY; SculptureCenter, New York, NY; the New York Film Festival, New York, NY; the Julia Stoschek Collection, Düsseldorf, Germany; International Film Festival Rotterdam, Rotterdam, the Netherlands; the Experimental Media and Performing Arts Center (EMPAC), Troy, NY; and the Jim Thompson Art Center, Bangkok, Thailand.

SRESHTA RIT PREMNATH (b. 1979, Bangalore, India; lives in Brooklyn, NY) is an artist and the founding Editor of *Shifter*, an issue-based journal featuring contemporary art, creative writing, and critical theory. Premnath also directs the BFA Fine Art program at Parsons School of Design in New York, NY. His work has been the focus of solo exhibitions at GALLERYSKE, Bangalore, India; Galerie Nordenhake, Berlin, Germany; Rodriguez Gallery, Poznań, Poland; Kansas Gallery, New York, NY; Contemporary Art Museum, Saint. Louis, MO; Nomas Foundation, Rome, Italy; and the Contemporary Art Gallery, Vancouver, Canada, among others. He has exhibitions in 2021 at MIT List Center for Visual Art, Cambridge, MA, and Contemporary Art Center, Cincinnati, OH. His group exhibitions include "The Matter Within: New Contemporary Art of India," Yerba Buena Center for the Arts, San Francisco, CA; "The Hollow Center," Smack Mellon, New York, NY; "Common Space," the Kitchen, New York, NY; "After Midnight," the Queens Museum, New York, NY; "So-Called Utopias," Logan Center for the Arts, Chicago, IL; "Cartography of Ghosts," the Drawing Center, New York, NY; and "L'Intrus Redux," Westfälischer Kunstverein, Münster, Germany, among others. He holds a BFA from the Cleveland Institute of Art (2003) and an MFA from Bard College (2006).

SUNG HWAN KIM (b. 1975, South Korea) has most recently exhibited his work at the National Museum of Modern and Contemporary Art, Gwacheon, South Korea; daadgalerie, Berlin, Germany; the 57th Venice Biennale, Venice, Italy; and Berwick Film and Media Arts Festival, Berwick, UK. With David Michael DiGregorio, he inaugurated the Asian Arts Theater, Gwangju, South Korea, with the operatic theater piece 피나는 노력으로 한 [*A Woman Whose Head Came Out Before Her Name*] (2015) and created two radio plays, commissioned by Bayerischer Rundfunk: *one from in the room* (2010), which won the Karl-Sczuka-Förderpreis, and *Howl Bowel Owl* (2013). His solo exhibitions include "Sung Hwan Kim," CCA Kitakyushu, Japan; "Life of Always a Mirror," Artsonje Center, Seoul, South Korea; "Sung Hwan Kim," the Tanks at Tate Modern, London, UK); "Line Wall," Kunsthalle Basel, Switzerland; as well as "Sung Hwan Kim, From the Commanding Heights ...," Queens Museum, New York, NY, and "Golden Times Part 2: Sung Hwan Kim," Haus der Kunst, Munich, Germany. His works have been shown in the Gwangju Biennale, Performa, Manifesta, Berlin Biennale, Rotterdam International Film Festival, and Rencontres Internationales Paris/Berlin, among others. He was a fellow at the Rijksakademie van beeldende kunsten (2004–05) and a recipient of Berliner Künstlerprogramm des DAAD (2015). His publications include *Talk or Sing* (distributed by Artsonje); *Ki-da Rilke* (distributed by Sternberg Press); and *When Things Are Done Again* (distributed by Tranzitdisplay). He is currently working on a new piece commissioned by GB Foundation for the Gwangju Biennale in 2021.

Born in Tokyo, **SYLVIA SCHEDELBAUER** moved to Berlin in 1993, where she has been based since. She studied at Berlin University of the Arts with Katharina Sieverding. Her films negotiate the space between broader historical narratives and personal, psychological realms mainly through poetic manipulations of found and archival footage. Her work has screened at the Berlinale, the Toronto International Film Festival, the International Short Film Festival Oberhausen, the London Film Festival, the New York Film Festival, and the Robert Flaherty International Seminar. Her awards include the VG Bild-Kunst Award, the German Film Critics Award, and the Gus Van Sant Award for Best Experimental Film. Schedelbauer was a 2019–20 fellow at the Radcliffe Institute for Advanced Study at Harvard University.

TAUSIF NOOR is a critic, curator, and graduate student in the History of Art Department at UC Berkeley, where he studies modern and contemporary art with a focus on South Asia. His research addresses intersections of art and politics, focusing on histories of nationalism and internationalism, postcolonialism, and Marxist thought. His criticism and essays can be found in *Artforum*, *Frieze*, *ArtAsiaPacific*, and catalogues for the India Habitat Centre in New Delhi, India, and Karma Gallery in New York, NY. He has curated exhibitions in Philadelphia, PA, including shows at FJORD Gallery, AUTOMAT Gallery (with Ginny Duncan), and Pilot Projects (with Lauren Downing), and has previously worked at the Whitney Museum of American Art, the Imperial War Museum in London, and the Institute of Contemporary Art at the University of Pennsylvania, where he was the Spiegel-Wilks Curatorial Fellow from 2017 to 2020.

VINAY HIRA is a multidisciplinary artist based in Manhattan, New York, NY. His self-referential aesthetic and varied, self-taught technique produce work that distorts the image of a charming, Commonwealth Brown boy—making audiences simultaneously experience familiarity and Otherness.

Hira is a trained marine scientist and plant pathologist who was flung into artistic notoriety while working in sterling bond investment in the bourgeois New Zealand suburbs. His work dips in and out of pop culture, existing in the liminality between eccentricity and instability, where our deepest desires and greatest insecurities threaten to spill from our mouths: it is his journey as both an artist and a human.

YARA EL-SHERBINI asks a lot of questions, such as: *How many squirrels has Iran arrested on suspicion of spying?* Using irreverent humor and playful forms, her works prompt slow form social action. "Forms of Regulation and Control," her first solo show in the US was curated by Naeem Mohaiemen at the CUE Art Foundation in 2020. She is also part of the duo YARA + DAVINA, who will be touring their large-scale public artwork *Arrivals + Departures* across the UK in 2021.

YAYOI SHIONOIRI serves as Executive Director to the Estate of Chris Burden and the Studio of Nancy Rubins, where she is responsible for stewarding Burden's art historical legacy and promoting Rubins's artistic practice. She also serves as US Alliance Partner to City Lights Law, a Japanese law firm that represents creators, innovators, and artists. She is a published specialist on art law. From 2015 to 2019, Shionoiri served as General Counsel and Head of Asia Strategy to Artsy, responsible for all legal matters of the company's global operations, advising on corporate transactions, intellectual property issues, technology startup management and operations, and digital media strategy. From 2011 to 2015, Shionoiri was the Associate General Counsel of the Solomon R. Guggenheim Foundation, providing legal services for matters including exhibitions and nonprofit operations. From 2008 to 2011, she served as Legal Advisor to Japanese contemporary artist Takashi Murakami, managing his contract negotiations and worldwide intellectual property rights. She received her AB from Harvard University (2000), her JD from Cornell Law School (2003), and her MA in modern art from Columbia University (2010). As a US-Japan Leadership Program Fellow and an Asia Society Asia 21 Young Leader, she actively contributes to the ongoing development of cultural collaborations and political ties across nations. She serves as Vice-Chair to the board of Recess Art and as an Advisory Panelist to the Serpentine Gallery's Legal Lab.

ZULFIKAR ALI BHUTTO (b. 1990, Damascus, Syria) is a visual artist, performer, and curator. Bhutto's work explores complex histories of colonialism that are exacerbated by contemporary international politics, unpacking the intersections of queerness and Islam through a multimedia practice. Bhutto was a curatorial resident at SOMArts Cultural Center in San Francisco, CA, where he cocurated "The Third Muslim: Queer and Trans Muslim Narratives of Resistance and Resilience" (2018). His work has been shown in galleries, museums, and theaters globally. He has spoken extensively on the intersections of faith, radical thought, and futurity at Columbia University, UC Berkeley, Stanford University, and New York University. Bhutto is based between Karachi and San Francisco, where he received an MFA from the San Francisco Art Institute in 2016.

CREDIT

p. 5: Byron Kim, "Is the Sky Still Blue?" was simultaneously written for the exhibition catalogue *Unconstrained Textiles: Stitching Methods, Crossing Ideas* (Hong Kong: Centre for Heritage, Arts and Textile, 2020).

p. 207: Martin Wong, "Dear Mom & Pop ... From Egg Foo Wong," 1978–79, graphite on paper scroll with envelope, 39 × 11-1/2 in. Courtesy Estate of Martin Wong and P·P·O·W, New York.

p. 104: Anni Albers, diagram showing draft notation (plain weave), ca. 1965. Plate 10 from *On Weaving*, 1965. Ink and pencil on gridded paper, 10-15/16 × 8-1/2 in. (27.8 × 21.6 cm). © 2020 Courtesy Josef and Anni Albers Foundation/Artists Rights Society (ARS), New York.

p. 143: Toshiko Takaezu, *#8*, 20th century, stoneware with glazes, 7-1/8 × 6 × 6 in. Courtesy Iris & B. Gerald Cantor Center for Visual Arts at Stanford University. Gift of the artist.

p. 148–58: Chitra Ganesh and Sung Hwan Kim, *Between You and Me*. The original version of this conversation was conceived for *Art Practical*, April 15, 2018.

PAPER MONUMENT
n+1 Foundation, Inc.
PO Box 26428
Cadman Plaza Station
Brooklyn, NY 11202-0921
www.papermonument.com

EDITORS
Dushko Petrovich and Roger White

ASSOCIATE EDITOR
Prem Krishnamurthy

MANAGER
Rachel Ossip

DESIGN
Abby Chen, for Wkshps

From Christopher K. Ho and Daisy Nam: Special thanks goes to Jane DeBevoise, who hosted Asia Art Archive in America's Leadership Camp: "Model Minority and Model Majorities," where we met and where many of these ideas originated. Chris additionally is grateful to Owen Duffy for his enthusiasm and selfless support. Daisy would like to thank Chris, Cindy, and Harper Lew as well as Lucy Kim and Gloria Sutton, whose sustained encouragement is invaluable. We owe much to *Paper Monument* series editors (and coeditors of this volume) Roger White and Dushko Petrovich, and to managing editor Rachel Ossip, for their guidance and editorial skills. Finally, we are indebted to those who came before us and those who will come after us.

Paper Monument would like to thank all our contributors for their time and effort, and our friends at *n+1* for their support.

Paper Monument is supported, in part, by public funds from the New York State Council on the Arts and New York City Department of Cultural Affairs in partnership with the City Council.

Best! Letters from Asian Americans in the arts

ISBN 978-1-7365079-0-2

Printed in the United States of America
First printing